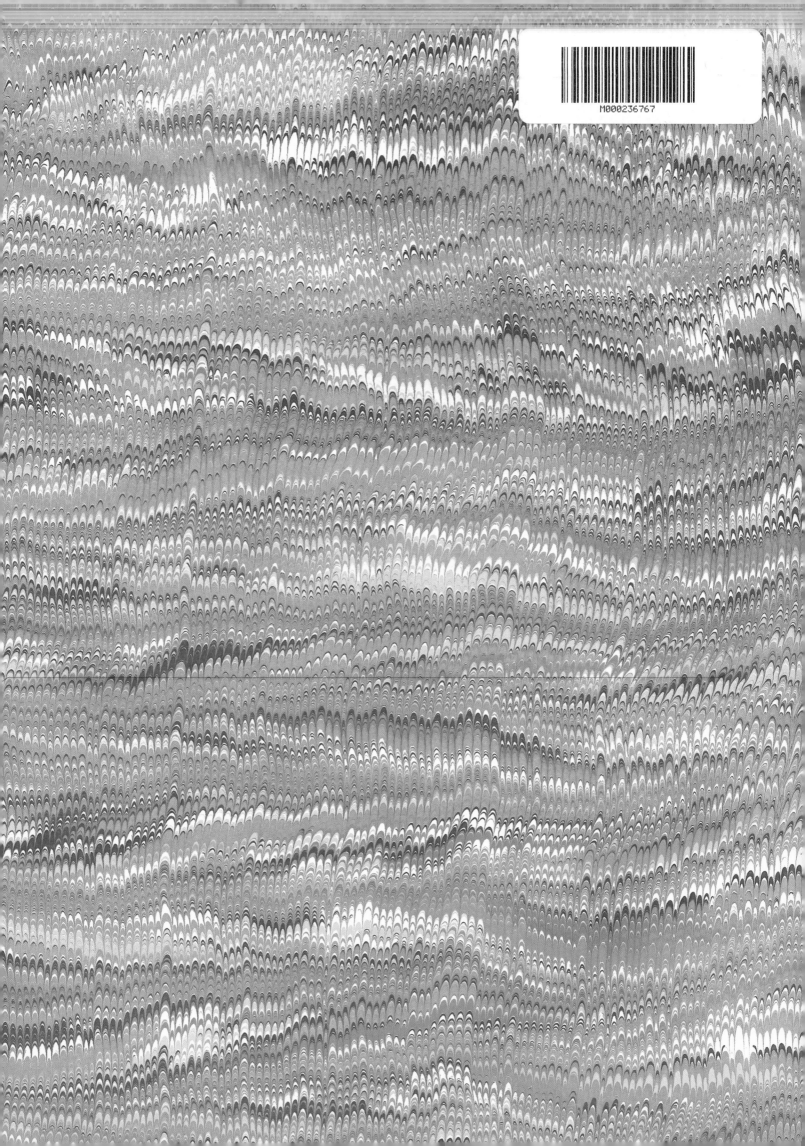

Army Blue

Army Blue

ARMY BLUE

The Uniform of Uncle Sam's
Regulars
1848-1873

John P. Langellier

Schiffer Military History
Atglen, PA

DEDICATED TO

RAYMOND S. BRANDES, SIDNEY B. BRINCKERHOFF, and JEROME A. GREENE

"The uniform gentlemen, is not a matter of individual, whimsical expression."

Lieutenant Colonel Owen Thursday (Henry Fonda)
Fort Apache (RKO) 1948

Book Design by Ian Robertson.

Printed in China.
ISBN: 0-7643-0443-7

We are interested in hearing from authors with book ideas on related topics.

Published by Schiffer Publishing Ltd.
77 Lower Valley Road
Atglen, PA 19310
Phone: (610) 593-1777
FAX: (610) 593-2002
E-mail: Schifferbk@aol.com.
Please write for a free catalog.
This book may be purchased from the publisher.
Please include $2.95 postage.
Try your bookstore first.

CONTENTS

FOREWORD

With this volume and the one to follow, John Langellier takes his place in the ranks of the foremost historians of American military uniform – if in fact he has not already reached that status with a series of previous publications. The focus of these two volumes is on the years of the Western Indian wars, and the Civil War insofar as the Regular Army's uniforms were concerned., extending to nearly the end of the nineteenth century.

The history of scholarly study of American military uniforms is not a long one. Colonel Albert G. Brackett made passing mention of the evolution of cavalry uniforms in his history of that arm written in 1863 and published in 1865. After that, one or two articles appeared later in the nineteenth century in illustrated newspapers of the era. Addition-ally, even before Brackett's work, colored military prints accompanied by descriptions of uniforms had been produced from time to time, but covered only the dress then currently in use. The most significant of these were rendered by Huddy and Duval around 1840 for the *U.S. Military Magazine*; the prints illustrating regulations for the newly prescribed Regular Army uniforms published by Horstmann in 1851 (reprinted in Appendix B of this volume); the chromolithographs-illustrated new uniform regulations produced for the Quartermaster Department in 1882 and 1888; and three prints published around 1900 to reflect the new uniforms adopted after the outbreak of the Spanish American War.

Only one notable title appeared during the nineteenth century which explored the history of U.S. Army uniforms, but it was outstanding and

Flanked by officers in their practical field dress, during the War with Mexico, Major General Zachary Taylor observes the Battle of Monterrey. Taylor, who later became president of the United States, demonstrated an aversion to uniforms, often donning civilian garb during campaigns, perhaps in part because, he like many officers, found regulation wear wanting, or as was the practice with some high ranking English officers, he preferred going in mufti, much as British gentry dressed in plain garb while outfitting their retainers in elaborate livery.

Gleason's Pictorial Drawing-Room Companion, one of the popular illustrated newspapers of the 1850s, reproduced images of the 1851-pattern uniform, garb that accommodated military fashion ideals versus functional clothing requirements. LC

precedent-setting. In 1889, the Quartermaster Department republished the twelve chromolithographed prints it had commissioned illustrator Henry Alexander Ogden to prepare of then-current uniforms in 1888, but with two additions. War Department clerks complied all general orders pertaining to American military uniforms, including Continental Army orders, covering the years 1774 to 1889, and the Department commissioned Ogden to execute thirty-two more color plates to depict the period represented by the compiled orders. The Quartermaster Department then published the entire work, consisting of the full text of the regulations and orders and forty-four chromolithographs (several of which appear in the Introduction of *Army Blue)* in a bound volume. In preparing his prints, H.A. Ogden did something that set his work apart from, and far ahead of, virtually all European military uniform illustrations and publications: for each print, he gave the year of adoption and discontinuance for the uniforms depicted, a characteristic that has tended to dominate American military uniform research and art ever since. As pioneering as Ogden's work was, however, it only was the beginning especially in that the work included many errors requiring future correction.

In the twentieth century the Quartermaster Department maintained its interest in depicting the history of the American military uniform, commissioning from time to time prints of uniforms as they were adopted.

As early as 1907 the department published another twenty-three chromolithographs by Ogden documenting the sweeping changes in the uniform made as a result of the 1902 regulations.

One other effort in the field of uniform history in the early twentieth century was Charles Lefferts' volume on the Revolutionary War uniform of both the Continentals as well as the British forces that the New York Historical Society published after World War I. Also after World War I, and extending well after World War II, the Quartermaster Department commissioned works from time to time by a number of artists who rendered illustrations of contemporary uniforms. Practically none of these, however, were published in color or made readily available in any form. Much later, the U.S. Army did commission three series of military prints by H.C. McBarron, Ogden's twentieth century successor as the dean of American military uniform illustrators. Yet these series were neither comprehensive nor systematic.

During World War II Americans serving in Europe encountered collections of prints illustrating the history of European uniforms. This exposure to foreign sources, together with their own service in the war, stimulated an interest in American military history after veterans returned to the United States. Some of these individuals began to collect genuine American military arms, uniforms, and equipments, and soon created a "run" on old Civil War-era military surplus supply houses such as Francis Bannerman and Sons of New York City and W. Stokes Kirk of Philadelphia, not to mention costume-renting companies among whose replica stock and fanciful costumes lay hidden authentic items.

One group of individuals even organized a nationwide historical society named "The Company of Military Collectors and Historians," which eventually became known simply as the "Company of Military Historians." Beginning in January 1949, the Company published a quarterly journal, *Military Collector and Historian*, along with a parallel series of sixteen hand-colored military prints per year known as *Military Uniforms in America*. The Company's publications provided the first serious focus on the history of the American military uniform since Lefferts' work, while *Military Collector and Historian* would grow more sophisticated and scholarly as time passed. Indeed, it remains the principal journal in the field.

Stimulated by this journal, new works on American military uniforms and equipments began to appear. For example, during the 1960s Thomas Yoseloff reprinted all seventy of Ogden's illustrations in two bound volumes, although with the first forty-four, he chose to reproduce a less-useful descriptive narrative by Henry Loomis Nelson which originally had been included with a privately-printed edition of the chromolithographs of the 1774-1889 illustrations in 1890.

Also in the 1960s, Sidney B. Brinckerhoff, director of the Arizona Pioneers' Historical Society (later the Arizona Historical Society) initiated a series of museum monographs, three of which he wrote himself, on various aspects of American military uniforms. The author of this foreword wrote two more in titles in that series on various aspects of the western Indian wars that illustrated the wealth of information found in the *Army and Navy Journal* and the published reports of the Ordnance Department and Quartermaster Department available in the serial or Congressional Documents volumes. These five monographs significantly impacted the field, providing a new stimulus for additional work.

At this point the historiography of American military uniforms entered a new phase initiated by two publications from the Smithsonian Institution that resulted from the research efforts of Edgar M. Howell and Donald Kloster, which together with articles and a monograph by

James Hutchins, for the first time drew in depth from official Quartermaster Department correspondence and other records in the National Archives.

Others joined the field: Duncan Campbell and William Emerson explored military insignia, including chevrons; Douglas McChristian of the national Park Service provided an excellent study of uniforms and equipments in the 1870s. Militaria dealer Jacques Noel Jacobsen made a whole range of pamphlet-sized reprints of regulations and early military catalogs available. Articles on American uniforms were included in such British periodicals as *Tradition* and *Military Illustrated*, along with a U.S. periodical *Military Images*.

Author of various articles, pamphlets, and monographs in the field, John P. Langellier has resumed his contributions to the literature, first with brief, heavily illustrated studies related to the Civil War and the Indian wars eras for the "GI" series, a joint venture by Greenhill Books of England and Stackpole of the United States, and finally with this volume and the one to follow, which provide a comprehensive history of the U.S. Army uniform from 1848 through 1902.

Dr. Langellier has devoted the time and resources to sit hour after hour, day after day, week after, for uncounted numbers of weeks, painstakingly researching all the correspondence and document files, orders and circulars, and contracts with military suppliers that comprise the extant records of the Quartermaster Department for the second half of the nineteenth century. Thus he has built on the more narrowly focused Smithsonian publications, the Arizona Historical Society monograph series, and the articles, monographs, and previous books by others to provide for the first time a scholarly history of the developments and innovations in American military uniforms since the Mexican War through the War with Spain. This profusely illustrated two-volume work published by Schiffer places him in the first rank of twentieth century historians of American military uniforms.

Gordon Chappell
Regional Historian
National Park Service
San Francisco

Another illustrated newspaper, *Harper's Weekly*, published an image of the light artillery uniform in its June 8, 1867 issue. The uniform was more ceremonial than the practical garb adopted during the Civil War. SI

In September 1872 *Harper's Weekly* was among the first publications to inform the public about the new uniform that was to replace the Union garb worn during the Civil War. SI

PREFACE

Over thirty years ago my mother came home from an auction with a small box of buttons she had purchased as a surprise for me. Inside were many nineteenth century military specimens with tiny tags indicating that they came from various battlefields and forts around the country. Intrigued with this treasure chest of history, I began to look for further information not only about these small brass artifacts from a bygone era, but also those that covered the U.S. Army uniform in general. At that time only a few scattered reference works were in print about these subjects. Frustrated in what the local public library had to offer, I succeeded in making my way to the Arizona Historical Society, where several important secondary and primary sources were available for use.

I should have been satisfied with what I found there. Instead the newly acquired knowledge compelled me to search for more information. For one thing, over the ensuing years, the number of articles, monographs, and books increased covering the period from the Mexican War to the end of the 1800s.[1] I even contributed a few modest works to the field, the first of which came about through the encouragement of Dr. Raymond Brandes, my mentor at the University of San Diego. While I was one of his graduate students, Dr. Brandes agreed to my proposal for an independent study about U.S Army enlisted dress uniforms of the 1866-1902 era. The Arizona Historical Society's executive director at that time, Sidney Brinckerhoff, wholeheartedly supported this project, and along with other members of the staff there, most notably Pierce Chamberlain, Thomas Peterson, and Jay Van Orden, provided considerable support to ensure that the extensive collection of uniforms and reference materials at the Society were accessible for the completion of my research. John Sukey and James Wertman, the friends from Tucson, also greatly contributed to this early project. Fortunately, Don J. McGee shared enthusiasm for the venture and published it in 1976 as *They Continually Wear the Blue*.

More titles followed, but all the while I felt compelled to produce a major publication that would synthesize the work of many other students of the subject, as well as allow me to incorporate the results of my own twenty-five years of haunting archives, libraries, museums, and private collections. In 1997, I finally succeeded in weaving thousands of notes and hundreds of illustrations into this volume covering the period from 1848 to 1873. Happily, Peter Schiffer agreed to undertake the publication. All the while, both Mr. Schiffer and military editor Robert Biondi proved patient partners in this project. While this volume represents the culmination of more than three decades of effort, it by no means is exhaustive, especially in that it contains only limited analysis of the type anthropologist Clifford Geertz terms "thick description."[2] Instead, although such an academic approach holds considerable merit, this publication takes a different course.[3] It chronicles the development of the uniform of the immediate post Mexican War era to the decade just after the Civil War. Among other things, this study attempts to give context as to why the uniform evolved over the years under consideration, and likewise demonstrates the difference between regulations and what actually was worn by the soldier in the Regular Army. Moreover, attention has been paid to lag between official adoption of new patterns, and when these items really reached the rank and file. Most significantly, the book features key uniform specimens and contemporary photographs from dozens of sources to complement the primary documents consulted in the National Archives and elsewhere, hopefully making it a useful tool for collectors, curators, and others who are interested in the U.S. Army uniform as it existed during the mid-nineteenth century.

The author owes a great debt to many individuals and institutions for their contributions to this study. In addition to those noted above, Robert G. Borrell, Sr., Wes Clark, Jerome Greene, Josh Landish, and Douglas McChritian kindly allowed me to photograph their fine collections. So did Glen Swanson, who despite a hectic schedule to open the Reno Battlefield Museum, volunteered his valuable time and talents to photograph the excellent specimens from his collection. Similarly, Gordon Chappell provided photographic support, expert advice, and graciously agreed to write the foreword, among his many contributions to *Army Blue*. Dr. Michael J. McAfee was another extraordinary colleague who went above and beyond the call of duty with copies of pictures from his collection as well as color photographs of pre-Civil War specimens in the collections of the U.S. Military Academy's West Point Museum.

Jim Hutchins, Don Kloster, Margaret Vining, and the late Dr. Ed Ezell, all of the Smithsonian Institution's Museum of American History, generously opened the important collections in their charge on several research visits, including during my tenure as a Smithsonian Fellow in 1985. J. Edward Green (then of the Presidio Army Museum in San Francisco), encouraged me to forge ahead with this project, and assisted whenever called upon for support.

What is more, Harry Roach, publisher of *Military Images*, facilitated contact with key private collectors, most notably Dr. William J. Schultz, who although at work on co-authoring his own monograph on antebellum uniforms, unselfishly provided several excellent pre-Civil War images for my use. Michael F. Bremer, Norm Flayderman, Eugene R. Groves, Greg Martin, Mr. and Mrs. V.J. Moran, Stephen Osman, and Herb Peck, also granted permission to draw upon their superb privately owned images.

At the former Wyoming Archives, Museums, and Historical Department, Paula Chovoya and Tom Lindmier always were ready to respond to requests for assistance. Steve Allie, director of the Frontier Army Museum of Ft. Leavenworth, Kansas, sent images from that institution's excellent photo collections. Chief Curator James Nottage, Research Center director Dr. Kevin Mulroy, and others at the Autry Museum of Western Heritage offered similar courtesies. Gail DeBuse Potter, former chief curator of the Museum of Nebraska History, made the collections in Lincoln accessible to me, and arranged for photographs of many artifacts to be taken. John Carter of that same organization likewise lent support, as did Tim O'Gorman and Luther Hansen, of the U.S. Army Quartermaster Museum. John Campbell of the North Carolina State Museum, along with Michael Winey and Randy Hackenberg of the U.S. Army Military History Institute at Carlisle Barracks, Pennsylvania also are due thanks. Renee M. Erwin, assistant curator of history at the Fort Worth Museum of Science and Industry, Sally Nelson Harb, librarian for Western Costume, and Scott Portman of the State of Wisconsin Historical Society are among others who provided assistance. Staffs of the Kansas State Historical Society, Montana Historical Society, the North Dakota Historical Society, the Utah Historical Society, the National Archives and Records Administration in Washington, D.C., and the Library of Congress, all rendered professional services as well.

Dr. Don Mrozek, my major professor at Kansas State University, suggested many important elements found in the book's introduction. Another colleague Dr. Vincent Transano, the U.S. Navy's Facilities and Engineering Command Historian, patiently read drafts of the manuscript and offered valuable comments on the text, as did Kurt Hamilton Cox. Additionally Mr. Cox helped with photography for the book and shared his own research for the text. Finally, my wife Deanna and daughter Erica indulged me for the over two years it took to complete the volume. To them and many others, I offer my sincere thanks.

NOTES

[1] See bibliography for a concise selection of many of the most notable titles.

[2] See, Clifford Geertz, *The Interpretation of Cultures* (New York: Basic Books, 1973).

[3] For an excellent example of an analytical review of military uniform in keeping with Geertz see, Scott Hughes Myerly, *British Military Spectacle: From the Napoleonic Wars through Crimea* (Cambridge, MA: Harvard University Press, 1996). Myerly goes beyond the usual descriptive, and often antiquarian approach to uniforms. As such, he offers a provocative model for others to follow.

INTRODUCTION

In the late eighteenth century the Thirteen Colonies made their bid for independence from Great Britain. Despite success in this undertaking the young country continued to owe an intellectual debt to the English, and indeed to many other Europeans as well. Perhaps nowhere was this situation more evident than in the United States Army. For over a hundred years, that institution searched for an identity which often took its cue from the other side of the Atlantic. In fact, from the time of the Revolution forward, a sometimes subtle but constant tension existed between employment of European military mores versus an "American" martial spirit.[1]

One group of military leaders envisioned the form the U.S. Army would take in terms of organization, tactics, equipment, and other material requirements from the point of view of "cultivated traditions" – recreating Old World models most notably from England and France.[2] An opposing camp looked to "vernacular . . . patterns and forms . . . in attempting to give satisfying order to the unprecedented elements in

A major general of the Mexican War era and various other officers, including officers of engineers and artillery, appear in relatively plain, practical campaign uniforms with shoulder straps to indicate rank and the ubiquitous 1839-pattern forage cap. Function tended to be more important than form during the conflict.

In 1848, after the war between Mexico and the United States ended, the ornate cap and coatee reemerged as ceremonial dress for Uncle Sam's Regulars. White worsted tape denoted infantry and yellow tape with red accent piping designated artillerymen. Musicians had red coatees in contrast to the dark blue of the rank and file. Yellow trimmed blue coatees marked dragoons, as seen for the sergeant depicted in the right background.

In 1851 a new uniform regulation, partly predicated on the concept that one outfit would serve for ceremonial and field or fatigue use, was issued. Several years passed before enlisted men received this outfit. Collars, cuffs, and caps displayed branch colors including Saxony blue for infantry, yellow for engineers, orange for dragoons, scarlet for artillery, and green for riflemen. Musicians had plastrons of matching branch colors.

All officers also had frock coats according to the new 1851 regulations, but unlike enlisted men, branch colors did not adorn the cuffs, collar, or caps. Double-breasted coats were worn by majors through colonels. Company grade officers (second lieutenants through captains) had single-breasted coats much as the troops they commanded, thereby visibly identifying them with their men. A French-inspired cloak coat was adopted for officers as inclement-weather wear.

which democracy and technology have [been] jointly introduced into the human environment . . ." in the United States.[3]

American versus European paradigms especially were evident and of paramount importance in understanding the United States Army during the mid to late nineteenth century. The garb adopted by the Regulars particularly was significant if one subscribes to the theory that: "Identification with and active participation in a social group always involves the human body and its adornment and clothing."[4] Furthering this argument, an early commentator on the subject contended that clothing originated from the wearing of badges or symbolic elements rather than from sheer necessity.[5] Thus, "the extreme form of" this type of "conventional dress is the costume totally determined by others: the uniform" which "unlike most civilian clothing . . . is often consciously and deliberately symbolic" in that "it identifies its wearer as a member of some group and often locates him or her within a hierarchy."[6]

This was not the case when uniforms began to develop in the seventeenth century. During the 1600s, early uniforms resembled civilian patterns, but because commanding officers had to raise and equip their men from personal resources they found it more economical to outfit their troops in one color of material, thereby beginning military uniforms.[7]

As time passed, however, uniforms became more complex. With this change they have been identified as one of the most innovative uses of clothing – the personification of governmental authority by individuals or groups.[8] Continuing this thread of reasoning these uniforms sup-

posedly separated "the limbs of authority from the common herd and secured immediate obedience."[9] Additionally, uniforms eventually were used "to distinguish friend from enemy." It then followed that "the uniform of the fighting man" came to be regarded as a necessity, at least in modern times, except in cases of guerilla war.[10]

According to another source it was this "manipulation of visual images," including uniforms that, "is especially significant in the exercise of power."[11] Further, this imagery was seen as "essential in communicating to soldiers the fundamental values embedded in the military model: bravery and duty, discipline, self-control, conformity, and hierarchy; unity and solidarity of purpose; motivation, efficiency, and self-sacrifice for a higher goal; and above all, loyalty to those in command."[12]

Fulfilling these various objectives meant that military dress was designed by those in control rather than by those who were to wear the uniform.[13] Thus martial attire is more than a statement of fashion. It is also "representative of the state it serves." This double imperative likewise carries over into two areas that usually are in opposition when it comes to the matter of militaria – "a pleasing aesthetic, on one hand, and a design that is both practical in providing protection for the body and comfortable to wear, on the other. . . ."[14]

The United States Army was created during the era when uniforms had been accepted by the major powers in Europe. Americans followed suit and adopted a garb that would set the soldiery apart from the general population, as well as differentiate comrade from foe. But for much of its history the U.S. Army was little concerned with avoiding confusion in conflict, given the decades of service in the American West against an unconventional enemy – various American Indian peoples, who wore no uniforms in the European sense.

Only the Mexican War and the Civil War gave rise to one of the basic reasons for the creation of uniforms in more recent history. Conversely, the latter confrontation took place during the coming of age of long-range weapons and other advances in ordnance that increasingly made it desirable to blend with one's surrounding in battle, rather than stand out.

Added to this dichotomy was the U.S. Army's role as servant to a republic headed by elected civilian officials. Democratic principles and the caste-like system of the military set up a duality. This was exaggerated further by one of the traits ascribed by some historians, including Frederick Jackson Turner, as a basic defining force of Americans – individualism.[15]

This individualistic bent runs counter to an extreme view that maintains, "the uniform was invented as a means to indicate the relationship of an individual to a group." Further, "the origin of the word itself (uniform: one form, all alike)" clearly defines that a man thus garbed "*shows by his clothing that he has given up his right to act freely as an individual but must act in accordance with and under the limitations of the rules of the group.*"[16]

Given these varied determinants, the problem of what constituted proper martial wear in the United States took on even more subtleties.

Little wonder than that Rufus Zogbaum, a prominent nineteenth century author and illustrator of matters related to the U.S. Army noted:

> The subject of what to wear always seems to be a vexed question in our little army, and the advantages of this or that pattern of coat or cap are discussed over and over again in all departments of the service, from headquarters of the general commanding the army to the barracks of a one company post on the remote frontier.[17]

While widespread dissatisfaction may have existed, no universal solution satisfied all critics. Significantly at least two main contrary perspectives can be traced when it came to uniforms.

On one hand, there were those who drew inspiration from foreign models. These men leaned toward dominant powers from abroad for answers as to what best suited the soldier in terms of attire. Arguably many conservative, older leaders fell into this category, but membership was not restricted to those who fit this profile. Certainly age was not the only motivation here, because as one scholar suggested this approach was "prompted by reverence for one imitated or it may be prompted by the desire to assert equality with him."[18] The prominence of French forces throughout much of the early nineteenth century, and the later rise of Germanic and British armies certainly contributed to changes in American martial attire. One might argue imitation of this

General officers also wore frock coats according to the 1851 uniform regulations, but had black velvet cuffs and collars to set them off from lower ranks. Their pompons likewise were distinct, as were their sashes which were buff rather than the crimson worn by all other officers except surgeons, whose sashes were green.

A short jacket was ushered in during 1854 for mounted troops (dragoons, light artillery, and mounted rifles). There also was a new cap with a single welt of facing in branch color adopted in lieu of the 1851-pattern that had solid facing material for all but ordnance and engineer troops. Sky-blue replaced Saxony blue in that same year for infantry facings and trim. The following year a French-inspired plaited coat was prescribed for all foot troops. The short jackets represented a concession to more functional wear given that tails were less practical for horse soldiers, while the 1855-pattern plaited coat demonstrated the continued interest in European martial attire that was driven more by fashion than form in most instances.

Winfield Scott was known as "Old Fuss and Feathers," in part because of his penchant for ornate uniforms. Depicted here on the eve of the Civil War, Scott clearly stands out from those whom he commands as the senior officer in the U.S. Army of the time.

Dark blue trousers to match coats and jackets gave a monotone appearance when adopted in 1858. This was a short-lived deviation from the two-tone look so long associated with the U.S. Army. A new hat was prescribed in that same year to replace the cap of the 1854-pattern. The transition was not immediate, however, because typically a lag existed between the adoption of new uniforms or clothing items and actual issue.

sort had ancient roots from hunters who donned the skins of their prey, to early warrior societies that took trophies from their fallen enemies to demonstrate their own prowess.

For those holding counter views the adoption of foreign styles constituted mere aping without substance. Many military men with this mind set, rather than looking to the Old World considered the conditions that existed in the New World. They opted for solutions that they believed fit the circumstances found in a vast, diverse country, in keeping with another of Professor Turner's pronouncements.[19] Often supporting simplified, practical concepts rather than solutions based solely on custom, this circle regularly championed the experimental or the expedient, while traditionalists eschewed such methodology.

The results of those who sought to put European patterns aside might be viewed by those who disputed them as "ungainly, crude, or awkward." Their products attempted to adapt to the physical environment, whereas those who clung to cultivated traditions could be accused of ignoring local conditions and even rejecting technological advances.[20] Because of the considerable strides in industrialization that occurred in the United States during the 1800s, failing to espouse machine manufacturing must have seemed unamerican to those who looked to technology and sought a uniform that met the needs of varied climatic conditions.

Reaction to the proponents of cultivated tradition by vernacular supporters no doubt increased considerably as the Victorian era wore on, given the "pragmatism" and other intellectual leanings of the 1880s and 1890s that drew from powerful sources. This was a period of rapid technological and economic development, the application of Darwin's

theories to the social milieu, and other forces of the times.[21] All these led to a general suspension "of approaches which are excessively formal" and could be viewed as "survivals" that no longer had relevance or meaning. Among other things this proclivity accounts for the fact that by the immediate post-Civil War period surgeons, the representatives of the scientific community, began to play a greater role in uniform development, heretofore mostly the realm of the quartermaster department.

This shift represented both the ascendancy of science as well as political realities of the period when the quartermaster general's power waned to some extent while other departments in the period of the bureau system, that predated the establishment of the general staff, gained power through various means. Erosion of the quartermaster general's status nonetheless did not spell immediate reform in military dress. Furthermore, the advocacy of new patterns was not just a product of the era after Appomattox.

In reality the movement could be traced to a least the 1840s. However, the existence of relatively large stocks of clothing produced for the Mexican War inhibited momentum for the abandonment of old styles in favor of new ones. A cost conscious Congress simply would not approve expenditures when what appeared to be perfectly good materials were on hand. Nevertheless, the desire for change continued. The outbreak of the Civil War added fuel to debate, but once more recommendations for certain styles fell by the wayside, although as in all wars, the effect was to make the uniform more utilitarian. The fighting dress of the soldier came to approximate civilian country or sporting clothes.[22]

Repeating the situation after the War with Mexico, the years after the American Civil War were ones where the existence of surplus uni-

By the late 1850s a floppy forage cap based on French headgear began to make its appearance. During the Civil War it gained widespread use in a number of patterns or designs, and came to be called a "bummer's cap" in slang of the era.

As the Civil War raged increasing numbers of officers and enlisted men put aside the more ornate antebellum uniform in favor of no-frills combat clothing. General U.S. Grant, seated in the center of this illustration by artist Henry A. Ogden, typified this trend.

form articles forestalled efforts to obtain new patterns. Massive production by the standards of that era had caused an overabundance in everything, including uniforms.[23] Quartermaster personnel knew the powers who controlled the coffers in Washington would not release funds for what some might look upon as frivolous fashion trends or examples of materialistic show that had caught on at many levels of late Victorian society. Lawmakers would frown upon those who desired to display wealth or class in hopes of gaining respectability, as the quartermaster general probably realized.

These perceptions and the desire to use up existing material impeded reform. This was considered in some circles as false economy because some of the clothing manufactured during the late war allegedly was of inferior quality. The items made during the war supposedly deteriorated after limited use, and in addition fit poorly because of ill cutting or scrimping on the part of contractors. Then, too, the clothing was faulted as inadequate to the varying climates served in by American troops.

While all these factors merely added to a basic phenomenon in that the exigencies of combat inevitably causes uniforms to become more utilitarian, restoration of peace drastically altered the situation.[24] In this atmosphere the inclination is toward "a general `smartening up'" which is to say it becomes "less important that troops should be able to endure the rigors of campaign than they should look smart on parade."[25]

With these various competing trends at play the summary of nineteenth century American author Henry Loomis Nelson was indicative of the widespread debate. He wrote: "there are few officers or men . . . who do not desire a radical change in their uniforms." Additionally it

The conclusion of fighting between North and South saw a return to the parade-ground uniform essentially as it had existed before the Civil War. Despite this, the major general depicted has elected to don a slouch hat in lieu of a chapeau or 1858-pattern hat, somewhat symbolic of the growing dissatisfaction and desire among many officers and enlisted men for a new uniform.

seemed the militia oftentimes preceded the regulars in the adoption of better articles of wear, while revisions from Washington supposedly had "been of a timid and conservative character as such a proponent for change noted." If the soldier constantly complained of his outfit, he had a right to, because American troops had "never worn anything to be proud of," nor had they "been clothed in the splendor which captivates the eye of the civilian and fills with pride the bosom of the enlisted man."[26]

The mention of gaining acceptance by civilians and instilling self-esteem in the soldier is a telling one. First of all, the innovation "that the esprit de corps and fighting spirit of a body of troops could be vastly increased by drilling them together and clothing them in the same garb" dated from the seventeenth century, and formed the very foundation that led to the creation of uniforms.[27]

As far as affirmation or notice of the military by civilians is concerned British fashion historian James Laver concludes this stems from one of three basic principles that govern all costume evolution, in this case "The Seduction Principle." Laver defines this as an attempt of the wearer to make his or herself "as attractive as possible to the opposite sex." In terms of uniforms this is manifested by patterns that "widens the military man's shoulders, narrows his hips, puffs out his chest, lengthens his legs and increases his apparent height."[28] The double impression sought, at least in the early forms of military clothing, was to in-

That new uniform came into being in 1872, complete with a helmet for mounted troops, following the lead of the Prussians, English, and other European powers, and a return to a cap with pompon for dismounted troops, along French and English lines. This cap for enlisted foot troops had a pompon (white for infantry, scarlet for artillery, and so forth). Mounted troops were to be issued a helmet. Enlisted cavalrymen had yellow plumes and cords, while those for light artillery were scarlet, and orange for signal service personnel. Officers' caps were surmounted by white or scarlet cock feathers respectively for infantry and heavy artillery, and light artillery officers, along with cavalry officers, followed enlisted men in terms of scarlet or yellow plumes respectively. Facings on the dress coats issued the other ranks included yellow for cavalry, scarlet for artillery, and medium blue for infantry.

timidate the enemy and to entice women, because in both cases the effect being sought is to convey an aura of physical power. One turn-of-the-century guide to prospective spouse hunters echoed the latter theory in a section delineating fifteen points that women found appealing in men. The discourse concluded with the assertion: "It is a well known fact that women love uniformed men. . . . The military man figures as a hero in every tale of fiction, and is said by good authority that a man in uniform has three more chances to marry than the man without uniform."[29]

Laver's second axiom is "The Hierarchical Principle" that: "establishes social position. It is the general principle governing male dress. In military costume it shrinks into a rigid ritualism of rank."[30] As a consequence, a dilemma arose. If the idea of the uniform was uniformity how could superiority of one individual over others be indicated? Usually this was accomplished by "the primitive measure of marking each successive rank, from below upwards," and "by an increase in decorativeness of the corresponding costume."[31] Here supposedly *Man's ingenuity came into play again, and he invented the insignia, the stripe, the epaulet, or some other variation in the uniform to indicate the difference in rank.*[32] Eventually, indication of rank became stereotyped by badges, particularly during times of war. In fact, as the nineteenth century wore on, the numerous nuances that set officer apart from enlisted man, and set one strata above another gradually declined.[33]

This phenomenon coincided with Laver's final tenet, "The Utility Principle." As the realities of war take hold, ornate, stiff peacetime uniforms give way to more practical loose garb. Eventually though these clothes also become formalized and less responsive to necessity, likewise requiring them "to be replaced by something easier." A new "battle dress" then appears, and according to Laver, the uniform it supplants becomes the "walking out" dress, that is a "smartened" version of the "battle dress" of the previous war." In other words, the "Ceremonial uniform is often the battle dress (formalized and fantasticated) of the *last war but one.*"[34]

Finally, Laver viewed the military uniform as the interplay between the seduction principle and the utility principle.[35] Laver concluded the utilitarian dominated, with the repercussion that the muted field uniform eventually gained the upper hand. This reduced the glamour of war and replaced it with the grim realities of modern combat.[36]

The same argument can be made regarding the uniform of the United States Army as it evolved in the last half of the 1800s. As presented in *Army Blue* the evidence indicates symbolism took second place to pragmatism. Individualism and egalitarianism gained considerably over hierarchical, authoritarian caste systems. Foreign influences waned, or were modified greatly. Civilian and military styles again tended to converge, as they had in earlier times. Considerable deviation from regulation was the norm for not only officers, but many men as well.[37] Finally, environmentally inspired vernacular eventually won out over cultivated tradition, thereby becoming "a cultivated tradition of its own."[38]

All but generals relinquished their sashes when the 1872 regulations came into force. In fact, from 1851 through the early twentieth century, this sash accented the somber dark blue coat and trousers with gold epaulets that continued as a mainstay for general officers, topped off by their chapeau de bras. The 1872-pattern coat for all other officers was double-breasted in clear contrast to all enlisted dress coat that were single-breasted, thereby ending a long standing tradition for at least company grade officers to appear in a garb similar to the rank and file on parade.

NOTES

1   Marcus Cunliffe, *Soldiers & Civilians: The Martial Spirit in America, 1775-1865* (New York: The Free Press, 1973), and Russell Weigley, *The American Way of War: A History of United States Military Strategy and Policy* (New York: Macmillan, 1973), both present provocative treatments on the U.S. military's search for identity.

2   John A. Kouwenhoven, *Made in America* (Garden City, NJ: Doubleday & Co., 1948), expands upon the idea of cultivated traditions versus vernacular in terms of architecture in the United States. Some of the same theoretical constructs have merit when applied to material culture and other outward manifestations of the U.S. Army during the Victorian era.

3   John A. Kouwenhoven, *The Beer Can by the Highway* (Baltimore: Johns Hopkins University Press, 1988), 141. Kouwenhoven defines the vernacular arts as, "the empirical attempts of ordinary people to shape elements of their everyday environment in a democratic, technological age." He states further, "The history of design...is essentially the product of dynamic tension between the cultivated and vernacular traditions," and points out "that cultivated forms have influenced vernacular forms" although the reverse is sometimes also true. Ibid., 132, and 172-173.

4   Ted Polehemus and Lynn Proctor, *Fashion and Anti-Fashion: An Anthropology of Ornament and Clothing* (London: Thames and Hudson, 1978), 20.

5   Herbert Spencer, *The Principles of Sociology* II (New York: D. Appleton, 1892), 174-210. J.C. Flugel, *The Psychology of Clothes* (London: Hogarth Press, 1940), offers an extensive treatise on the numerous reasons why clothes are worn. Mary Ellen Roach and Joanne Bubolz Eicher, eds., *Dress, Adornment, and the Social Order* (New York: John Wiley Sons, 1965), 5, acknowledges, "numerous attempts have been made to discover the motives" for humans to dress and adorn themselves, but all these explanations can be reduced to two basic "categories, expressive and instrumental." To clarify what is meant, "The expressive function involves the emotional and the communicative aspects of dress." This includes the range from establishing individuality to expressing group affiliation.

6   Beyond this, "Clothing may also be instrumental, involving rational use of dress in goal-directed behavior. Clothing may be utilitarian and protective; it may be used to attain desired rewards." Sometimes all these imperatives can be operating together; at others they may prove to be exclusive or at odds. Alison Lurie, *The Language of Clothes* (New York: Random House, 1981), 17 and 19.

7   James Laver, *British Military Uniforms* (London: Penguin Books, 1948), 9.

8   Lawrence Langner, *The Importance of Wearing Clothes* (New York: Hastings House, 1959), 127.

9   Ibid., 128.

10 Ibid., 131.

11 Myerly, *British Military Spectacle*, 10.

12 Ibid., 11.

13 Put another way, "control over the design of military uniforms symbolized authority and power. Ibid., 45.

14 Ibid., 34.

15 According to Frederick Jackson Turner, "The Significance of the Frontier in American History," reprinted in Ray Allen Billington, ed., *The Frontier Thesis: Valid Interpretation of American History?* (New York: Holt, Rinehart and Winston, 1966), 16, the nation's history was influenced by Westward expansion which was "productive of individualism."

16 Langner, *The Importance of Wearing Clothes*, 131-2. Myerly, *British Military Spectacle*, 40-1, suggests the uniform was "a badge of servile status" in England, in that "the subservient position of those in military uniform, which resembled the traditional livery worn by servants of the nobility...conveyed the power, grandeur, and taste of the master." To heighten this effect, the civilian master often dressed "in simple clothing to emphasize the contrast between himself and his handsome, sharply dressed menials. This is similar to the practice of many older officers wearing mufti whenever possible, even in reviews."

17 Rufus Fairchild Zogbaum, "Army Uniforms," *Harper's Weekly*, May 4, 1897, 4.

18 William Henry Flower, "Fashion in Deformity," V *Humboldt Library of Popular Science Literature* 28: 2.

19 According to Turner, "at the frontier the environment is at first too strong for man. He must accept the conditions which it furnishes, or perish, and so he fits himself into the Indian clearings and follows the Indian trails. Little by little he transforms the wilderness, but the outcome is not the old Europe...." Turner, "The Significance of the Frontier," 11.

20 Kouwenhoven, *The Beer Can by the Highway*, 145 and 183.

21 Morton White, *Social Thought in America: The Revolt Against Formalism* (Boston: Beacon Press, 1957), 6.

22 Laver, *British Military Uniforms*, 14.

23 These cycles coincide with what has been referred to as the "wave pattern," which although originally applied to British aviation history also bears a certain validity when it comes to other military development in the United States. The model set forth proposes a sequence of "peacetime equilibrium, disturbed by rearmament, then settling into the controlled activity of full wartime production; and when the war is over, renewed instability due to disarmament, phasing into new equilibrium." Robin Higham, *Air Power: A Concise History* (New York: St. Martin's Press, 1962), 3.

24 Laver, *British Military Uniforms*, 16.

25 Ibid., 16.

26 Henry Loomis Nelson, "Reform in Army Uniforms," *Harper's Weekly*, August 30, 1890, 682.

27 Laver, *British Military Uniforms*, 9. Myerly, *British Military Spectacle*, 58, contended "the fantasy of the uniform with all its association...was especially appealing to those who wanted to bolster self-esteem and sexual appeal." Further, Myerly noted the uniform served other functions from recruiting, imposition of discipline, entertainment, projection of power, and boosting or morale.

28 Laver, *British Military Uniforms*, 23.

29 B.G. Jeffries and J.L. Nichols, *Know Thyself or The Royal Path to Happiness* (New York: J.L. Nichols Co., 1903), 18.

30 Laver, *British Military Uniforms*, 23.

31 Flugel, *The Psychology of Clothes*, 130.

32 Langner, *The Importance of Wearing Clothes*, 134.

33 Laver, *British Military Uniforms*, 15.

34 Ibid., 24-5.

35 Ibid., 24.

36 Langner, *The Importance of Wearing Clothes*, 134.

37 This was not a uniquely American approach, however, in that British leaders often deviated from the regulation dress, even though their Prussian or other continental counterparts might have viewed this as a "crime." In England, however, this was looked upon "as a sign of" the officer's "political status as a free-born Briton." Indeed, older, more experienced officers in England not uncommonly preferred mufti as a means of demonstrating their independence. Myerly, *British Military Spectacle*, 69-70. To some extent this same tradition existed in the United States.

38 Kouwenhoven, *The Beer Can by the Highway*, 172 and 183.

Stephen Watts Kearny in the uniform of a colonel of the First Regiment of Dragoons as prescribed from 1833 through 1851 for dress wear. LC

1

CONSTABULARY DUTY, 1848-1860

Detail of collar of 1833 through 1851 dragoon officer's coatee of Richard Mason, who had been charged with delivering patterns of the uniforms for the Regiment of Dragoons when it was formed in 1833. LC

In 1846 the United States began to flex its nationalistic muscles against its southern neighbor, Mexico. For sixteen months, propelled by a spirit of Manifest Destiny, the Americans turned their martial might against formidable Mexican forces. When hostilities ceased, the *norteamericanos* had obtained considerable territorial gains from their former foe. The 1848 Treaty of Guadalupe Hidalgo brought an official peace between the two nations, and opened up a vast new area in what is now the western United States, including all of California and New Mexico, as well as most of today's Arizona.[1] This region soon grew in national importance.

As such, by 1850, dozens of installations came into existence across the vast new holdings west of the Mississippi River. It was there foot soldiers and mounted troops, who together represented the majority of the regulars at the time. On occasion they campaigned against American Indians; built roads; provided escorts; or served as a constabulary detailed from Kansas to California, positioned between the borders with Canada and Mexico.

Another segment of this military body was posted to coastal fortifications along the Atlantic seaboard and where key harbors or other strategic sites existed around the country. Artillerymen garrisoned these fortifications. Both forces taken together totaled less than 11,000 officers and men as the entire United States Army. In fact, the 1850 the strength of the U.S. Army stood at 10,763, with 2,109 being posted at 33 stations east of the Mississippi and the remainder garrisoned at 67 posts west of the Mississippi. A decade later that number has increased slightly to a total of 16,006 with the lion's share, 13,143, deployed to the West.[2]

Maintaining a far-flung, albeit relatively small complement of fighting men, challenged an even more numerically constrained support component. This in-

Front view of the 1833 through 1851 dragoon uniform for second and first lieutenants. Company grade officers were to have light blue trousers with double 3/4" wide yellow stripes of facing material on the outer seams, and field grade officers dark blue ones with gold lace double leg stripes. A cap with gold festooned triple weave cord and cap line was surmounted by a white horsehair plume. The sash was to be orange silk, but in this case Second Lieutenant James Clyman, for whom the uniform was made in 1833, elected to procure a yellow one. CSPRD

Side view of the 1833 through 1851 dragoon second lieutenant's uniform. CSPRD

cluded the Quartermaster Department, for the most part an eastern-based operation. From his office in Washington, D.C., the quartermaster general, who from 1818 until his death on June 9, 1860 was Thomas S. Jesup. This dynamic officer essentially created the Quartermaster Department. According to one historian Jesup's "long tenure, together with the unbroken, lengthy span of service of some of his subordinate officers, gave a continuity to Quartermaster training, methods, and procedures that had been utterly lacking in the past." During Jesup's administration, then he shaped the department that was charged with diverse responsibilities, including the design, procurement, production, and distribution of clothing.[3] This presented no easy task given a limited budget, far-stretched supply lines, and other difficulties.

The cost of shipping items to troops during the Mexican War and to the garrisons that were established afterwards in the West, particularly represented a significant drain on the quartermaster's budget. As a consequence, local commands in the West sometimes had little in the way of spare clothing and equipment.

It was not for want of supplies that these shortages existed because the Quartermaster Department had increased production during the late

OPPOSITE: Captain Thomas Swords wears the dress uniform of a dragoon officer complete with twisted gold and silver shoulder cords (aiguillettes) that were required for members of the regimental staff (in Swords' case the regimental quartermaster). Three gold lace loops on the cuffs indicate his rank, as do the gold epaulets with 1/4 bullion fringe. Facings were yellow for dragoons, white for infantry, and scarlet for artillery. This uniform was prescribed from 1833 through 1851. WPM

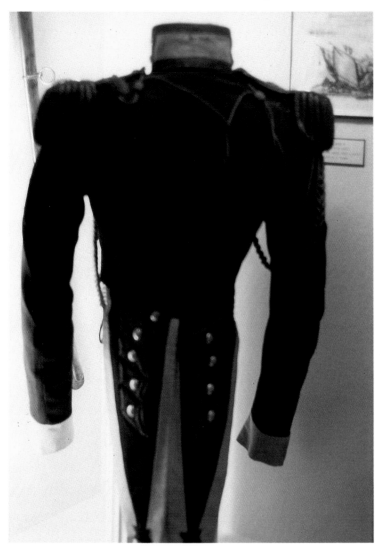

Rear view of Kearny's dragoon colonel's 1833-pattern coatee. MOHS

Field grade dragoon officers had four gold lace loops on their cuffs to indicate rank on the dress uniform coatee from 1833 through 1851. Gold epaulets with 1/2-inch gold bullion fringe, a silver eagle, and silver regimental numeral also indicated the rank of colonels and their unit. Finally, as of 1847, colonels commanding line regiments could don a chapeau with red and white cock feathers in place of the dress cap. MOHS

The regulation artillery officer's cap for dress wear from 1832 through 1851, with scarlet cock feathers. Michael McAfee Photograph. WPM

Captain Lucian Bonaparte Webster, commanding Battery C, First U.S. Artillery, poses with blue 1832 through 1851 dress uniform appropriate to his rank and assignment, including scarlet cock feathers from his cap, and scarlet trim and facings on his uniform coat. The buttons, epaulets, belt plate, saber knot, insignia on the cap, and lace ornamentation on his coatee were all to be gold color. The sash was to be crimson silk. Regulations prescribed a white buff belt for artillery officers above the rank of major, or for those serving as adjutants or quartermasters of their regiment, while all other officers were to have shoulder-belts. Captain Webster has elected to avail himself of the waist belt with interlocking buckle.
PAH&MC

From 1833 through 1851 the regulation belt plate for dragoons was a gilt rectangle with a wreath and Old English script "D", both in silver. WSHS

Topographical Engineer officer in the 1839 to 1851 dress uniform. Gold buttons bore a shield and the Old English letters "T.E." The gold embroidery on the collar and cuffs is worked over a dark blue velvet background. Surgeons and paymasters had similar coatees and chapeau but the background for the collar and cuffs was black velvet, while the embroidery on these coatees was of different design. WPM

war by adding ten times the number of seamstresses and tailors than it had employed before that conflict. This meant there were large stocks of garments on hand when the fighting stopped, the numbers being sufficient for many years to come in terms of clothing the small army of the 1850s. Despite this fact, transportation problems caused many men to be clothed in items that did not conform to the regulations. One army inspector general described this group as being "very imperfectly uniformed" – a relatively common plight during the antebellum period for the troops in the West, and occasionally in the East as well.[4]

Besides logistical obstacles, differing points of view as to what constituted the proper garb for Uncle Sam's regulars presented yet another challenge to quartermaster personnel, and contributed to a lack of uniformity when certain individuals sought to provide their own outfits. European models seemed compelling to some, with English models holding sway in the 1830s through 1850s, when French dominance began to hold sway. But varied environmental conditions, especially for the majority of the army serving on "frontier duty," caused a grassroots response "for a more practical uniform for field wear to replace the tight-fitting, parade-ground dress which had been in use for so many years."[5] Such contrary opinions concerning function versus fashion, coupled with fiscal concerns when it came to continued issuance of existing stocks, were key factors when it came to the uniform provided not only from 1851 through 1860, but also for some decades beyond.

Regardless of these sometimes polemical approaches, the styles adopted in the 1830s seemed outmoded to a number of soldiers in the late 1840s and early 1850s, in keeping with general trends in men's clothing that began to evolve gradually away from the breeches, pantaloons, and coatees or tailed coats of the early nineteenth century to frockcoats and trousers starting around 1815. By 1850 the civilian middle class embraced these changes in pursuit of "sensible, comfortable and practical" outfits, with a "marked preference for looser shapes."[6] In that same year Secretary of War George Crawford responded to statements of dissatisfaction when it came to martial attire. On February 13, 1850 he approved General Orders No. 2, that included in its first paragraph a rationale for issuing this directive, a candid explanation seldom found in orders. Crawford indicated:

A large number of the Officers of the Army, probably more than half, have applied since the war with Mexico, to have a uniform less expensive, less difficult to procure, and better adapted to campaign and other service. Their opinions, reasons and wishes are entitled to attention and respect; and it is important that the garments and equipments shall protect the persons of the wearers, preserve their health and make them efficient. . . .

In these few sentences the secretary of war summed up the main arguments of those who placed purpose over appearance when it came to the uniform. Among other features of the garb proposed to meet this group's demands was that, unlike previous regulations that mandated one type of headgear for dress and another for field, one cap was adopted for both situations. Officers were to obtain something akin to the 1839-pattern forage cap but with new insignia and bands around the crown to coincide with a color scheme adopted for each branch, the old 1832-pattern dress cap being seen by many as ill-adapted to the service while the forage cap was preferred.[7] Another cap, evidently designed along the lines of the old 1833-pattern leather forage cap, but instead of dark blue wool, was to serve double-duty for enlisted men.[8] A plume was to be added for gala occasions and omitted for undress duties.[9]

A British military periodical lauded the direction being advocated by the Americans remarking that it was, ". . . good common sense in the article of dress, and a disposition to yield to the wishes of the soldiery in adapting their costume to their personal comfort." Despite an endorsement from a major martial power and possibly similar responses from many observers in the U.S. Army, this relatively practical combat kit was not adopted for enlisted men at least, although some officers evidently procured the new outfit and were allowed to retain their purchases by General Orders No. 25, War Department, August 23, 1850. Conversely, the same order made it clear that enlisted men were not to adopt the new outfit after all.

The reason for this change was quite simply, ". . . so much clothing was on hand from the Mexican War there was no need to procure any additional stocks for some years." In fact, the quartermaster general pointed out that more than a million dollars worth of clothing from the Mexican War remained in storage at Schuylkill Arsenal, the army's central clothing establishment in the Philadelphia area.[10] With ample supplies on hand and constant Congressional requirements to be frugal, the quartermaster general saw a new uniform as, "injudicious and highly prejudicial to the interests of the Army."[11]

Some individuals were pleased that the proposed change was halted by the surplus stocks. For instance, a Topographical Engineer officer wrote from Oregon Territory in October 1850, "I am not sorry that they suspended our new uniform." Perhaps the writer was happy with the status quo because the Topographical Engineers already had an expensive and quite distinct uniform in keeping with their elite status. After all, a new uniform would have required the officer to purchase another outfit, one that would have been more generic, thereby making him stand out less from his fellow officers.

Others disagreed with this approach. In fact, some officers evidently purchased the new uniform soon after it was sanctioned, thereby prompting permission for this group to wear the new outfit "for the present time," according to General Orders No. 25. Consequently, the momentum for change continued, leading to the formation of another uniform board to review the matter. Such boards were called into existence from time to time and became a common thread in the history of uniform development during the second half of the nineteenth century. This particular one convened pursuant to General Orders No. 40, War Department, December 31, 1850. Meeting early the following year, the group reviewed comments from the field, factoring this information into its deliberations. Moreover, it considered ". . . various collections of drawings exhibiting dress in use in Foreign Services, and having in view the character of the frontier service most likely to be required of American troops for many years to come."

Once more this statement summarized the double imperatives operating when it came to the army's uniform. Practical concerns still were weighed against precedent of how military forces in other countries were attired. In many respects European military styles gained the upper hand, although this flew in the face of mid-nineteenth century civilian trends to abandon "padded chests" and "full coat skirts."[12] Finally, the fact that the uniform board proposed one basic outfit for nearly all purposes, with minor modifications for garrison and field wear, countered the pro-

The regulation 1839 to 1851 Topographical Engineer coatee of Captain George W. Hughes. WPM

pensity in Victorian society as a whole, "for clothing to be appropriate to the person's station in life, to the occasion and to the time of day."[13]

All these varying points were evident in the uniform board's report, a document that was the basis for General Orders No. 31, Adjutant General's Office, June 12, 1851. Starting at the head, this directive inaugurated the use of a cap of dark blue cloth with a crown fashioned from four upright pieces that rose from 5 3/4-inches to 6 1/4-inches in front and from 7 1/4-inches to 7 3/4-inches in back was to be worn by ranks from private to the most senior major general who commanded the army (although Winfield Scott clung to the chapeau despite this headpiece's disappearance from mention in the 1851 regulations). Some

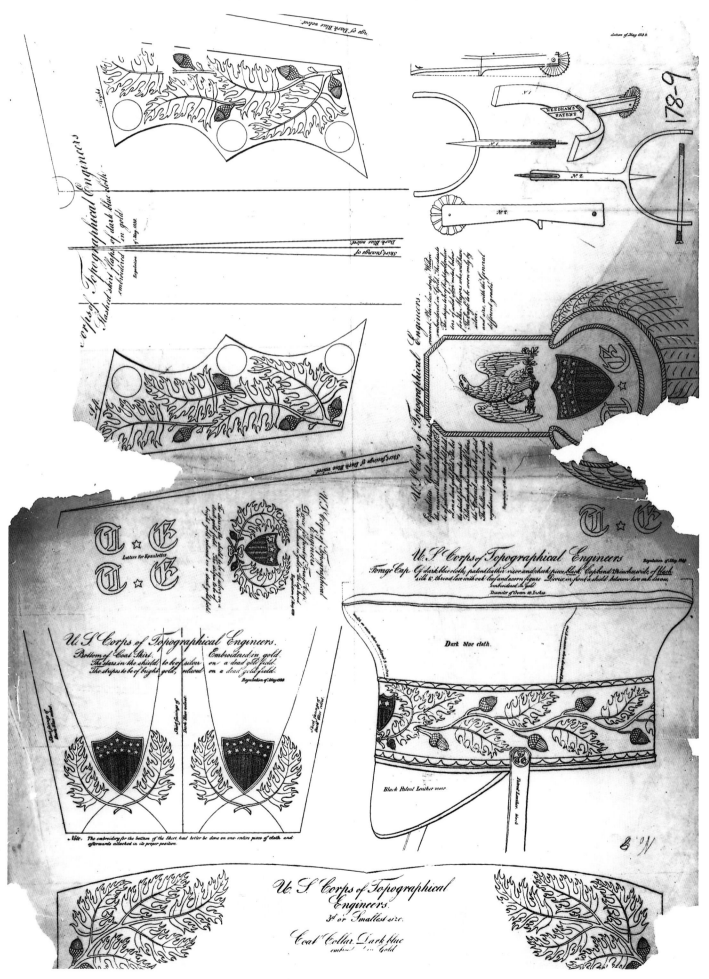

Details of collar, cuff, tails, epaulet, and 1839-pattern forage cap for Topographical Engineers as illustrated in an original specification drawing. NA

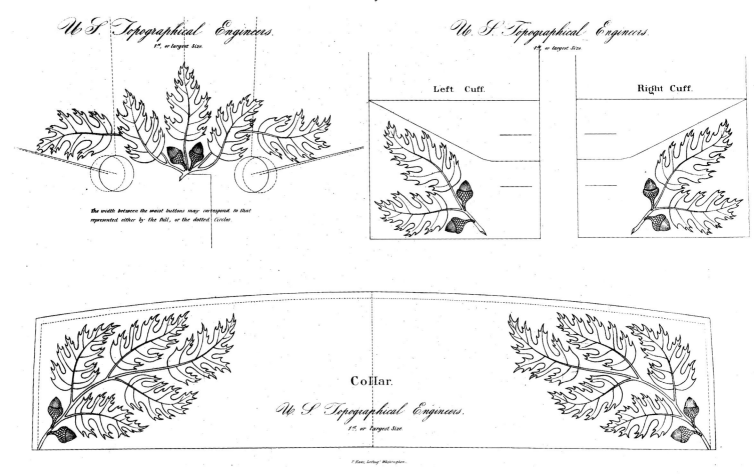

Detail of collar and cuff embroidery on dark blue velvet background for Topographical Engineers from 1839 to 1851. NA

of these early examples even had bodies made of gutta purcha, produced by a process patented by John Rider and John Murphy that allowed cloth to be vulcanized, thereby offering a potential weather resistant application for military clothing. Others would be made by a relatively new piece of technology in the manufacturing process – the sewing machine. The new machine, however, soon would be employed for only non-critical portions of the cap, that is the decorative band, and for producing chevrons, both articles not subject to heavy wear, unlike coats, shirts, and trousers, that were ordered to be made by hand, this process then being deemed as producing more durable goods.[14]

Whether made by hand or machine, or with bodies of gutta purcha or felted cotton and rabbit fur, all caps were to have a black 2 1/4-inch visor and a leather adjustable chin strap with yellow metal buckle. Pompons were basic, too, those for generals being shaped like an acorn and made of gold embroidered net, 3-inches long. Officers and enlisted men had spherical worsted pompons that were color-coded as follows: Adjutant General's Department – lower two-thirds buff, upper third white; Inspector General's Department – lower two-thirds buff, upper third scarlet; Judge Advocate – white; Quartermaster Department – lower two-thirds buff, upper third light or Saxony blue; Subsistence Department – lower two-thirds buff, upper third royal or ultramarine blue; Medical Department – lower two-thirds buff, upper third medium or emerald green; Pay Department – lower two-thirds buff, upper third dark olive green; Corps of Topographical Engineers and Corps of Engineers – lower two-thirds buff, upper third black; Ordnance Department – lower two-thirds buff, upper third crimson; artillery – scarlet; infantry – light or Saxony blue; mounted riflemen – medium or emerald green;

dragoons – orange; aides-de-camp – buff; adjutants of regiments – same as for Adjutant General's Department; and regimental quartermasters – same as for Quartermaster Department.

Enlisted men of artillery, dragoons, infantry, and rifles had the same color pompons as their officers, whereas enlisted engineers wore yellow and ordnance enlisted personnel were assigned crimson. Furthermore, enlisted versions were attached to a yellow metal ring, 2/3-inch in diameter by 1/3-inch deep, with a yellow metal spread eagle, 1 3/4-inches between the tips of he wings attached to this in order to hold the accessory on front of the cap. Officers had a gold net base ring which was permanently affixed to a gold embroidered spread eagle. Pompons always were to be worn when epaulets were used by officers. In turn, pompons could be removed when shoulder straps were substituted as a means of indicating officer's ranks. Conversely, enlisted men always were to have their pompons in place, in theory at least, unless the cap cover was being employed.

The insignia for this headgear consisted of the silver embroidered script "T.E." in a gold embroidered wreath for topographical engineers and a similar arrangement for officers of the engineers, excepting that a silver embroidered castle was placed in the center of the wreath instead of the script letters. Generals, adjutant generals, inspector generals, and officers of the Judge Advocate Corps, Pay, Quartermaster, Subsistence, and Medical Departments had the same type of gold wreath but in the center appeared "the letters U.S. in old English characters." A gold embroidered flaming bomb was established for ordnance officers, while crossed sabers with a silver numeral above was assigned to dragoons, crossed cannons with the numeral above went to artillery, a perpendicu-

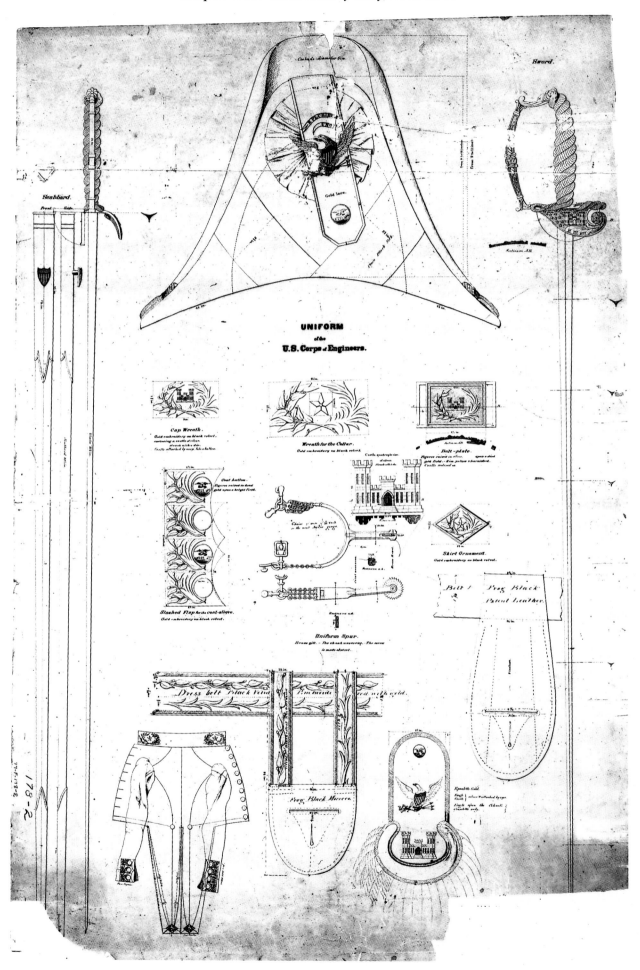

Specification drawings for Corps of Engineer officers' dress uniforms through 1851. Unlike the "Topos," the coatees were single-breasted. NA

lar trumpet with numeral in the bend was the identifying element for mounted rifles, while a gold embroidered bugle (hunting horn) with silver regimental numeral in the bend was to be used by infantry officers. In turn, enlisted caps exhibited a stamped yellow metal turreted castle for engineers and a shell and flame for Ordnance Department personnel. The other branches simply had stamped sheet brass 1-inch high letters for their respective companies.

An 1852 newspaper account noted the cap was "very nearly that of the French and some other European army regulations."[15] The coats meanwhile resembled France's line infantrymen coats which that nation had begun issuing in 1845 as a response to its experience in North Africa, an environment that had certain similarities to parts of the American West.[16] In the U.S. Army, lieutenants and captains were to have versions that resembled those issued to the men in general cut, with the exceptions of being of better quality cloth, and of having three small buttons at the cuffs while enlisted versions had only two. Moreover, officers' coats were plain, without the branch trim or facings allotted to the other ranks, the colors selected to designate the soldiers following those specified for the cap.

Nine buttons closed the front of both company grade officer and enlisted frock-coats, the button patterns varying to identify the wearer's branch. Field grade officers also had the same buttons as their respective branch, excepting those not serving in one of the combat arms who were authorized a general staff button. Engineers and topographical engineers were a special case. They had their own distinct buttons. All majors, lieutenant colonels, and colonels were further distinguished by double-breasted frocks with seven buttons in each row. For all branches

and arms the buttons were now of gold color or brass, unlike the pre-1851 era when infantry had silver. The design of the 1851 buttons likewise differed from those of earlier times.

Generals likewise had double-breasted coats, but the button arrangements varied with brigadier generals having eight buttons in each row paired off in sets of two, major generals having nine buttons grouped in threes and the commanding general having leeway to design his own outfit, an option Winfield Scott followed in that he retained the coatee with gold embroidered oak leaves on his collar and cuffs of the type authorized in the 1847 regulations well into the mid 1850s. After that, he had a double-breasted frock similar to that of other generals but with the turn-over collar and cuffs bearing embroidered oak leaves. This was in contrast to the collars and cuffs of other generals' coats which were covered in plain black velvet.

Shoulder straps and epaulets provided the means to indicate the rank of officers. From the 1830s to 1851 epaulets were gold for all officers, except those in the infantry, who had silver epaulets, and majors who had a silver and gold combination described below.

Generals had silver stars to indicate rank, with one, two, or three being prescribed for a brigadier, major general, and the major general commanding the army. Colonels were authorized silver eagles except infantry colonels who wore gold versions. Lieutenant colonels had the same style as colonels, but without eagles, and majors had gold straps with silver bullion for the infantry, and silver straps with gold bullion for all other branches. The bullion from majors through generals was to measure 1/2-inch in diameter and be 3 1/2-inches long, that for captains 1/4-inch, and for lieutenants, 1/8-inch with a length of 2 1/2-inches. The

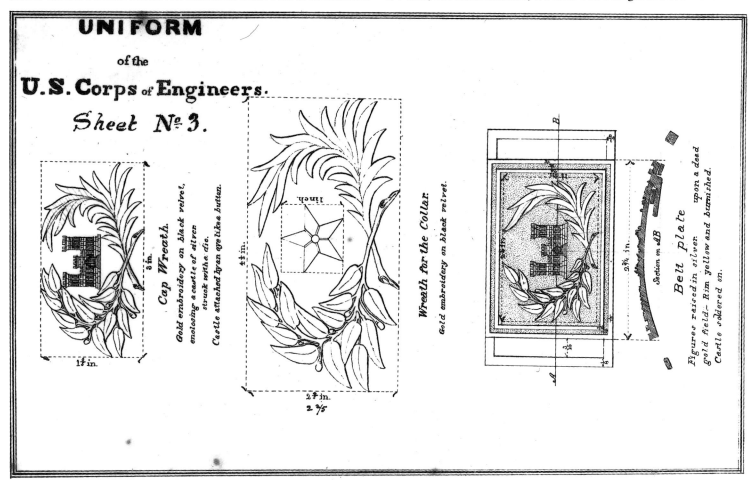

Detail of cap wreath, collar devices, and 1841-1846 belt buckle for Corps of Engineer officers. NA

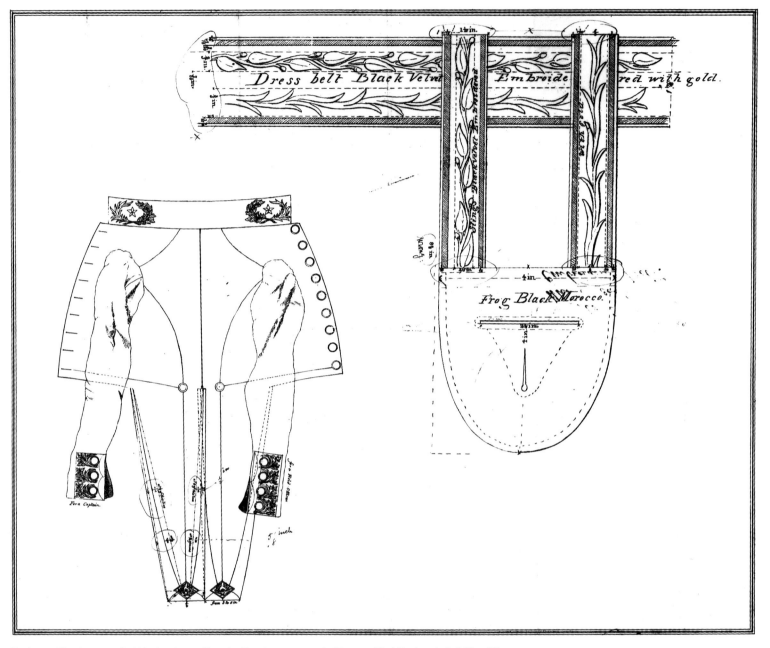

Engineer officer's coatees had black velvet cuffs and collars in contrast to the Topographical Engineer's dark blue. NA

bullion size was maintained after the new uniform of 1851, but gold was adopted as the universal color at that time when the system of bars, oak leaves, and eagles came into play for more precise indication of rank, as did a more elaborate system for indicating corps or branch.

Similarly, shoulder straps of not less than 3 1/2-inches in length nor more than 4-inches, bore an eagle for colonels, beginning in 1832 when these devices were adopted for field and general garrison (a special version was prescribed for dragoon officers in 1839). The eagles were silver on a dark blue background bordered by 1/4-inch gold embroidery, for all but infantry colonels, who had gold devices with a silver embroidered border. Gold leaves, one at each end of the strap indicated lieuten-

ant colonels of all corps and branches save infantry, who had silver leaves instead. Conversely, majors had silver leaves where the border was gold, and gold leaves for infantry. Parallel double bars at each end of the strap matched the border and were reserved for captains, while a single bar matching the border designated first lieutenants. Infantry second lieutenants had plain dark blue centered straps with silver borders, and all other second lieutenants had the same pattern but with gold borders. The 1851-patterns modified this scheme in that the centers were dark blue for generals and staff officers but in scarlet for artillery, orange for dragoons, and so forth, while the borders in all cases were gold. Finally, stars for general officers, eagles for colonels, and oak leaves from lieu-

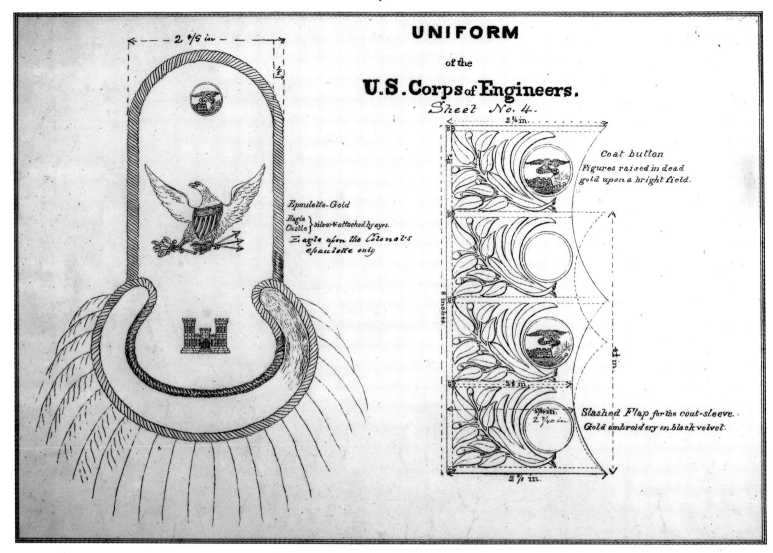

UNIFORM

of the

U.S. Corps of Engineers.

Sheet No. 4.

Epaulette-Gold

Eagle & Castle } silver & attached by eyes.

Eagle upon the Colonel's epaulette only

Coat button
Figures raised in dead gold upon a bright field.

Slashed Flap for the coat-sleeve.
Gold embroidery on black velvet.

Cuff detail with appropriate gilt buttons for the coatees of Corps of Engineer officers. The epaulets were all of gold, except for majors who had silver fringe with gold straps. Epaulets for the colonel bore an eagle, whereas all other officers below that rank were distinguished by the size of the fringe rather than by insignia of the type found on shoulder straps (i.e., oak leaves or bars). All were to have silver castles, however, to indicate that they were engineers. NA

tenant colonels all were to be silver, while oaks leaves for majors, double bars for captains, and single bars for second lieutenants were of gold embroidery only.

Silk sashes were another method to differentiate officers from rankers. For instance, generals had buff silk sashes, and also had the another distinction – a Russian (red) leather sword belt that was adorned with three gold embroidered stripes on the body and two on the sword slings. All other officers had plain black leather belts generally worn over crimson silk sashes, except surgeons who were to have emerald green sashes. These silk accessories wrapped around the wearer's waist twice, and were to be tied just behind the left hip. The exception was when an individual served as officer of the day, in which instance the sash was worn "scarf fashion" across the chest from the right shoulder to tie behind the left hip. Red worsted sashes were authorized for senior non-commissioned officers, first sergeants, ordnance sergeants, and hospital stewards.

Epaulets, similar to those of officers, presented yet another method of depicting the rank of enlisted personnel. These were of worsted, in branch color, and had three types of fringe that varied in size to differentiate the rank and file, in a scheme that paralleled officers as of 1851. The post-1851 fringe was 3-inches in length but the diameter varied beginning with privates and corporals whose bullion was 1/8-inch, ser-

geants who had 1/4-inch, and non-commissioned staff who had approximately 1/2-inch bullion. A similar concept was used to distinguish mounted troops in that three forms of brass (bronze was authorized for mounted rifles) shoulder scales were sanctioned for privates, corporals through sergeants, and non-commissioned staff.

Chevrons offered another manner to indicate rank for non-commissioned officers. Worsted tape identified corporals through first sergeants, and silk was used for the regimental non-commissioned staff. Two specialist ratings also were added in 1851, one for pioneers and another for hospital stewards.

The forerunner of these chevrons first appeared in the U.S. Army during the early 1800s. Over the decades, the original, simple designs evolved into a more complex system. These were to be worn on both sleeves of the uniform coat, jacket, or overcoat for non-commissioned officers above the elbow with the points facing downward.[17] Made of 1/2-inch wide silk for non-commissioned staff officers (ordnance sergeants, sergeants major, and regimental quartermaster sergeants), they consisted of 1/2-inch worsted tape, similar to that found on mounted jackets as trim, for all other NCOs, they were sewn separately on a background of blue material that matched the uniform, or occasionally to the coat itself. The chevrons measured an average 7 1/2-inches across and went from seam to seam of the sleeve.

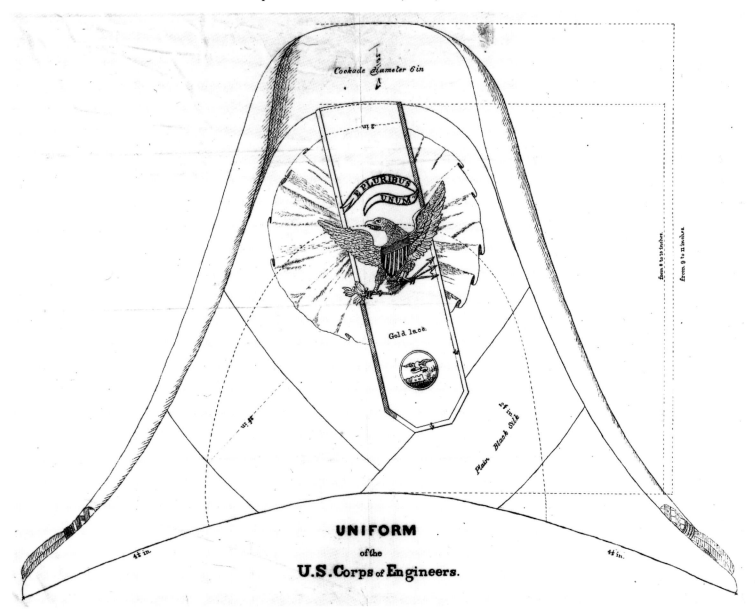

The Corps of Engineer officer's chapeau 1840-pattern was to have three black ostrich feathers. NA

The rank of sergeant major was three bars and an arc of three bars silk; a quartermaster sergeant - three bars and a tie of three bars; an ordnance sergeant - three bars and a star; first sergeant - three bars and a lozenge; a sergeant - three bars; a corporal - two bars; and a pioneer - two crossed hatchets of cloth, of the same color and material as the edging of the collar. These were to be sewn on each arm above the elbow in the place indicated for a chevron (the hatchets of a corporal to be placed above and resting on the chevron). The head of hatchet was upward, its edge outward, of the following dimensions, viz.: Handle - 4 1/2-inches long, 1/4-inch to 1/3-inch wide. The hatchet was to measure 2-inches long, 1-inch wide at the edge.

All chevrons were to be the color of the wearer's respective branch. Hospital stewards, who through 1857 did not have a specific uniform but evidently wore what was issued to the local garrison where they served, proved the exception (in 1857 these men adopted ordnance sergeant's uniforms, but replaced the chevrons and hat trim of this rank with the special rank device mentioned hereafter, and with a wreath that partially encircled a Roman German silver or white metal "US"). Hospital stewards did have a specific rank device, though, consisting of 1 3/4-inch wide emerald green band of facing cloth embroidered on the

outer edges by 1/8-inch yellow silk, as opposed to crimson, the color which adorned the collar and cuffs of their frock-coats. These differed from other NCO patterns in that they were "half" chevrons and ran obliquely downward from the outer to the inner seam of the sleeve, at an angle of about thirty-degrees with a horizontal, parallel to, and 1/8-inch distant from, both the upper and lower edge. The band went at a diagonal above the elbow with the lower portion angling forwardmost. A 2-inches long caduceus, also embroidered with yellow silk, the head toward the outer seam of the sleeve, was to appear in the center.

Service was to be indicated for all non-commissioned officers, musicians, and privates, who "served faithfully for the term of five years," by "a mark of distinction, upon both sleeves of the uniform coat, below the elbow," these diagonal devices being 1/2-inch wide. Service stripes extended from seam to seam, the front end nearest the cuff, and 1/2-inch above the point of the cuff, and were of the same color as the edging on the coat. An additional half chevron, above and parallel to the first, for every subsequent five years of faithful service was prescribed, the distance between each being 1/4-inch. Service in war was indicated by a light or sky-blue stripe on each side of the chevron for artillery, and a red stripe for all other corps the stripe was to be an 1/8-inch wide.

Major General William Jenkins Worth's 1840-pattern chapeau was topped by black upper and white lower swan feathers plume as was regulation for his rank. FWS&HM

Detail of cockade on Worth's 1840-pattern chapeau. FWS&HM

Additionally, branch or regimental affiliation for enlisted men was to be designated by collar insignia made of sheet brass. For example, a castle was to be affixed on both sides of the collar for engineers with a similar requirement of a flaming bomb being substituted for ordnance men, these insignia following the scheme established for caps. Conversely, block numbers rather than the company letters prescribed for caps indicated the regiments of artillery, dragoons, infantry, and mounted rifles.

In all instances trousers (except for generals and officers serving in a regiment) were to be of plain sky-blue kersey, a kind of coarse narrow cloth, woven from long wool and usually ribbed, that, "could be produced by weaving blue and white threads together" to produce a blue gray shade that was less expensive to produce than dark blue. A less complex trim was adopted for the 1851 trousers as compared to the previous 1847 regulations.[18] An 1/8-inch welt to match the color of the soldier's branch or corps was let into the outer seams, the exception being for generals who had plain trousers without welt and officers not serving with regiments whose welts were to be buff. Further, infantry enlisted men and officers, whose Saxony blue would not have be visible against the sky-blue trousers, were to have welts of dark blue. Moreover, mounted troops had reinforcing added to the inner legs of their trousers and on the seat to prolong use given the wear and tear of riding.

Black leather ankle-length bootees or Jefferson right and left boots served as footwear, the former items being for foot troops while brass spurs with leather straps could be worn with either type of footgear for mounted troops. All enlisted men were to receive leather neck stocks in theory to maintain the man's erect gaze. On the more utilitarian side, the government authorized such items as a gray flannel shirt, white linen undershirt and drawers, and a white stable frock to cover the uniform

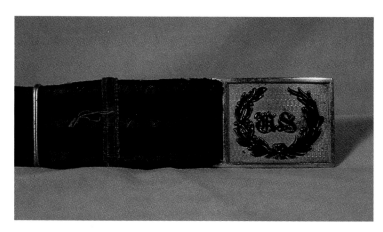

Worth's belt plate was typical of the style adopted by general officers and staff officers of the 1830s through 1851. Corps of Engineers officers also were to obtain this design of belt plate after 1846 to replace their earlier plate with silver castle within a wreath. FWS&HM

when the horse soldiers groomed the mounts or performed other similar fatigue tasks.

Accoutrements formed another part of the issue. Both the 1839-pattern oval plate for the waist belt or the new 1851-pattern rectangular brass plate that bore an eagle as well as a separately applied german silver wreath were among the accoutrements worn with the enlisted uniforms. So were various edged weapons and small arms, ranging from the 1840-pattern non-commissioned officer's sword held by an over-the-shoulder sling that had a brass circular plate bearing an eagle in the center, to musician swords, Roman-inspired short swords for heavy artillerymen, and the heavy cavalry saber, sometimes known as the "wrist breaker" in more recent times.[19] Leather saber knots likewise were provided to mounted troops, as were the buff leather dyed black or black harness leather saber belts with eagle buckle, cap pouch, carbine cartridge box, and the carbine sling. Pommel holsters of leather were used at first until belt mounted versions appeared later in the decade.[20]

A patent leather saber belt was common for officers who, in addition, had gold lace saber knot, gilt spurs, tall black leather boots, black cravats, and even gauntlets. These were some of the other accessories that officers could purchase and which set them apart from their men.

Even cold weather garments distinguished soldiers from their superiors. For enlisted men a great coat of matching material to that of the trousers existed, closely approximating the iron-gray overcoat or capotes adopted by the French Infantry in the late 1820s.[21] Originally it had a standup collar and an unlined, nondetachable outer cape which closed with small eagle buttons of the type found on the jacket. This cape covered the chevrons of the wearer, thereby making it difficult to distinguish non-commissioned officers. The coat itself was double-breasted with six large 1851-pattern eagle buttons in each row for mounted troops and single-breasted for foot soldiers.

Officers' overcoats differed from those of the men in a number of ways, most notably being of dark blue cloth, at the time a more expensive hue to produce from imported indigo than light blue that could be made by intermixing white and blue threads. Officers could wear their coats with or without capes. This handsome cloak coat closed by the means of four frogs of black silk cord down the chest and a long loop *chelleat* at the throat. The option existed for the collar to be a standing type or a stand and fall cut depending upon the wearer's choice. Rank was displayed by a flat black silk braid measuring one-eighth of an inch. Arranged on the lower sleeves in a special pattern, five braids denoted a colonel, four a lieutenant colonel, three a major, two a captain, and one a first lieutenant. Alas, the poor "shave tail's" sleeves sported no braid!

Not surprisingly this overcoat also drew its inspiration from the French officer's caban of the period.[22] Thus, troops in the United States were supposed to be clad much as their counterparts across the Atlantic, although departures from this ideal, both permitted and otherwise, were not uncommon – a state of affairs that continued through most of the Victorian era.

This fact contrasted with the intent of General Orders No. 31 that directed colonels of regiments and corps to ". . . enforce this order; and Generals and other Inspecting Officers will notice deviations from it." When offenders were found, they were subject to court martial for "disobedience to orders."

General Orders No. 31 likewise revealed another typical circumstance in that "articles of the old uniform already manufactured for en-

William Worth in the uniform of a major general of the 1832 through 1851 era. FWS&HM

listed men" were to "be issued until exhausted" providing they were "first altered, so far as practicable, to correspond with the new pattern." But "in no instance" were "the two different patterns" to be issued to "troops stationed at the same post." This statement added one further complication to an already problematical supply system.

More to the point, budgetary constraints meant that old patterns, modified or not, would have to be exhausted, at least for privates and non-commissioned officers (officers had to purchase their own uniforms unlike their subordinates who were furnished their clothing by the government) before substantial dispersal of the new patterns could be accomplished. Here, as in previous times, and on many occasions in the future, the desire to replace old items with new articles was impeded, resulting in considerable lag-time between the exhaustion of sufficient quantities of old patterns and the issuance of new patterns.[23] Sometimes, too, old and new patterns were combined such as when the cap with pompon was authorized to be issued, when available, with the old swallow-tailed coat.[24]

At least some observers lauded the direction the army had attempted to take, even if in practice years passed before implementation occurred. For instance, an article in a Boston newspaper of the era indicated: "We think that, altogether, these changes [as set forth in General Orders 31] in the dress of the army are important. We are most heartily tired of the swallow-tailed coats that have so long prevailed; and as to the caps heretofore worn in service, they were disgraceful."

One reminiscence focused on the new cap, and went so far as to state, "the Dragoons and [Mounted] Rifles exulted in what was known as the 'Albert Hat' with orange and green pom-poms."[25] Another critic

Front and rear views of Worth's 1832-pattern major general's coatee. FWS&HM

took an opposite stand on the matter finding the hat, "a rather preposterous sort of affair" that would not be worn by any of the officers "until obliged to do so." Continuing, he noted that although the cap was "worn in the French and many other services" the invention was laughable.[26] Indeed, a contemporary cartoon by Topographical Engineer George Derby even depicted St. Peter at the gates of heaven turning away a newly departed officer with the words, "You can't enter here in that cap, old fellow."

Such negative comments to the contrary the 1851-patterns actually were adopted, at least in certain situations. For one thing, as noted previously, officers were compelled to buy their regulation uniform to comply with orders, while certain units had need of the new issue earlier than others.

For instance, from its formation in 1846, the Regiment of Mounted Rifles never had a dress uniform. This factor and the near depletion of the regiment's clothing supplies prompted the quartermaster general to approve the issue of the frock-coat with green facings and worsted epaulets along with sky-blue mounted reinforced trousers with a 1/8-inch green welt, and the cap surmounted by a pompon, all of the 1851-pattern.

Some heavy artillery companies received their 1851-pattern caps and coats in relatively short order, too, there being fewer men in these units as compared to the infantry. Their scarlet trimmed coats, caps, and trousers started to be available as early as August 1851, with most companies being clad in the new issue by the middle of 1853. This did not preclude them from obtaining the white jackets and trousers through 1854. What is more, by fall 1854 replacement of their former yellow trimmed sky-blue wool jackets began.[27] Unissued 1832-pattern jackets that had been in stock, but retrimmed with scarlet worsted lace on the collar and shoulder straps, was a revision that was set in motion by General Orders No. 24, Adjutant General's Office, June 29, 1852.[28] These refurbished garments could be coupled with the 1839-pattern forage cap, of which considerable supplies existed until the late 1850s.[29] By 1855 quantities of the sky-blue jackets likewise were exhausted to the point that supposedly heavy artillery performed "fatigue duties in their shirts or cut their old frock-coats into jackets."[30]

Similarly, the former pattern distinctive dark blue uniform jacket having a collar piped in scarlet and matching trousers with scarlet piping down the outer seams of the legs, remained the fatigue or work uniform for ordnance men for several years to come. Engineer enlisted

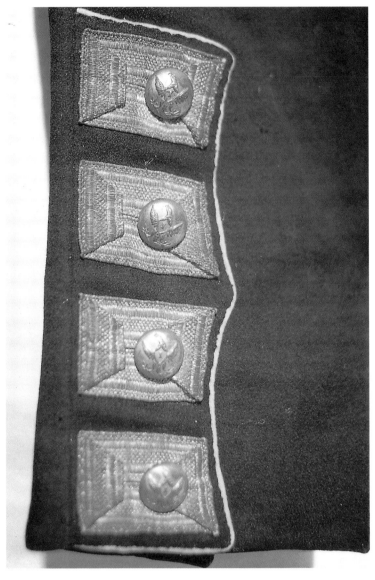

Cuff detail of a field grade infantry officer's 1832-pattern coatee. Four loops were worn by field grade officers of infantry, dragoons, and artillery, while captains of these three branches had three loops, and lieutenants had two. A similar scheme was used by infantry and light artillery enlisted men, with four loops being worn by regimental non-commissioned staff officers, three by sergeants, and two by corporals, privates, and musicians, but in worsted lace rather than in silver or gold lace as was prescribed for officers. WC

fatigue uniforms likewise remained of the pre-1851 style. These outfits consisted of a dark blue jacket with a black velvet collar piped in yellow, a forage cap with black velvet band that bore the castle insignia in brass on the front, and sky-blue trousers with a black welt.[31] For dress purposes, however, yellow piping was added to convert this portion of the uniform to the 1851 standard. Also, white cotton jackets and trousers substituted for summer fatigue wear through approximately 1858.[32] Finally, white cotton canvas "overalls" were strictly an engineer work issue. These garments were, "to cover the whole of the body below the waist, the breast, the shoulders and arms, with narrow wristband buttoning with one button. . . ." They were to fasten at the neck, "behind with two buttons, and at the waist behind with buckle and tongue."[33]

Given that the engineer soldiers were stationed at the U.S. Military Academy at the time, these special uniforms were in keeping with the nature of the work of the troops as well as set them apart as an exclusive element within the army. This was also the situation with the West Point bandsmen, who in accordance with the 1851 uniform regulations were to don a dark blue frock-coat with ten enlisted engineer buttons down the front. The collar was to match the coat, but be set off by 4-inch facings on either side in red, as were the cuffs. Double 3/4-inch wide red stripes were to run down the outer seams of the light blue trousers, a space of 1/8-inch being prescribed in between the stripes. The 1832 artillery type enlisted cap with a plume and cord, along with red worsted epaulets made up other elements of the band's parade dress.[34]

Undress was to consist of a dark blue cloth jacket with nine small buttons on the front. Red worsted binding "trimmed along the top of the collar" and "two small buttons with loops of the same binding," were placed "on each side of the collar." Shoulder straps also had the matching red binding. In this the West Point musical group exhibited a departure from the uniform prescriptions for other bands in the army in that the other military bands were to "wear the uniform of the regiment or corps to which it belongs."

That is not to say bands were identical in appearance to the musicians assigned to companies because General Orders 31 went on to authorize the commanding officer of a corps or regiment to "make such *additions* in ornaments as he may judge proper." It should be noted that this same or nearly identical wording was to be found in previous uniform regulations, including that of 1847. In this, as in past and future

Detail of collar and epaulets of a colonel of infantry's 1832-pattern uniform. WC

Rear insignia on the coat tails of an 1832-pattern infantry officer's coatee. WC

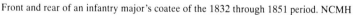

Front and rear of an infantry major's coatee of the 1832 through 1851 period. NCMH

instances, bands enjoyed considerable latitude in their appearance when compared to the rank and file as a whole.[35]

Another nonstandard item of the early 1850s was the so-called "Andrews hat" a piece of headgear nicknamed for Colonel Timothy P. Andrews, the commanding officer of a special unit that existed briefly during the Mexican War, the Voltiguers. Andrews had asked for permission to have "broad-brimmed soft felt," hats "of a pearl or stone color, capable of being looped up, but with a stiff brim when let down, and with an orifice for ventilation on each side of the crown that might be closed at pleasure. . . ." This forerunner of the drab campaign hat never reached Andrews' men, although in fact 500 were made, the lion's share of which went to the Second Dragoons in Texas during 1851.[36]

As one more means of using up old stocks the quartermaster general sanctioned the issue of white cotton jackets and trousers of the type that had been provided earlier in the century, thereby making a warm weather outfit available for work details and campaigning, a situation that continued until 1855. It should be noted that officers serving with mounted troops also had the option of wearing a plain dark blue cloth jacket for stable wear, with either one or two rows of buttons, according

to whether the individual held company or field-grade rank. The collar was the same as for the frock. Shoulder straps constituted the means to indicate rank.[37] The vest was another optional accessory in blue, white, or buff, with small officers buttons of the type worn at the cuffs. Further, all officers could procure a plain blue body coat "with the button designating the respective corps, regiments, or departments, without any other mark or ornament upon it." Under no circumstances, however, was this item to be "considered as a dress for any military purpose."[38]

The men had no such latitude, the "swallowtail" or coatee of the 1830s pattern remaining the standard issue item for nearly all troops despite the new 1851 orders. This fact was most evident in the West where one inspector general reporting from the Pacific Coast and New Mexico indicated that the soldiers had only the old pattern clothing available. To make matters worse, these garments were believed to be "defective in cut" in that generally the pantaloons were "too short in the leg, and too small at the foot" while the coats were "too narrow." Additionally, on a few occasions the men had to buy shoes, socks, and shirts "at very high rates" from the sutlers (civilian contract merchants at the post) because "the Government failed to have these articles on hand," or because, as in the case of the white issue flannel shirt, shrinkage was so bad "after washing as to" render the item "unfit for service" unlike ones made of colored flannel.[39]

So it was that the 1851-pattern, as far as enlisted men were concerned, saw spotty service, mixed with older issue, and a certain number of expedients. Even as the articles of clothing were being made available General Orders No. 1, Adjutant General's Office, January 20, 1854 changed the course of things once more, and dictated yet different uniforms from those adopted in 1851, although of a similar cut at least for enlisted foot troops and for all officers.

On one hand this document disposed of trouser welts for enlisted men, as well as the facings for their coats. Instead piping in branch colors, as had been used by engineer soldiers and ordnance men, were to trim the collars and cuffs. As far as facings were concerned, the color of infantry changed from Saxony blue to sky-blue. Worsted epaulets were discontinued too. Thereafter all enlisted men were to be issued brass shoulder scales, previously solely the prerogative of horse soldiers.

Buttons also were changed to one style for enlisted men. Prior to 1854 they were of brass with an eagle device that bore a "D" for dragoons, an "I" for infantry, and so forth on the chest of the eagle. The new buttons retained the eagle but the designating letters were discontinued.

Another change resulting from this general order was the adoption of short jacket for mounted troops, not unlike the old 1833-pattern dragoon "roundabout," thereby beginning the phase-out of the long frock for mounted artillery, dragoons, and mounted rifles. Twelve brass buttons closed the new mounted jackets, the fronts of which were plain except in the case of trumpeters and bandsmen, where a special lace ornamentation probably was added. This trim replaced the plastron of the 1851-pattern for all musicians. In addition, the collars were cut at a forty-five degree angle rather than being square as had been the case with the pre-1851 jackets.

The same type of worsted tape was sewn at the cuffs, collar, around the edges, and at the rear of two padded pillow-like projections (nicknamed "bounty jumpers" by some enlisted men) designed to help hold

Mexican War era artillery colonel's epaulets with ties to attach to the coatee. WC*

Major of Seventh Infantry 1832-1851 pattern epaulets. The straps of infantry officers' epaulets were silver as was the fringe, except for majors, who had gold fringe with a silver strap for infantry and silver fringe with gold straps for all other branches. The regimental numeral was placed toward the end of the strap nearest the shoulder, often on a light blue circle enclosed by embroidery, although plain metallic numerals or embroidered numerals without cloth branch color backings are found on many epaulets, especially of pre-Mexican War vintage. NCMH

the saber belt in place on the jackets of mounted troops. Once again, the color of all trim indicated the branch, with artillery jackets being set off in scarlet, dragoons trimmed in orange, mounted rifles edged in emerald green, and so forth, following the precedence established in 1851. Moreover, numerals were retained on the collars for the combat arms as were the flaming bomb or castle for ordnance men and engineers respectively, although because of the tape on collars of mounted jackets, dragoons, light artillery, and mounted riflemen evidently ignored these brass devices in some instances.

This was but one example of disregard for issue items, especially when troops took to the field. Despite a trend in the field to strip away frills, General Orders No. 4, Adjutant General's Office, March 26, 1855, ushered in an even more elaborate type of trousers. These were to be plaited in lieu of the plain ones that were adopted in 1851. Moreover, a frock-coat with fuller-skirts than previously worn was prescribed for foot soldiers and officers. The design once again took its inspiration from the French, in this case from the *chasseurs-à-pied* model.[40] This new outer garment continued to be single-breasted with nine buttons down the front for enlisted men and company grade officers. Moreover, the color remained dark blue wool for all with the piping around the collar and cuffs in branch colors for dismounted enlisted men also con-

Front and rear view of an infantry lieutenant's 1832-pattern uniform. White trousers that were authorized for officers from May 1 to September 30 in linen or cotton, as a concession to hot weather. WPM

Captain Henry Little, Seventh U.S. Infantry, wore a white buff sword belt rather than the over-the-shoulder belt prescribed by the regulations, except for certain positions on the regimental staff including all field grade officers. Deviations from the authorized uniform were not uncommon even in dress given the variations available from different tailors and military suppliers, along with personal tastes. Little became a captain on August 20, 1847. He resigned his commission on May 7, 1861 to become a brigadier general officer in the Confederacy. USAMHI

tinuing in service. Given the cut, field grade officers and generals probably would not avail themselves of the more voluminous skirts. The two new infantry regiments created in March 1855, the Ninth and the Tenth, not only were to don these new coats and trousers, but also were to have chasseur style waistbelts and saber bayonets to affix to their model 1855 rifles, the former accoutrement and edged weapon once more being a French derivative.[41]

Many soldiers probably were less than enthusiastic about the latest European trends. Evidently men in the West increasingly discarded or supplemented regulation items for more functional wear. According to the recollections of an enlisted man of Company B, First Dragoons, in the early 1850s his troop pressed blue shirts into service to replace their "regulation uniform" when in the field. Further, they purchased "drab hats" as a substitute for issue caps.

A second memoir mentioned that some infantrymen in Texas who had been converted to mounted service in 1853, "to increase our resources in sending out scouting parties against Indians," were led by an officer who opted for "a dragoon fatigue jacket, with gold shoulder straps and buttons, a broad brimmed slouched sombrero, and a pair of boots, with sheaths of leather to waist, to protect from the underbrush. . . ."

He also had a "belt full of pistols, a sword buckled to his side, and a six-shooting rifle" as well as "a powder-flask hanging from his belt. . . ." The observer further recorded, "The shirts worn on these occasions. . . . are composed of a dark blue check material, warranted *to last a week*, and are in great demand where laundresses are scarce." These were "termed 'Old Hickories,' cost exactly fifteen cents, and are generally used by hunting and scouting parties in this part of the world." Likewise, "The men were equipped something like their officers. . . ."[42]

Similarly, by 1855 another Texas-based unit, the Second Dragoons, adopted pragmatic civilian clothing consisting of: "corduroy pants; a hickory shirt or blue flannel shirt, cut down in front, studded with pockets and worn outside; a slouched hat and long beard, cavalry boots worn over the pants, knife and revolver belted to the side and a double barrel gun across the pommel, complete the costume as truly serviceable as it is unmilitary." In 1856 the Lone Star State additionally was the scene of another U.S. Army organization, the Mounted Rifles, drilling "with blue flannel hunting shirts and felt hats."[43]

A year later a strike force sent against the Cheyennes from Fort Leavenworth, Kansas included Companies E and K of the Sixth Infantry and Companies C, F, I, and K of the First Cavalry. One of the infan-

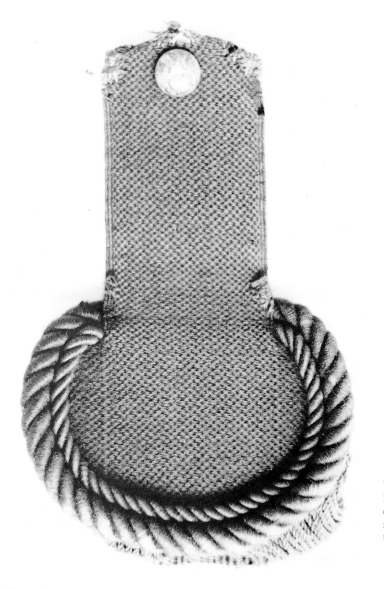

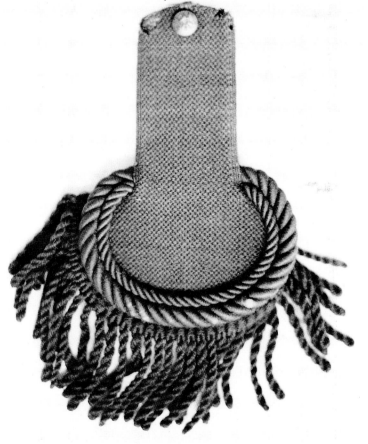

Worsted epaulete for the coatee of sergeants and orderly (first) sergeants of heavy artillery, engineers, infantry, and ordnance had fringe similar to that of company grade officers in terms of diameter and length, thereby providing an additional visual tie between the non-commissioned officers and the officers within a company. The color coincided with the branch facing or trim. USA

Worsted "strap" for engineer soldiers, heavy artillery, infantry, ordnance, and musicians, for wear with the coatee on both shoulders below the rank of sergeant. The color coincided with the branch facing or trim. USA

1832-pattern infantry private and corporal coatee with white lace and trim, along with silver buttons. **SI**

ABOVE: Dragoon corporal dress uniform of the 1833-pattern with M1839 saber belt and M1840 saber. The uniform was issued through the early 1850s. Note the cuffs differed markedly from those of infantry, heavy artillery, engineers, and ordnance. The branch color was yellow, although the horsehair plume on the cap was white. Additionally, yellow .5-inch stripes of facing material were to b worn no the trousers for privates and corporals. **WPM**

try sergeants with the column stated: "You should see us here in our prairie outfits; don't imagine a uniform. Every man is wearing a broadbrimmed hat, each of a different color; white trousers of rough material; a woolen shirt of red, green, blue, or brown – in short, of every color, usually open in the front and worn like a coat; the shoes (we still have shoes though who knows how soon we may have to wear moccasins) with the uppers slashed wherever they might chafe in marching." Further, the rankers and non-commissioned officers stowed or discarded their bayonets and swords, but all carried "long hunting" knives and many toted five-or six-shot revolvers, as well as issue rifled muskets. Enlisted men and officers could hardly be told apart, a democratic but highly unusual state of affairs in the Victorian era military. This situation prompted the diarist to mention the assembled field force looked "more like Polish Scythemen than" they did U.S. Army regulars.[44]

Similarly, when President James Buchanan's administration decided to curtail what was perceived as a Mormon separatist movement in Utah Territory, another force gathered at Fort Leavenworth, Kansas in 1857. Among the 2,500 regulars was the Fifth Infantry regiment. The men of this unit apparently had the 1839-pattern forage cap and old mounted

Infantry private, dress uniform, 1832-pattern. SI

A sergeant in the 1833-pattern dragoon dress uniform. The trousers and coatee of this type continued to be issued through the early 1850s in some cases, sometimes in combination with the 1851-pattern cap. Such measures were not uncommon, particularly in times of changeover from an old pattern uniform to a new pattern. Additionally, sergeants had double yellow stripes of facing material on their trousers, after the fashion of company officers. SI

uniform jackets. The jackets either retained the color trim of that had been applied to them at the arsenal, such as green for mounted rifles, or may have been without lace because the dark blue tape that replaced white in 1852 as the color for infantry fatigue jackets would not show up on the dark blue wool garments. The infantry overcoat, and, probably, heavy boots and with mufflers, completed the marching order.[45] In contrast, each company of the Tenth Infantry regiment in the expedition was allowed:

> to wear shirts and hats, provided they were all alike, the knapsack to be carried in the wagons. Accordingly, to commence on the right, Capt. Gardner, gray shirts, black hats; Co. B, Co., I, your humble servant [Captain Jesse Gove, who recorded this event], gray and gray hats, the only ones in the command and they are splendid; Co. C, Capt. Tidball, white shirts; Co. F, Lt. Forney, white; Co. G, Lt. Williams, light blue shirts, black hats; Co. H. Capt. Tracy, white shirts; Co. K, Capt. Dunovant, dark blue and black hats; Co. E., Lt. Dudley, gray and black hats.

Similarly, during 1858, in the Pacific Northwest, "The artillery and infantry wore blue flannel shirts drawn up over their uniforms and belted at the waist; the dragoons had a similar dress of grey flannel. The officers had adopted the same, with slouched hats. The only marks of their rank were shoulder straps sewed to the flannel."[46]

Such field expedients arose in part because of heightened military activities, especially in the West. Responding to these situations, the United States Congress deemed it necessary to add two new mounted regiments to the standing force on March 3, 1855. These were the First and Second Cavalry regiments. Colonel Edwin V. Sumner assumed command of the First, while Colonel Albert Sidney Johnston took the reins of the Second Cavalry.[47]

For the first five years of service the two regiments gained considerable laurels, yet hard field duty took its toll on men, mounts, equipment, and uniforms, the last-mentioned element reflecting a mix between earlier 1854-pattern garb assigned to mounted units, with a notable exception.

The 1833-pattern enlisted dragoon dress cap had yellow worsted cords. The cap began to be phased out after new regulations were adopted in 1851. SI

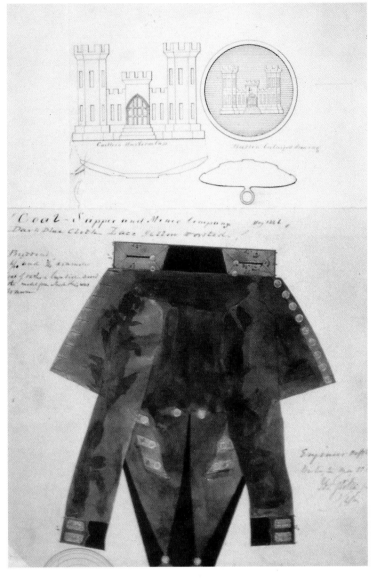

Details of the 1846-pattern button, cap insignia, and coatee for enlisted personnel of the U.S. Company of Sappers, Miners, and Pontoniers. The design of all these components paralleled those for officers with the exception of the cap (shako) and stamped sheet brass cap insignia that also had been adopted for the headgear of cadets at the United States Military Academy several years prior. NA

This was a black felt hat that looped up on the right side, and supplied with a leather chin strap attached to the inside sweat band, was the crowning glory of these cavaliers. The pattern had been favored by Colonel Sumner who sat on the board that specified the cavalrymen's gear and who had seen similar types of headwear in Belgium. He particularly liked the Belgian *chasseur à pied* head dress which he described as, "a hat with a medium sized brim, turned up on the left side, . . . with a cockade, and a small black feather in full dress."[48]

In fact, this hat was similar to the American cavalry hat that this group selected. The prescribed hat ultimately was adorned with a gold-wire festooned cord hanging from the top of the crown and a second cord of the same material terminating in acorns for officers. This accessory was placed at the base of the crown. Enlisted men wore similar cords but of yellow worsted. Another difference that distinguished officers from rank and file entailed an embroidered eagle device, the U.S. Coat of Arms, to hold the right brim in place against the crown. Additionally, a spray of three ostrich feathers appeared on the left side of the

hats worn by majors through colonels while a pair of these feathers were prescribed for lieutenants and captains. Enlisted personnel had only one feather and a simple brass button with a stamped sheet brass eagle of the type that had been attached to the pompon on the 1851 and 1854-pattern caps, along with a strand of yellow worsted cord as a loop attachment. Issues for enlisted troopers also bore a large stamped sheet brass company numeral on the front, while officers wore a gilt embroidered regimental numeral. Leather chin straps completed the hat for both officers and men.

This hat provided the most distinguishing feature of the 1855 cavalryman's outfit because the enlisted jacket differed little from that worn by the other mounted regiments, light yellow lace being the only distinct element (the old color for dragoons). No doubt, as regularly proved the rule, the new hats and jackets took some time to procure. For this reason, the 1854 cap with bill as provided to engineer soldiers with a yellow welt may have been issued while the horse soldiers awaited their new hat.[49] The standard mounted overcoat also was issued, although as protection against rain, a gutta-purcha (rubberized material popular during this period) talma was one more item unique to the two cavalry regiments.

For weapons the troopers received a mixed lot of firearms and accoutrements, thereby attesting further to the experimental nature of the units when they first took the field. The issue was as follows:

Three squadrons of each regiment were to be armed with the rifle-carbine of the pattern manufactured at the Springfield Armory, and one squadron of each with the removable-stock carbine, with the barrel ten to twelve inches long, as might be found best by experiment. One squadron of the First Cavalry was to be armed with the breech-loading Merrill Carbine, and one squadron of the Second Cavalry with the breech-loading Perry carbine. Colt's navy revolvers and dragoon sabres for both regiments; one squadron of each to be provided with gutta-purcha cartridge boxes.

Some trial gutta-purcha saber scabbards and "pistol cases" (holsters) saw limited use too. Carbine slings also were provided with the exception of those carrying the pistol-carbine or the Perry carbine.

Although certain of these experimental accoutrements represented efforts by the Ordnance Department to cope with campaign conditions, the Quartermaster Department did not always respond to pragmatic needs, especially when it came to cold weather. As one enlisted man of the 1850s lamented: "overshoes, mittens, gloves, leggings or other extra wraps were not then provided by the Government, nor kept for sale, and men made for themselves out of old blankets, skins, pieces of old canvas and cast-off clothing, anything that necessity prompted them to invent for protection from the bitter cold." While facing the bitter winters at Fort Pierre in today's South Dakota, infantryman Eugene Bandel also recorded that soldiers bought tanned hides from Indians to make into clothing for the cold season. Bandel had a deerskin coat, buffalo-calf trousers with the fur side in, and headgear consisting of wolfskin

Rear view of an 1832-pattern artillery officer's coatee. WC

By the mid-1840s light artillery enlisted men gradually gained coatees that essentially were identical to those of dragoon troops, except for the use of scarlet facings accented by yellow worsted lace in lieu of the all yellow scheme for dragoons. They likewise wore a cap with scarlet sidelines and horsehair plume that resembled the dragoon cap. WPM

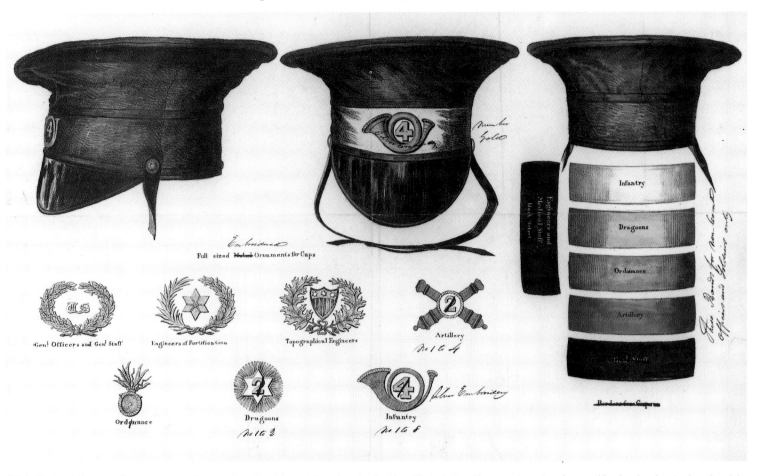

Originally the 1839-pattern forage cap was to have a colored band for each branch and embroidered insignia for officers, as shown here in a specification drawing that introduced the new cap. Both ideas essentially became optional when the cap finally was adopted. NA

with the fur worn on the outside. Additionally, he had two pairs of moccasins, an ornamented pair of deerskin worn under a second larger pair of buffalo-calf leather.[50]

Besides the cold, the need to traverse long distances, often over rugged terrain, took its toll on footgear. In some cases issue shoes deteriorated to the extent that "men were barefoot," a circumstance of no little concern in a country "where rattlesnakes are numerous, and scorpions and tarantulas abound, and where cactus and the Spanish bayonet often grow ranker than grass, and where" foot soldiers "often have to march for miles over solid rock." Another problem was that, "Shoes of untanned deer or ox hide" did not hold up in wet climates, thereby causing further need to procure footwear. Shoes became scarce commodities the farther a unit progressed from its supply base. Thus, shoes that fetched $1.78 before a unit marched out now brought $5.00 a pair, if a supply could be located on the trail, a sum that was equal to approximately half a month's base pay for a recruit on his first campaign.[51] In the field, uniforms disintegrated too, causing no little consternation, and inspiring occasional ingenuity, such as converting wagon covers into "white summer pantaloons" but even then the price could be dear – $2.50 for a pair.[52]

This example of an 1839-pattern forage cap has the silver embroidery U.S. enclosed by a gold embroidered wreath, the insignia that came to be standard for general officers and staff officers. WC

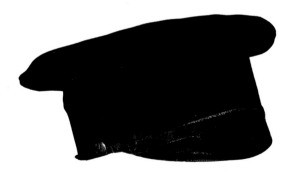

Officer's 1839-pattern forage cap worn by Lieutenant James Duncan, Second Artillery, was another of the many variations of this cap available between the time of its adoption and the final discontinuance of the cap in the 1850s. Michael McAfee Photograph. WPM

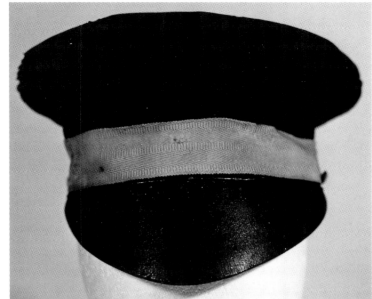

Front, rear, and interior view of an 1839-pattern Second Dragoons enlisted forage cap. Note the worsted yellow cap band that was a trademark of the regiment. The band of the First Regiment of Dragoons had a double row of yellow lace or facing that went around the base of the cap and a regimental numeral in front. Tom Shaw Photograph. MNHS

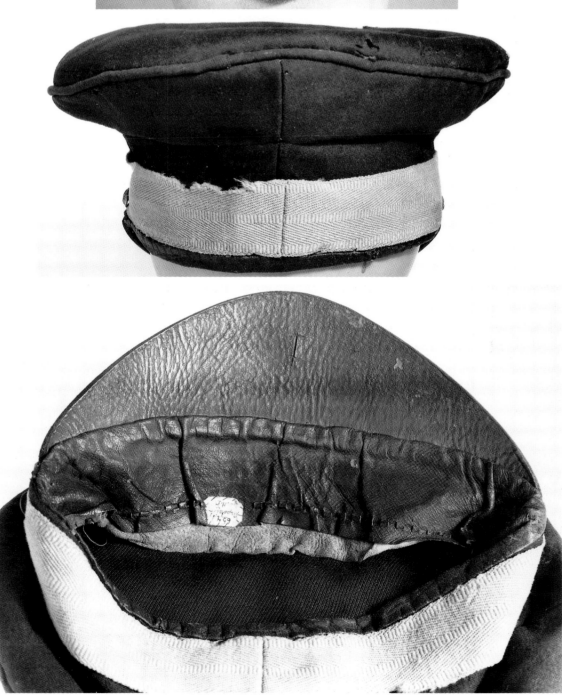

Lieutenant George Gordon of the Regiment of Mounted Rifles wears the 1839-pattern forage cap with eagle device bearing an "R" in the center to designate the wearer as an officer of that unit. WJS

Second Lieutenant Bezaleel Wells Armstrong, West Point Class of 1845, was assigned to the First Dragoons upon graduation and transferred to the Second Dragoons in 1846. Although the dress uniform was to be worn with the cap and gold cords, he instead wears the 1839-pattern forage cap with the addition of a six-pointed gold embroidered star of the type that was sewn to the rear of each tail of the coatee. The latter garment was dark blue wool with yellow facings on the tails, cuffs, and collar. Epaulets of gold attached to the shoulders to indicate rank and regimental affiliation (a silver "1" or "2" being attached on the ends of these accessories) while gold lace decorated the collar and cuffs, although Armstrong's non-regulation gloves obscure this detail. HP

An unidentified infantry major has elected to apply a silver bugle device to the front of his 1839-pattern forage cap of the type that was made for the lower tails of the dress coatee. The shoulder straps have dark blue centers to match the frock coat, the edge is silver embroidery, and the oak leaves gold embroidery for infantry majors. JCN

Second Lieutenant Parmenas T. Turnley of the First U.S. Infantry has on an 1839-pattern forage cap without insignia, and the officer's single-breasted blue wool frock coat which was to have at least eight but up to ten buttons, depending on the height of the officer. The buttons were to be silver with an eagle motif. A shield with an "I" was on the eagle's breast for infantry officers and enlisted men. Shoulder straps for infantry second lieutenants had plain dark blue centers with a silver embroidered border of approximately 1/8-inch. USAMHI

First Dragoon officer Cave Johnson Couts holds a riding crop, and wears a rakishly positioned 1839-pattern forage cap with embroidered dragoon star. Also note the 1839-pattern straps unique to dragoon officers (although worn by at least one Topographical Engineer and perhaps some Regiment of Mounted Rifles' officers). HL

Charles May gained considerable fame in the war against Mexico. Here he wears the optional double-breasted coat of a field grade officer of the late 1840s, with the distinctive dragoon shoulder straps that remained regulation until discontinued in 1851. LC

Captain Nathan Boone also wears the distinctive shoulder straps prescribed for dragoon officers from 1839 through 1851 to indicate rank in the field and on campaign. These were of dark blue wool to match the frock coat with a gold border and gilt crescents at the end. The rank insignia and regimental numeral appeared on these accessories. SHSM

On the way to Utah troops also found footgear a problem. In April 1858, Captain Albert Tracy, commanding Company H of the Tenth Infantry indicated: "For the want of shoes, my men have come to be nearly barefoot. A few moccasins have been picked up, at fabulous rates, which answer a very excellent purpose – for those who have them." This meant officers kept busy requisitioning "clothing for the men, shoes and stockings" all of which were "needed very much." Eventually the government provided some relief in this matter by sending out a supply of buffalo overshoes in the spring of 1859 to be issued to guards and men on detached service, but only after the troops had arrived in Utah and had suffered considerably during the march there.[53]

An enlisted dragoon bound for Utah echoed the plight of the troops as they proceeded westward writing in August 1858: "We are illy prepared to encounter" cold weather "for more than one half of the command is bare-footed, and but few of us can boast a whole pair of trousers or a jacket complete." Carrying spares presented a problem given the limited capacity of the knapsack, and the relatively small size of the baggage train.

The knapsack of the period consisted of a rigid wooden frame with an India rubber flap. Regulations called for it to be painted black, Those for artillery" to be "marked in the centre of the cover with the number of the regiment only, in figures of one inch and a half in length, of the character called full face, with yellow paint." Infantry knapsacks were to be marked in the same manner but in white paint, while ordnance

men were to have yellow crossed cannon applied in lieu of the regimental number. Inside the letter of the company and a number assigned to the soldier to designate his gear, was prescribed for all. Haversacks with the number and name of the regiment were issued as well, these cotton items with nonadjustable shoulder straps being used to carry rations. They were to be worn with the canteen on the outside and both being slung on the left side "on marches, guard, and when paraded for detached service."

It seems dragoons also carried the knapsack on the Utah Expedition. These articles were small as well as cumbersome which meant that the overcoat could not be accommodated, thereby being relegated to the supply train. When a cold snap brought unexpected snow, the infantrymen were caught in their woolen shirt without their protective outer garments.[54]

The shortcomings of the knapsack that weighed nearly nineteen pounds when fully packed, also meant soldiers tended to lighten their load on the march when they could not stow their personal belongings on the pack train. Disposal of gear as a result caused, "many a good coat and other items of clothing" to be thrown away by the soldiers.

Thus, whether the issue wore out or the men discarded items, or for both reasons, they faced a problem once away from their base of supply. This situation became most evident once the force found it could not obtain replacements for worn materials at Fort Laramie. The men therefore were compelled to do without or turn to other sources to meet their

When the Regiment of Mounted Rifles was established its officers and men wore the dragoon field uniform but with dark blue trousers rather than sky blue, and the trouser stripes were black with a yellow border. The gold or brass buttons were to have an "R" in the shield that was on a spread-eagle. Captain Benjamin Roberts, shown here around 1847, served with the regiment during the Mexican War and has on the waist length dark blue wool jacket with gold lace trim, which although not mentioned in orders or regulations was applied to many officers' garments in a fashion similar to the worsted lace of the other ranks. He wears standard shoulder straps rather than the special epaulete-like ones of dragoons, and evidently his gilt buckle for his saber belt bears a script "R." USAMHI

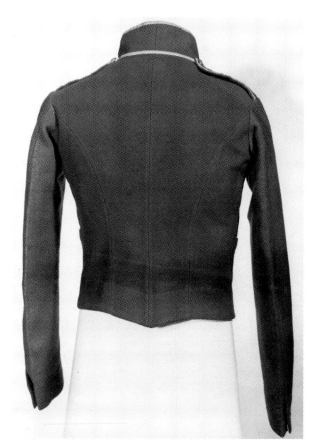

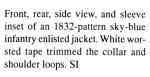

Front, rear, side view, and sleeve inset of an 1832-pattern sky-blue infantry enlisted jacket. White worsted tape trimmed the collar and shoulder loops. SI

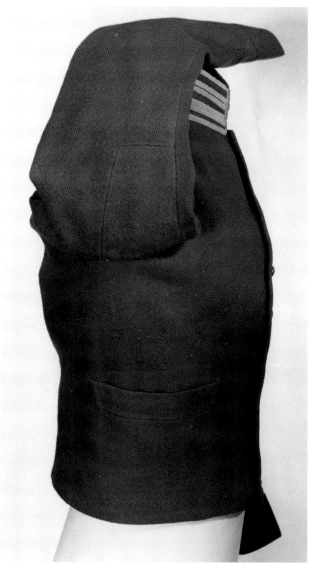

Front, rear, and side view of an 1833-pattern enlisted dragoon jacket. Enlisted men of the Regiment of Mounted Rifles wore the same jacket but had an "R" on the center of their buttons while those for dragoons bore a "D." SI

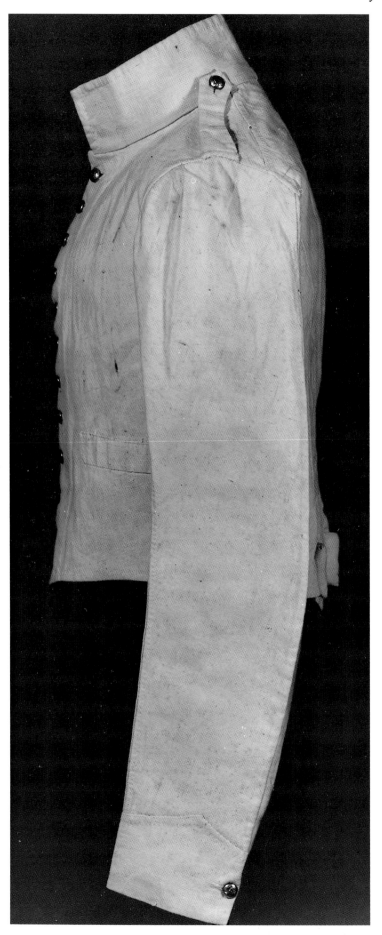

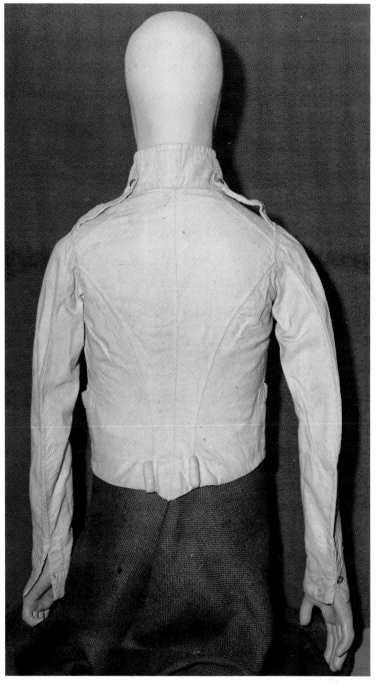

Rear view white cotton drilling summer enlisted fatigue jacket. WPM.

requirements.[55] Some troops took advantage of the fact "soldier's clothes and feathers" appeared attractive to local Indians who agreed to trade for "old jackets and `tar bucket' hats" (1854-pattern) in exchange "for buffalo robes, moccasins, and other articles. . . ."[56]

By barter or other means men of the Utah column attempted to replace their worn government issue or improve on what they had received from the army, adopting buckskin trousers, "mountaineer's leggings, coming up over the knee and tied with a string, coat of buckskin or anything you choose," as Captain Jesse Gove commented. He went on to comment how wonderful it was

Side view of the white cotton drilling enlisted jacket, in this case for a dragoon. Only one button rather than two closed the sleeve on this item designed to add to the comfort of the soldier during the warm seasons. While difficult to keep clean, this outer garment was one of the few options a soldier had to cope with the heat, and as such was issued from the 1830s through the 1850s. SI

to see the uses that buckskin can be put to. It serves everything in the wearing apparel line. There are several kinds of skins, antelope, deer, elk, and mountain sheep. The mountain sheep is much the finest and makes the handsomest garments.

For this reason, Gove availed himself of a pair of buckskin trousers made by a local Indian woman, and indicated he intended "to get a coat trimmed with beads" along with some moccasins, although he preferred shoes to his type of footgear.[57] By his own admission in a letter to his wife, the captain could afford to be selective in that he was better outfitted than most with:

> three buffalo robes and in case of necessity . . . my wolf's robe. So you see I cannot suffer from want of clothing, and you know that I have ten government blankets. Besides, I have a large supply of other clothing, better and more of it than any other officer in the command.

Gove went on to make known his good fortune in letters about how he had on his "white shirt, collar, fancy gray shirt, and am really dressed up and never felt better."[58] He even mentioned he had "plenty of handkerchiefs and other clothes" including "three or four beautiful shirts" and a military vest, gloves, and stocking.[59] Unlike most others on the expedition Gove could state: "My great luck lies in the fact that my wardrobe is extensive for such a campaign." He was doubly blessed in that "everything like wearing apparel" was very costly, but he did not have "to buy a dime's worth, nor shall I need to do so for 6 months to come. You know what an elegant outfit I got just before I left [Fort] Ridgley," he told his spouse.[60]

Sixth Infantry Sergeant Eugene Bandel was a "clothes horse" much as Gove seemed to be. The sergeant indicated he never had "been obliged to keep on wearing a dirty shirt when, as sometimes happened, six weeks would pass without a clean one being issued to us. This was impressive given the fact that Bandel customarily wore "three shirts (two flannel and one cotton. . . .)" He stated he also wore "drawers summer and winter, and that while on the march I changed my socks daily and other underwear twice a week. . . ." This meant that his knapsack, which he carried, and his trunk that was hauled in a baggage wagon were "well filled" – no mean accomplishment given the limited space in the knapsack and in the wagons. What is more, Bandel indicated, "Clothing – that is, extra clothing – costs a good deal." Besides the price of purchase, he found it necessary to "have all his clothes (uniform and trousers altered after drawing them from the government" at the cost of five dollars each month. This refitting of the issue was a common practice and a source of complaint among soldiers who noted that the army failed to provide properly fitted garments.

Tenth Infantry officer Albert Tracy might have envied Bandel in that his own uniform was "so worn and battered, and so rough and coarse of grain" when he returned from Utah, a new "outfit of citizen's clothing" seemed imperative, although costly at $48 for a suit.[61] Perhaps this situation may have caused Tracy to regret that he was not named to a board "to improve on army uniforms," a goal he had failed to attain in 1858.[62]

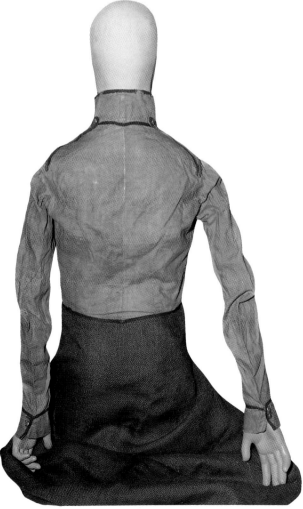

Front, rear, and side view of an officer's summer fatigue jacket. The binding and wings are adaptations of the basic pattern but are not regulation. WPM

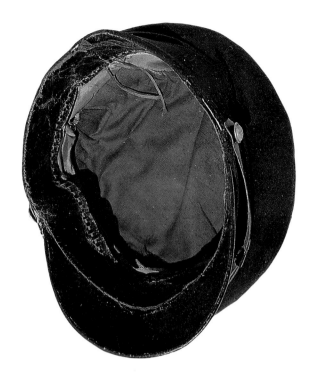

Front, side, and interior of Major General Zachary Taylor's 1839-pattern forage cap. WC

(top) Regiment of Mounted Rifles, (bottom) detail of buttons and collar for an 1832-pattern artillery officer coatee, and (right) infantry buttons, all of the Mexican War era. WC

Front and rear view of 1851-pattern enlisted shoulder scales for mounted troops, left: musicians, privates, corporals; middle: sergeants and first sergeants or orderly sergeants; right: non-commissioned staff. The scales were prescribed for mounted troops only, until 1854 when all enlisted men were to adopt them in lieu of the worsted epaulets that had been prescribed for dismounted enlisted men. SI

Worsted epaulets in branch colors were to adorn the shoulders of musicians, privates, and corporals in the engineers, infantry, heavy artillery, and ordnance, according to the 1851-uniform regulations. The fringe was 1/8-inch in diameter. As of 1854, these epaulets were to be replaced by brass shoulder scales.

The 1851-uniform regulations called for worsted epaulets for the regimental non-commissioned staff of engineers, infantry, and heavy artillery, as well as ordnance sergeants and hospital stewards, to have a fringe with a 3/8-inch diameter. In 1854, brass shoulder scales were called for as replacements for the worsted epaulets.

As of 1851, facings of branch color covered the collars and cuffs of all enlisted men except engineers and ordnance personnel. This image is of a private of infantry in the 1851-pattern uniform. ERG

Engineer and ordnance enlisted men had welts of yellow and crimson respectively to set off the collars and cuffs on the 1851-pattern enlisted coats. A stamped sheet brass castle flanked either side of the collar for engineer privates and non-commissioned officers as well, while a pair of flaming bombs were to be affixed to the collars of ordnance enlisted personnel. The epaulets were yellow worsted for engineers and crimson for ordnance. It appears this individual wears staff officer's buttons rather then the prescribed Engineer Corps buttons. USAMHI

The 1851-pattern officer's cap. Infantry officers had a gold embroidered bugle with silver regimental number, in this case a "7" for the Seventh Infantry. SHSW

Brevet Major John F. Lee posed in the 1851-pattern uniform of a judge advocate general with white pompon and double-breasted frock coat with seven staff buttons in each row, the standard for field grade officers. The welt on the dark blue trousers was to be 1/8-inch buff facing material. PAF

Paymasters and surgeons had special gilt swords marked "PD" (Pay Department) and "MD" (Medical Deparment) to designate their status. The same letters appeared on their gold epaulets, while their pompons were buff on their lower two-thirds and emerald green on the upper third for surgeons and dark olive green on the upper third for paymasters. The individual seen here is Surgeon Robert Little Brodie. WJS

Black velvet collars and cuffs set off general officers according to the 1851 uniform regulations. Placement of buttons indicated rank, such as four pairs of staff officer's buttons for brigadiers. The sash was to be buff silk net. The cap band was black velvet and the pompon a gold embroidered net acorn. MJM

A young second lieutenant appears in the regulation company grade uniform prescribed in 1851, including a single-breasted dark blue wool frock coat with nine gold buttons and the tall cap with removable Saxony blue pompon and embroidered hunting horn device, the insignia for infantry officers. He wears shoulder straps, which were prescribed for field and general garrison wear, over the epaulets, a deviation from regulations that was not uncommon during the 1850s. The size of the fringe of the epaulets is that of a subaltern, the bullion being 1/8-inch in diameter. The fact that there are no indications of rank marks this unknown officer as a second lieutenant. USAMHI.

1851-pattern artillery officer's cap. The regimental numeral was to be in silver and the artillery crossed cannon insignia in gold embroidery or metal simulated embroidery. All other officers had a similar cap the differences being the color of the pompon and the insignia on the front. RB

Other officers did make their influence felt when it came to recommendations concerning uniforms. For instance, George B. McClellan, a first lieutenant of engineers who was promoted to captain and transferred to the First U.S. Cavalry Regiment, served as a member of a U.S. military commission sent abroad to observe the Crimean War from 1854 to 1856. Before returning from that duty McClellan studied various European armies. He paid special attention to foreign equipment and uniforms. One of his most noted recommendations from this study was the saddle that eventually would be adopted as the standard for the United States cavalry, and that continued as the basic issue through the history of that branch.

Over the decades, this saddle overshadowed clothing that McClellan proposed, which subsequently were adopted. For instance, he recommended that shoulder scales be dispensed with for enlisted men, and the epaulet discontinued for regimental officers (both were deleted in 1872). Further, he thought, "For service on the prairies, the men should have" a simple garb consisting of "the ordinary dark-blue sailor's shirt, cut open in front, and provided with a lining and pockets" along with "a loose flannel coat, leaving the uniform coat in garrison."[63] While such a shirt would be some time in coming, the sack coat McClellan sought was adopted in fairly short order, ultimately proving one of the most utilitarian items produced by the Quartermaster Department in the nineteenth century. Beginning on November 28, 1857 this rudimentary but effective garment was approved for mounted troops. The item soon be-

Front and side of an artillery 1851-pattern enlisted cap. Similar caps were issued to all other enlisted men, but the bands were to be in branch colors, except for engineers who had a pair of yellow welts and ordnance men who were to have crimson welts. RB

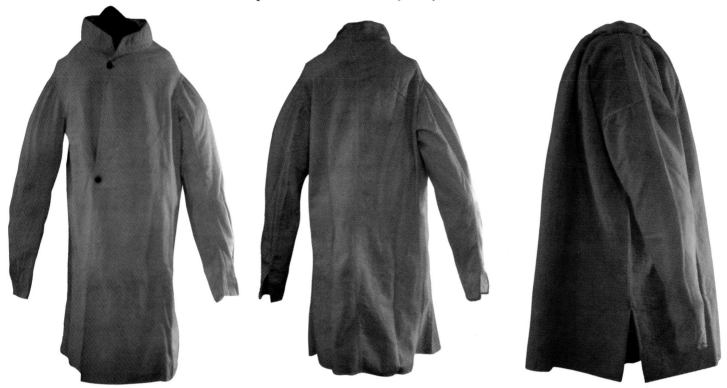

Front view of stable frock as issued from the late 1840s through the early 1860s. TC

Rear view of stable frock. TC

Side view of stable frock. TC

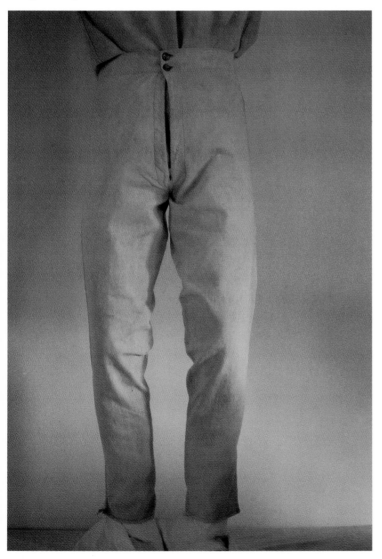

Front 1851-pattern underdrawers. TC

Rear 1851-pattern underdrawers. TC

Front 1851-pattern enlisted foot overcoat. TC

Rear 1851-pattern enlisted foot overcoat. TC

came standard for all troops after March 1858 as the well known, and relatively popular four-button blouse.

McClellan also mentioned the desirability of a less cumbersome cap that would be more in keeping with fatigue and field wear than the stiff 1854-pattern. He postulated that mounted troopers at least should have:

> a police cap, without visor, and of such a nature that it can be folded up and carried in the pouch [saddlebags], or wherever is convenient; the Scotch bonnet, Turkish fez, a Greek cap of knit or woven wool, a flexible cap of the shape of the old forage-cap – any of these would answer.

Additionally, McClellan mentioned the French forage cap with a conical top and large straight visor as another type of headgear that would serve this need. During the mid-1840s this *bonnet de police à visière* began to be issued to French troops, and in time became associated intimately with that nation's military as the *képi*.[64] The year

McClellan's report was published (1857) the engineer officer who commanded the Company of Sappers, Miners, and Pontoniers stationed at West Point asked that his organization might be given a hat similar to the cavalry received in 1855, or the 1839-pattern forage cap be reinstated, in either case for fatigue wear. By March 31, 1857 Secretary of War John B. Floyd looked favorably on this request, but instead sanctioned a sample cap of a new design to be made for consideration. In fact, two prototypes were constructed of the *chasseur* pattern, one costing $1.00 with a high crown, and another that was priced at $.87 1/2, with a lower crown. The taller type was endorsed. As a result, the Schuylkill Arsenal produced a sufficient quantity of these for all enlisted engineers, the first seventy-four being issued to those men posted to Fort Leavenworth. There were also a like number of cap covers sent at the same time, although it is unknown what either the cap or the covers looked like exactly.[65] The idea was that the cap would be issued in alternating years over a soldier's five year enlistment, thereby reducing costs as well as providing a more workman-like piece. (See Table 1 for the allowance of clothing as specified in the paragraph 1036, *Regulations for the Army* in 1857, before the issue of the new forage cap.)

Front 1851-pattern enlisted mounted overcoat. TC

Rear 1851-pattern enlisted mounted overcoat. TC

CLOTHING	Table 1 FOR FIVE YEARS				
	1st.	2d.	3d.	4th.	5th.
Cap, complete	2	1	2	1	1
Pompon	1	....	1	....	....
Eagle and ring	1	....	1	....	....
Cover	1	1	1	1	1
Coat	2	1	2	1	2
Trowsers	3	2	3	2	3
Flannel shirt	3	3	3	3	3
" drawers	3	2	2	2	2
Boatees, pair	4	4	4	4	4
Stockings, pair	4	4	4	4	4
Leather stock	1	....	1	....	....
Great-coat	1	....	....	....	....
Stable-frock (for mounted men)	1	....	1	....	....
Fatigue overalls for eng'rs and ordnance	1	1	1	1	1
Blanket	1	....	1	....	....

Mounted men may receive one pair of "boots and two pairs of "bootees" instead of four pairs of bootees.

Side 1851-pattern enlisted mounted overcoat. TC

Detail of lining of 1851-pattern enlisted overcoat. TC

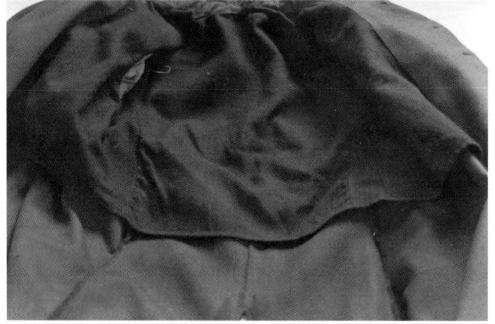

Belted back of both the 1851-pattern enlisted foot and mounted overcoat. TC

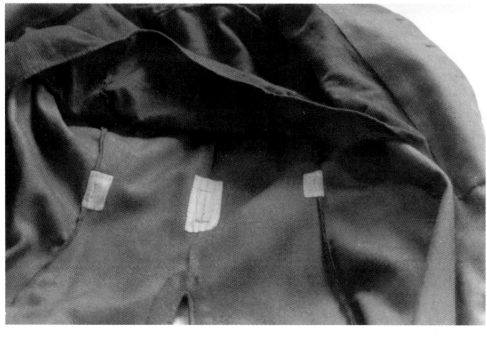

1851-pattern enlisted overcoat interior. TC

A private of dragoons in the 1854-pattern uniform jacket of an enlisted man with the cap called for in the same year. All facings for dragoons were orange lace on the collar around the edges, and cuffs, and orange piping set off the lower portion of the cap from the upper portion. Shoulder scales were brass. This same cap and coat remained regulation until 1858, although the latter garment continued in use for some years thereafter. SI

In 1854 mounted enlisted men were to replace the frock coat with a jacket having twelve eagle brass buttons. Branch colors were depicted by worsted lace, scarlet being present here for this light artillerymen who holds an M1840 light artillery saber. The cap is the 1854-pattern with scarlet welt for artillery, but bears no company letter, perhaps indicating that the individual was an unassigned recruit. MJM

Later, in the summer of 1858, Brevet Major William H. French, the artillery officer who commanded Fort McHenry, Maryland noted his men removed the "stiffening of their" 1854-pattern caps, "to wear them on fatigue." Although this apparently was not an uncommon expedient, the officer found the appearance unsightly. Because of this he advocated a "light, comfortable, military" cap that also was "cheap" to produce. To make his point he had four samples made, one each for artillery, cavalry, infantry, and staff, and sent these along to the adjutant general. Despite the fact that this suggestion did not go through normal military channels of the time, it did reach the secretary of war, and from there went to the quartermaster general. Having made the rounds, approval for adoption came relatively soon with the promulgation of General Orders No. 13, War Department, November 30, 1858 that read:

For fatigue purposes, Forage caps, of pattern in the Quartermaster General's Office, will be issued, in addition to hats, at the rate of one per year. Dark blue cloth, with a cord or welt around the crown of the colors used to distinguish the several arms of service, and yellow metal letters in front to designate companies. For unassigned recruits dark blue cord or welt around the crown and without distinctive badge.

The same general order permitted officers to obtain such a cap "with dark welt and distinctive ornament, in front, of the corps and regiment." Evidently these insignia were to be of the type worn on the 1854-cap for officers, while it seems likely that a 1-inch high sheet brass regimental number of the type worn on the collar prior to 1857 for enlisted coats and jackets, would have been affixed to the caps of the other ranks.

The 1858-pattern forage cap received mixed reviews, true to prior changes in issuance. However, it apparently appealed to others as indicated by the fact that officers at the Artillery School had petitioned for permission to obtain the headpiece even before it was announced that it would be issued throughout the army. This same group also sought a means to address the problem of soaring temperatures and humidity at Fort Monroe, Virginia, where the Artillery School was located. As a consequence, attendees there would receive a special summer outfit consisting of cotton overalls and a "round straw hat" for officers and enlisted men alike, while the former body could buy a white linen coat.[66] Later, a more detailed directive stated: "Officers will wear the prescribed uniform for the army, on parades and guards until on or after the 5th inst. [June 5, 1858] when white linen, or drilling overalls will be substituted for the woolen general wear." The order continued, "For general wear the same or, a plain white straw hat with a black ribbon and with-

Corporal of the Tenth U.S. Infantry in 1854-pattern coat. WJS

Private of heavy artillery in 1854-pattern coat. WJS

Sergeant of heavy artillery in the 1854-pattern cap and coat. WJS

Emerald green half chevrons of facing material embroidered with yellow silk were called for in 1851 to designate hospital stewards. USAMHI

out lining or facings on the rim and a white linen or drilling coat and overalls. A blue flannel uniform coat may be worn on other than parade and court martial duties." This lighter weight version of the officer's frock helped relieve the brass from heat and humidity, while the men also had some relief from these conditions in that they could adopt the straw hat and white overalls for parades and guard mounts.[67]

By late June the special outfit was on hand for officers and men alike. Once available the latter group were directed to place the proper buttons and shoulder straps on their frocks, but under no circumstances were they to substitute the new even more functional sack coat.

It seems probable that the cut of this frock-coat would follow the new pattern adopted in 1858. This was a less elaborate version of the 1855 coat, the plaits being eliminated as was the case with brass numerals on the jacket and coat collars for enlisted men. The plaits for trousers no longer were required at this time too, while 1/8-inch welts were retained in the branch color for officers, including a gold welt that was

1854-pattern enlisted caps had welts in branch colors rather than facing material bands, much like those for engineers and ordnance men of the 1851-pattern. SI

The 1854-pattern dragoon bugler or musician jacket had orange worsted tape on the front rather than a plastron as had been the case for the 1851-pattern coat. In 1854 a jacket similar to that worn before 1851 for all troops was again prescribed for mounted soldiers, including light artillery and mounted rifles personnel with green for mounted rifles, orange tape for dragoons, and scarlet for light artillery. A cap with a pompon and welt of the same color cloth was combined with this outfit which supposedly was to serve for all garrison functions and field service. Brass shoulder scales and collar numerals were to be worn by all troops, mounted or dismounted as of 1854 to designate regimental affiliation through 1857. Welts with branch colors on the outside seams of the trousers also were dispensed with by General Orders No. 1, January 20, 1854. SI

In 1854 welts replaced facing material bands on the caps of enlisted infantry, artillery, dragoons, and mounted rifles. This example is for an infantryman. The color was changed for infantry in that year too, from Saxony to sky-blue. TC

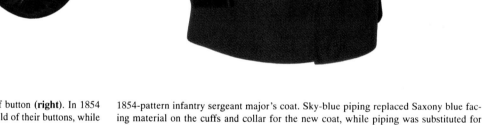

Staff officer's coat button (**left**) and enlisted 1854-pattern cuff button (**right**). In 1854 only line officers were to have the letter of their unit in the shield of their buttons, while those for enlisted men were not, unlike previous patterns. JG

1854-pattern infantry sergeant major's coat. Sky-blue piping replaced Saxony blue facing material on the cuffs and collar for the new coat, while piping was substituted for facing on the cuffs and collars of heavy artillery coats as well. SI

adopted for staff officers and generals. Further, the plain seams of non-commissioned officers trousers once again were to be set off by leg stripes. Now 1 1/2-inch worsted stripes were prescribed for sergeants, and 1/2-inch for corporals. Privates were to have no such adornment.

The leg stripes and welts were to be in branch colors in all cases even for infantrymen whose light blue at last would show up against the dark blue trousers. The reason for this was that the 1858-pattern trousers also were to be dark blue cloth to match the coat, and thus the infantry facings of light blue for the coat, cap, chevrons, and the like would now be visible.

There was one exception to all this, in that light artillerymen perhaps never wore the new dark blue trousers, especially after 1860 when they were permitted to retain sky-blue ones. It should be noted that the same order that called for the retention of sky-blue trousers for light artillery also prescribed a special, "round jacket, according to pattern, of dark blue cloth, trimmed with scarlet, with the Russian-knot the prescribed insignia of rank to be worked in silver in the centre of the knot" as an undress garment for light artillery officers.

While many of these initiatives represented streamlining measures, not all the Quartermaster Department's efforts were so directed. Three types of headgear of the 1850s further indicated the bent of some individuals toward show rather than more mundane concerns. Certainly the reappearance of the chapeau de bras for field officers and those of the general staff represented a less than practical initiative, and marked a reversion to pre-1851 fashion.[68]

So, too, did a second headcover, one that evidently came into being because of a movement in 1857 among certain light artillery officers to return to a cap adopted for this elite arm in 1844. Sometimes known as the "Ringgold cap" after Major Samuel Ringgold, whose "flying artillery" had achieved considerable stature in the 1840s' military establishment, the idea of this cap was resurrected years later. At first, the quartermaster general approved the use of the 1854-pattern cap with horsehair plume in scarlet for light artillery units that requested them according to letters of October 25, 1858, and January 25, 1859. By February 12, the cap also was modified to have scarlet cords much as they had in the 1840s. In fact, 1844-pattern Ringgold caps were provided at first

Front of the 1855-pattern *chasseurs-a-pied* inspired single-breasted frock coat with its full pleated waist that was to be worn by foot troops through 1857. Actually, production and issue of this item, as with most articles of the uniform, lagged from the time of adoption to the date when the troops received the garments. In some cases, certain patterns never saw universal issue, as possibly was the case with these pleated trousers. TC

Private (probably heavy artillery) with the 1854-cap and 1855-pattern chasseurs coat. WJS

because the head of the quartermaster depot in Philadelphia thought the 1854-pattern cap could not bear the weight of the plume. Soon thereafter, an artillery officer came up with a scheme to reinforce the newer cap, and thereafter that pattern was modified to be issued to those batteries requesting them, a practice confirmed by General Orders No. 20, War Department, August 6, 1860. Even then, commanders had the option of requisitioning the cap, or they could obtain a hat that was to be adopted by all branches of the army in 1858, thereby resulting in a mixture of two styles depending on the desire of the individual commanding officer.[69] This second type of headgear took its inspiration from the former 1855 cavalry hat. Authorized by General Orders No. 3, Adjutant General's Office, March 24, 1858, several differences existed that distinguished the piece from the 1855-pattern cavalry issue, one change being the elimination of the festooned cord on the crown, and another the discontinuation of the leather chin strap. The acorn tips on enlisted hat cords likewise were replaced with small fringed tassels. These and other details were set forth in General Orders No. 3 as follows:

For Officers: Of best black felt. The dimensions of medium size to be as follows:

> Width of brim, 3 1/4 inches,
> Height of crown, 6 1/4 inches,
> Oval of tip, 1/2 inch,
> Taper of crown, 3/4 inch,
> Curve of head, 3/8 inch,
> The binding to be 1/2 inch deep, of best black ribbed silk.

*For Enlisted Men. Of bl*ack felt, same shape and size as for officers, with double row of stitching, instead of binding, around the edge. To agree in quality with the pattern deposited in the clothing arsenal.

Trimmings

For General Officers: Gold cord, with acorn-shaped ends. The brim of the hat looped up on the right side, and fastened with an eagle attached to the side of the hat; three black ostrich feathers on

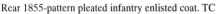
Rear 1855-pattern pleated infantry enlisted coat. TC

Side 1855-pattern pleated infantry enlisted coat. TC

the left side; a gold embroidered wreath in front on black velvet ground, encircling the letters U.S. in silver, old English characters.

For Officers of the Adjutants General's, Inspector General's, Quartermaster's, Subsistence, Medical and Pay Departments, and the Judge Advocate, above the rank of Captain: The same as for General Officers, except the cord, which will be of black silk and gold.

For the same Departments, below the rank of Field Officers: The same as for Field Officers, except that there will be two feathers.

For Officers of the Corps of Engineers: The same as for the General Staff, except the ornament in front, which will be a gold embroidered wreath of laurel and palm, encircling a silver turreted castle on black velvet ground.

For Officers of the Topographical Engineers: The same as for the General Staff, except the ornament in front, which will be a gold embroidered wreath of oak leaves, encircling a gold embroidered shield, on black velvet.

For Officers of the Ordnance Department: The same as for the General Staff, except the ornament in front, which will be a gold embroidered shell and flame, on black velvet ground.

For Officers of Dragoons: The same as for the general Staff, except the ornament in front, which will be two gold embroidered sabres crossed, edges upward, on black velvet with the number of the regiment in silver in the upper angle.

For Officers of Cavalry: The same as for Dragoons, except the sabres will be reversed, with the number of the regiment in the lower angle.

For Officers of Mounted Rifles: The same as for General Staff, except the ornament in front, which will be a gold embroidered trumpet, perpendicular, on black velvet ground.

For Officers of Artillery: The same as General Staff, except the ornament in front, which will be gold embroidered cross-cannon, on black velvet ground, with the number of the regiment in silver at the intersection of the cross-cannon: The brim of the hat to be looped up on the left side, and the feathers to be worn on the right side.

For Officers of Infantry: The same as for Artillery except the ornament in front, which will be a gold embroidered bugle, on black velvet ground, with the number of the regiment in silver within the bend.

Front 1855-pattern pleated foot soldier's trousers. Note that there is no welt or leg stripe, this ornamentation having been discontinued in 1854. TC

Rear 1855-pattern pleated foot soldier's trousers. TC

Side 1855-pattern pleated trousers. TC

Waist 1855-pleated trousers. TC

Cuff detail 1855-pattern pleated trousers. The button could be attached to a leather or cloth strap that helped keep the cuff in place when worn under the sole of the foot. TC

For Enlisted Men: The same as Officers of the respective corps; except that there will be but one feather, the cord will be of worsted, and the badges yellow metal, to be worn in front.

All the trimmings of the hat are to be made so that they can be detached; but the eagle, badge of corps, and letter of company, are to be always worn.

This last requirement would be ignored more often than not over the passing years. Also in regard to insignia, cavalry officers and all enlisted men in the combat arms (artillery, cavalry, dragoons, infantry, and mounted rifles) previously had no hat insignia beyond either regimental numerals for officers or company letters for enlisted men for their 1851 or 1854-pattern caps, while the other officers and men did so and continued to use the same scheme set forth in 1851. This change placed everyone on the same footing. It likewise should be noted that hospital stewards received a further distinction with the adoption of the hat in that they were to have buff and green hat cords, the two colors combined making them unique among enlisted personnel. Moreover, the two hues closely approximately the half chevron these enlisted medical men had been provided since the early 1850s.

Additionally, General Orders No. 24, War Department June 24, 1858, made a further adjustment, perhaps for the sake of uniformity. This directive indicated that dragoons and cavalrymen would have the sabers worn with the edges placed upwards rather than reversed from each other as in the past. The only difference would be that the regimental numeral would be located above the sabers for dragoons and below the sabers for cavalry.

The hat was not issued in large quantities until the following year. Soon thereafter one cavalry officer suggested that the chinstrap again be provided as with the 1855-pattern, a suggestion the quartermaster general sanctioned for cavalry and dragoons, at least for a limited time.[70]

Another cavalry officer reacted to the hat in less positive terms writing, "If the whole earth had been ransacked, it is difficult to tell where a more ungainly piece of furniture could have been found." He went on to indicate the 1858 hat was "somewhat more unwieldy" than its 1855 progenitor. It seemed "that the soldiers take great delight in seeing into what ludicrous shapes they can get their hat. . . ." He concluded that the hat reminded the viewer of a stage costume piece worn by "Fra Diavolo," the title character to "one of the most frequently performed operas of the 19th century."

Captain Jesse Gove, an officer serving in Utah held a different opinion of the matter recording: "We see by the papers that the uniform is to be changed. The cap or hat to be black and ostrich feathers. That will please you, but the other changes are disapproved by everyone here in the army."[71] During April 1858 Captain Gove's company was stationed in today's western Wyoming. His company was the only one in the regi-

Front 1854-pattern light artillery musician or bugler's jacket. RB

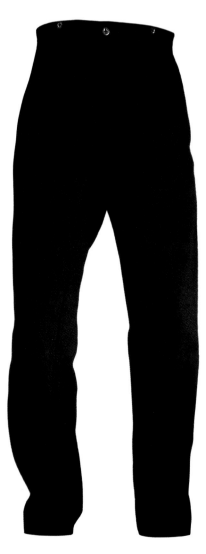

Front 1855-pleated mounted trousers. TC

Rear 1855-pattern pleated mounted trousers. TC

Front 1855-pattern cavalry enlisted jacket. TC

Rear 1855-pattern cavalry enlisted jacket. TC

ment at that time to have received the "cavalry hat" as he called it, and he thought the men "looked splendidly."[72] He also underscored that the hat had a "black ostrich feather like Kossuth hats, turned up on the right side."[73]

In a second instance, on May 27, 1858, Gove mentioned Kossuth hats were combined with worn uniforms, or interspersed with the old 1854-pattern cap, while on outpost duty. The men also had set aside the knapsack for:

A blanket tightly rolled up and bound round their chests, passing over their right shoulder and round their left arm, to be used for protection against and cold, a tin plate was tied to the blanket, while the haversacks contained provisions for twenty-four hours.

A few days later, a more formal gathering of Gove's company took place. He reported with pride the men had on their good uniforms, with their accoutrements and arms "were bright and glistening."[74]

On yet one more occasion, during February 1859, Captain Albert Tracy had a different experience. While on parade, a snowstorm covered the troops, some in the 1854-cap with pompons, others in "kepis," and still some in the felt hats, "with broad or looped up brims, and plumes

of ostrich" that "were simply a mess, and shocking to behold" once drenched in the cold, moist flakes. Tracy concluded: "In the 5th Infantry, the loss and demoralization in brand new hats and plumes, is said to be something fearful. In our own regiment it was not light."

The mixture of hats also was found in Nevada when a campaign was launched in 1860 against a local Indian group, the Piutes. Some of the forces sent there were men from Company H, Third Artillery stationed in the San Francisco area, and a detachment from the Sixth U.S. Infantry dispatched from Benicia, California. According to a newspaper account the artillery, "wore blue frock-coats, dark mixed pants, (officers with red stripes down the outside of the pants), the regular army military hat, with letter II [sic], in gilt, on front, without pompoon [sic], cartridge box, water cup and sack." In turn, "the infantry company wore short blue frock-coats [four-button sack coats], light blue pants, black Kossuth hats, with left brim turned up and fastened with a gilt *attache*, gilt bugle in front, and surrounded with blue cord and tassels, water cup and sack, and cartridge box."[75]

This report and the practices of the Utah expedition underscored a number of trends that existed by 1860. First, for the most part the stock of Mexican War surplus finally had been exhausted. Still, the mixture of old issue and new continued to be in vogue with articles of various

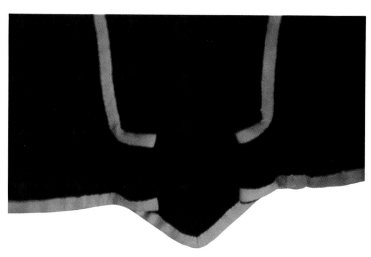

Detail rear skirt 1855-pattern cavalry enlisted jacket. TC

Side 1855-pattern cavalry enlisted jacket. TC

Detail collar 1855-pattern cavalry enlisted jacket. Note the brass regimental numeral that was in keeping with the collar insignia called for on the coats of foot troops. Because the lace for the mounted jacket somewhat obscured these devices, it is possible that they were not always worn by the cavalry, dragoons, horse artillery, or mounted riflemen. TC

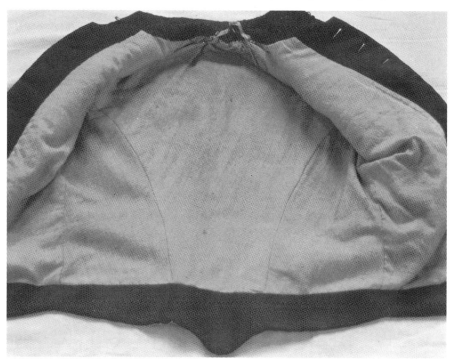

Lining of 1855-pattern enlisted cavalry jacket. TC

Front 1855-pattern cavalry enlisted hat. TC

Detail right side 1855-pattern cavalry enlisted hat. TC

Right side 1855-pattern cavalry enlisted hat. TC

Rear 1855-pattern cavalry enlisted hat. TC

Left side 1855-pattern cavalry enlisted hat. TC

Detail of rosette to hold the single black ostrich feather for 1855-pattern cavalry enlisted hat. TC

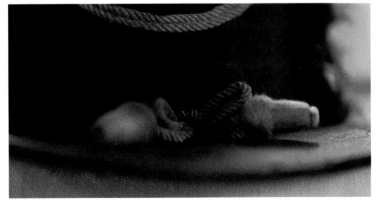

Acorns on the 1855-pattern enlisted cavalry hat cords. TC

Front of the four-button sack coat that began to be issued as a practical work and combat garment beginning in 1859. It soon became popular and was manufactured in large quantities during the Civil War for wear by the Union Army. TC

Rear 4-button sack coat. TC

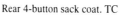

patterns introduced throughout the 1850s seeing service side by side. Additionally, the idea of a single uniform fulfilling dual purposes for garrison and field usage, as had been the direction taken with the 1851-pattern, was challenged as some individuals came to promote different garments specifically designed according to circumstances. This was a direction that had come into its own in the civilian sector, when the former practice of work clothing and dress wear being one garment began to give way to a variety of outfits made possible by the increased availability and reduced costs of ready made clothing.

But in the army, this trend toward specialization was still in flux, given the voluminous workmanlike four-button sack coat was employed simultaneously with the more formal, restrictive frock, indicating that the subject of what constituted the best article of clothing based upon

1855-pattern cavalry officer's hat. SI

Captain George B. McClellan, First U.S. Cavalry Regiment, (far right) wears the single-breasted company grade officer's frock coat with nine buttons. Major Alfred Mordecai (left seated) and Major Richard Delafield (center seated) wear the double-breasted frock of field grade officers with seven buttons in each row. Both hold the 1851-pattern officer's cap, Delafield's displaying the castle insignia of engineers, a device that is repeated on his gold epaulets. His pompon was to have the upper third in black and the lower two-thirds in buff, while Mordecai, as an ordnance officer was to have a pompon with the upper third in crimson and the lower two-thirds in buff. USAMHI

the assignment at hand was not resolved. The ambivalence demonstrated by composite clothing forms characterized the dozen years after the Mexican War. Resolution of the desire to cut a military figure, while at the same time address pragmatic concerns continued at the heart of the debate over the U.S. Army uniform by 1860, causing Captain Gove to ponder, "Why cannot they get some officers on their boards that have some sense and idea of good taste?"[76]

This question characterized the ongoing dialectic about appearance versus functionality that had surfaced after the Mexican War. In the ensuing dozen years much had taken place to accommodate the two divergent perspectives, yet whole areas of importance, such as winter campaign wear, had been ignored officially. The final solution to the equation still was forthcoming, however, particularly because the issue was to be subsumed by smoldering sectional differences that were about to ignite the nation in a civil war.

Surgeon Albert Myer, serving in Texas in the mid-1850s, has put aside almost all indications that he is a U.S. Army officer except for his M1851 eagle belt plate and some of his accoutrements. Adopting civilian clothing, accessories, and equipage was a frequent response when government issue items did not meet local environmental conditions, or when personal preference took precedent over official policy. NA

Brevet Second Lieutenant Orlando Poe of the Topographical Engineers appears in the regulation uniform for the mid-1850s, although he has elected to obtain an old style 1839-pattern forage cap rather than the 1851-pattern cap. The welt on his dark blue trousers was to be buff. His gilt coat buttons were to bear a shield with the letters "T.E." The sword is an M1850 foot officer's sword. USAMHI

Brevet Second Lieutenant William Proctor Smith cuts a similar figure to his fellow Topographical Engineer, O.M. Poe. The sash was to be crimson silk. USAMHI

Second Lieutenant William Spencer served with the Second U.S. Infantry during the mid-1850s when this portrait was taken. He has armed himself with a Colt revolver and a dagger for this photo session and wears his sash scarf style which was regulation for the "officer of the day." The 1/8-inch welt on his trousers was dark blue. Again, the forage cap is the 1839-pattern. SEO

Captain Thomas Wood of the First Cavalry has retained the gold cords on his 1855-pattern hat but has added the new gold embroidered crossed saber devices prescribed in 1858. Originally cavalry officers wore this insignia with edges downward per General Orders No. 3, Adjutant Generals Office, March 24, 1854. Woods wears his shoulder straps over his epaulets, a practice that began to be discontinued by the late 1850s. USAHI

David Hunter was the colonel of the First Cavalry Regiment. He wears the regimental numeral in silver below his gold crossed saber devices on the 1858-pattern hat as was regulation for cavalry officers. Dragoon officers were to wear their regimental numerals above the sabers per General Orders No. 7, Adjutant General Offices, June 24, 1858. USAMHI

Second Lieutenant Charles Bowman displays the numeral "1" in silver below his officer's hat insignia in keeping with the directive for cavalry officers to do so set forth in General Orders No. 7, Adjutant General Offices, June 24, 1858. WPM

First Lieutenant Roger Jones of the Regiment of Mounted Rifles 1858-pattern officer's hat with it distinctive perpendicular gold embroidered trumpet ornament appears next to him. A silver numeral "1" appears in the loop of the trumpet, although there was no reason to designate the regiment with a numeral because it was the only regular army mounted rifle outfit in existence. Jones cradles an M1850 foot officer's sword and his single-breasted dark blue wool frock coat indicate that he is a company grade officer, while his epaulets further establish his rank and regiment. From 1858 through 1861 his trousers would have been dark blue with an 1/8-inch emerald green welt let into the outer seams for mounted rifle officers. USAMHI

Infantry bandsmen with the Utah Expedition depict the diversity of coats and headgear worn in the field in the late 1850s, including what appears to be a number of 1854-pattern caps that have been compressed to provide a forage cap. The non-commissioned officer in the center has on an 1839-pattern forage cap and a triple row of buttons, probably indicating that he is the principal musician or chief trumpeter. USHS

Infantry troops at Camp Scott in today's Wyoming also illustrate the mixture of uniforms worn on the Utah Expedition. The trousers are sky-blue, despite the fact that dark blue ones were prescribed in 1858. Typically there was a lag between new uniform regulations and actual issue of the clothing once produced. Further, the troops in the field tended to adopt their oldest, most worn clothing rather than have new items ruined from heavy field wear. USHS

Wearing out old clothing seems to be the case for this infantry sergeant major (Fifth Infantry?) who evidently is ready for the Utah Expedition of the late 1850s, although he has on the old 1832-pattern infantry jacket with white worsted tape and the 1839-pattern forage cap with an officer's style bugle device. He does have an up-to-date revolver and holster that he might have donned as a prop for this portrait or purchased for use on the expedition. The sword is the M1840 non-commissioned officer type. The sash was to be crimson worsted. WJS

The enlisted forage cap of the late 1850s was to have a welt around the top (accept for recruits who had no welts) in scarlet for artillery, orange for dragoons, yellow for cavalry and engineers, crimson for ordnance, and emerald green for mounted riflemen, a practice which was discontinued by 1861. Here a dragoon of the 1858 era stands to horse at Ft Leavenworth, Kansas in the pre-1861 forage cap with the 1854-pattern mounted jacket trimmed in orange worsted lace. LC

Second Lieutenant Kirby Smith, while taking solar reading in Utah during 1858, wears his blue wool forage cap and a dark blue short "stable" jacket of the type usually associated with officers serving in mounted regiments. His trousers are sky-blue without welts, contrary to regulation calling for dark blue trousers in that year. LC

In the late 1850s Second Lieutenant Kirby Smith of the elite Topographical Engineers (later to become a general officer in the Confederate Army) went to Utah with a major surveying expedition. An embroidered wreath with shield in the center indicates his branch on the front of the blue wool forage cap, a pattern of headgear unique to engineers from 1857 through 1858, when the secretary of war ordered that it be adopted for all branches and ranks. The transition was gradual, but by the Civil War this cap was typical. NA

Colonel P.G.T. Beauregard, as superintendent of the U.S. Military Academy, obtained an engineer officer's forage cap of the 1858-pattern. This early model differs from later forage caps in that it seems to be a cross between the 1839-pattern and the "bummer's" cap of the Civil War. WPM

In this circa 1860 image Lieutenant Bowman has elected to procure an enlisted sky-blue wool mounted overcoat rather than the officer's dark blue wool "cloakcoat." His cape, however, is longer than the 1851-pattern issued. Obtaining such a coat not only was less costly but allowed an officer to be less conspicuous when serving on campaign in that he blended more readily with his troops. WPM

Sergeant Herman O. Renaldo wears the infantry forage cap of the 1858-pattern with sky-blue welt around the crown, as does his unknown comrade. He also has on the dark blue trousers with 1.5-inch worsted lace leg stripes of a sergeant of infantry, as called for in 1858. VJM

The collar of the 1858-pattern coat essentially was identical to the 1854 and 1855-patterns. So, too, were the cuffs of the 1858-pattern coat. AHS

The waist of the 1858-pattern coat, however, returned to a non-pleated cut as seen for in this example from the rear. AHS

1858-pattern engineer sergeant coat. SI

In 1858 dismounted men were again to have a single-breasted frock coat with nine buttons down the front made without pleats. This coat was to be worn with the 1858-pattern hat for formal occasions. Trim was yellow for engineers (depicted here for a first sergeant), scarlet for heavy artillery, crimson for ordnance and hospital stewards, and sky blue for infantry. In addition, a special lace design ornamented the front of musician's coats as seen in this case for an infantry bugler. Dark blue trousers were regulation from 1858 through 1861 and from that year through 1872 sky-blue trousers were worn with this uniform. WPM

In 1858 a new hat, which took its inspiration from a pattern issued to the First and Second Cavalry regiments from three years earlier, was prescribed for all troops. This fur felt headpiece eventually was to looped on the left side for foot soldiers and on the right side for mounted troops (although considerable variation existed as seen in period photographs). Company letters and the regimental number affixed to the front of the crown. A black ostrich feather and worsted cords which ended in tassels, unlike the old cavalry version that had acorn tips, also were prescribed as was a sheet brass eagle device which was used to hold the turned up side in place. The example shown here is for a mounted rifle trooper of Company G, as indicated by the green cords and brass insignia. The perpendicular trumpet insignia is one of two types known to exist. It is unclear which of insignia was correct for this hat. Gordon Chappell Photograph.

1851 through 1872 Infantry first sergeant chevron of worsted lace. AMWH

1851-1872 ordnance sergeant of silk lace. SI

1851 through 1872 infantry sergeant major chevron of silk lace. SI

Before the Civil War the United States Military Academy Band had a dark blue 1858-pattern coat that also was distinguished by the addition of a plastron in yellow and three rows of buttons. All trim was yellow as well. A lyre insignia appeared on the 1858-pattern hat. Trousers were light blue. The drum major had an officer's type frock coat with gold epaulets and gilt aiguilettes, along with a baldric and sash. MJM

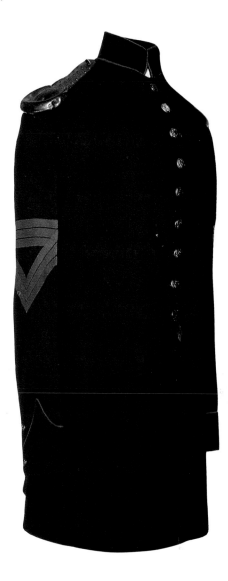

1858-pattern ordnance sergeant coat. SI

Plaited trousers and the plaited coats were discontinued by General Orders No. 3, March 3, 1858, for this pattern of coat, the example here being for a heavy artillery regimental quartermaster sergeant. Dark blue trousers were adopted by the same order with 1/8-inch welts for officers, .5-inch stripes in worsted branch colors for corporals, and 1.5-inch stripes for sergeants, also in worsted branch colors. SI

1858-pattern coat collar, infantry. Kurt Cox Photograph. JML

A private in the 1858-pattern frock coat showing the detail of the collar. WS

A service dress uniform also was provided to the Military Academy Band around 1859, and it eventually replaced the yellow plastron coat around 1861. The trousers were dark blue and the coat was the 1858-pattern. MJM

NOTES

1   refer to K. Jack Bauer, *The Mexican War 1846-1848* (Lincoln: University of Nebraska Press, 1992), for a concise overview of this conflict between the United States and its southern neighbor.
2   For an overview of the U.S. military history for the dozen years following the Mexican American War consult, Robert M. Utley, *Frontiersmen in Blue: The United States Army and the Indian, 1848-1865* (New York: The Macmillan Company, 1967), 1-210, and Edward M. Coffman, *The Old Army A Portrait of The American Army in Peacetime 1784-1898* (Oxford: Oxford University Press, 1986), 42-211.
3   Erna Risch, *Quartermaster Support of the Army: A History of the Corps 1775-1939* (Washington, DC: Office of the Quartermaster General, 1962), 301.
4   Ibid., 184.
5   Chester L. Kieffer, *Maligned General: A Biography of Thomas S. Jesup* (San Rafael, CA: Presidio Press, 1979), traces the forty-two year career of this officer.
6   Ibid., 253.
7   Robert W. Frazer, ed., *New Mexico in 1850: A Military View* (Norman: University of Oklahoma Press, 1968), 126, 140, 148, and 164. Conversely, men of the Third Infantry posted to New Mexico at the time tended to fare better than the mounted troops, with the exception of one company who had no woolen clothing on hand, white cotton jackets and trousers evidently being the only uniform items available at the time. Ibid., 121, 133, 155, 168, 172, and 176. According to a letter from Fort Brady, Michigan, in November 1852, the men of Company A, Fourth Artillery also experienced shortages, in this instance of flannel shirts and pantaloons. This lack of clothing illustrated the problem was not confined to the West alone. CCF, Box 1147, RG 92, OQMG, NA.
8   Frederick P. Todd, *American Military Equipage 1851-1872* (New York: Charles Scribner's Sons, 1980), 30-1; 45-50, discusses France's domination when it came to the U.S. Army uniform of the 1850s, whereas Edgar M. Howell and Donald E. Kloster, *United States Military Headgear to 1854 Catalog of United States Army Uniforms in the Collections of the Smithsonian Institution*, Vol. I (City of Washington: Smithsonian Institution Press, 1969), 26, points to England's influence in early times. In fact, the head of quartermaster clothing bureau even requested that an officer on tour of England in 1832 ask for patterns be sent back from that country for use in the United States. This letter included the tacit admission, "for I perceive we have copied the English in most of the changes which have been made..." in the uniform. J. Garland to J.E. Wool, August 10, 1832, LS, Clothing Bureau, OQMG, RG92, NA.
9   Howell and Kloster, *United States Army Headgear to 1854*, 56. The 1847-1851 garb is described in *Regulations for the Uniform of the United States Army 1847*. See Appendix A for a reprint of this regulation. Also consult Ron Field, *Brassey's History of Uniforms: Mexican-American War 1846-48* (London: Brassey's Ltd, 1997), for more on military clothing of the period. Finally, additional official correspondence concerning the uniform board of 1844 is located in Document File B 136, 1844, Box 150, AGO, RG94, NA. Additional correspondence related to the uniform from 1844 through 1854 can be found in LR, AGO, RG94, Microcopy 567, Roll 282, NA.
10 Penelope Byrde, *Nineteenth Century Fashion* (London: B.T. Batsford Limited, 1992), 88-98, briefly traces this evolution in men's wear. For terms such as "coatee," see the Glossary on pages 334-336.
11 Byrde, *Nineteenth Century Fashion*, 99.
12 General Orders No. 2, WD, February 13, 1850.
13 Howell and Kloster, *United States Army Headgear to 1854*, 56-7, describes both

caps and offers details from, Colonel Sylvester Churchill, one of the two inspectors general of the period, who reported that over fifty percent of the officers he spoke to about the uniform favored a more streamlined uniform that dispensed with the coatee and cap, these being replaced by frock coats and forage caps.
14 The forage cap of leather was discussed in 1832 and the pattern furnished in 1833. Additional information on this headpiece is found in, Ibid., 36-9.
15 Ibid., 56-7.
16 *United Service Gazette*, April 13, 1850. The British themselves were in the process of abandoning the "unserviceable 'smartness' the uniform had reached in 1848" for "looser...French models; France being, until 1870, the nation with the highest military reputation." Laver, *British Military Uniforms*, 36.
17 Risch, *Quartermaster Support of the Army*, 302.
18 On April 2, 1794, an Act of Congress called for the establishment of four arsenals to provide for the needs of the American army. A few years later the first of these was founded on Gray's Ferry Road, and became Schuylkill Arsenal, so named because of the river on which it was located. At first, both clothing and ordnance stores were provided by the facility, but after the War of 1812, with the building of Frankford Arsenal in New York, only quartermaster items were provided. L.C. Baird, "The Philadelphia Quartermaster Intermediate Depot," VI *Quartermaster Review* No. 6 (May-June 1927), 18-9.
19 Thomas Jesup to C.A. Waite, April 22, 1850, LS, C&E Br., Vol. 12, OQMG, RG92, NA. Thomas Jesup to P. St. George Cooke, November 28, 1855, Vol. 14, ibid., reiterated why the 1850 change was halted writing: "when a former Secretary of War, on the recommendation of a few Officers of the Army, ordered a change of the uniform, there was a large war stock on hand of the old pattern sufficient for several years supply of the reduced Peace establishment." The quartermaster general went on to conclude: "The change was most injudicious at the time, and under the circumstances in which it was made—The great extension of our Territories had quadrupled the expenditures of the Military Establishment; Congress alarmed at these expenditures, was reducing the most necessary appropriations...." This reply was in response to Cooke's query why his regiment was still in old patterns. Jesup explained that he was required by Congress to issue existing stocks as long as sufficient serviceable items remained on hand. Not until the mid-1850s did clothing made for the Mexican War dwindle to a degree that new patterns could be obtained and issued on a widespread basis.
20 Robert V. Hine and Savoie Lottinville, eds., *Soldier in the West: Letters of Theodore Talbot During His Services in California, Mexico, and Oregon, 1845-53* (Norman: University of Oklahoma Press, 1972), 151.
21 Brevet Lieutenant Colonel Joseph H. Eaton to Adjutant General, April 28, 1851, and Adjutant General to Major General Winfield Scott, May 22, 1851, File U.12, 1851, AGO, RG 94, NA.
22 Byrde, *Nineteenth Century Fashion*, 98.
23 Ibid., 110.
24 Howell and Kloster, *United States Army Headgear to 1854*, 63 and 67.
25 Thomas Jesup to Nechard & Co., March 31, 1859, C&E Br., Vol. 17, OQMG, RG92, NA.
26 Howell and Kloster, *United States Army Headgear to 1854*, 40-53, offers more details about the 1851-cap.
27 "New Uniform for the U.S. Army," *Gleason's Pictorial Drawing-Room Companion* (March 22, 1852), 328. For depictions of the French version of the cap adopted in the 1840s see, Robert H. Rankin, *Military Headdress: A Pictorial History of Military Headgear From 1660 to 1914* (London: Arms and Armour Press, 1976), 32 and 34. It is interesting that the previous pattern of cap that had been adopted in 1832 and subsequently issued to all but dragoons and mounted artillery also had French roots, as did its replacement of 1851 that, "was almost an exact copy of the

form adopted by the French in 1844." Howell and Kloster, *United States Army Headgear to 1854*, 64.

28 Todd, *American Military Equipage*, 55; and R.J. Wilkinson-Latham, *Collecting Militaria* (New York: Arco Publishing, Inc., 1976), 26.

29 David F. Johnson, *Uniform Buttons, American Armed Forces, 1784-1848 (Watkins Glen, NY: Century House, 1948 (2 Vols., provides visual references to the differences between pre-1851 and post-1851 buttons).*

30 Mendel L. Peterson, "American Army Epaulettes 1814-1872," III *Military Collector and Historian* No. 1 (March 1951): 1-14, covers the evolution of this form of military rank indication.

31 Prior to 1851 regulations for the infantry, ordnance, engineers, and heavy artillery enlisted men called for worsted epaulets in the branch colors of white, crimson, yellow, and scarlet respectively, with 1/8-inch diameter fringe measuring 2 1/2-inches for all but privates who were to have "half fringe" that measured approximately 1/2-inch in length. The epaulets of engineer non-commissioned officers were of silk and worsted was the material for all others. Additionally, non-commissioned staff officers (sergeant major, quartermaster sergeant, and chief musician) had a worsted aiguillette attached the left epaulet similar to the type worn by regimental field grade and staff officers.

32 For additional information on early chevrons consult, William K. Emerson, *Chevrons: Illustrated History and Catalog of U.S. Army Insignia* (Washington, DC: Smithsonian Institution Press, 1983), 28-9, and 39-44.

33 The practice of providing coats or jackets with chevrons already affixed was common during the pre-Civil War era, a typical example being found in manifests for supplies to artillerymen at Fort Monroe, Virginia and Fort Moultrie, South Carolina in April 1856. See correspondence from G.H. Crosman to R.W. Potter, April 15, and April 16, 1856, Joint Collection, University of Missouri, Western Historical Manuscript Collection, Columbia, State Historical Society of Missouri.

34 Todd, *American Military Equipage*, 31.

35 The regulation adopted in 1847 had various schemes for trousers ranging from a buff or gold 1 1/2-inch wide stripe on dress trousers for generals, to no stripes or welts at all for undress and the white trousers. See Appendix A for particulars.

36 J. Duncan Campbell and Edgar M. Howell, *American Military Insignia 1800-1851* (Washington, DC: Smithsonian Institution, 1963), 38-40, and 43-49, depicts waistbelt and shoulder-belt plates of the pre-Mexican War era through 1851. Ibid., 25-31, and 41-2, illustrates several types of insignia for the same period, as does William K. Emerson, *Encyclopedia of United States Army Insignia and Uniforms* (Norman: University of Oklahoma Press, 1996).

37 Harold L. Peterson, *The American Sword, 1775-1945* (Philadelphia: Ray Riling Books, 1965), remains the standard for edged weapons of the period under consideration.

38 Accoutrements of the 1851 through 1872 period are treated in some detail in Todd, *American Military Equipage*, 184-230, and as such are not described more fully here.

39 John Mollo, *Military Fashion* (New York: G.P. Putnam's Sons, 1972), 158.

40 According to W.Y. Carmen, *A Dictionary of Military Uniforms* (New York: Charles Scribner's Sons, 1977), 35, this garment "was a very loose overcoat, almost a shaped cloak of heavy cloth lined with red worn by French officers, inspired by the North African campaigns of the 1830s and 1840s."

41 It should be noted that GO No. 31 required officers to cease wearing the old uniform no later than January 1, 1852. Most commonly, civilian companies, such as William H. Horstmann & Son of Philadelphia or Smith, Crane & Co. of New York would offer the items required for officers. "Late in 1851", however, "the Secretary of War authorized officers to purchase kersey, and wool overalls at cost from the Army Clothing Establishment. Jefferson Davis, when he became Secretary, withdrew this privilege, but Secretary [John B.] Floyd restored it by permitting officers at remote stations to purchase enlisted men's clothing and other items at reasonable prices." Todd, *American Military Equipage*, 38.

42 According to Thomas Jesup to Philip St. George Cooke, April 28, 1855, C&E Br, Vol. 14, OQMG, RG92, NA, some old pattern uniforms were still in stock and being sent to certain units nearly four years after a new pattern had been mandated.

43 Todd, *American Military Equipage*, 354, cites the allowance of the new cap to be worn with the old swallow-tailed coat for dress occasions.

44 "New Uniform for the U.S. Army," *Gleason's Pictorial Drawing Room Companion* (March 22, 1852), 328.

45 Albert G. Brackett, *History of the U.S. Cavalry, (New York: Harper & Brothers, 1865),* 160. Sidney B. Brinckerhoff, *Military Headgear in the Southwest, 1846-1890* (Tucson: Arizona Pioneers' Historical Society, 1963), 5, states, "This design hat was first worn by French soldiers in Algeria during the 1830's, and later was favored and worn by Prince Albert, consort of Queen Victoria of Great Britain," and thus the reference to the style by Brackett, although in fact the cap adopted in England was not exactly of the style worn in the United States, thereby making this term incorrect.

46 Hine and Lottinville, *Soldier in the West*, 168. During an 1854 inspection of numerous Western posts Inspector General Sylvester Churchill asserted the nearly two of every three officers he polled about this cap objected to it. Sylvester Churchill to Secretary of War Jefferson Davis, February 27, 1854, File No. B, 136, 1854, U.S. Army Commands, RG98, NA.

47 Based on a survey of officers serving at nine garrisons in the West made between 1853 and 1854 fourteen of the respondents liked the 1851-pattern cap and its pompon, while thirty-six disapproved of the new design, as well as preferred short

plumes to pompons. The commander of the First Dragoons took a somewhat different stand in that he thought the hat suitable for all troops except dragoons, being "heavy, heating and painful to the head when used in the sun, wind, or at a rapid gate." Howell and Kloster, *United States Army Headgear to 1854*, 64.

48 Prior to 1851 enlisted mounted riflemen had the dragoon jacket and cap, while black stripes bordered in yellow worn on dark blue trousers were the only means of setting off mounted rifle enlisted men from dragoons. Additionally, buttons were to bear an "R" in the center of the eagle device rather than the "D" for dragoons. There was no dress uniform, the unit having been raised in wartime. Officers had crimson sashes rather than the orange of their comrades in the dragoons. They, too, had the dark trousers with black stripes bordered in yellow. Moreover, prior to 1851 they had a spread eagle device with an "R" in the center as prescribed by GO No. 18, WD, June 4, 1846.

49 GO No. 13, AGO, May 21, 1853, for example listed specific artillery and infantry companies that were to be issued old patterns exclusively drawn form stocks throughout the army. These were Companies B and D, Third Artillery; Companies C and K, Fourth Artillery; Companies E, H, and K, First Infantry; Companies A, B, C, G, F, and K, Second Infantry; Companies D and F, Third Infantry; Companies B, F, G, and H, Fourth Infantry; Companies A, B, C, D, E, F, H, and K, Sixth Infantry; Companies A, B, D, E, and I, Seventh Infantry; and Companies A, B,C, D, E, F, G, H, I and K, Eighth Infantry. Conversely, an example of the sporadic issue of the new pattern occurred on September 1, 1853, when Company F, Second Dragoons, serving in Texas, received 100 caps complete with pompons, letters, covers, eagles, and rings, as well as 100 coats and shoulder scales, along with 100 old pre-1851 fatigue jackets with numbers. John R. Elting, ed., *Military Uniform in America,* Vol. III (Navato, CA: Presidio Press, 1982), 4. The reason these dragoons finally obtained the new outfit was because of the near exhaustion of the old pattern by spring 1853, thereby making it possible for quartermasters to provide articles of the 1851-pattern.

50 John R. Elting, ed., *Military Uniforms in America* Vol. II (San Rafael, CA: Presidio Press, 1977), 122, offers brief information on the pre-1851 artillery uniform variations.

51 Todd, *American Military Equipage*, 375-6. It should be noted GO No. 24 applied to other combat arms besides the heavy artillery, and read in part as follows: "Measures will be taken by the Quartermaster Department to issue, for fatigue purposes, to the troops of all arms, the sky-blue cloth jackets now on hand in the Department; the trimmings first altered to correspond to the arm for which the clothing is designed."

52 Some officers preferred the old forage cap, as was the case, in 1854, of the commander of the First Dragoons, "who complained bitterly about the unsuitability of the [1851] cap for wear in the field and especially for fatigue duty, and requested for his unit a reversion to the 1839-pattern forage cap. Edgar Howell, *United States Army Headgear 1855-1902: Catalog of United States Army Uniforms in the Collections of the Smithsonian Institution* (Washington, DC: Smithsonian Institution Press, n.d.), 12.

53 Todd, *American Military Equipage*, 376. Supposedly this was the case with light companies (mounted artillery) too, according to ibid., 377.

54 Ibid., 392.

55 GO No. 18, AGO, June 4, 1846, had prescribed this uniform previously. Consequently, old patterns of engineer enlisted uniforms were maintained after 1851, in keeping with a general trend throughout the army.

56 Todd, *American Military Equipage*, 390-1.

57 GO No. 31, AGO, June 12, 1851.

58 For a slightly earlier West Point Band uniform description see, GO No. 18, AGO, May 23, 1850.

59 From 1820 to 1850 the West Point band wore white uniforms trimmed in red, and the practice was revived from 1867 to 1873, according to Elting, *Military Uniform in America*, Vol. II, 94.

60 GO No. 31, AGO, June 12, 1851. The West Point band uniform essentially was that of the artillery, and would be replaced by direction of the secretary of war in 1852, when that official sanctioned what was a standard engineer musician's uniform of the 1851-pattern, including the cap with yellow pompon and brass castle. Fifteen coats and caps were supplied for this purpose, in the latter case with yellow worsted epaulets, "and a supply of yellow cloth for fashioning plastrons, and enough yellow binding and cord to replace all red on coats, fatigue jackets, and pants." Todd, *American Military Equipage*, 407. When this change was completed, the Military Academy's bandsmen conformed more closely to the prescription of GO No. 31.

61 Thomas C. Railsback and John P. Langellier, *The Drums Would Roll: A Pictorial History of U.S. Army Bands on the American Frontier, 1866-1900* (Poole, England: Arms and Armour Press, 1987), provides several photographic examples of the varied uniform worn by bandsmen during the period under discussion.

62 *A Medical Report upon the Uniform and Clothing of the Soldiers of the U.S. Army, 15 April 1868* (Washington, DC: Surgeon General's Office), CCF, Box 1171, OQMG, RG92, NA, hereinafter referred to as the "Woodhull Report."

63 Howell and Kloster, *United States Army Headgear to 1854*, 54.

64 Todd, *American Military Equipage*, 354 and 365.

65 A half dozen years later, in 1857, light artillery officers were granted the same latitude in that they could obtain a plain dark blue cloth jacket for stable duty according to the *Regulations for the Army of the United States 1857* (New York: Harper Brothers, Publishers, 1857), 446.

66 GO No. 31, AGO, June 12, 1851.

67 Robert W. Frazer, ed., *Mansfield on the Condition of Western Forts 1853-54* (Norman: University of Oklahoma Press, 1963), 58. See ibid., 42, 43, 47, 49, 50, 52, 55, 58, 149, 150, 154, and 165, all indicating that of a dozen posts mentioned, only one, Fort Reading, had new pattern uniforms available, the rest of the garrisons all being in the pre-1851 pattern.

68 Ibid., 41 and 165.

69 "The term 'Light-Artillery' for many years was loosely used to include 'horse' or 'flying' artillery in which all personnel were individually 'mounted' or 'harnessed' artillery, in which some personnel were individually mounted and the remainder rode on caissons and limbers. In the Civil War, the term generally indicated the artillery which accompanied the army in the field as opposed to fortress or siege artillery." Howell, *United State Army Headgear, 1855-1902*, 22.

70 "In 1839 a battalion of *chasseurs à pied* was formed at Vincennes" France, and adopted "a uniform based on African models." By 1840 ten battalions were formed, all in single-breasted tunics. Mollo, *Military Fashion*, 166. "Although trained as light infantry, the Chasseurs wore stiff shakos, plaited frock coats and epaulets as did all French infantry" of period. Michael J. McAfee, "U.S. Army Uniforms of the Civil War Part VI: Zouaves and Chasseurs," IV *Military Images* No.3 (November-December 1982): 14. This style, along with a belt-mounted cartridge box, in lieu of the old crossbelts, served as a models for the American military, as did the tactics employed by the chasseurs (light infantry), that seem well suited to the new rifled longarms that fired American versions of the French Minié bullet. These weapons began to phase out smoothbores in 1855 for U.S. infantrymen. Gregory J.W. Urwin, *The United States Infantry: An Illustrated History, 1775-1918* (London: Blandford Press, 1988), 85-6.

71 Philip Katcher, *U.S. Infantry Equipments 1775-1910* (London: Osprey Publishing Ltd., 1989), 28, and 38, depicts and briefly mentions this new equipage. Also see, Stephen J. Allie, *All He Could Carry: US Army Infantry Equipment, 1839-1910* (Ft. Leavenworth: Frontier Army Museum, 1991), 4-17, for a synopsis on the transition from Mexican War era accoutrements, weapons, and tactics to those of the American Civil War.

72 Percival G. Lowe, *Five Years A Dragoon And Other Adventures on the Great Plains* (Norman: University of Oklahoma Press, 1965), 83.

73 Teresa G. Viele, *Following the Drum: A Glimpse of Frontier Life* (Lincoln: University of Nebraska Press, 1984), 224-5.

74 Joseph H. Parks, *General Edmund Kirby Smith* (Baton Rouge: Louisiana State University Press, 1954), 90.

75 John Van Deusen Dubois, *Campaigns in the West, 1856-1851* (Tucson: Arizona Pioneers Historical Society, 1949), 114.

76 Ralph P. Bieber, ed., *Frontier Life in the Army* (Glendale, CA: Arthur H. Clark, 1932), 124.

77 Ibid., 140.

78 For background on this somewhat obscure phase of U.S.Army history read, Leroy R. Hafen, ed., *The Utah Expedition 1857-1858: A Documentary Account of the United States Military Movement Under Colonel Albert Sidney Johnston, and The Resistance by Brigham Young and the Mormon Nauvoo Legion* (Glendale, CA: The Arthur H. Clark Company, 1982).

79 Todd, *American Military Equipage*, 380 and 384.

80 Otis G. Hammond, ed., *The Utah Expedition, 1857-1858; Letters of Capt. Jesse A. Gove, 10th Inf., U.S.A., of Concord, N.H. to Mrs. Gove, and special correspondence of the New York Herald* (Concord: New Hampshire Historical Society, 1928), 15.

81 Lawrence Kip, *Army Life on the Pacific: A Journal of the Expedition Against the North Indians...in the Summer of 1858* (New York: Redfield, 1859), 122-3.

82 John F.Callan, *The Military Laws of the United States, Relating to the Army, Volunteers, Militia, and to Bounty Lands and Pensions from the Foundation of the Government to the Year 1863, To Which are Prefixed the Constitution of the United States. (With an Index Thereto,) and a Synopsis of the Military Legislation of Congress During the Revolutionary War* (Philadelphia: George W. Childs, 1863), 435-6.

83 George F. Price, *Across the Continent with the Fifth Cavalry* (New York: D. Van Nostrand, Publisher, 1883), 11-22, gives an overview of the formation of these regiment with an emphasis on the Second Cavalry that would be redesignated the Fifth in 1861.

84 The following was taken from GO No. 13, AGO, August 15, 1855.

85 Sumner's Report on Trip to Europe, microfilm, LR, M-567, Roll 506, AGO, RG 94, NA. According E.V. Sumner, A.S. Johnson, J.E. Johnston, and W.J. Hardee to Jefferson Davis, July 19, 1855, LR, Ordnance, RG156, NA, the enlisted hat was to have an eagle device, although the only known surviving specimen does not.

86 Howell, *United States Army Headgear 1855-1902*, 1-5, offers further details on this piece of headgear.

87 Elting, *Military Uniform in America*, Vol. III, 6.

88 Price, *Across the Continent with the Fifth Cavalry*, 29-30. Also see, *ARSW, 1855*, Vol. 1, 7-8, for more on rifled weapons being adopted universally and several experimental breech loaders being considered.

89 Lowe, *Five Years A Dragoon*, 45.

90 Bieber, *Frontier Life in the Army*, 221-2.

91 Ibid., 128-9.

92 Ibid., 167. In 1854, Secretary of War Jefferson Davis succeeded in persuading Congress to increase the pay of soldiers which had been frozen from 1833 to 1854. At that point the base for an infantry private rose from $7 to $11 a month. Artillery privates and those in the mounted arms received $12 a month. The pay increased to either $13 or $14 for a corporal; $17 to $18 for a sergeant; and $20 or $21 for an orderly sergeant (first sergeant), depending on the branch. Occasionally enlisted men could obtain supplemental income as bounties and extra pay for fatigue duties (when serving as laborers, mechanics, or teamsters) or special locality pay, such as was the case in Oregon and California in 1850. Ibid., 105; Averam B. Bender, *The March of Empire* (Lawrence: The University of Kansas Press, 1952), 122-3, and 261; and William Addleman Ganoe, *The History of the United States Army* (Pishton: Eric Lundeberg, 1964), 231.

93 Bieber, *Frontier Life in the Army*, 167.

94 J. Cecil Alter, ed., *The Utah War Journal of Albert Tracy, 1858-1860* (Salt Lake: Utah Historical Society, 1945), 4-5, and 15.

95 Risch, *Quartermaster Supply of the Army*, 303.

96 Harold Langley, ed., *To Utah With The Dragoons* (Salt Lake: University of Utah, 1974), 44. The anonymous correspondent indicated he ruined his trousers by sliding down rocks and leaving behind "shreds of blue" on the sharp points. He also lost a boot, thereby forcing him to wear the remaining one mismatched with a shoe that he was fortunate to have with him. Ibid., 46 and 60.

97 *Regulations for the Army of the United States 1857*, 14.

98 Langley, *To Utah With The Dragoons*, 46, 52, and 75.

99 Bieber, *Frontier Life in the Army*, 268-70.

100 Writing from that post in today's Wyoming the quartermaster officer there, E.E. Babbit, told Assistant Quartermaster D.D. Tompkins that it was impractical to provide troops uniforms from the supply trains headed to Utah, although this smacked more of an excuse than a real reason. Babbit to Tompkins, July 26, 1858, LR, Microfilm M-567, Roll 584, AGO, RG 94, NA.

101 Langley, *To Utah With The Dragoons*, 39.

102 Hammond, *The Utah Expedition*, 86. As noted in Sumner's Report, Letters Received, AGO, RG94, NA, leather jerkins (associated with the roundheads during the English Civil War and later in the Spanish borderlands by *soldados de cuera*, the lancers who garrisoned presidios in the eighteenth and early nineteenth century) offered a potential item of issue for the American horse soldier, although this 1854 observation was not placed into practice. Nevertheless, privately purchased buckskin garments were found among the troops in the field, especially officers, from the 1830s through the 1880s.

103 Hammond, *The Utah Expedition*, 44 and 151.

104 Ibid., 72. Elsewhere Gove reiterated he had the four robes, plenty of blankets, and garments, "so it is not for want of clothing that is to embarrass me. I am splendidly provided for in this respect." Ibid., 75.

105 Ibid., 39.

106 Ibid., 105.

107 Ibid., 117.

108 Bieber, *Frontier Army Life*, 231, and 241-4.

109 Alter, *Utah Journal of Albert Tracy*, 116.

110 Ibid., 9.

111 For a reprint of McClellan's letter on this subject and a description of the 1859 model of the saddle and horse equipments consult, Randy Steffen, *The Horse Soldier 1776-1943*, Vol. II (Norman: University of Oklahoma Press, 1978), 53 and 58-63.

112 *Report of the Secretary of War, Communicating the Report of Captain George B. McClellan, (First Regiment United States Cavalry) One of Officers Sent to the Seat of War in Europe 1855 and 1856*, Executive Document No. 1, Senate, Special Session (Washington, DC: A.O.P. Nicholson, Printer, 1857), 248.

113 Todd, *American Military Equipage*, 354; and GO No. 3, WD, March 24, 1858, that authorized the sack coat for all troops.

114 *Report of the Secretary of War, Communicating the Report of Captain George B. McClellan*, 248.

115 Howell, *United States Army headgear, 1855-1902,* 13.

116 Ibid. It should be noted that in 1857 a blue *chasseur* model cap began to be worn by cadets at the United States Military Academy. Ibid., 96, n140.

117 Brevet Major William H. French to Colonel Samuel Cooper, August 11, 1858, Letters Received, File 102-F-1858, AGO, RG94, NA.

118 Petition dated October 13, 1858, File 349B, 1858, ibid. A circular dated December 1, 1858, from the Adjutant General's Office, indicated that from that date "the coat and hat are only to be issued to permanent parties at depots and rendezvous" while the "forage cap and sack" were to "be issued, instead, to all unassigned recruits. They will then receive the dress uniform now on joining their regiments." Microfilm Collections, Box 82, U.S. Army Military History Institute, Carlisle Barracks, PA.

119 GO No. 5, AGO, May 19, 1858.

120 GO No. 77, Headquarters of the Artillery School, June 7, 1858, Post Returns of Ft. Monroe Artillery School and Post General Orders, September 12, 1854-July 18, 1860, Records of US Army Commands, RG98, NA.

121 GO No. 101, June 28, 1858, ibid. The Artillery School outfit was short lived, however, being discontinued in September or October 1858. GO No. 169, September 23, 1858, and GO No. 203, ibid., September 28, 1858, ibid.

122 These alterations were ushered in by GO No. 3, WD, March 24, 1858.

123 GO No. 20, AGO, August 6, 1860, authorized the sky-blue trousers for light artillery, as well as permitted the round jacket.

124 GO No. 31, HQA, June 12, 1855, allowed general officers and field grade officers who had held brevets as general officers to wear the chapeau they had been authorized in 1847, so long as it was on ceremonial occasions when not serving with troops. GO No. 3, WD, March 24, 1858, extended this practice to all field officers for general wear and to staff officers. Finally, GO No. 27, WD, December 22, 1859, modified the earlier order permitting, "all officers of the General Staff, and Staff Corps, to wear, at their option, a light French chapeau, either stiff crown or flat...." Officers below the field rank would have two feathers and those of field rank would have three.

125 Howell, *United States Army Headgear 1855-1902,* 23, and 96-7. Evidently old white horsetail plumes remaining from the 1833-pattern dragoon enlisted cap still were in stock and were dyed to the proper color for artillery. Todd, *American Military Equipage,* 378.

126 Ibid., 23.

127 GO No. 2, WD, February 13, 1850, had called for insignia for enlisted men, but this directive was rescinded before it could take effect. According to, Campbell and

Howell, *American Military Insignia,* 31, the trumpet for the 1858-pattern mounted rifles enlisted hat insignia was that proposed in 1850, but Gordon Chappell, "Dress Hat of the First Regiment of Mounted Rifles, 1858-1861," XXII *Military Collector and Historian* No. 2 (Summer 1970): 58-8, disagrees.

128 F.C. Townsend and Frederick P. Todd, "Branch Insignia of the Regular Cavalry, 1833-1872," VIII *Military Collector and Historian* No. 1 (Spring 1956): 1-5, traces changes in the cavalry and dragoon insignia.

129 Howell, *United States Army Headgear 1855-1902,* 7.

130 Brackett, *History of the U.S. Cavalry,* 160-1. Fra Diavolo was a brigand chief (tenor) in an *opéra comique* production of the same name by Daniel-Francois-Esprit Auber and Eugène Scribe. First performed in Paris on January 28, 1830, by 1907 this opera had played in Paris no less than 900 times. In addition, within two years after its premier, it was performed abroad and formed part of the repertory of many houses including in New York. The inspiration came from a French play that made its debut in 1808 as *Fra Diavolo, chef des brigands dans les Alpes.* Stanley Sadies, ed., *The New Grove's Dictionary of Opera,* Vol. II (New York: Grove's Dictionary of Music Inc., 1992), 268-9.

131 Hammond, The Utah Expedition, 164.

132 Ibid., 150.

133 The reference to the style of the hat was derived from Louis Kossuth, who had attained considerable international fame in his efforts to free Hungary from Austrian rule, and who achieved a certain popularity among Americans after a visit to the United States. Kossuth's image was that of a democratic freedom fighter, complete with dashing broad brimmed hat. In more recent times this headgear has been referred to as the "Jeff Davis" or "Hardee" hat, the latter after William J. Hardee, who also cast his lot with the Confederacy, although no contemporary references can be found using this terminology. Evidently these nicknames are of more recent origin, perhaps being invented by collectors and militaria dealers.

134 Hammond, *The Utah Expedition,* 278.

135 Ibid., 278.

136 Alter, *The Utah Journal of Captain Albert Tracy,* 55-6. This is one of the earliest uses of the term "kepi." Presumably it referred to the forage cap adopted in the late 1850s. According to Brinckerhoff, *Military Headgear in the Southwest,* 8, the term was a "French word of German origin to describe a military hat."

137 "Movement of Troops," Sacramento *Daily Union,* May 29, 1860.

138 Claudia B. Kidwell and Margaret C. Christman, *Suiting Everyone: The Democratization of Clothing in America* (Washington, DC: The Smithsonian Institution Press, 1974), traces this aspect among its core themes.

139 Hammond, *The Utah Expedition,* 164.

Winfield Scott was the major general commanding the U.S. Army at the outbreak of the Civil War. Although a Southerner by birth he remained loyal to the Union. True to his nickname, "Old Fuss and Feathers" donned a uniform of his own design with gold embroidery accents to his black velvet collar and cuffs. His embroidered dress belt also differed from the 1851-pattern belt prescribed for general officers. MJM

2

ARMY BLUE,
1861-1865

On April 12, 1861, cannon fire directed at Fort Sumter, South Carolina, triggered the American Civil War. Some men could not wait to enter the fray. These patriotic individuals shared the enthusiasm of West Pointers who were anxious to "bid farewell to cadet gray and don the army blue."[1] The fact is, blue was not the only hue worn by the Northern forces when the conflict erupted.

Militia and volunteers, who joined the standing army after Abraham Lincoln's call for reinforcements to fight the Confederates, marched off in a wide variety of uniforms. Some had taken up arms in their civilian clothing, being distinguished as soldiers only by their weapons and accoutrements. Others found simple, rather nondescript outfits in gray, ample. Several adopted more elaborate European-inspired costumes such as French Zouave-like garb, towering Napoleonic bearskins, British havelocks (named after the English officer, whose distinguished service in India just a few years earlier had popularized the device), feathered Italian *bersaglieri* headgear, Scottish kilts and tartan trews, and green ensembles for Irish American groups (and eventually for sharpshooters).[2]

Even regulars presented a mixed appearance, such as the U.S. Army engineers who mingled sky-blue or gray "shell" jackets with dark blue trousers, and oil cloth covered forage caps as their fatigue dress when posted in the Washington, D.C. area during April 1861.[3] While this and other uniforms that the troops were arrayed in during the opening months of the war provided a rich tapestry to casual observers, it violated one of the basic functions of a military uniform – identification of friend from foe. Ignoring this tenet meant "the confusion promoted in the field by the use of varied colors . . . resulted in some instances of Union soldiers firing on each other." As a result orders eventually "were issued forbidding the use of any color but the established colors of light and dark blue."[4]

Besides these coats of many colors, "The clothing of the troops were in the first months" of the conflict "all too likely to be shoddy."[5] This term originally meant "a woolen yarn obtained by tearing to shreds refuse woolen rags," that was combined with some new wool to make "a kind of cloth." It soon took on a different meaning as, "Worthless material made to look like material of superior quality."[6] In 1864, a

Once the Civil War erupted cadets at the U.S. Military Academy were anxious to put aside their gray uniform and don "Army Blue." MJM

West Point cadets also had a plain dark blue frock coat with matching trousers and "furlough cap" when they were on leave that resembled the Regular Army company grade officer's uniform of the Civil War. MJM

A private of the Seventh New York has the chasseur style cap which was gray to match the color of his regiment's uniform – one example where the traditional dark blue uniform was not used by Federal forces. Kurt Cox Photograph. WCC

The lower-crowned chasseur style forage cap was popular with some individuals and units, such as this example for an engineer officer. Kurt Cox Photograph. JML

newspaper reporter depicted the material in an even more derisive manner describing shoddy as "A villainous compound, the refuse stuff and sweepings of the shop, pounded, rolled, glued, and smoothed to the external form and gloss of cloth, but no more like the genuine article than the shadow is to the substance."[7]

For these and other reasons, orders eventually called for the universal use of blue, but not before several permutations of the issue uniform had come about. In fact, even before the war erupted, some minor alterations had been made to the clothing that would become the norm during the clash between North and South.

One of these changes came with General Order No 4, War Department, February 26, 1861, that discontinued the colored welt for enlisted forage caps, the resulting piece of headgear becoming the dominant "bummer's cap" seen so frequently in photographic images of the era, although it received mixed reviews from wearers. Some thought it was "useful and even natty," having "room for a wet sponge, green leaves, a handkerchief, or protection against the sun in the top," while its ". . . slanting visor fits easily against the forehead."[8] Others countered it was a "waste of cloth, too baggy, and caught the wind."[9]

In addition to discontinuing the welt on forage caps, General Orders No. 4 added gutta purcha talmas, previously unique to cavalry troopers, as part of the table of clothing allowance for dragoons and mounted rifles. Moreover, the same order reversed the previous practice established by General Orders No. 3 of March 24, 1858, that singled out infantry and artillery officers as the only ones to loop their hats on the left side and wear their ostrich plumes on the right. Thereafter, they would follow the practice of all other officers and loop their hats on the right, this change perhaps resulting from the fact that when the "carry arms" was executed from the saber drill the hat brim would interfere with the blade.

Shortly thereafter, General Orders No. 6, War Department, March 13, 1861, retained this scheme for officers but directed that from that point forward enlisted men in dismounted units were to have their brim hooked on the left, while hats for mounted troops would turn up the right. Additionally, the same order specified that enlisted insignia would include the branch devices above which went a 1-inch brass company

Second Lieutenant George C. Round was one of the early signal service officers. His low-crowned forage cap bears the crossed flag and torch device used by several signalmen during the Civil War as a cap badge. The overcoat appears to be a sky-blue kersey mounted pattern with an added dark collar. Officers were allowed to wear enlisted overcoats in order to blend more readily with their troops. USAMHI

Infantry officer's "McDowell" pattern forage cap. Kurt Cox Photograph. JML

Profile officer's "McDowell" pattern forage cap. Kurt Cox Photograph. JML

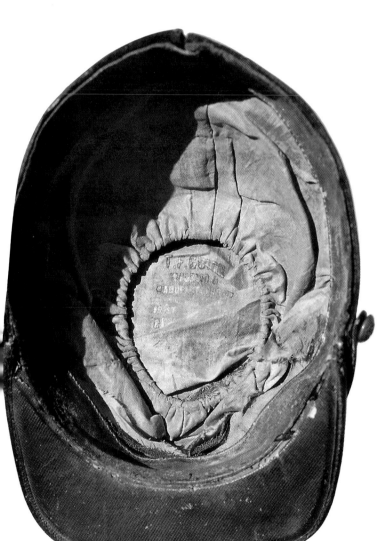

Another example of lining for an officer's forage cap. Kurt Cox Photograph. JML

Lining of officer's chasseur pattern forage cap. Construction varied from maker to maker.
Kurt Cox Photograph. JML

The light artillery trumpeter on the left has a "McDowell" pattern forage cap with sloping visor and the one on the right wears the standard 1861-pattern forage cap with artillery insignia evident, although not called for by regulations. MJM

Detail of button and chinstrap for a typical Civil War issue enlisted forage cap, referred to as a "bummer's" cap by some individuals during the 1860s. Kurt Cox Photograph. JML

Enlisted 1861-pattern forage cap of the type issued through the early 1870s. The welt in branch color around the crown was discontinued as of General Orders No. 4, February 26, 1861. Kurt Cox Photograph. JML

Emmett Underwood, an infantry sergeant major has applied an officer's style forage cap insignia to his "McDowell" pattern cap perhaps to indicate his status as the senior non-commissioned officer of his regiment. Such modifications were not uncommon. MJM

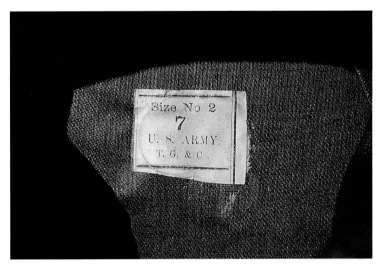

Maker's label from one of many firms that produced chasseur style forage caps during the Civil War. Kurt Cox Photograph. JML

Example of an enlisted chasseur pattern forage cap. Kurt Cox Photograph. JML

letter surmounting a 5/8-inch regimental number where applicable. However, the order retained the differentiation of dragoon officers from cavalry instituted earlier, in that the regimental silver numeral went above the crossed sabers in the former instance and below them in the latter situation.

In addition, General Orders No. 6 set forth that officers would wear their respective hat badges on the front of the forage caps, although these often tended to be smaller in size, or sometimes of metal made to simulate embroidery. Enlisted caps were to bear on the brass 1-inch company letter in front, although this practice varied greatly, some individuals adopting the insignia made for the 1858-pattern hat affixing it to the front of the cap or more often to the crown, while others eschewed all devices and wore only plain headgear.

More important, this order established what eventually became the basic "look" of the Civil War Union soldier.[10] Despite this, the uniform did not remain static.

For one thing, old distinctions among mounted troops began to disappear after dragoons and mounted rifles were converted to cavalry regiments as of August 3, 1861. At the same time another mounted regular regiment was added to the force, the Sixth U.S. Cavalry (known briefly as the Third U.S. Cavalry from May to July).[11] With the reorganization of all mounted units into one arm, the dragoons and mounted rifles were to discontinue their previous distinctive colors and adopt yellow trim, as soon as their old issue had been exhausted. A former Second Dragoon officer observed his regiment seemed to take advantage of this loophole, retaining their "cherished orange" for some two years thereafter.[12]

Preservation of regimental characteristics aside, the Civil War began to erode such traditions. For one thing, the invention of more accurate, long range weapons made concealment of rank a concern among officers. One means of dealing with this situation was provided by General Orders No. 102, War Department, November 25, 1861, that allowed sky-blue enlisted overcoats to replace the dark blue officers' pattern "in

time of actual field service." On one occasion the assistant adjutant general of the II Corps, Army of the Potomac was able to take advantage of this order as a sort of disguise. By putting on his enlisted overcoat atop his uniform, he was able to pass among the enlisted men and overhear their candid remarks as the troops waited on the skirmish line before a major battle.[13]

Eventually such a means of gathering the views of the rank and file would come to an end in that General Orders No. 286, War Department, November 22, 1864, authorized a circlet of the color of the branch bordered by gold embroidery to be sewn to each cuff of the enlisted overcoat when worn by officers. The center of the circle was to bear the wearer's rank thereby making it possible, upon close inspection at least, to again differentiate officers from enlisted men.

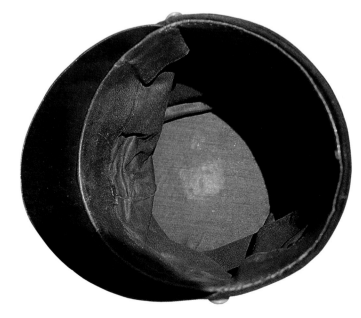

Lining of an officer's "McDowell" forage cap. Kurt Cox Photograph. JML

Second Lieutnant F.V. Farquhar of the Corps of Engineers wears the 1858-pattern hat for his branch with two black ostrich feathers as a company grade officer. He has on the nine button frock coat with engineer buttons accented by a crimson silk net sash. His epaulets were to be plain gold with only a silver castle, although the castles are not evident in this portrait. Dark blue trousers with a gold 1/8-inch cord were standard throughout the Civil War for staff officers, a practice which included engineers. The sword is the M1850 foot officer's sword. USAMHI

Captain George Meade was a Topographical Engineer at the outbreak of the war although he was destined to be promoted to major general of volunteers and gain fame as the Union commander at Gettysburg. Before this rise he sat for a portrait wearing the forage cap with sloping visor that came to be known as the "McDowell" pattern after Irvin McDowell, another federal general during the war. Meade's shoulder straps are fastened under his epaulets, perhaps being of a type that was permanently affixed to the frock coat, making it necessary to place the epaulets over the straps when full dress was required. USAMHI

Assistant Surgeon Samuel W. Crawford wears epaulets with Old English "M.S" in a wreath as regulation for the Medical Service. His M1840 Medical Officer's sword also is regulation while the sash was to be emerald green rather than the crimson silk assigned to the staff and line. Crawford was the surgeon at Fort Sumter, SC when that bastion of the Union fell to the Confederacy. USAMHI

Dark blue trousers had been called for in 1858 through 1861 for all officers and soldiers as seen here for this first lieutenant of the First Artillery whose tightly tailored single-breasted company grade frock coat with nine artillery officer's buttons is the pattern adopted in 1851 and which remained regulation through 1872. The centers of the shoulder straps were to be scarlet and the single bar at each end gold embroidery to indicate branch and rank. RB

U. S. Regulation Buttons.

GENERALS & STAFF.	INFANTRY.	ARTILLERY.	CAVALRY
  No. 169.	No. 171.	No. 173.	No. 175.
No 170.	No. 172.	No. 174.	No. 176.

RIFLE.	ENGINEER.	TOPOGRAPHICAL ENGINEER.	ORDNANCE.
No. 177.	No. 179.	NO. 181.	No. 183.
No. 178.	No. 180.	No. 182.	No. 184.

No. 185. Navy Coat.	No. 186. Navy Jacket.	No. 187. Navy Vest.	No. 188. Shield	Button. No. 189.
No. 190. Marine Coat.	No. 191. Marine Jacket.	No. 192. Marine Vest.	No. 193. N. Y. State Line	No. 194. Button.
No. 195. Revenue Coat.	No. 196. Revenue Jacket.	No. 197. Revenue Vest.	No. 198. N. Y. State Staff	No. 199. Button.

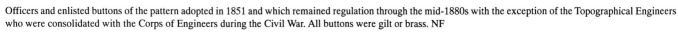

Officers and enlisted buttons of the pattern adopted in 1851 and which remained regulation through the mid-1880s with the exception of the Topographical Engineers who were consolidated with the Corps of Engineers during the Civil War. All buttons were gilt or brass. NF

The 1858-pattern infantry officer's hat was to bear a gold bugle device with silver regimental numeral, in this case for the Fifth U.S. Infantry. Once again, the dark blue trousers were regulation from 1858 through 1861, when General Orders No. 108, December 16, called for sky-blue trousers for all enlisted men and line officers. Previously only light artillery troops were to wear sky-blue. MJM

Hat Cords.

No. 63.

Gilt and Silk Machine Hat Cord.

No. 64.

Gilt and Silk Twisted Hat Cord.

The 1858-pattern officer's hat was to have gold and black cords that terminated in acorns, except for generals whose hat cords were to be gold. NF

SCHUYLER, HARTLEY & GRAHAM'S

Hat and Cap Ornaments for Officers.

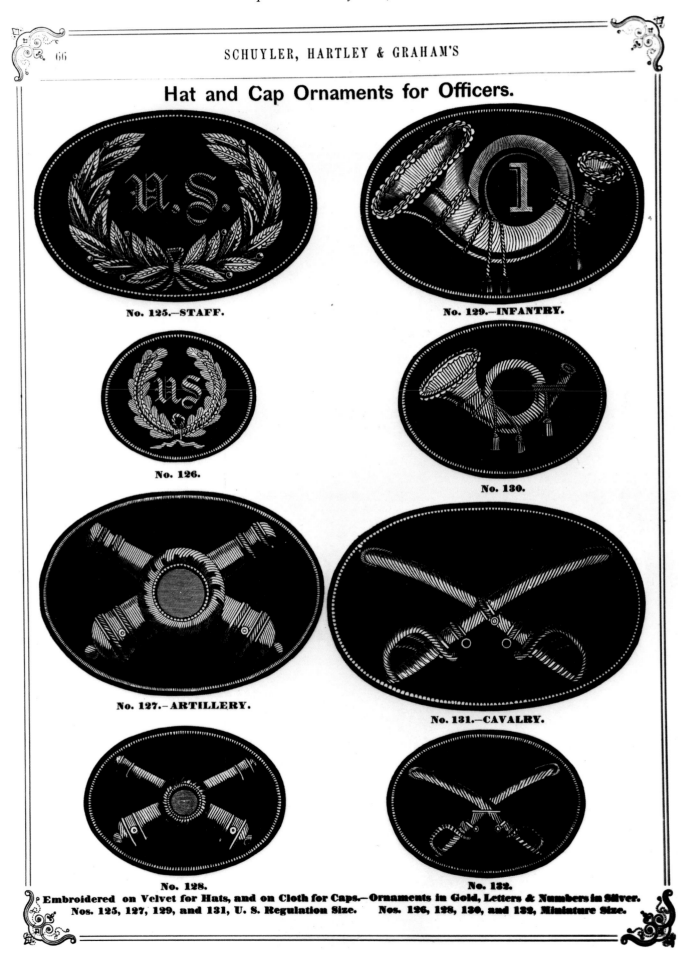

No. 125.—STAFF.

No. 129.—INFANTRY.

No. 126.

No. 130.

No. 127.—ARTILLERY.

No. 131.—CAVALRY.

No. 128.

No. 132.

Embroidered on Velvet for Hats, and on Cloth for Caps.—Ornaments in Gold, Letters & Numbers in Silver.
Nos. 125, 127, 129, and 131, U. S. Regulation Size.   Nos. 126, 128, 130, and 132, Miniature Size.

Officers' hat and cap insignia usually were embroidered gold devices with silver regimental numbers, the smaller ones being worn mainly on the forage cap or non-regulation slouch hats. There were metallic versions as well, which were less expensive and more practical for field wear. Many officers purchased these less costly devices during the Civil War. NF

Not only did General Orders No. 3, March 24, 1858 usher in dark blue trousers with 1/8-inch welts for officers (sky-blue being the color of infantry as seen here), but also the cocked hat or chapeau was again made optional for wear by generals and field grade officers. As the commanding colonel of the Eleventh Infantry, Erasmus Keyes has elected to obtain such a chapeau in lieu of the 1858-pattern hat. He wears the double-breasted frock coat with seven buttons in each row as was regulation for field grade officers from 1851 through 1872. MJM

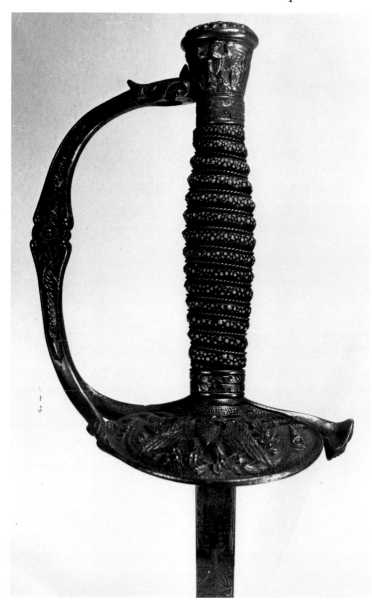

The M1860 staff and field sword gradually began to replace both the M1850 staff officer's sword and the M1850 foot officer's sword. The latter two weapons were to be discontinued or replaced by the smaller bladed M1860 by the early 1870s.

Unidentified cavalry officer in the 1851-pattern cloak coat that was regulation until 1872. The low crowned forage cap is the chasseur type favored by many officers during the war. MJM

Another similar wartime adjustment allowed shoulder straps to be replaced by simple rank devices similar to those worn from the later nineteenth century to the present day. These were to affix to the shoulder, but sometimes individuals applied them to the collar. Finally, epaulets, sashes, and forage cap badges were no longer required in accordance with General Orders No. 286, and consequently "saved many lives," in the estimation of one writer.[14]

Other means of dealing with officers being recognizable to their troops, yet less conspicuous to the enemy included miniature shoulder straps, and a special type devised by George Evans (Patent No. 37,142, December 9, 1862) that enabled an officer to remove or reattach his straps quickly and with ease.[15] This pattern also had the added advantage of making it possible to clean a coat or jacket without its straps in place, or for epaulets to be substituted with the straps removed.

Stamped metal shoulder straps offered another practical option in that they could be fabricated rapidly and would cost less to produce. Gideon Robinson even developed a form of strap that could be made by coiling wire around a half-round mandril that would form the outer border. This method was cheaper than embroidery.[16] Thus, the cost of re-

placement was relatively inexpensive when straps were damaged, soiled, or a promotion obtained. This was a boon to officers, all of whom had to buy their uniforms and accessories.

Another change that brought about a degree of similarity between men and officers had to do with trousers (referred to as "trowsers" as of General Orders No. 6, March 13, 1861). These were returned to sky-blue for all regimental officers and every enlisted man except those in the ordnance who retained dark blue, in accordance with General Orders No. 108, Headquarters of the Army, December 16, 1861. Worsted leg stripes were retained with this general order for sergeants and corporals, all in branch colors, although dark blue was reinstated for infantry, and crimson was prescribed for hospital stewards as well as ordnance sergeants. Welts in 1/8-inch facing material of the same branch colors as for enlisted men were required for officers in the combat arms, while 1/8-inch gold cord remained the trim for general staff and staff corps officers on their dark blue trousers. Dark blue trousers also persisted for general officers, but the gold welt prescribed in 1858 was deleted, the new regulation clearly indicating no "stripe, welt, or cord down the outer seam."

Major Robert Anderson eventually had to surrender his command to the Confederates after Fort Sumter took a pounding from their heavy guns. He was an artillery major at the time and wears the 1851-pattern overcoat with three gallons to indicate his rank, as well as the 1851-pattern field grade officer's frock coat. RB

Badges Worn on Sleeve of Overcoat, to designate Rank.

No. 141.
HOSPITAL STEWARD'S
Chevrons—Silk, Embroid-
ered on Green Cloth.

No. 142.
1st LIEUTENANT — One
Braid—⅛ inch Black Silk
Braid.

No. 143.
CAPTAIN—Two Braids.

No. 144.
MAJOR—Three Braids.

No. 145.
LIEUTENANT-COLONEL—
Four Braids.

No. 146.
COLONEL—Five Braids.

No. 147.
GENERAL—Five Braids.

Overcoat silk braid for the 1851-pattern officer's overcoat. Second lieutenants had plain sleeves. Note also the hospital steward half-chevron worn on enlisted overcoats, blouses, and frock coats. NF

First Lieutenant David Hamel of the Sixth New York Heavy Artillery posed around 1864 for this portrait. He has elected to use a similar insignia to the overcoat rank device, but probably in gold lace rather than black silk, to depict his rank. This was a redundant practice, however, in that he also has shoulder straps of a first lieutenant of artillery on his stable jacket. Light artillery officers were permitted to procure stable jackets per General Orders No. 20, August 6, 1860. MJM

Miniature Shoulder Straps.

**No. 96.
COLONEL.**

**No. 97.
LIEUTENANT-COLONEL.
Major same as Lieutenant-Colonel, but Gold
Embroidered Leaves.**

**No. 98.
2d LIEUTENANT.
Medium Strap.**

**No. 99.
CAPTAIN.**

**No. 100.
1st LIEUTENANT.**

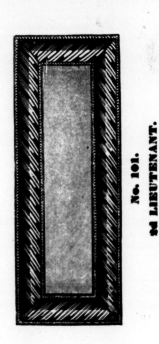

**No. 101.
2d LIEUTENANT.**

Shoulder straps were the more traditional means of indicating officer's ranks on the field uniform, being adopted as early as the 1830s. By 1851 they had evolved to a rectangular frame with black or dark blue centers for staff and general officers, and light blue or medium blue centers for infantry, scarlet for artillery, orange for dragoons, emerald green for mounted rifles and, as of 1855, yellow for cavalry. Blank straps indicated a second lieutenant, for a first lieutenant one gold bar at each end of the strap was prescribed, two gold bars for a captain, gold oak leaves for a major, silver oak leaves for a lieutenant colonel, and a silver spread eagle for a colonel. Brigadier generals had a single silver star and major generals a pair of silver stars. Borders were gold. Sizes of the straps and the types of borders differed from various makers. There also were simulated metallic straps that were easy to replace or even remove in the field, a consideration of some concern as snipers began to seek out officers as targets. NF

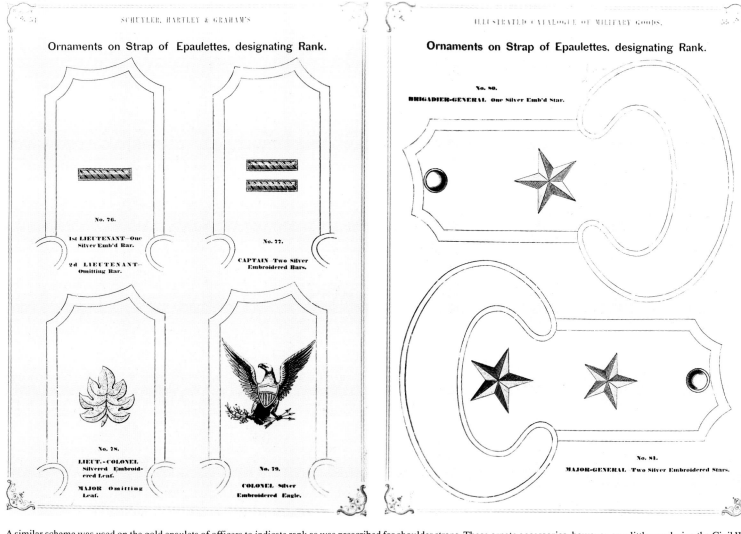

SCHUYLER, HARTLEY & GRAHAM'S

Ornaments on Strap of Epaulettes, designating Rank.

No. 76.

1st LIEUTENANT—One Silver Emb'd Bar.

2d LIEUTENANT—Omitting Bar.

No. 77.

CAPTAIN Two Silver Embroidered Bars.

No. 78.

LIEUT.-COLONEL Silvered Embroidered Leaf.

MAJOR Omitting Leaf.

No. 79.

COLONEL Silver Embroidered Eagle.

ILLUSTRATED CATALOGUE OF MILITARY GOODS.

Ornaments on Strap of Epaulettes, designating Rank.

No. 80.

BRIGADIER-GENERAL One Silver Emb'd Star.

No. 81.

MAJOR-GENERAL Two Silver Embroidered Stars.

A similar scheme was used on the gold epaulets of officers to indicate rank as was prescribed for shoulder straps. These ornate accessories, however, saw little use during the Civil War when hard campaigning and a desire for officers to appear less noticeable to the enemy were concerns. NF

Front and rear view of epaulets of a first lieutenant of the Seventh Infantry. The size of the fringe, as well as the insignia on the epaulete indicated rank. Japanned tin canisters were common storage cases for the epaulette. RBM

Large fringe and a silver spread eagle provided the means to indicate that this epaulete was for a colonel. The numeral indicated the regiment and the blue backing behind the number was the branch color for infantry. Kurt Cox Photograph. JML

Detail of typical underside of officer's epaulets of the 1851 to 1872 period with the metallic hinged fastening device and clip bearing the maker's marks. Kurt Cox Photograph. JML

Shoulder straps could be affixed in a number of ways ranging from directly sewing them to the coat to brass clips that passed through some form of attachment such as eyelets or loops of thread. Sometime ties similar to shoestrings were used to secure the straps in position as well. Kurt Cox Photograph. JML

Some officers purchased larger straps with double gold embroidered borders such as this example for a first lieutenant of artillery. Kurt Cox Photograph. JML

Colonel of infantry shoulder strap. Kurt Cox Photograph. JML

Major Benjamin Rohren was the surgeon of the Tenth Pennsylvania Reserves. He elected to depart from U.S. regulations as others did by adding an "M.S." for Medical Service to his shoulder straps. Kurt Cox Photograph. JML

"Extra Rich" shoulder strap of second lieutenant of infantry with double gold embroidery border. Kurt Cox Photograph. JML

Major Rohren also wore the "M.S." rather than regulation "U.S." on his forage cap. Kurt Cox Photograph. JML

An assistant surgeon (captain) was another medical officer to employ the "M.S." device on his shoulder straps and hat insignia. WSHS

France's influence was evident in many uniforms worn in the United States before and during the Civil War, not the least of which was the zouave style as seen here. The outfit took many forms and was worn by troops of both North and South. MJM

Reinforcement of the seat and inner legs continued for mounted troops, of matching sky-blue kersey that was to measure 11-inches across at the buttocks and 6 1/2-inches wide at the knee, tapering to 3 1/2-inches at the bottom cuff for medium sizes according to the 1865 quartermaster manual, a document that further demonstrated efforts to codify the uniform in that previous pattern uniforms had been made without written specifications.[17]

This type of innovative approach did not guarantee uniformity however, as could be determined by such basic indicators as the fact that some 22,000 pairs of the old dark blue trousers still were on hand at Philadelphia as late as October 1864.[18] Presumably these would be available for issue alongside sky-blue pairs, although their use possibly was mostly restricted to Ordnance Department personnel and some volunteer units.[19]

In part this type of situation arose because no one "was prepared by training or experience to cope with the logistical problems of the army" when so large a force had to be mobilized and quickly sent to the field.[20] Consequently, producing and maintaining stocks sufficient to meet the needs of a huge Union force taxed quartermasters throughout the four years of fighting. These demands for clothing caused the quartermaster to harken back to the Mexican War experience. Not only were thousands of seamstresses and tailors added at Schuylkill Arsenal to hand finish the cloth section prepared by government cutters, but also workers were added to provide labor for new depots in New York City; St. Louis; Cincinnati and Steubenville, Ohio; along with operations at

Quincy and Springfield, Illinois; Boston; Detroit; Indianapolis; and Milwaukee. Contracts were let with firms that could procure material and fabricate uniforms as well.[21] These initiatives improved output, while new technology, such as introduction of machines that tested the strength of cloth, represented other efforts to employ the latest industrial methods.[22] Nonetheless, quality seemed to vary as did the cut and appearance of garments supplied by the numerous sources available.[23]

Diversity also continued because several volunteer units held steadfast to their distinctive outfits. The *zouave* style that had been so popular on the eve of the war was one such holdover from the days of antebellum pomp.

In the 1830s, North African-based troops were first drawn from Berber warriors known as *Zouava*. They donned the distinctive *Tirailleurs Algerian* (Turcos) garb associated with the region where they served. Soon, "the French Zouave regiments captured the romantic fancy of the world much as the Foreign Legion of today. . . ."[24] Many imitators in United States militia organizations found their baggy pantaloons, fezes, leggings, and short jackets irresistible. The rage swept North and South before the war. Some stalwarts were reluctant to give up their finery despite trends toward regular army patterns, and thus wore this picturesque costume through much of the war.

Furthermore, the sway of France went beyond militia and volunteers as evidenced by the importation of 10,000 uniforms and complete equipments from a Parisian military supplier. In August 1861, M. Alexis Godillot received a contract that included *habit tuniques*.[25] These were

French inspiration was evident in the deliberations of the 1862 uniform board for whom these illustrations were produced. Despite the board's recommendation for change, the patterns adopted in the mid-through late-1850s prevailed as the Federal uniform during the Civil War. NA

Another illustration produced for the 1862 uniform board reveals a proposed new scheme for depicting rank and organization that was somewhat of a hybrid of pre- and post-1851 patterns. NA

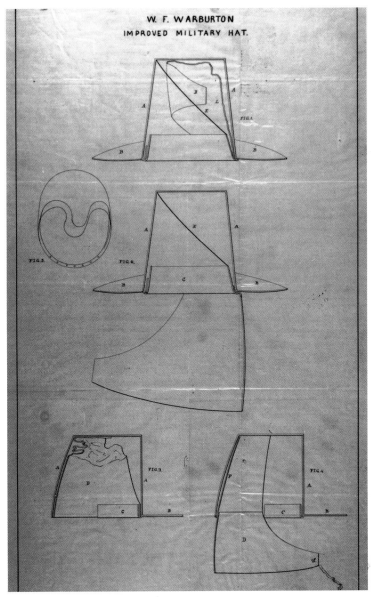

Many inventions and suggested improvements to the uniform were proposed during the Civil War such as this hat and cap patented by W.F. Warburton. Most of these suggestions never were produced. NA

the short frock-coats with side slits issued to the elite Imperial Guard *Chasseurs* in 1854, and subsequently adopted for all French infantry in 1860.

By November 1861, when the shipment arrived from Paris, the outfits mainly were distributed to troops stationed near Washington, D.C. Among them were the Eighteenth Massachusetts, the Sixty-second and Eighty-third Pennsylvania, and the Forty-ninth and Seventy-second New York Infantry Regiments.[26]

Despite the smart figure they were supposed to cut, these outfits generally were found to be too small for the average Yankee. Because of this shortcoming thought was given to cutting up the unissued garments for use in the manufacture of other clothing, or to provide fabric for canteen covers. As it turned out, the officer in charge of the clothing and equipment office found refurbishing of some of the largest sizes served "a few musicians and Bands of the Colored Regiments, but none remain large enough for men, altho' fitted for the use of boys." The most practical course of action for the remaining stock of the goods from France seemed to be sending the items to auction.[27]

This failed effort at importation did not dissuade certain officers from looking toward French modes for the American soldier. In fact, it seemed that the question of outfitting the federal forces was far from decided despite the problem with the outfits from Paris and the publication of the 1861 uniform regulations as guidelines.

Pursuant to Special Orders No. 31, Adjutant General's Office, February 11, 1862, a number of regular and volunteer officers met to deliberate "what changes or additions should be made to the uniform of the Army."[28] Board members included Daniel Butterfield, Winfield Scott Hancock, Irvin McDowell, Philip Kearny, George Stoneman, and George Sykes. These men made many recommendations, some of which had been inspired from French models. The board even had several French uniform plates available to them as part of their deliberations. Nevertheless, some of the members were proponents of the regular army uniform.[29] Foreign inspiration or not, many individuals on and off the board seemed bent on a new uniform.

The divergent opinions echoed previous debates on the topic. As an example, Hancock opted for forage caps for general officers and dis-

Some 10,000 *chasseur de Vincennes* uniforms were imported from France for issue in the United States to such Union units as the Eighty-third Pennsylvania Volunteer Infantry Regiment. This even included the leather cap or shako with cock feathers. The jackets were dark blue with yellow piping and served as an inspiration for the 1872-pattern mounted coat several years later. KSHS

Front, rear, skirt piping, and belt loop of an imported *chasseur de Vincennes* uniform coat. KSHS.

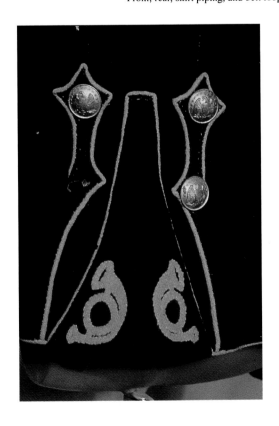

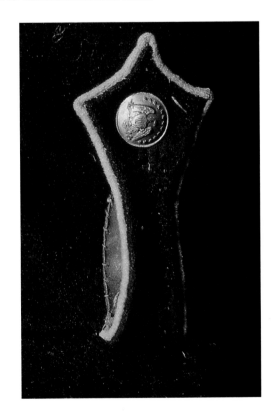

In 1859 the light artillery regained a cap that was reminiscent of the one adopted in the 1840s with horsehair plume, cords, and lines. This officer's model from Charles Parsons has the plume and "tulip" holder removed thereby making it possible to see the detail of the insignia. WPM

Light artillery officers also were permitted to wear a Russian knot of gold cord on their shoulders, as a further distinguishing feature of their uniform as of 1860. There were a number of patterns available for purchase. NF

Charles Parsons was an officer of the Fourth Artillery when he wore his light artillery officer's cap. WPM

The regimental numeral on this artillery officer cap appeared above the trunnions of the cannon insignia rather than at the intersection which was more typical. He carries an M1850 foot officer's sword. Some other light artillery officers utilized light cavalry sabers of the 1859-pattern or light artillery M1840 sabers among other variations. MJM

Captain J.E. Smith, Second U.S. Artillery's light artillery cap, epaulets, and leather carrying case. HO

Private Aherns, Battery B, Second U.S. Artillery, trimmed his light artillery cap with obsolete insignia. MJM

A light artillery bugler in the uniform of the 1861 through 1872 period regulation dress. USAQM

An unidentified principal musician of the Civil War in the light artillery cap. He wears an 1858-pattern frock coat rather than the jacket. The belt is special private purchase and the chevrons based on those of a sergeant major with the addition of a star in the center, there being no rank devices provided for principal musicians at the time. MJM

In the late 1850s mounted artillerymen again received permission to wear a dress cap with horsehair plume and cords. This example was manufactured during the Civil War. RB

Side view 1860s light Artillery enlisted cap. RB

pensing with epaulets "on active service." He also sought light blue coats with short skirts for foot troops in the *habit tunique* style, and the discontinuance of trouser stripes for corporals. The quartermaster general himself was a strong advocate for this style of light blue jacket and trousers, and even recommended that no more dark blue cloth be purchased after existing contracts ceased.[30]

Taking another approach, a sample pair of sky-blue trousers with full peg cuffs and a 3 1/2-inch waistband was presented that closed at the top with two buttons. These had a white worsted cord that was recommended for infantry privates and corporals and infantry sergeants were to have a white 1 1/2-inch stripe on their pairs. Because white had been the infantry branch color prior to 1851, this proposal may have been founded in part from a desire to return to tradition.

The concept was to issue the same style trousers to artillery and cavalry troops too, but with 1 1/2-inch scarlet stripes for sergeants of

All members of this band wear the light artillery cap with the exception of the principal musician or drum major who has on a bearskin as well as a baldric. Bands could be attired in varied ways in that their uniform was prescribed by the regimental commander and paid for from regimental funds, raised from the rank and file. LC

First Lieutenant Abraham Ryerson, Fifth New York Independent Battery procured a stable jacket with gold braid on the cuff much like the Confederate form of designating rank (although two loops were used by the South for first lieutenants). The collar also is trimmed in black velvet and accented by gold lace piping, as an example of the many variations of uniforms that existed during the Civil War, particularly among volunteer units. Kurt Cox Photograph. JML

A captain with a Wisconsin infantry regiment also improvised his rank insignia along Confederate lines using three gold lace bars on each side of the collar. He likewise opted for a three-quarter length cape rather than an overcoat and a double-breasted field grade officers frock coat rather than the more common single-breasted company grade type. WSHS

artillery and 5/8-inch stripes for enlisted artillery personnel, and the same width stripes for cavalrymen, but of yellow. Further, artillery, cavalry, and infantry officers were to have two 5/8-inch stripes set 1/4-inch apart, much like the 1847 regulations. These were to be scarlet, yellow, or white respectively. An 1/8-inch crimson welt was advocated for ordnance officers, 1 1/2-inch black velvet was deemed appropriate for engineer officers, and black silk of the same width for quartermasters. The proposal went on to suggest 1 1/2-inch light blue cloth stripes for the subsistence department, 1/8" gold braid for inspectors general, and two stripes of 7/8-inch gold braid 1/4-inch apart for adjutants general. Plain trousers were thought best for signal officers, judge advocates, and the Pay Department.

Another suggestion came from George Stoneman, an officer who began his martial career with the dragoons. He wanted a double-breasted coat with a yellow plastron front for all save musicians, who would have the same trim as worn on their jackets and coats since the mid-1850s. He carried on his fashion pronouncements by suggesting a yellow sash for all officers, essentially the hue formally associated with

generals. Additionally, Stoneman asked for sky-blue pantaloons "made loose around the hips with broad waist band, re-enforced, split from the foot and to button up near the top of the boot." Officers and sergeants were to have double yellow stripes on their trousers as they had during the 1833 to 1851 era for the dragoons.

Several more proposals advocated streamlining. Abolishing leather neck stock, shoulder scales, epaulets for all but general officers, discontinuance of the double-breasted cavalry enlisted overcoat, and the substitution of sky-blue overcoats for the dark blue cloak coat worn by officers, all were proposed. Further, all agreed the full dress hat should cease to be issued, as should the cap for infantry, while a new hat was suggested for foot troops. The consensus was, however, the forage cap was adequate for mounted soldiers, and that the light artillery cap should continued for this organization with the same insignia and cords as in the past but evidently of a slightly different design in that a sample was made up as a model. Discussion even included the Signal Corps, and arm that had been under consideration but not yet established, crossed silver flags being proposed for officers of the department as their insignia for both the cap and collar. Finally, it appeared that company grade officers might be allowed to do away with sashes, so long as a more ornamental sword belt was prescribed for them.

This plan was abandoned when another member of the board moved dark blue coats and sky-blue trousers should be retained "as prescribed by existing orders." This motion was approved.

Despite a number of contrary pronouncements this was the direction finally taken in regard to the uniform. In fact, the board disbanded without adopting new patterns. As one writer pointed out, "It is impossible to trace the final correspondence in this matter, or to find out who turned down the Board's proposal, but it is clear that the U.S. Army came within a narrow margin of adopting a chasseur uniform. . . ."[31]

Nonetheless, after the board disbanded, other individuals continued to seek "improvements in the outfit of the troops," as exemplified by an 1863 letter to the quartermaster department from Captain J.H. Jones.[32] This company commander with the Sixtieth New York Volunteers believed the jacket issued by his state was better suited for the field than the federal frock-coat. For one thing the frock-coat cost $7.21 to produce versus the New York style jacket that could be made for $5.45. Not only was the frock more expensive, but also it remained serviceable only about half as long as the jacket. Further, the jacket was

easier to keep clean, and was "handier" in that it had no tails to get in the way on campaign.

Besides practical arguments, Jones addressed the issue of fashion, thereby indicating that function could not be separated from form in the mind of many individuals of the era. Jones maintained, "Most men look more trim, neat, & soldier-like in a jacket than a dress coat." The light artillery jacket seemed ideal in this regard, except that the collar was too high and should be reduced to above one inch, with no trimming. He found such a jacket "far preferable to the blouse after the first of Sept." In addition, the jacket allegedly was "always far neater & more trim in appearance," as well as was warmer than the blouse for the fall, winter, and spring months. Jones concluded: "So far as I know there is but one mind on this question among those in the field. Can we not hope then if it be not too great a revolution that this great reform may be inaugurated when the fall & winter clothing is issued."

Jones closed with a final note that he endorsed the remainder of the infantry clothing as then provided. To a great degree it seemed that others concurred because Union troops tended to take on the appearance of the regulars as the war progressed.

Another commentator wrote from the field that devices for majors and lieutenant colonels should be changed, given that they appeared so

This Wisconsin infantry major followed U.S. Army regulations in his choice of the double-breasted 1851-pattern field grade officer's frock coat and crimson silk sash. WSHS

Infantry colonel's 1851-pattern frock coat of Civil War manufacture. Kurt Cox Photograph. JML

Company grade Union cavalry officer's frock coat. Kurt Cox Photograph. JML

Rear of First Lieutenant B.F. Hosford, Battery E, Second Connecticut Heavy Artillery's 1851-pattern single-breasted nine button officer's frock coat, crimson sash, and sword belt. Kurt Cox Photograph. JML

Rear field grade officer's frock coat 1851-pattern. Kurt Cox Photograph. JML

Numerous variations of the federal four-button sack coat were adopted during the Civil War including this custom-made example for an infantry officer. Kurt Cox Photograph. JML

Rear variant infantry officer's sack coat or blouse. Kurt Cox Photograph. JML

Officers and enlisted men alike obtained many types of slouch hats for wear on campaign instead of forage caps of other types of military headgear. This example has an officer's hat cords. Kurt Cox Photograph. JML

First Lieutenant B.F. Hosford not only added a regulation officer's black and gold cord to his slouch hat but also selected a typical artillery officer's badge to adorn the front of his hat. Kurt Cox Photograph. JML

Another form of old headgear that represented a cross between the 1858-pattern regulation hat and a slouch hat was worn by some officers. This type of headwear was referred to by some as a "Burnside" hat after Union General Ambrose Burnside. The example here was for a staff officer or general. Kurt Cox Photograph. JML

Lining with maker's label for an officer's type "Burnside" hat. The manufacturer, Warnock and Co., was one of many firms that produced uniform items during the war and thereafter. Kurt Cox Photograph. JML

much alike. He thought the former rank should be a gold shield with crossed halberds on the center of their shoulder straps, while the latter might use a silver shield with crossed swords in the same manner.[33] A second individual believed that a silver flag for majors and a silver shield for lieutenant colonels would be more appropriate still, because this proposal made all field grade officers' devices silver in contrast to the insignia for company grade officers who displayed gold bars.[34] Following a similar bent, systematizing seemed desirable to one individual who opted for a total revision of the adornment employed by commissioned officers. He proposed the use of a single, double, or triple star combination for all commissioned ranks, except the most senior general holding overall command of the army who was to have two crossed batons and an American eagle as his symbol of office, the placement of the buttons on the wearer's coat distinguishing single-breasted garments for company from field officers and general officers with their double-breasted coats respectively.[35]

Another advocate called for the adoption of a universal device to be displayed by all officers of the regular army which was to be, "a *Castle* of gold one and one half inches long and one and a quarter in height, the letters U.S. in old English of silver on centre tower...." From this basic design small silver chains were to hang down from which crossed sabers, cannon, and other specific unit emblems were to be suspended.[36]

While many recommendations were rejected, the quartermaster general's office did adjust to certain wartime changes in the composition of the Union forces. For instance, on March 3, 1863, the Topographical Engineers merged with the Engineer

A first lieutenant of the Fourteenth U.S. Infantry wearing a "Burnside" hat with his dress uniform including epaulets, crimson sash, and sky-blue trousers with dark blue 1/8-inch welt as prescribed in 1861. MJM

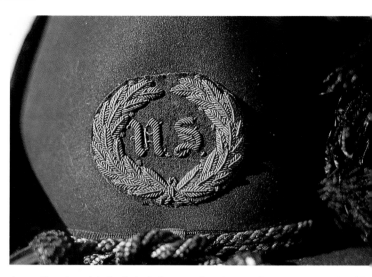

Staff officer's hat insignia on black velvet background. These insignia came in many sizes and varied quality. Kurt Cox Photograph. JML

A second version of the hat insignia for generals and staff officers demonstrate the differences from one maker to another. Kurt Cox Photograph. JML

Artillery officer's hat and cap insignia. The crossed cannon are embroidered in gold but the regimental numeral has been added separately in metal as an inexpensive means to produce large quantities of the basic insignia then affix numbers to distinguish the wearer's unit. Kurt Cox Photograph. JML

Cavalry officer's hat insignia. This version bears no regimental number meaning it never may have been worn or the wearer did not deem it necessary to depict his unit designation, a practice that was not uncommon during the Civil War. Kurt Cox Photograph. JML

Volunteer infantry officer's hat insignia that followed federal regulations. Kurt Cox Photograph. JML

Side piece for officer's 1858-pattern hat. Kurt Cox Photograph. JML

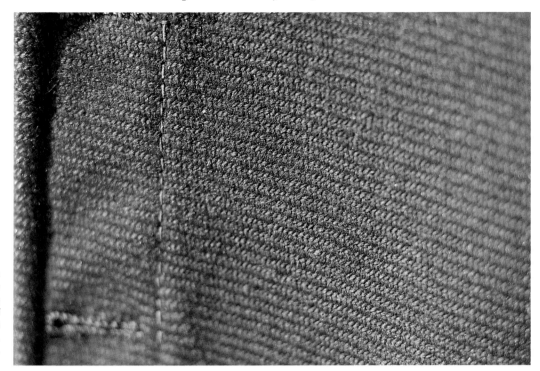

Closeup of enlisted overcoat Kersey of Civil War manufacture with button hole. The black thread of the button hole has turned brown with age. Kurt Cox Photograph. JML

Front enlisted foot overcoat 1851 through 1871 of Civil War manufacture. Kurt Cox Photograph. JML

Rear enlisted foot overcoat 1851 through 1871 of Civil War manufacture. Kurt Cox Photograph. JML

This unidentified infantryman in an enlisted foot overcoat depicts how closely the sky-blue of the coat and the trousers prescribed in 1861 matched in hue. The chasseur forage cap, however, was of dark blue cloth, as were most forage caps regardless of pattern. MJM

Standard cuff of 1858 through 1872 enlisted frock coat, in this case for an infantryman. SI

Variant of 1858 through 1872 enlisted infantry coat cuff with three rather than the standard two buttons. Such variations were not uncommon given the many contractors employed to produce the uniform during the Civil War. Kurt Cox Photograph. JML

Corps, and all differentiation ceased between the two elements shortly thereafter.[37]

Another early "casualty" during the opening salvos of the War Between the States was the artillery cap that had been adopted with scarlet plume and cords in the 1850s. Few units drew this type of headgear from stocks, and even before the war some light companies opted for the 1858-pattern hat in lieu of the cap. Then, toward the end of 1863, a revitalization of the cap as an item of issue arose, mostly because of certain light batteries being assigned to garrison duty or as occupation forces "at established posts."[38] For some reason, despite the fact that a number of the caps were on hand, in 1864 the quartermaster department let a contract for more caps, these costing $2.89 each as opposed to the previous $1.06. The increase in price may have stemmed from inflation, given rising costs during the war. Although the reasons for an escalation in the amount paid for the caps cannot be determined with certainty, its physical appearance is not a matter of speculation because of the rather detailed description provided by the 1865 quartermaster manual and the presence of numerous existing specimens.[39] The manual prescribed:

Uniforms caps for light artillery – of six sizes; the following are specifications for caps, No. 3 medium size, viz: body of cap made of stiffened felt, so as to preserve its form; made on sample block, and covered with dark blue forage cap cloth; diameter at base, 7 1/2 inches; at crown, 5 3/4 inches; covered at top with stiff glazed leather, of best quality, extending over body 3/4 of an inch; sewed strongly at 4 points, – front, rear, and sides, with 5 stitches each, and depressed in the crown 5/16 inch; and a band of thin glazed leather, best quality, 1 1/8 inches wide encircling base; height of cap in front, 5 3/4 inches; in rear, curved, 7 3/8 inches; circular vizor of stiff glazed leather, 11 3/4 inches long, inside edge, and 19 inches on outside edge, breadth in the middle, 2 3/4 inches, strongly sewed on body with 20 stitches; sweat leather of black morocco of best quality 3/4 of an inch wide, sewed on exterior of base of ca, and folded inside; a small piece of morocco, 1 1/2 inches long and 1 inch wide, sewed inside body of cap, 1 1/2 inches from the top, with ten stitches, leaving a loop to receive the whalebone stick of hair-plume; two chin straps of glazed leather, best quality, 5/8 inch wide, one of which to be 8 inches long, having sewed at one end a

Front 1858-pattern infantry sergeant frock coat. Kurt Cox Photograph. JML

Rear 1858-pattern infantry sergeant frock coat. Kurt Cox Photograph. JML

strong 7/8 inch buckle, of No. 19 brass; at the other end a yellow vest button, with a piece of No. 18 iron wire, 2 1/2 inches long, looped in the eye of the button, with which to fasten the end of the strap to the cap, and having a glazed leather slide attached to the strap, through which to pass the other end of the strap after it has been buckled; the other chin strap of soft glazed leather, of same quality and width of short chin strap and 12 1/2 inches long, and having 4 holes, punched at equal distances, to receive the tongue of buckle when on the cap; the other end of this strap is fastened to the hat by a yellow vest button, with wire, similar in all respects to that described above for fastening the other end of the strap to hat.

Brass crossed cannon, – stamped on thin sheet brass, No. 28, representing 2 cannon crossing each other at the trunnions, muzzles upwards; length 3 1/2 inches; breadth at breech of cannon, 5/8 inch; breadth at muzzle, 1/2 inch provided with 4 brass wire loops, 3/8 inch long, strongly soldered on the back to fasten them on hat.

Brass bugles, – stamped on a thin sheet of brass, No. 28, length, 3 1/2 inches; height across a crook, 1 1/2 inches; provided with 2 iron wire loops, one of which is 3/8 inch and the other 1/4 inch long, strongly soldered on back of bugles to fasten them to hat. [Why the infantry enlisted insignia was described here is unknown because the cap supposedly was restricted to light artillerymen]

The Medal of Honor was introduced during the Civil War, ultimately becoming the nation's highest recognition for valor under fire. This is the pattern presented from the 1862 through 1890s to men in the U.S. Army.

An unidentified sergeant of infantry wears the 1858-pattern frock coat trimmed in sky blue and holds the 1858-pattern hat. The trouser stripes were to be 1 1/2-inch dark blue worsted lace. The belt and the sword bayonet are part of the M1855 rifle equipments. MJM

The "hash marks" (service chevrons) on this infantry first sergeant's sleeves indicate that he had completed twenty-five years of "faithful service." This image depicts the uniform as it often was worn from 1861 through the early 1870s. MJM

The 1858-pattern enlisted infantry hat was to be looped on the left side according to regulations for foot troops. SI

Not only has this private of the Sixteenth U.S. Infantry decided to loop his 1858-pattern hat on the right side, contrary to regulations, but also he has added an additional number, in this case a "3" to further identify him as a member of the Third Battalion of his regiment. Regulations called for the company letter and regimental number only. MJM

Although this corporal of the Eighth U.S. Infantry has looped his hat on the left side per regulations he likewise has creased the crown to give it the appearance of a "Burnside" hat, thereby deviating from the prescribed manner of wearing the hat. MJM

Detail of sweatband for an enlisted 1858-pattern hat. Kurt Cox Photograph. JML

A pioneer of heavy artillery was to wear brassards of scarlet facing cloth above the elbows on the sleeves of the frock coat. The 1858-pattern hat was to be looped on the left side for heavy artillery to indicate their status as foot troops. USAQM

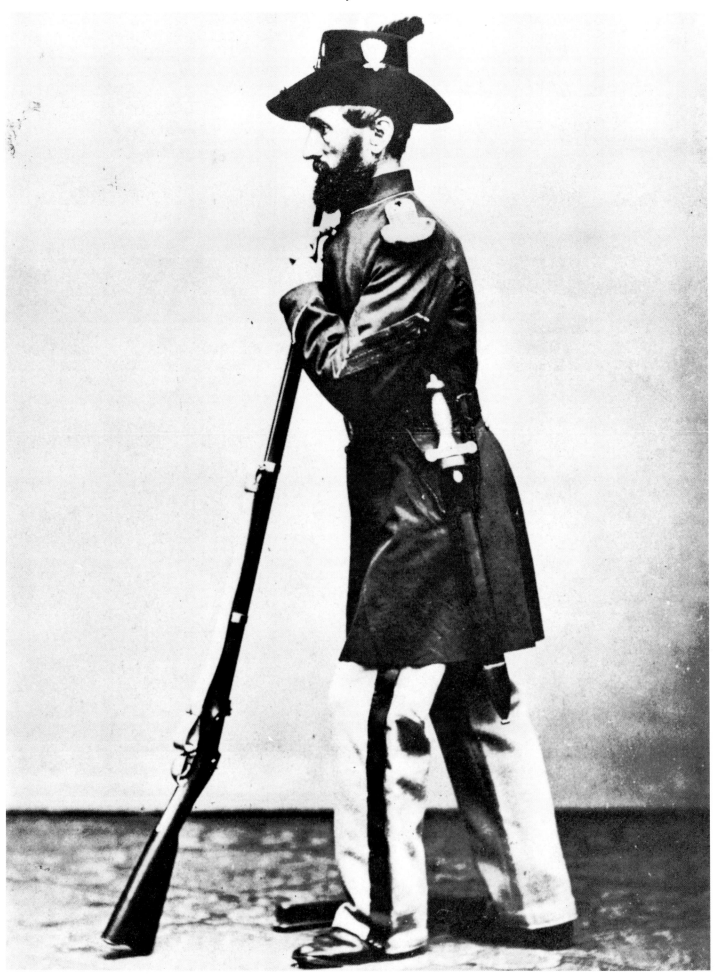

The uniform of a sergeant of heavy artillery has the M1833 short sword that was a distinguishing feature for non-commissioned officers of this branch. USAQM

In 1864, this private of the Third Pennsylvania Heavy Artillery has creased his 1858-pattern hat to make it appear more like a slouch hat or "Burnside" hat. MJM

1858-pattern enlisted artillery (scarlet) and infantry (sky-blue) hat cords. JG

1858-pattern heavy artillery enlisted hat. SI

Horse-hair plumes, – of bright scarlet, fast color, length 15 inches; circumference at the base, where it is encircled by a brass ring, 3 1/4 inches; height; diameter of brass wire wing 1/8 inch; securely plaited and fastened for a distance of 4 inches on a square piece of whalebone, 8 inches long and 1/4 inch square; the plume to be secured at its lower end, around the whalebone, by a piece of red morocco 3/4 inch wide, sewed around it.

Tulip, for horse-hair plume, – A thin sheet brass, No. 28, tulip of 4 leaves, strongly soldered to shell and flame of same metal; length from bottom of shell to top of tulip leaf, 3 1/4 inches; length of tulip proper 2 1/4 inches; diameter measured across top of tulip leaves, 1 inch, opening at top to receive the plume; at button of tulip proper a round opening, 1/2 inch in diameter; a strong loop of

brass wire, 1-16 [1/16] inch diameter, 3/4 inch long, forming a rectangle, and strongly soldered to inside of shell, so as to pass through the cap and hold the tulip and plume.

Eagle, for light artillery cap, – of thin sheet brass, No. 28, holding in the left talon 3 arrows, and in dexter talon and olive branch, and with beak turned to the right; height from talons to beak, 2 inches; breadth, from tip to tip of wings, 3 inches; breadth, from arrow points to tip of olive branch, 2 inches; a strong brass wire loop 1/2 inch long and 3/8 inch broad, securely soldered on back of eagle, to pass through the cap and hold the lower end of plume stick.

Cord and tassel for light artillery caps, – to be made of scarlet worsted braided cord, (with cotton filling inside of cord,) and braided

1858-pattern heavy artillery enlisted frock coat. Kurt Cox Photograph. JML

1858-pattern enlisted heavy artillery enlisted hat. Some light batteries also wore this hat in lieu of the cap with cords and horsetail plume. In the field, certain insignia also was discarded and the piece worn more like a slouch hat. Kurt Cox Photograph. JML

OPPOSITE: Louis Benz and his dog appeared in the West Point Yearbook for 1865. Benz, a Prussian by birth, spent forty years as a musician at the United States Military Academy. He has removed the side piece from his 1858-pattern hat so that the brim is flat, a practice that was fairly common. He wears a four-button sack coat and holds a B-flat keyed bugle. MJM

After December 1861 sky-blue trousers with the dark blue four-button sack coat and 1861-pattern forage cap began to be one of the standard uniforms for campaign wear in the Union army. MJM

Some Union army enlisted men, such as this Private P. Delmedge, Fourth U.S. Artillery, opted for a sack coat that more closely conformed to civilian wear of the era. The vest was optional for officers and enlisted personnel alike, but often was worn in blue to match the coat and with appropriate military buttons. MJM

Mounted troops often preferred the jacket for field or campaign wear, as seen here for this light artillery private who has affixed 1858-pattern hat insignia to the crown of his forage cap, although this was not called for by regulations. The trousers have reinforcing from the seat to the cuffs inside the thighs as was prescribed in the case of mounted troops. MJM

Light artillery sergeant's 1854-pattern jacket with proper scarlet worsted lace trim. Kurt Cox Photograph. JML

The U.S. Sixth Cavalry was formed early in the Civil War as part of an expansion of the Regular Army. This image might be a portrait of a new recruit to that unit in his 1855-pattern jacket and 1858-pattern hat looped on the right side as was called for in the case of mounted troops. MJM

on a carrier machine, about guage [sic] 5 or 3-16 [3/16] inch thick; two plaits, with about 2 1/4 inch cord between them; the one for the front of cap 14 inches long, and the one for back of cap 17 inches long; from each plait is 6 feet of cord, with round plaque, 2 5/8 inches in diameter, (made of 3 gimps,) and a tassel, attached to the end of each cord; these two cords pass through a tassel and two small slides, and about 4 inches about the plaques; to have a small loop netted on, by which to attach and suspend the plaques from a button on the breast of the coat. The tassels (three in number,) are to be of solid worsted, with a netted head, about 2 1/2 inches long, including head; the skirt or fringe of tassels, composed of from 809 to 90 ends of bullions; the cord and tassels to weigh about 3 1/2 ounces.

Scroll and ring, for light artillery caps, – The scroll to be made a circle, sheet brass, No. 28, 1 inch in diameter, corrugated, convex 1/4 inch; a hole in the centre in which is inserted a double loop of brass wire 3/4 inch long, projecting 1/4 inch on outside and 1/2 inch inside, strongly soldered on inside of scroll; a double ring of stout brass wire, 1/2 inch diameter, passed through the outer loop, from which to hang the tassel cord.

While the quartermaster manual went to great lengths to provide makers with everything they needed to know to manufacture the caps for enlisted men, this was not the case officers. This practice was typical of the entire period. It is not surprising then that the officers' versions tended to differ from those of the rank and file. For one thing, the plaits and the cords were of gold wire for officers, and the insignia gold embroidered. For the most part the type of crossed cannon devices and the Arms of the United States style of eagle that was used to loop up the 1858-pattern officer's hat brim were typical for artillery officers' caps. The tulip likewise lacked the shell and flame. It appears that officers usually did not have leather tops or reinforcing bands around the base of

Front 1855-pattern cavalry enlisted jacket of Civil War manufacture. Kurt Cox Photograph. JML

Front 1855-pattern cavalry trumpeter's jacket of Civil War manufacture. Kurt Cox Photograph. JML

their caps either. Because officers obtained their uniform components from numerous sources, the quality and certain details differed from one man to the next.

In fact, some officers had no specific information to go by early in the war with regard to their garb. This was the case for chaplains, whose uniform finally was prescribed for the first time late in 1861.[40] Early chaplains were to have a rather nondescript outfit consisting of a single-breasted black frock-coat with standing collar and nine self-covered buttons. Plain black trousers and a plain black hat or a forage cap, presumably of plain black, served as headgear on all occasions, although a chapeau could be obtained for dress wear. Three years later General

1858-pattern cavalry enlisted hat. Kurt Cox Photograph. JML

Orders No. 247, War Department, August 25, 1864, modified the uniform in that a "herringbone of black braid" was to adorn the button holes and buttons of the coat, and the headgear could bear the staff officer insignia of the Old English "U.S." in a gold wreath applied to a black velvet background. Again the chapeau could be substituted "on occasions of ceremony."

Having tended to clothing for those who met spiritual needs of the soldiers, federal authorities began to address another new addition to the army's organization, the hospital corps that was established to assist surgeons and hospital stewards. The creation of this group bespoke of changes in the structure of the military establishment, and resulted in a directive that these enlisted specialists were to have "the undress uniform of a private soldier, with a green half chevron on the left forearm."[41] It remains unclear whether this practice was followed.

It seems more probable that another innovation having to do with medical support, the ambulance corps, did see some use, albeit on a sporadic basis. As an example, in August 1862, privates serving with the corps in the Army of the Potomac were authorized: "a green band, one and one quarter inches broad, around the cap, a green half-chevron, two inches broad, on each arm above the elbows, and to be armed with two revolvers;" a point that indicated these men were not looked upon as non-combatants as they would be with the promulgation of the Geneva Convention. In turn, non-commissioned officers were "to wear the same band around the cap as the privates, chevrons two inches broad, and green, with the point toward the shoulder, on each arm above the elbow."[42] During the following year, this order was modified slightly in that the green cap band was to measure only

A young cavalry trumpeter in the 1855-pattern jacket for cavalry musicians. The lace was yellow worsted. SH

1 1/4", while no dimensions were given for the chevrons or half-chevrons.[43]

By January 1864, the Army of the Cumberland issued General Orders No. 2 that adopted the scheme established for the Army of the Potomac's ambulance train. The ambulance train for the XVIII Army Corps in the Department of North Carolina took a slightly less elaborate approach, simply calling for a broad red band to be applied to the hat that knotted on the right side.[44] By the time Congress created an Ambulance Corps for the Union army in 1864, the secretary of war was given the latitude of providing a suitable uniform design for the officers and men, although no such action seems to have been taken.[45]

Another new organization, the Invalid Corps, was launched on October 10, 1863, "recruited in the main from partially disabled soldiers in general hospitals and convalescent camps in various states" where these men provided guards and staffs for Union medical facilities. Later, in March 1864, the name changed to the Veteran Reserve Corps, in part because the old designation was abbreviated "IC," shorthand for "inspected and condemned," a term that had been used by the military for

Rear 1855-pattern cavalry enlisted jacket. Kurt Cox Photograph. JML

During the Civil War this cavalryman has applied non-regulation cloth saddler's knife to the sleeves of his 1855-pattern jacket to indicate his specialty. It was nearly a decade later before this type of insignia would be adopted officially for saddlers. Additionally, gauntlets were not issue items until the 1880s. Prior to that time they had to be purchased.

Three Union infantrymen appear in their four-button sack coats and forage caps. The private standing in the center has an oil-cloth forage cap cover.

Special trefoils accent this bandsman's frock coat, while double leg stripes with contrasting color borders are evident as just two variations on a theme in that regimental commanders could make "such *additions* in ornaments" as they judged proper, when it came to the regiment's band. MJM

Another bandsman, in this case from the Seventeenth U.S. Infantry, also has special leg stripes with borders and custom trim on the chest of his frock coat along with an interlocking belt plate to hold his sword belt and M1840 musician's sword in place. Additional braid appears on the chasseur forage cap. MJM

An engineer sergeant major in the 1861 through 1872 regulation dress uniform, including multiple service chevrons in yellow worsted to indicate that the man had served decades in the ranks. The hat may be a non-regulation substitute for the 1858 pattern, or has been creased partially in a non-regulation style. MJM

This Seventeenth U.S. Infantry bandsman's cuffs and collar are covered in facing material similar to the 1851-pattern coat, although the image is from the Civil War. MJM

The distinctive garb for hospital stewards evolved between 1857 and 1861. In the latter year the basic outfit finally was set as a single breasted nine-button frock coat with crimson piping around the collar and at each cuff. A green half chevron with yellow borders and a yellow silk thread embroidered caduceus was placed in the center of the device and these were worn at downward angles above the elbow. By 1861, sky-blue trousers with a worsted 1 1/2-inch crimson stripe ran down the seams of the trousers. A red worsted sash wrapped around the waist two times and tied at the left (as was prescribed for all non-commissioned officers from first sergeant or orderly sergeant and above) where a model 1840 non-commissioned officers sword was suspended by either an over the shoulder belt, or after 1868 by a belt frog. The 1858-pattern hat with a cord of buff and yellow and a gilt wreath enclosing a silver "U.S." all formed the dress uniform from 1861 through 1872. USAQM

The 1858-Hospital Steward frock coat was to be trimmed in crimson and display the emerald green half chevrons with yellow thread embroidered caduceus and border above the elbow. SI

The size and design of hospital steward chevrons often varied from one individual to another. Headgear also was a matter of choice, as seen here where a small officer's type cap insignia is worn on a chasseur forage cap. MJM

discarded surplus. The other motive for the renaming was expansion of eligibility to veterans who although able bodied did not wish to reenlist for combat duty at the expiration of their first term of service. Under the new title, their mission expanded to guarding bridges, prisoners of war, railways, and government property, among other assignments.[46]

Early on a uniform was prescribed for enlisted personnel of the Invalid Corps.[47] The standard dark blue forage cap and kersey trousers were of the type issued to other soldiers, but the jacket was similar in cut to the cavalry shell, with the exception that it was polka-skirted. Also, the color was light blue to match the trousers. In effect this was the uniform General W.S. Hancock suggested and Quartermaster General Montgomery Meigs endorsed as part of the 1862 board's recommendation for issue to the entire army. Dark blue lace trimmed the collar, cuffs, and shoulder loops, the last component being another departure from regular army uniforms of the period, although these loops represented a return to the roundabouts issued in the 1830s through the 1850s. In fact, with the exception of the skirts, the jacket was similar to that worn by the infantry in previous times.

In turn, officers of the Invalid Corps were to be attired in light blue frock-coats, set off by dark blue velvet collars and cuffs. Trousers were

matching light blue highlighted by a double dark blue stripe on the seams, each stripe to measure 1/2-inch wide, with a 3/8-inch space between them. Shoulder straps were dark blue velvet, and headgear the standard forage cap.[48] These patterns were retained after the name change and for the remainder of the existence of this wartime organization, although bandsmen in these units evidently adopted colorful non-regulation uniforms and the French leather shako imported early in the war from Paris.[49]

Another innovation of the war was the result of improved communication methods, that in turn gave birth to the Signal Service.[50] Dr. Albert Myer, a U.S. Army surgeon, was to head the organization.[51] He would be joined by a small command of less than 100 officers and men, with provisions for lieutenants through a colonel as well as privates and sergeants. Originally Myer, as chief signal officer, was to have the uniform of a major of the general staff, which presented no problem because his uniform from the Medical Service was identical and of the same rank as that prescribed for his new office. All other officers assigned to the Signal Corps likewise seemed to retain whatever dress they had obtained when they entered the service.

Then, on August 22, 1864, General Order No. 36, Headquarters of the Signal Corps, called for a badge to set off commissioned officers.

In 1863 the Invalid Corps (redesignated the Veteran Reserve Corps in March 1864) was authorized a "polka-skirted jacket." Once again the color was not dark blue. Instead the jacket was sky-blue "cut like the jacket for the United States cavalry" with dark blue lace trim, and sky-blue trousers with dark blue leg stripes for corporals and sergeants. Chevrons also were dark blue as seen here for a corporal with 1/2-inch leg stripes and an M1840 non-commissioned officer's sword (perhaps a prop from the photographer given that only sergeants or first sergeants and the regimental non-commissioned staff were to carry such badges of office). MJM

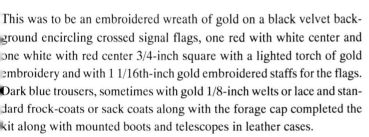

Front view Invalid Corps (Veteran Reserve Corps) private's jacket. Kurt Cox Photograph. JML

Rear view Invalid Corps (Veteran Reserve Corps) enlisted jacket. Kurt Cox Photograph. JML

This was to be an embroidered wreath of gold on a black velvet background encircling crossed signal flags, one red with white center and one white with red center 3/4-inch square with a lighted torch of gold embroidery and with 1 1/16th-inch gold embroidered staffs for the flags. Dark blue trousers, sometimes with gold 1/8-inch welts or lace and standard frock-coats or sack coats along with the forage cap completed the kit along with mounted boots and telescopes in leather cases.

For enlisted personnel, the same general order prescribed:

Crossed signal flags, red and white, on dark blue cloth. *Size of flags*: three-quarters of an inch square; centre, one-quarter of an inch square; length on staff, three inches. Sergeants will wear the designation of the corps placed in the angle of the chevron upon the left sleeve. Privates will wear the designation of the corps in the same position on the left sleeve as the chevron of sergeants.

In some instances, it appears privates took it upon themselves to have the new insignia applied to both sleeves. Regardless of this type of deviation, the flag device provided a distinctive element, the remainder of the enlisted signal uniform was a hodgepodge of whatever was available with everything from ten-button single breasted frock-coats to stan-

dard mounted cavalry jackets without trim being evident in photographs of the period.

The desire to identify with a particular unit was not lost either. Previous to the Civil War the company was the basic building block of the regulars, with the regiment only infrequently being brought together.[52] After the conflict between the North and South began, however, divisions, corps, and armies came into existence. Corps Badges eventually were adopted for a number of reasons, one of which was to produce unit identity to build cohesiveness and esprit. In addition, a somewhat more tangible reason for the institution of these insignia was to prevent "injustice by reports of straggling and misconduct through mistake as to the organizations" that such individuals belonged to, or so the XI Corps commander so reasoned.[53]

At first this practice began informally with Major General Philip Kearny's Third Division, III Corps. The general, according to one account, dressed down an officer he presumed to be under his command, only to learn that the man was from another unit. Supposedly Kearny wished to avoid a recurrence of this kind of episode. On June 28, 1862, he ordered a red flannel 2-inch square swatch to sewn to the caps of officers serving in his corps.[54] After Kearny was killed in action, his replacement directed that the practice would continue in honor of the fallen general. Eventually many enlisted men in the XI Corps elected to follow suit, even though no orders existed authorizing this action. Thus the so-called "Kearny Patch" was born.[55]

By February 10, 1863, the First Division of XI Corps likewise opted for a square or diamond patch to set off the personnel of this unit. From then on, corps after corps gradually inaugurated its own version of the badge, according to one source especially after "Fighting Joe" Hooker assumed command of the Army of the Potomac "to identify corps, divisions and brigades on the march or battlefield. As such one veteran asserted: "They were useful in many ways and tended to strengthen the *esprit du corps* [sic]" of those who wore them.[56]

Often these badges were crescents, stars, and other signs that in past times had adorned magical clothing, perhaps consciously or unconsciously suggesting another meaning for the corps badge as a good luck charm![57] By the conclusion of the fighting all but two corps had some form of badge available as a morale booster.

Kearny's death likewise gave rise to another decoration, the Kearny Medal, a semi-official device adopted on November 29, 1862, for officers and men who had served with that officer in battle.[58] This was not the only medal to be struck during the War, nor the first. In fact, the Sumter Medal and the Pickens Medal both were issued in May 1862, after being approved and paid for by the New York State Chamber of

Commerce for men who had served in the defense of these two forts at the outbreak of the conflict. These included the Kearny Cross that supplemented the Kearny Medal, after March 13, 1863; the XVII Corps (McPherson) Medal; the Gillmore Medal; the Butler Medal for Colored Troops; and other decorations. There were also badges from various veterans groups akin "to modern service medals" including the Aztec Club of 1847 for the Mexican War duty, the Military Order of the Loyal Legion of the U.S., the Society of the Army of the Cumberland, the Society of the Army of the Potomac, the Society of the Army of the Tennessee, and the Grand Army of the Republic.[59]

The last mentioned device was designed similarly to the only decoration established by the U.S. government during the war, the Medal of Honor. Congress first authorized it for the U.S. Navy and Marine Corps by act of December 21, 1861. By July 12, 1862, the U.S. Army received its own version of this outward sign of valor. The following year, the medal, which originally had been prescribed solely for "the conflict at hand," was granted permanent status.[60] By war's end, "Some 1,500 would be awarded, and the standards for receiving the honor varied from heroism to simple political expedience."[61]

The early Army medal was a five-pointed bronze star attached to an American eagle with crossed cannon suspended from a ribbon of thirteen alternating red and white stripes capped by a blue stripe. In

Detail of worsted lace and 1854-pattern enlisted eagle button on the collar of an Invalid Corps (Veteran Reserve Corps) enlisted jacket. Kurt Cox Photograph. JML

Shoulder loop and collar of Invalid Corps (Veteran Reserve Corps) enlisted jacket. Kurt Cox Photograph. JML

Closeup of sky-blue kersey of Invalid Corps (Veteran Reserve Corps) jacket. Kurt Cox Photograph. JML

Signal Private Hamilton Clark obtained gauntlets and a chasseur type forage cap as part of his outfit. The red and white crossed flags on his right sleeve are of the type authorized for signal service enlisted men in 1864. MJM

An 1858-pattern enlisted infantry hat with corps badge (2nd Division, V Corps). Kurt Cox Photograph. JML

(**Below**): While not universally adopted, corps badges saw wide usage in the Union army being made from of a range of materials and in varied sizes, and worn in several ways on coats and headgear. MJM

1861-pattern enlisted forage cap with corps badge (lst Division of both XII and XX Corps). Kurt Cox Photograph. JML

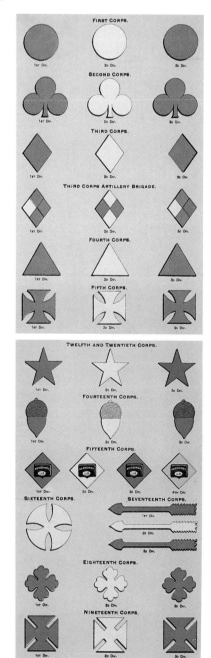

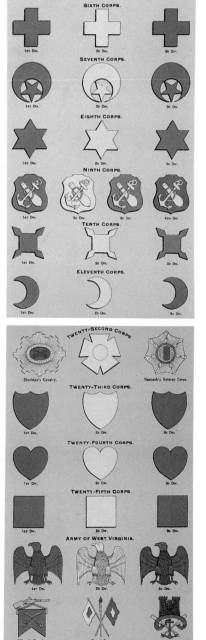

Wesley Merritt wears a more typical uniform of a general officer, this one being for a brigadier general, with a double-breasted frock coat having black velvet cuffs and collar and eight staff officer's buttons grouped in twos. A single silver star in the center of the black backed shoulder straps provided another means to indicate the rank of a brigadier general. Note the trousers are plain dark blue to match the frock coat and without welt or stripe. LC

Major generals were to have nine buttons in each row on their uniform frock coats, grouped in threes. Two silver stars indicated rank as well on the shoulder straps as seen here for Major General Alfred Terry. WCC

rows of buttons placed in sets of threes for a total of nine in each row also remained from the previous practice for not only the major general commanding the army, but also for all major generals.[64]

These fine points probably meant little to Grant, however, who was known for dressing in plain garb, with a nondescript black civilian slouch hat, and an ever present cigar.

Not all Yankee generals were so disposed though, some donning elaborate uniforms *à la fantaisie*, including George Custer whose velvet double-breasted jacket inspired by Napoleonic cavalrymen Marshal Murat, was just one of his picturesque personal wardrobe options.[65]

For the most part, however, after five years of Civil War, the early spectacle of gaily glad troops had given way to more mundane, serviceable kits. By 1865, with Robert E. Lee's surrender at Appomattox, the picture of a no-nonsense four-button sack and "bummer's cap" clad army had achieved widespread acceptance as the embodiment of a victorious Union soldiery. That imagery remained for generations to come, yet some of those who remained in the service after the federal forces disbanded challenged this symbol, not as revisionists or iconoclasts of what the Union uniform had come to represent, but instead based on pragmatic issues, personal views, or individual experiences as to what they thought was best suited for the heirs of Mr. Lincoln's army.

Brigadier General William Wells' blouse was a double-breasted type that resembled a civilian coat save for the staff officer's buttons grouped in twos similar to the placement of buttons on a general officer's frock coat. Such nondescript garb was not uncommon, especially for senior officers who often adopted practical field uniforms as the Civil War raged. Kurt Cox Photograph. JML

turn, a bronze bar with pin back surmounted the ribbon, allowing the wearer to display the medal from his chest. The first contract called for William Williams & Son, Philadelphia, to produce the medal at a cost of $2.00 each for a preliminary production run of 2,000.[62]

While the adoption of these additional insignia, medals, and uniforms predominantly was generated by the creation of new organizations, one final development that arose from the Civil War experience affected only one individual in terms of martial badges. This was U.S. Grant, whose elevation to the rank of lieutenant general in recognition of his assumption of command of the Union army resurrected a grade that had been only been granted to George Washington and Winfield Scott up to that time.[63] The outward symbol of this reinstated position was three stars on shoulder straps and epaulets, the center star being the largest on the straps, while the stars on epaulets were to descend in size from 1 1/2-inches in diameter at the crescent to 1 1/4-inches in the center, and 1 1/8-inches toward the collar. For all intents this scheme was an adaptation of the previously assigned emblems of the major general commanding the army, but now retitled lieutenant general. In keeping with this precedent the button arrangement on the frock-coat of two

Captain Rollo Phillips, Company E, Twelfth Regiment Light Infantry (Eighty-fifth Pennsylvania) adopted a slouch hat for use in the field as did many others during the war. NSHS, Museum Collections, #2733-3-3

Colonel J.K.F. Mansfield of the Inspector General Corps combined some elements of a chapeau or the Andrews hat with some of the insignia and accessories of an 1858-pattern hat and evidently obtained a buff-colored sash to indicate his promotion to brigadier general early in the war. Despite the fact that inspectors were to be the watchdogs of army regulations, Mansfield opted to modify the uniform according to personal preference as so many others did before, during, and after the Civil War. MJM

Many officers did follow the regulations in their choice of headgear, however, as seen in this 1858-pattern cavalry officers hat (First Cavalry). Company grade officers were to have two black ostrich feathers and field grade three on the right side. The left side was to be looped up and held in place by an eagle device. Note the edge of the brim is trimmed in tape. Kurt Cox Photograph. JML

1858-pattern infantry officer's hat. Kurt Cox Photograph. JML

Staff officer's 1858-pattern hat. Cords for all officers except generals were to be gold and black mixed while those for generals were to be gold only. JML

NOTES

1 Philip Egner and Frederick Mayer, eds., *Songs of the United States Military Academy West Point, New York* (West Point: Egner and Mayer, 1925), 10. This song, *Army Blue*, was adopted by the Class of 1864 as it own, although it continued to be heard at the Military Academy over generations.

2 Many Union volunteers adopted this regulation in whole or in part, while others ignored them, and appeared in distinct outfits, as evidenced in such publications as: Marfé Ferguson Delano and Barbara C. Mallen, *Echoes of Glory: Arms and Equipment of the Union* (Alexandria, VA: Time-Life Books, 1991); Albert W. Haarmann, "The Blue and the Gray," VI *Military Images* No. 6 (May-June 1985): 16-23; Francis A. Lord and Arthur Wise, *Uniforms of the Civil War* (Cranbury, NJ: Thomas Yoseloff, 1970); J. Phillip Langellier, *Parade Ground Soldiers: Military Uniforms in the Collections of the Wisconsin State Historical Society* (Madison: State Historical Society of Wisconsin, 1978); Michael J. McAfee, "Militia of `61," VIII *Military Images* No. 1 (July-August 1986): 16-24; Michael J. McAfee and John P. Langellier, *Billy Yank: The Uniform of the Union Army, 1861-1865* (London: Greenhill Books, 1996); Robing Smith, Brassey's *History of Uniforms: American Civil War Union Army* (London: Brassey's Ltd., 1996); and Frederick Todd, *American Military Equipage, 1851-1872*, Vol. II (n.p.: Chatham Square Press, 1983), to name but a few sources that offer pictorial and other evidence of diversity among non-Regular Army troops in the Northern forces. Because of the extensive information provided by these and other titles, including many articles in *Military Collector and Historian* and *Military Images* (see bibliography and additional end notes in this chapter for further references), the Civil War receives limited treatment in this publication.

3 Todd, *American Miliary Equipage*, 390-1. This source also indicated that the unit carried the "U.S. rifle M1841, altered to .58 caliber, with saber bayonet." The accoutrements included the two-piece "US" buckle with the Sappers and Miners belt, from which a saber bayonet was suspended by means of a frog.

4 Risch, *Quartermaster Support of the Army*, 354-5. Such confusion existed on both sides. For example, the First Minnesota went into the first battle at Bull Run (Manassas) in little more than black trousers, forage caps or black slouch hats, and scarlet shirts, and were mistaken by the Confederates in several instances as being the Fourth Alabama, because they also dressed in a similar garb. Richard Moe, *The Last Full Measure The Life and Death of the First Minnesota Volunteers* (New York: Henry Holt and Company, 1993), 44; 58-9.

5 Russell F. Weigley, *Quartermaster General of the Union Army: A Biography of M.C. Meigs* (New York: Columbia University Press, 1959), 5.

6 According to *The Oxford Universal Dictionary of Historical Principles*, (Oxford: The Claraden Press, 1955, 3rd ed.), 1877, the term's first meaning appeared as early as 1832, but by 1864 it had come to refer "to, or dealing in shoddy goods." For this and additional definitions see Glossary on page 334-336.

7 Robert Tome, "The Fortunes of War," XXIX *Harper's New Monthly Magazine* (June 1864), 227-8.

8 *United States Army and Navy Journal*, November 14, 1863, 180. Hereafter referred to as *A&NJ*, date, and page.

9 Ibid., September 12, 1863, 26.

10 This entire order was incorporated into the *Revised Regulations for the Army of the United States, 1861*, that bore an August 10, 1861 date with the secretary of war's approval. This slightly later version differed from GO No. 6 only in the numbering scheme of the paragraphs and in the addition of one other detail, a 3-inch strip of gold lace, 1/2-inch wide, placed in the middle of a green cloth 3 3/4-inches long by 1 1/4-inches wide that was to be worn by medical cadets. See Appendix C for a complete rendition of the 1861 uniform regulations.

11 Price, *Across the Continent With the Fifth Cavalry, 103-4.*

12 Theo F. Rodenbaugh, *From Everglade to Canyon with the Second Dragoons* (New York: D. Van Nostram, 1875), 237-8.

13 Moe, *The Last Full Measure*, 4.

14 Francis A. Lord, *Civil War Collector's Encyclopedia: Arms, Uniforms, and Equipment of the Union and Confederacy* (New York: Castle Books, 1965), 232.

15 Ibid., 232.

16 Ibid., 232, indicates this was Patent No. 37,056, December 2, 1862.

17 George Hampton Crosman, United States Military Academy Class of 1823, oversaw the production of this manual. Mark M. Boatner III, *The Civil War Dictionary* (New York: David Cay Company, Inc., 1959), 210. "Quartermaster Manual, 1865," Chapter Sixteenth, 22 (unpublished MS), OQMG, RG92, NA, gives additional details on the four sizes that were produced during the war. For materials "Footmen's trowsers" were to be made of "2 yards 15 inches of 3/4 sky blue kersey; 1/2 yard of 7/8 unbleached drilling, 5 suspender buttons, 5 shirt or fly buttons; 1 1/2 inches of black or dark blue linen thread, No. 30. For ordnance men, dark blue kersey." Mounted pairs required "3 yards 8 inches of 3/4 sky blue kersey; 1/2 yard of 7/8 drilling; 8 suspender buttons; 13 shirt or fly buttons; 8 skeins of dark blue linen thread, No. 30; 1 1/2 inches black or dark muslin." The sizes would be cut as follows: No. 1 to be 41 1/2" length, 31" leg seam, 32" waist; No. 2 to be 42 1/2" length, 32" leg seam, 34" waist; No. 3 to be 43 1/2" length, 33" leg seam, 36" waist; No. 4 to be 44 1/2" length, 34" leg seam, 38" waist. Ibid., 26. Buckles also were called out in these specifications, presumably for a rear fastening strap. These were of two sizes, numbers 7 and 11, japanned iron, the larger gauge presumably being for leather neck stocks, and the smaller for trousers. Both had double tongues and were to be of "best quality." Ibid., 18.

18 A.G. Robinson to S. Biggs, October 4, 1864, Vol. 24, C&E Br., OQMG, RG92, NA. A.G. Robinson to J.G. Johnson, September 13, 1864, ibid.; A.G. Robinson to J.G. Johnson, October 1, 1864, ibid.; and A.G. Robinson to D.G. Thomas, October 4, 1864, ibid., also refers to this matter. Additionally, A.G Robinson to D.H. Vinton September 30, 1863, ibid., inquired, "If there are on hand any pants of the French Blue Cloth at all similar to" a sample that had been sent to Philadelphia, and even if "not so fine" as the sample, a dozen specimens were to be sent to New York to determine whether these trousers were suitable for sale to officers.

19 Light blue seemed dominant, however, at least from rather extensive pictorial evidence found in Francis Trevelyan Miller, ed., *Photographic History of the Civil War* (New York: Review of Reviews, 1911) 5 vols., and William C. Davis, ed., *The Image of War 1861-1865* (Garden City, NY: Doubleday & Company, 1981-83) 5 vols.

20 Weigley, *Quartermaster General of the Union Army*, 165.

21 Risch, *Quartermaster Supply of the Army*, 348-52.

22 Other measures that were taken in an attempt to maintain quality were noted in correspondence from G.H. Crosman to Chief Inspector, Schuylkill Arsenal, September 30, 1864, Vol. 24, C&E Br., OQMG, RG92, NA, that mentioned a "new machine made for the purpose" of testing the strength of cloth had been introduced. This innovation continued as indicated by ibid., A.J. Perry to D.H. Vinton, Vol. 30, ibid, stating two machines were on hand at Schuylkill Arsenal, two at the Office of the Quartermaster General, and one at Jeffersonville Arsenal in Indiana. A detailed analysis of the fairness of the results of these machines is found in, M.C. Miegs to G. Gibson, August 3, 1868, Vol. 30, ibid.

23 Review, Risch, *Quartermaster Support of the Army*, 348-57; Weigley, *Quartermaster General of the Union Army*, 182-3; Fred Shannon, *Organization and Administration of the Union Army, 1861-1865* (Cleveland: Arthur H. Clark Co., 1928), 2 vols.; and K.W. Munden and H.P. Beers, *Guide to Federal Archives Relating to the Civil War* (Washington, DC: National Archives, 1962), 287-300, for background on logistical operations for Lincoln's forces during the war.

24 Michael J. McAfee, "What Is A Zouave," I *Military Images* No. 2 (September-October 1979): 14.

25 CCFiles, Box 1172, OQMG, RG92, NA.

26 Todd, *American Military Equipage*, 46; McAfee, "U.S. Army Uniforms of the Civil War Part VI," 14-5; and Delano and Mallen, *Echoes of Glory*, 148.

27 G.H. Crosman to M.C. Meigs, March 3, 1864, CCF, Box 1171, OQMG, RG92, NA. Crosman also suggested that gray uniforms made for the Twenty-seventh Pennsylvania be sold at auction, because that unit received a substitution of "the regular army colors" and had no need for "about one hundred suits" left at the depot as a result. As such, the movement away from gray continued.

28 Other boards of the period assembled from time to time to investigate such things as "the merits of certain military hats," as was called for by Special Orders (S0) No. 308, AGO, November 18, 1862; SO No. 31, AGO, February 11, 1862, for the purpose of reviewing Lieutenant Colonel W. King's "Cavalry Raiding Equipment;" SO No. 22, AGO, January 22, 1865, to study Woods' infantry equipment; and SO No. 62, AGO, February 8, 1865, regarding the matter of Weston's shoulder brace equipment. The fact that these bodies periodically were summoned bespoke of a willingness to look to new solutions for uniforms and equipment.

29 Source for the foregoing 1862 board information are found in, CCF, Boxes 1170 and 1171, OQMG, RG92; and LR, A723, 1866, Box 1278, Pt. 1, AGO, RG94, NA.

30 M.C. Meigs to E.M. Stanton, January 22, 1862, CCF, Box 1170, OQMG, RG92, NA.

31 Todd, *American Military Equipage*, 46.

32 J.H. Jones to M.C. Meigs, August 17, 1863, CCF, Box 1170, OQMG, RG92, NA, contain's this volunteer officer's opinions as cited above.

33 *A&NJ*, September 24, 1864, 70.

34 Ibid., October 22, 1864, 133.

35 Ibid., October 29, 1864, 156.

36 Ibid., May 6, 1865, 583.

37 William H. Goetzmann, *Army Exploration in the American West New Haven: Yale University Press, 1965),* 432. According to ibid., 433, "Though the war caused the destruction of the Corps [of Topographical Engineers], its officers played a larger part in the outcome of hostilities than any other comparable group." Two years earlier a plan had been considered to establish an enlisted component to the Corps of Topographical Engineers, with 150 men to complement the officers of that organization. The 1863 merger with the Corps of Engineers would have meant the disappearance of the enlisted corps. If indeed that body ever mustered into Union service, it was to be issued "Top. Eng. forage caps." Letters to Gordon Chappell from John Elting, July 17, 1976, and August 12, 1976, referencing the work or Roger Sturke.

38 Howell, *United States Army Headgear, 1855-1902*, 23 and 25.

39 Ibid., 24-5.

40 GO No. 102, WD, November 25, 1861. For examples of several variation of uniforms worn by Union chaplains see, Michael J. Winey, "Clergy in Uniform," IV *Military Images* No. 6 (May-June 1983): 8-12.

41 Circular No. 4, Surgeon General's Office, June 5, 1862.

42 GO No. 147, Head-quarters, Army of the Potomac, August 2, 1862, Camp Near Harrison's Landing.

43 GO No. 85, Head-quarters, Army of the Potomac, August 24, 1863, Ambulance Corps/Ambulance Train.

44 GO 85, XVIII Army Corps, December 30, 1862.

45 Todd, *American Military Equipage*, 398.

46 Ibid., 411. Also see, Philip Katcher, "They were well thought of...' The Veteran Reserve Corps, 1863-1866," VI *Military Images* No. 1 (July-August 1984): 20-4.

47 GO No. 124, WD, May 15, 1863.

48 GO No. 158, WD, May 29, 1863.

49 Todd, *American Military Equipage*, 412.

50 It is interesting to note that the one exception to the Signal Corps preeminence in communications was the telegraph, a separate Military Telegraph Service being established in November 1861 to operate this means of transmitting information. Because the service was "in the main civilian" no uniform was prescribed, although GO No. 14, Army of the Tennessee, July 5, 1864, allowed an undress uniform for operators in the Department of Tennessee. Todd, *American Military Equipage*, 402.

51 Max L. Marshall, ed., *The Story of the U.S. Army Signal Corps* (New York: Franklin Watts, Inc., 1965), offers more information on the evolution of this organization and its first chief.

52 Various type of insignia continued in use for the regiment from stamped sheet brass devices called for with the 1858-pattern cap to special signs adopted by individual units such as the Fifty-Sixth New York (X Legion), who wore a white Roman numeral inside a shield, and the 124 Regiment from Orange County, New York, who adopted a simple orange ribbon attached to their coats to set them off from other units. Seward R. Osborne, "They Wore An Orange Ribbon," XXXVIII *Military Collector and Historian* No. 1 (Spring 1986): 40.

53 Circular, Army of the Potomac, March 21, 1863. This document directed that a crescent would represent the corps, with the first division having red, the second division white, and the third division blue versions, according to a plan that paralleled other corps. The XI Corps' badge was to be affixed to the top of the forage cap, and inspectors were to ensure that the devices were "worn as directed." Moreover, when the "badges were lost or torn off" they were to be replaced immediately. Additionally, provost-marshall were to "arrest as stragglers all other troops found without badges, and return them to their commands under guard." This same approach was taken by the Department of the Cumberland, GO No. 62, April 26, 1864.

54 E.D. Townsend, *Anecdotes of the Civil War in the United States* (New York D. Appleton and Company, 1884), 168-9, and John D. Billings, *Hardtack and Coffee* (Boston: George M. Smith Co., 1888), 256.

55 Todd, *American Military Equipage*, 93-4. For additional information on corps badges consult, Wendell W. Lang, Jr., "Corps Badges of the Civil War," Pt. 1, VI *Military Images* No. 6 (May-June 1986): 16-25; Pt. 2, VIII ibid. No. 1 (July-August 1986): 8-15; Pt. 3, VIII ibid. No. 3 (November-December 1986): 16-26; Pt. 4, IX ibid. No. 3 (November-December 1987): 6-15; Marius B. Peladeau and Roger S.

Cohen, Jr., "Corps Badges of the Civil War," XXIII *Military Collector and Historian* No. 4 (Winter 1971): 103-12; John M. Wike, "The Wearing of Corps and Division Insignia of the Union Army, 1861-1865," IV *Military Collector and Historian* No. 2 (June 1952): 35-8; and Stanley S. Phillips, *Civil War Corps Badges and Other Related Awards, Badges, Medals of the Period: Including A Section on Post Civil War and Spanish American War Corps Badges* (Lanham, MD: S.S. Phillips, 1982).

56 Moe, *Last Full Measure*, 222, quoting William Lochren, adjutant of the First Minnesota.

57 Lurie, *Language of Clothes*, 29, contends that one of the original uses of clothing beyond providing protection from the elements may have been for magical purposes.

58 Only 320 of these decorations were issued according to, William Styple, "The Kearny Medal," IX *Military Images* No. 3 (November-December 1987): 18-9.

59 For more information read, Todd, *American Military Equipage*, 109-13; Howard Michael Madaus, "Massachusetts Mystery Medal," VIII *Military Images* No. 3

(November-December 1986): 14-15; and James W. Wike, "Individual Decorations of the Civil War and Earlier," V *Military Collector and Historian* No. 3 (September 1953): 57-64.

60 *Above and Beyond: A History of the Medal of Honor from the Civil War to Vietnam* (Boston: Boston Publishing Company, 1985), 4-5.

61 Ibid., 15. Actually, the original number was over 2,100 according to, Todd, *American Military Equipage*, 112.

62 Ibid., 109 and 112, and *Above and Beyond*, 5.

63 John R. Elting, Dan Cragg, and Ernest Deal, *A Dictionary of Soldier Talk* (New York: Charles Scribner Sons, 1984), 184. Elihu B. Washburne, a Illinois congress man introduced a bill to create the rank of lieutenant general, which passed both houses and became law on February 26, 1864, "with the implied understanding that General Grant was to fill the position." He did so on March 9, 1864, when Lincoln presented the commission directly to him at the White House. Horace Porter, *Campaigning With Grant* (New York: Bonanza Books, 1961), 17-18, and 21.

64 Todd, *American Military Equipage*, 357.

65 Ibid., 358.

In the years immediately following the Civil War, three new chevrons were authorized for non-commissioned officers assigned as company quartermaster sergeants (**left**): regimental hospital stewards (**bottom**): and regimental commissary sergeants (**right**). The company quartermaster sergeant chevron, which had been used by some Union volunteer units during the war, was adopted for the Regular Army in 1866 and remained regulation through 1872. The other two types of chevrons were adopted in 1867 and abolished in 1870.

Mixing of issue items with privately purchased articles continued after the Civil War much as it had before the war. For instance although a non-commissioned officer, this hospital steward elected to buy an officer's company grade frock coat and a chasseur pattern forage cap with small embroidered cap wreath as worn by surgeons and staff officers to form parts of his uniform in this circa 1870 image. Similarly, the belt is an officer's style private purchase although the trousers and sash appear to be regulation. FLARNHS

3

CONTINUALLY WEAR THE BLUES,
1866-1873

Much as the Crimean War had influenced the British military, the American Civil War impacted the United States Army.[1] In fact, the experiences of the 1861-1865 era fostered a spirit of reform in the American military that gathered momentum right after Appomattox. This mandate for change surfaced in such areas as tactics, weapons, and others arenas related to the how the regular army would operate after peace returned to the strife-ridden country.[2] The movement even included how the United States Army would be garbed.

Ultimately several factions debated the question of what the federal troops should wear. One group clung to tradition. They felt that the late war had been won by blue-clad Yankees who numbered among the finest fighting men ever to bear arms. It seemed sacrilegious to violate their memory by adopting a new outfit. One popular post Civil War tune summed up this position when it proclaimed:

England has its Grenadiers,
France has its zoos-zoos . . .
The U.S.A. never changes they say;
But continually wear the blues.[3]

Those who disagreed with the traditionalists attacked the issue from two basic points of reference. One side argued that the martial attire of the 1860s lacked distinction. Consequently, it should be replaced, preferably with an outfit based upon European models.

Another revisionist approach expressed less concern for the dictates of Continental and British fashion. Instead, this group desired to obtain more practical garb or clothing that was seen as better for the health and comfort of the troops, or provided a response to varied environmental conditions where scattered forces faced everything from blazing heat to freezing cold over a vast continent.

All the parties made their positions known either in writing or by their actions. For example, the conservatives regularly presented their side in official correspondence. Quartermaster General Montgomery Meigs especially championed the old Union Army's uniform provided by his personnel.

Three sergeants from the cavalry detachment serving at West Point, during the mid to late 1860s, illustrate the continuance of Civil War issue uniforms including the four button sack coat and the twelve button mounted jacket. The collar of the non-commissioned officer on the left appears to be lower than the regulation pattern. MJM

Another West Point-based cavalry enlisted man of the years immediately following the Civil War has custom corporal's chevrons in yellow worsted lace on his jacket and has acquired a chasseur- style forage cap on the front of which he has placed a small privately-purchased saber insignia. MJM

Cavalry trumpeters and light artillery trumpeters and musicians continued to wear the jacket with lace trim on the chest during the years immediately following the Civil War. MJM

Although a Georgian by birth, Meigs entered the U.S. Military Academy on an appointment from Pennsylvania, graduating fifth in his Class of 1836. He entered the Corps of Engineers thereafter. At the outset of the Civil War, Meigs became the commander of the Eleventh Infantry Regiment for only one day. The following day he moved up to brigadier general to assume the office of quartermaster general, having been favored by Abraham Lincoln to fill a vacant post that had been sought by many others, including William Sherman. Meigs remained as quartermaster general until retirement in 1882. During the clash between the North and South he performed yeoman service, deserving considerable praise for his ethical and dedicated performance of difficult duties. After that conflict, however, he became combative and conservative, but because of his dedicated service during the war his tendency toward protectiveness of the Quartermaster Department and its reputation was understandable.[4] Given Meigs' personal beliefs, Lieutenant Colonel Innis Newton Palmer, who commanded Fort Laramie, Wyoming Territory, found himself at odds with the quartermaster general. When Palmer conducted an inspection of quartermaster stocks on hand at his post he was dismayed. In communications directed to a member of the Inspector General's Department Palmer reported a lack of the two largest sizes made at the time. He "found only eight of the 'size 4' [the biggest standard issue] and twelve 'size 3'" on hand in a box of eighty jackets. All these were "much smaller than government specifications required." Palmer asserted that the "numbers 1 & 2" were so diminutive as to be of use only "for small boys." Trousers, overcoats, drawers, and footgear

all presented the same problem while insignia, according to Palmer, also were of extremely poor quality. This meant that rather than being able to clothe nearly a whole regiment, as indicated by the inventory on hand he barely could outfit a company. Palmer concluded these deviations stemmed from corrupt contractors.[5]

The contention that the quality of the uniform deteriorated as a result of wartime contract difficulties was a common charge. Some observers insisted that the items of apparel manufactured during the War Between the States were of lesser quality than ante bellum issue, being poorly fabricated and of inferior material. This was the conventional wisdom throughout the Department of the Atlantic, according to the inspector general there, who found the clothing in good condition but of poor quality, and universally of small sizes.[6]

Meigs conceded the clothing was "of coarser texture perhaps than is considered by some desirable . . . ," but he went on to say the reason for the difficulty with sizes was from the practice of company officers allowing their men to draw larger clothing in order to have them cut down and tailored.[7] Meigs denounced this routine as "waste and extravagance" for which there was "no sufficient excuse."[8]

A quartermaster in New Orleans even was warned about commanding officers who circumvented the standard tariffs the department had established based on long years of experience. These officers ignored the established standards and ordered nothing but large sizes.[9] Another ramification of men being allowed to draw only the largest sizes was that undue proportions of small sizes were left in stock. As a conse-

In this circa 1870 photograph Fifth Infantry bandsmen at Ft. Leavenworth, Kansas wear specially made uniforms, including worsted epaulets and caps similar to light artillerymen. The drum major towers in a white "bearskin." FAM

In this 1869 picture from Ft. Leavenworth, Kansas a sergeant leans against a field piece in a modified 1859-pattern four-button sack coat, the outer breast pocket being an addition not available on issue blouses. Chevrons with three stripes to indicate rank appear above the elbow, points down. These were to be worsted wool in sky-blue for infantry, yellow for cavalry, and scarlet for artillery. Once again, it appears that the chevrons here were custom made. The leg stripe were of 1 1/2-inch worsted tape for sergeants through 1872 in the color that matched the chevrons except for the infantry NCOs who had dark blue leg stripes. Finally, this non-commissioned officer has a privately purchased hat but has elected to draw the worsted hat cord, although this accessory apparently was far from popular in the field. FAM

quence, inspectors heard complaints about significant quantities of clothing that were on hand at various posts considered unfit for issue. This situation was brought about, in Meigs' estimation, by the neglect of officers in the field to see to the distribution of proper sizes in the first place.[10] One recommendation to halt this procedure called for a physical description of the recruit next to his name to assure the size ordered was correct, and of equal importance to provide up-to-date data to establish a realistic ratio of sizes for distribution to posts around the country.[11]

For some this action seemed to be a case of too little too late as a bit of doggerel titled "Private Blow," penned by a soldier for an 1867 Christmas program, satirized:

You ought to see the coat I wear,
And, then, the trousers, such a pair!
There's no such uniform, I swear,
In any decent army.[12]

While amusing this ditty once more underscored a general complaint that existing uniform components often did not fit the common soldier.[13] In fact, much as the hero of "Private Blow" one soldier of the late 1860s experienced an exaggerated, but telling incident. With his own tailored uniform being cleaned, the individual was forced to wear unaltered issue clothing for dress parade. Finding these too large he had a bunkie help him stuff the oversized garments with four handkerchiefs, three towels, a pair of shirts, and a like number of drawers. Additional impromptu preparations included folding up the cuffs of the coat sleeves and legs of his trousers, both being overly long. Hoping to escape notice, the unfortunate man took to the rear rank of his company, only to be discovered when his movement to execute the manual of arms and to march made the whole affair come undone. Soon the man was hobbling, then hopping as the trouser legs covered his feet, and the stuffing started to fall out on the parade ground to mark the path of the unfortunate Beau Brummel.[14]

This type of occurrence, although probably an extreme example, was the reason that company tailors had to be called on to correct the faulty government issue.[15] The men who provided this service were fellow soldiers rather than specialists assigned these duties. One tailor was authorized per company, although not every unit or garrison had one.[16] Their skills varied as did the amount they charged, this second point being a bone of contention, as was the fact the tailors were exempt from most military duties. Yet they drew the same pay as their comrades, in addition to what they received for their work.[17] One officer wrote that in order to render the "uncouth" and "totally unfit" shape of

The 1858 pattern black hat was not popular. Sometimes troops in the West substituted the forage cap even for parade as seen here for men of Company C, Third U.S. Infantry, at Fort Larned, Kansas, in 1867. Otherwise, the brass shoulder scales, frock coat, and other items are the regulation dress wear. KSHS

Infantry officers at Ft. Bridger in today's Wyoming demonstrate the diversity which existed in uniforms worn in the West from 1866 through 1872. All but one of the standing officers are lieutenants and captains which is indicated by their single breasted nine button frock coats. The tall man in the 1858 hat is a field grade officer (major through colonel) because of the fact that he has a double-breasted frock coat with seven infantry officers buttons in each row. The three military men on the far left wear shoulder straps which were authorized for marches, fatigues, campaigns, and similar duties while the rest of the party have their epaulets atop their shoulders. An embroidered bugle device is evident on the man with the early form of bicycle. He also has the 1/8-inch dark blue welt let into the seams of his sky blue trousers that was regulation for all infantry officers regardless of rank. The two seated officers who flank the white bearded post sutler, have on civilian coats without an indication of their rank. Except for their forage caps, it would be difficult to determine that they were in the army. The individual standing in front of the doorway has his sash over the shoulder which was the badge of office for the officer of the day. NA

Private William O. Tyler of the Seventh U.S. Cavalry wears a four-button sack coat made during the 1860s and an 1872-pattern forage cap, thereby indicating the mixture of new and old issue that continued in the period after the Civil War. In fact sack coats of Civil War manufacture continued to be used well into the 1870s. GM

Field grade officers continued to wear the double-breasted frock coat after the Civil War, as this cavalry major or lieutenant colonel does here. Instead of placing the crossed sabers of his branch on the front of the forage cap, this insignia is affixed to the crown as was often the case with enlisted insignia, but less so for officers. FSHM

the clothing distributed by the quartermaster into something presentable many company commanders compelled the "men to have their clothing altered and refitted, and even where they do not, a man's pride and comfort compel him to do so" at a charge of from eight to ten dollars.[18]

Because soldiers had no special allowance for tailoring, the cost for correcting such deficiencies had to "be made good out of their monthly pay" thereby raising many hackles.[19] This also led to questions as to why the government could not supply correctly fabricated clothing in the first place rather than requiring company tailors who were viewed by some as "pests of the service" that did as much harm as good when attempting to rectify the poor job done at the depots.[20]

Despite this and similar censure it seems that the quartermaster could provide for diverse measurements, if an 1866 request from Company A of the Engineers at West Point was any indication. Among the require-

ments were three pairs of trousers with a 40-inch waist, another three with a 44-inch girth, and one more for a man with a 45-inch waist complemented by a coat that required a 17 1/2-inch neck with a 42-inch chest. The man also needed a pair of sack coats and a greatcoat in the same proportions.[21] None of these dimensions were covered by the existing standard cuts, given that the largest waist size of the period was 36-inches, thereby requiring special tailoring in such cases. These special requirements were seen as exceptions, however, in that the individual soldiers in the case noted were of greater stature than the supposed average for whom the four uniform sizes were made.

In addition to reproach about improper sizes, the lack of standard shades of cloth came under fire. Reports drew attention to the fact that when assembled troops appeared in formation, they were anything but uniform.[22] Based upon inspections in the field, ". . . it was not uncom-

Captain George Wallace Graham of the Tenth Cavalry adopted a non-regulation black velvet roll collar, or turned over his standing collar to expose the lining on what probably is a waist length jacket for field wear, although his high white starched dress collar is not in keeping with campaigning. Graham's low-crowned forage cap has gold embroidered crossed sabers with a silver embroidered "10" to designate his regiment while his shoulder straps with yellow background displaying gold oak leaves indicate his branch of service and his brevet rank of major which he received on September 17, 1868. FAM

n this circa 1870 photo a lieutenant of Ordnance Department, holds his 1858-pattern hat and wears his crimson silk sash over the shoulder as was prescribed for the officer of the day. Gold epaulets continued to serve for dress wear through 1872. RBM

The special Engineer Corps buttons are evident on this captain's company grade frock coat as are his extra rich shoulder straps with dark blue or black backing in this circa 187 portrait. RBM

This image taken just prior to the 1872 uniform change depicts the cape that some officers obtained as a protection against inclement weather. The cape was dark blue cloth and closed with a black mohair loop. The 1/8-inch welts called for on officers' trousers are evident as well. RBM

Waist, side, and rear of uniform trousers of the pre-1872 era worn by Colonel Nelson A Miles with the proper 1/8-inch dark blue welt let into the seams. Some of the features of these trousers would be adopted officially in the mid-1870s, such as the belted back and "springbottom" cuffs, the former feature even being indicated in the quartermaster manual produced late in the Civil War. WC

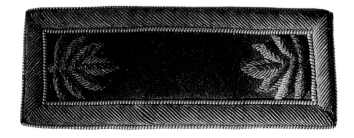

Typical early 1870s' shoulder strap of a lieutenant colonel of infantry. JML

Privately purchased slouch hats remained popular headgear for field duty, such as this example that belonged to Major Marcus A. Reno of the Seventh U.S. Cavalry. WC

This infantry private at Ft. Larned, Kansas has looped his hat on the right side as authorized for foot troops from 1868 through 1872. SFTC

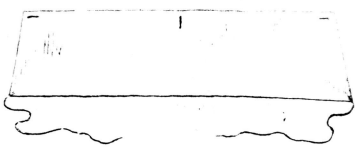

The 1868 army surgeon general's report likewise noted field expedients used by some U.S. troops to address cold weather, such as a detachable flap that could be added to the forage cap much like the one that had formed part of the 1839-pattern issue enlisted cap. NA

Some foreign clothing items seemed desirable for adoption in the United States according to the Woodhull Report. A "stiff dress hat" after the French and English shakos (**top**), a cloth fatigue hat (**middle**), and (**left**) seemed likely candidates for troops in the U.S. Army. NA

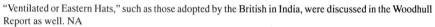

"Ventilated or Eastern Hats," such as those adopted by the British in India, were discussed in the Woodhull Report as well. NA

This example of a nineteenth century solar helmet with cork body covered in light cloth was of the type depicted in the Woodhull Report and purchased by some individuals in the United States following the lead of the English and other colonial powers. JG

LEFT & RIGHT: Another item reviewed by the surgeon general's study was a folding hat based on the short-lived, limited issue "Andrews" hat adopted at the end of the Mexican War. NA

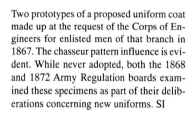

Two prototypes of a proposed uniform coat made up at the request of the Corps of Engineers for enlisted men of that branch in 1867. The chasseur pattern influence is evident. While never adopted, both the 1868 and 1872 Army Regulation boards examined these specimens as part of their deliberations concerning new uniforms. SI

mon to see five or six different shades of color in the coats, and also in the trousers of the same company."[23]

To this allegation Meigs replied:

> The Army trousers are generally of strong cloth, though not of standard color. That it was not possible to command in all the war contracts and purchases. The supply of trousers on hand is nearly consumed, and new ones are being made of good cloth, of which abundance of excellent quality is still in store from the supply delivered towards the close of the war, when the Department was providing for an army over a million strong.[24]

Meigs did not ignore the varying hues, however. A directive was sent to quartermasters instructing them to ship uniform items from the depots in packets that contained the same shades and which were marked on the outside of the packaging with that information.[25] Later, Meigs required that "only cloth fully up to standard is to be used in making garments . . . in quality, color and strength." He allowed new size 3 and 4 trousers to be made up for mounted and dismounted troops to provide for adequate supply.[26] He even directed: "the patterns by which garments are cut out" were to be reviewed by a skilled tailor to ascertain if improvements could be made. Likewise, while Meigs acknowledged "There is a good deal of complaint" he thought "that the patterns are good," but "perhaps to meet the common desire for room for remaking, it might be well to cut the trousers a little fuller."[27]

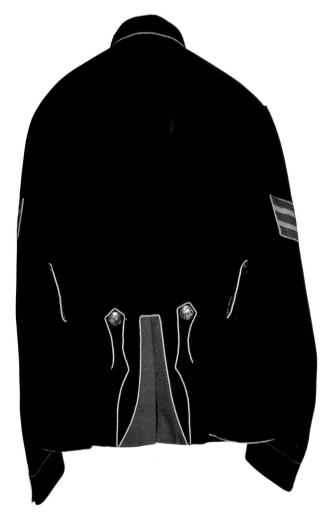

Rear of the proposed engineer enlisted coat that was prepared in 1867 but not adopted. SI

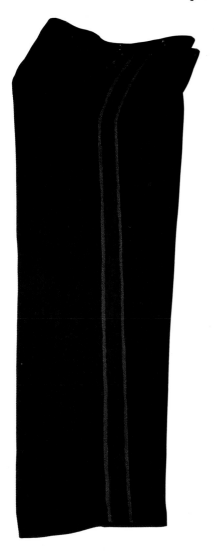

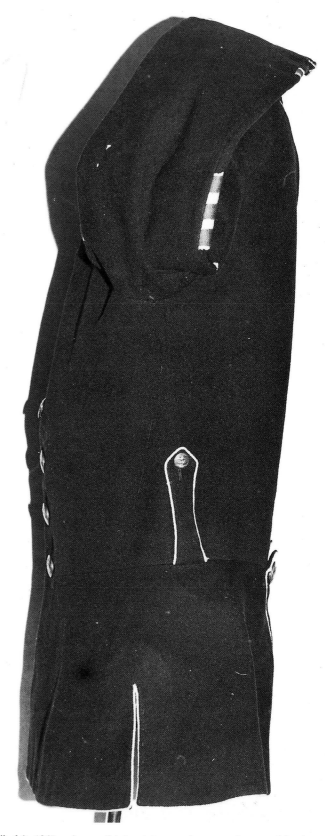

The trousers made up in 1867 for the proposed Engineer Corps enlisted uniform had scarlet leg stripes with white piping, a feature that would be adopted for non-commissioned engineer officers in 1872, although of facing material rather than of worsted as was the case of the prototype. SI

For a time, the department even allowed issuance of additional cloth to enlarge smaller sizes insofar as the larger ones had been exhausted in the system.[28] This practice continued for a few months. Soon manufacture of larger sizes resumed so that material ceased to be issued for such conversions.[29]

These actions were pragmatic and in keeping with Meigs continued staunch support of the existing quality and cut of the uniform, yet he demonstrated a certain flexibility, and made concessions where appropriate. While constantly countering criticism, Meigs acknowledged that some inferior items remained in the quartermaster's hands, but for the most part the "irregular and inferior materials" that were a byproduct of outfitting a million-man force, had been disposed of through sale or other means. The quartermaster general went on to accept, "The clamor for variety, for change, influences officers and soldiers, as well as the rest of mankind," but the "cry for a new uniform" seemed to be based on the recollections of older military men who looked back "to the days long before the war." This was a time when "clothing was made in small quantities for a small army" and as such seemed "much better than that made" afterwards. This perception, Meigs noted, ignored, "The improvement of American machines and manufacture" that had brought about better means of making clothes. All these views seemed to Meigs, "a good deal like our grandfathers' lament over the want of the fine peaches they had in their remote youth."[30]

Detail of the 1867 engineer enlisted prototype coat's construction around the sleeve and side. SI

Meigs also took pride in the fact that he could outfit the peacetime U.S. Army with clothing on hand without requesting new appropriations from Congress. He noted: "The Treasury cannot afford to throw away several millions of dollars worth of strong serviceable clothing...."[31]

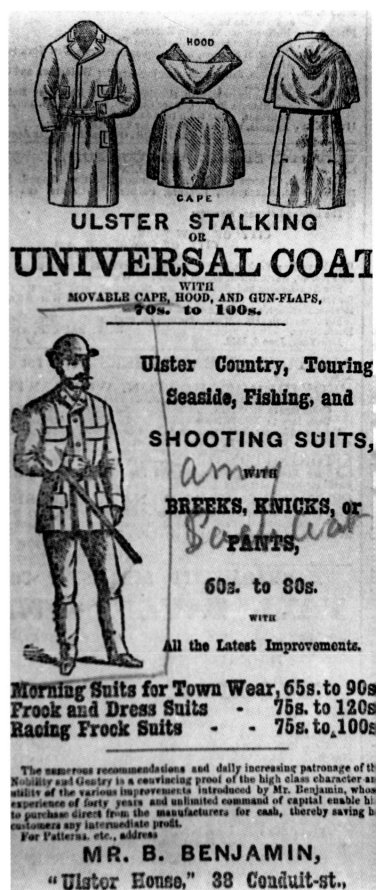

Captain Cyrus G. Dyer, Second Rhode Island Volunteer Infantry was one of many officers who donned a plaited blouse during the Civil War. These garments had been inspired by British civilian sports wear and adopted by some English militia units in the 1860s. MJM

Advertisment showing the "Ulster Stalking or Universal Coat," an English hunting garment of the 1860s that influenced the adoption of the plaited blouse for enlisted personnel as a field garment. NA

Two prototypes of the plaited blouse were made for the 1868 board and later examined by the 1872 board – one in cadet gray and one in drab or "butternut." White silk cord decorated the collar, plaits, yoke, and cuffs. SI

Rear of one of the prototypes made up for the 1868 board and reviewed by the 1872 board. SI

In 1872 not only were infantrymen authorized to hook their hat up on the right side, but also a new brace system was produced for issue to some infantry units, including a "Hoffman" swivel bayonet scabbard as seen here being worn by a private of the Fourth U.S. Infantry. The mixture of new equipment and old pattern uniforms, or vice versa, was not uncommon. MJM

In a similar defensive diatribe, this time to General of the Army William T. Sherman, Meigs asserted:

> The present uniform has continued with little change since the rebellion broke out. In the revolutions of fashion and tastes, it happens that many officers desire change in patterns, outfit and the color of dress of the Army. This is natural, but this Department must advise that the United States be not put to the cost of any change which will render useless the large stock of clothing, left in depôt at the close of the war, upon disbandment of an army of one million soldiers.[32]

Meigs reinforced his remarks with the contention that when clothing was sold as surplus it fetched only a fraction of its original cost being "exclusively of military material and make." Further, with from forty-five to sixty million dollars of clothing and material on hand it seemed inconceivable to Meigs that a change in pattern could be contemplated. In his eyes economy required the use of the old uniform until the supply is exhausted." Here Meigs referred to the remaining stocks of nearly 300,000 mounted jackets that were in storage as of 1866, with an even greater number of trousers on hand, along with more than a million sack coats.[33]

A plaited "Swiss" blouse was one of several concepts espoused by an 1868 surgeon general's study, sometimes referred to as the Woodhull Report. NA

Light artillery units were given a cap with scarlet cords and horsetail plumes. These bandsmen of the Third Artillery at the Presidio of San Francisco, around 1866, have adopted the standard horse artillery dress uniform for their parade outfit, with the exception of the bandmaster (standing to the left front) who has a bearskin and specially made non-regulation chevrons. The officer in the frock coat looking over the bandmaster's shoulder probably is the regimental adjutant in his company grade uniform. GGNRA

Charles Hendy (first row center) was the hospital steward at Ft. McPherson, Nebraska, in 1873. He appears in the nine-button plaited blouse adopted the previous year for enlisted men as a general garrison, fatigue, and field garment. The buttons are the type worn by staff officers, including surgeons. The collar, cuffs, and front yoke of the coat were to be piped in branch colors, in Hendy's case emerald green for hospital stewards. He has the half chevrons made of green facing material with caduceus embroidered in yellow silk thread. The edges also were to be piped in yellow. The emerald green leg stripes were to be 1 1/4-inches wide. His 1872-pattern forage cap bears a gilt wreath with silver "US" as another indication of his position as a hospital steward. Hendy is flanked by four cavalry privates in their 1872-pattern dress uniforms. UPM

The enlisted 1872-pattern cavalry dress helmet had yellow cords and a yellow horsetail plume, while those for light artillerymen were to have scarlet and signalmen orange cords and plumes respectively. Gordon Chappell Photograph.

Side buttons for the 1872-pattern helmet were to display crossed sabers for cavalry troopers and signalmen and crossed cannon for light artillerymen. LBNB

Only when these sizeable numbers of clothing articles were expended could something new be considered, although even then Meigs doubted that a majority really desired to "throw aside the uniform in which officers & men so well and gloriously served and saved their country .. ," motives that Meigs thought outweighed "changing tastes." Meigs reinforced this belief suggesting that the old uniform "was good enough to make campaigns in, and it ought to be good enough for the more inactive duties of the present military state of the country."[34]

Another officer echoed the position held by Meigs and other orthodox believers. This writer concluded, "better the old faded uniform, whose worn appearance is of itself an evidence of your services and respectability" than new frills.[35] With this argument in place, the half dozen years after the Civil War's end saw little revision from the regulations adopted in 1861.

Many opposed continuation of old patterns though. Nowhere was dissatisfaction displayed in more open terms than in the pages of the *Army and Navy Journal*, the semi-official voice for mid-nineteenth-century American military men.[36] Letter after letter to the editor appeared in the publication venting dissatisfaction with U.S. Army attire. Denunciation of the regulation garb which remained on hand from the Civil War was widespread.

Various approaches were advanced to address the matter. These ranged from the simple to the complex. For instance, one advocate called for the adoption of a universal device to be displayed on the headgear of all officers of the regular army. This was to be, "a <u>Castle</u> of gold one and one half inches long and one and a quarter in height, the letters U.S. in

Rear view of William Williams' 1872-pattern dress helmet. Williams was a trooper in the Seventh Cavalry and survived the ill-fated Little Bighorn engagement. Gordon Chappell Photograph. LBNB

nterior with contractor's label of Sergeant Williams' 1872-pattern cavalry helmet. Gor-
on Chappell Photograph. LBNB

old English of silver on centre tower. . . ." From this basic design small silver chains were to hang down from which crossed sabers, cannon, and other specific unit emblems were to be suspended.[37]

Another man expressed his abhorrence to troops being permitted "to wear every imaginable style and color of hat or cap that he may be possessed of."[38] Other officers much preferred the traditional staff officer's chapeau as a replacement for dress wear.[39]

Another advocate waxed eloquent over the merits of the metal helmets worn by Cromwell's roundhead cavalry in England during the seventeenth century, reflecting the fine "effect of a regiment of cavalry equipped like the Ironsides, with the addition of an eagle, in dark metal, surmounting a steel cap.[40] He went on to lavish praise on the helmet of the Czar's army that he though "exceedingly beautiful and serviceable" as was that of the Austrian dragoons which supposedly was "well ventilated, sword-proof, and graceful, and not expensive," in contrast to the "ugly and heavy" model won by the Kaiser's forces.[41]

Two more letters to the editor called for Russian-style helmets for cavalry and pasteboard-stiffened caps with pompons.[42] One of these two writers conceded it was "impossible, in these utilitarian days, to dream of the revival of 'pomp and circumstance of glorious war' which made Frederick's and Napoleon's armies spectacles to admire," but he still felt "elbow grease, discipline, soap, and rotten-stone will achieve miracles" when it came to maintaining a smart appearance. He proposed:

> Give a soldier a simple but striking uniform, and it will elevate him in his own esteem. Honest pride is a quickener of manly sentiment. But what we want most is a *corps d'elite*, organized on the principle of Napoleon's 'Old Guard,' with a distinctive uniform, the badge of that merit which served as an initiatory passage into its ranks.[43]

One more self-appointed fashion expert rejected the frock-coat finding it, "unsightly and the reverse of neat and trim. . . ." Additionally he thought it interfered with the use of the sword and sash. Betraying class consciousness, the man wanted to replace the frock because at a distance of even "a couple of hundred yards" it became difficult to distinguish enlisted personnel from their officers.[44] In conclusion, he believed when fine feathers seemed in order a swallow-tailed coat was the proper thing for those holding commissions because he contended, "the object of full dress is *display, not service*."[45]

For others, retaining the old patterns seemed adequate so long as the material and cut was upgraded.[46] Simplicity had appeal as well, this faction decrying any attempt to introduce more ornamentation.[47]

Taking a complementary approach, concern was expressed over the "alarming degree of disease and mortality" attributed to the "constricting coats and badly distributed weights." What was needed was a halt to "the heresy that the use of clothing is to hold a soldier in place." It was time for Americans forces to abandon "the rigidity of the British and Prussian types, so long regarded the necessary mode in the military world."[48]

Photograph showing the front view of the official pattern for the dress helmet adopted in 1872 for officers of light artillery and for cavalry officers. The plume was to be scarlet for artillery and yellow for cavalry. The socket that held the plume has been removed from this photograph. Upon careful examination it can be seen that the "helmet plate" was rendered in paper for this official photograph taken for the Quartermaster Department, perhaps because no specimen of the brass or gilt plate was available. NA

Side view of the official pattern of the 1872 officer's helmet, in this case for light artillery because of the crossed cannon devices on the side buttons. The side buttons also have horizontal lines instead of stippling usually found on enlisted helmets. Also, the gold cords festooned to the front and back of the helmet are separate from the breast cord, another difference from enlisted helmets. The tassel is separate here as well, an uncommon feature in most surviving examples. Moreover, the cords are hung from scroll and rings found on enlisted helmets rather than the scroll and hook more commonly used on officers' models. NA

Expanding on this line of thinking that eschewed European models for American ones, and took the additional tack of focusing on scientific and medical rationales when it came to the subject of clothing, a report issued by the U.S. Army's surgeon general offered new perspectives and directions that previously had been little considered in the United States. Based on the opinions and observations of 168 officers this document bespoke of a general complaint about the quality of the uniform. These comments appeared:

> . . .to vary in character at different posts, but each is condemned by some one or another, and the more important by all. Equally prominent is the shameful carelessness in the cut and make. . . . All who allude to it regard it as a serious hygienic defect that the men cannot be reasonably comfortable until the clothing provided by the government is remade or substituted by other at personal expense (an often great) expense. . . . The men become dissatisfied, consider they are neglected, and the discipline and morale of the army are materially impaired.[49]

Besides problems with the clothing itself, the same report indicated the role played by perceptions about the uniform. Because so many veterans took some or all of their issue home after being discharged from the Union Army the men who remained in service disliked the fact: "laborers in the streets and hackmen on their boxes" were clothed in old uniforms. This destroyed "the caste feeling in the soldiery which is essential to the highest development of martial qualities. . . .[50]

Detail of First Lieutenant William W. Cooke, Seventh U.S. Cavalry's 1872-pattern dress helmet showing the scroll and hook most commonly found on officers' helmet to keep the gold cord in place. Note the screen ventilator that also forms part of officers' helmet. CSPM

Captain Gunther Sebastian, like many officers of his time commanded a troop of cavalry while in his advanced years. Promotion was slow for most officers serving in the years afte[r]
the Civil War. Sebastian wears the company grade uniform prescribed for dress purposes in 1872 including the top-heavy helmet with steep rear visor. The plume is yellow horseha[ir]
and the cords on the helmet and his chest are of metallic gold thread. The gilt eagle device on the front of the helmet bears a silver number "4" to indicate Sebastian's regiment, as d[o]
his shoulder knots. The saber seems to be an enlisted model of the pattern adopted in the late 1850s. KSHS

This Fifth U.S. Cavalry officer's 1872-pattern helmet with the less drastic front and rear visors was one of the variations available for purchase by officers from military suppliers, in this case the New York firm of Baker and McKenney. HO

Lieutenant Colonel George Custer's 1872-pattern helmet. SI

Front and side view of an 1872-pattern infantry enlisted cap. The piece of headgear somewhat resembled the "stiff cap" discussed in the Woodhull Report. Gordon Chappell Photograph.

Moreover, the government's policy to transfer uniform items to the Freedmen's Bureau and to sell surplus garments on the open market raised even more objections. In a statement fraught with racial overtones a further submission to the *Army and Navy Journal* claimed, "almost every idle, dirty, individual both black and white . . . is dressed either partially or totally in soldier's garb," leaving a blue mix as the best option remaining in the author's opinion.[51]

Some feared that once men had lost their sense of identity with the uniform they would weaken in "discipline, tune, and morale."[52] This letter spoke for many who felt the uniform no longer distinguished the military from the civilian sector thereby defeating a primary function of specialized martial array. Coupled with the allegation that items disposed of from quartermaster supplies were charged at one-fourth the price to dealers as the value assigned to the same articles issued to soldiers, the matter of surplus stock sales was a volatile one.[53]

Meigs' department could respond that the cost of clothing the soldier had dropped from $42.86 in 1860 to $36.20 in 1868.[54] This fact and the policy of the government to charge soldiers the "average actual cost" for items offered arguments to quiet debate on surplus sales. Further, such clothing sales were made from stocks that "would not be issued for several years" as a means of reducing the burden of storage at depots and "partly from the apprehension that if kept till needed for issue, it [the clothing] would or might deteriorate." This action brought considerable money to the national coffers "at a time of difficulty" for the treasury.[55]

As such, Meigs claimed only the inferior items were sold, and in turn the men availed themselves of buying uniform items from the post trader at a lower rate than the quartermaster costs, thereby achieving savings in this way. Neither poor quality or high prices were the real issue to Meigs, then, who retorted:

Typical contractor's label in the top interior of an 1872-pattern enlisted cap. AHS

1872-pattern enlisted heavy artillery cap. SI

I do not believe that the clothing is generally of bad quality. I have worn much of it myself – do wear it – whenever I am placed in circumstances of living similar to those of the troops. I find that not only men, but officers on the frontier wear many government articles, such as trousers, shoes, shirts, and drawers, as the cheapest and most desirable, most serviceable suitable clothing, obtainable.[56]

Similarly, Meigs repeated, "in each and every case" clothing issued to troops was "made from the best stock at the time on hand." Because there was more than ample quantities in storage, the department followed this practice rather than have these items be subject to "the risk of loss from fire, or damage while in store. . . ."[57]

Further, the department sought ways to preserve those items in storage by taking precautions against fire and experimenting with moth proofing processes. This latter effort included sending 10,000 yards of kersey trouser cloth of standard color to a contractor to be subjected to a process to prevent moth damage.[58] The same formula also was to add a degree of waterproofing, although this seemed to be a less successful application judging from a field test conducted in 1872. The conclusion was that not only did the chemical treatment make little if any differ-

ence in shedding water, but also it seemed to discolor or darken the material to which it was applied, at least in those instances where sky-blue kersey was concerned.[59]

Another course of action was taken with items deemed inferior and not worthy of such measures to protect them. These were disposed of, along with certain stocks that were excess for other reasons, such as Zouave uniforms or Veteran Reserve Corps uniforms, and thus could be sold because there was "no further demand for this kind of clothing."[60] There had been one exception to this disposal plan in that some Veteran Reserve trousers and jackets were held back to be dyed dark blue to be issued to "prisoners whose clothing allowance" had been "cut off by sentence of court martial, or as deserters awaiting trial, or convicts who were not entitled in the first instance to clothing."[61]

With many clothing items being sold or converted perhaps some officials in the Quartermaster Department became retrospective and sought to preserve the fruits of their labor from the Civil War and earlier. The result was the establishment of "a museum at Schuylkill Arsenal Philadelphia in which" the department "proposed to exhibit the various styles of uniforms worn by the Army of the United States, since the foundation of the government."[62]

1872-pattern heavy artillery sergeant major's coat. The regimental numerals were supposed to be affixed on either side of the collar. SI

1872-pattern principal musician of heavy artillery coat. Regimental numerals in stamped sheet brass were called for by regulations to be affixed to either side of the collar. SI

Regardless of having to fabricate some older items, the first specimens set aside for this museum would be the envy of any modern collector. The inventory included dozens of French-made pieces from a sharpshooter's mounted overcoat to hussar and Imperial Guard jackets, coats, and the like.[63] As time passed, the inventory grew, and began to include pattern pieces of U.S. Army regulation uniforms, as well as some reproductions of uniforms that had been used in the past but no longer were available.

For this reason a request went out to the superintendent of the U.S. Military Academy at West Point for the loan of old or worn cadet uniforms so that a pattern could be produced and specimens (reproductions) made for use in the museum.[64] This practice evidently was not unusual. For instance, in "Clothing For Soldiers," the *Philadelphia Inquirer* of January 7, 1888, provided a brief sketch of the museum as it had developed over two decades. According to the article, neglect had reduced many of the items to a deteriorated state. As such, replacements were fabricated to represent some of the earlier pieces, these items possibly being the ones exhibited as part of the Smithsonian Institution's bicentennial exhibit recreating the Philadelphia centennial.

Another source of information about uniforms of the era came about by accident. The Quartermaster Department arranged for photographs of enlisted uniforms to be taken. Evidently these were to serve as guides for production of clothing, although it is not clear when the thirty-eight glass plate images were made.[65] It is known that copies were available

Colonel Nelson A. Miles, Fifth U.S. Infantry, 1872-pattern cap with cock feathers removed to show insignia. The hunting horn was regulation for infantry officers, from 1872 to 1875. WC

Infantry Second Lieutenant R.E. Thompson has obtained the new double-breasted dress coat with seven buttons in each row that was adopted in 1872 for company grade officers (second lieutenants through captains). The belt is gold lace with four horizontal silk stripes in blue. The gold knots have blue centers with the regimental numeral in silver and rank devices of the same type as found on the shoulder straps (plain for second lieutenants, a silver bar for first lieutenants, two silver bars for captains, a gold oak leaf for majors, silver oak leaf for lieutenant colonels, and a spread eagle for colonels. Trouser stripes were 1 1/2-inches wide and in dark blue for infantry officers. He also wears the 1872-dress cap. USAMHI

This side view of an infantry officer's dress cap is of the pattern adopted in 1872 and which remained in service until 1881. Flat gold cord trimmed the cap which had a gold embroidered hunting horn device on the front (replaced by crossed rifles in 1875) that bore the regimental numeral in silver in the center. White cocks' feathers rising five inches from the top of the cap were held in place by a gilt sheet brass ball and socket for infantry officers and scarlet feathers were assigned to heavy artillery officers who also had gold embroidered crossed cannons in lieu of the hunting horn. NA

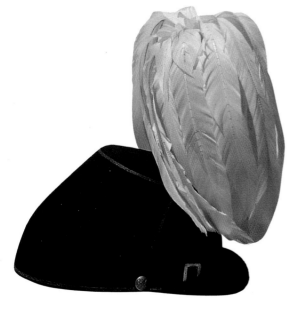

Side view of Colonel Miles' 1872-pattern cap with cock feathers in place. WC

Interior of Colonel Miles' 1872-pattern officer's dress cap. WC

One of several types of ventilators used with the 1872-pattern officer's dress cap, in this case the "Brasher" type that would be used primarily on the 1876-pattern campaign hat. JG

after the Civil War for distribution to various depots and at least one military supplier, Horstmann of Philadelphia. Some sets of these prints were hand-tinted to depict the color of facings prior to the decision to discontinue producing the images at the beginning of 1867.[66]

Efforts to save historical examples of uniforms bespoke of a certain conservative element in the Quartermaster Department that resisted change of almost any sort. This included denying requests for issuing overalls to infantrymen and white Berlin gloves to enlisted personnel for dress wear.[67] A patent ventilator for hats and caps was proposed and rejected too.[68] This same fate befell a new shirt, despite testimonials that it was a good product as the sample sent for inspection confirmed. Despite this, the quartermaster general's response was simple and typi-

cal: "There is now . . . a very large stock of flannel shirts in store – sufficient for several years."[69]

This is not to say that everything remained as it was during the height of the Civil War. One minor experiment resulted from replacement of sewn on buttons with patented shank lock buttons that were held in place by a rivet. After a brief trial, however, these buttons were determined not be an improvement over old types or less expensive.[70]

Contrary to this experiment, other concessions were made, usually as a result of some changes in rank structure or tactics during this period. In the former instance Grant's promotion to general in 1866 necessitated a new four star shoulder strap and epaulet, and a new button pattern on his frock coat. This was double-breasted as for all generals,

1872-pattern heavy artillery officer's dress cap with cock feathers removed to show the Second U.S. Artillery insignia. RB

Second Lieutenant Daniel M. Taylor, served with the First U.S. Artillery until 1874. He wears the 1872-pattern company grade dress for heavy artillery officers. The cock feathers, centers of the knots, the three horizontal stripes on the company grade gold lace sword belt, and 1 1/2-inch trouser stripes all were to be scarlet. RBM

Front of 1872-pattern heavy artillery officer's cap with cock feathers in place. JG

Detail of typical "tulip" or socket that held the cock feathers on the 1872-pattern officer's cap in place. JG

but in this case had twelve staff officers buttons in each row, grouped in fours. In turn, Sherman became lieutenant general with three stars (Grant's old device) and a coat that was the same as a major general (double-breasted with nine buttons in each row placed in groups of three).[71] None of this affected the army as a whole, however, in that only officers had to purchase these new items.

At less lofty levels, two new non-commissioned ranks were created, lasting but a brief period through 1870. These required new chevrons. The first was for company quartermaster sergeants who would have worsted (although silk examples also exist) stripes in the color of their respective branch with three chevrons pointing downward and a tie of a single bar above. The same order clarified that the regimental quartermaster sergeant would have chevrons with three ties bars above, all to be made of silk.[72] Moreover, during spring 1867, silk regimental commissary sergeants' chevrons were added for infantry, artillery, and cavalry having three stripes pointing down and an angular tie or vertex pointing up (a distorted mirror image).[73] The third rank was for a regimental hospital steward, who was to have the same chevrons as sergeants of their respective unit with the addition of caduceus device that was issued separately embroidered in dark blue silk on an oval of the

This sealskin cap was bought by Colonel Nelson A. Miles as a means of protection against cold climates, particularly on campaign. Army issue did not adequately address harsh winter conditions until many years after the Civil War, thereby necessitating the private purchase of foul weather gear such as this. WC

George Custer posed for the camera in his garb for a hunting expedition with Russian royalty in 1872. He donned a buckskin suit and fur cap to look the part of a frontiersman, as much as for the practical aspects of this type of outfit. RBM

Private Howard Weaver, Troop A, Seventh Cavalry, wears the 1872-pattern campaign hat. He also has on the 1872-pattern plaited blouse, in this case with yellow cord for cavalry. GM

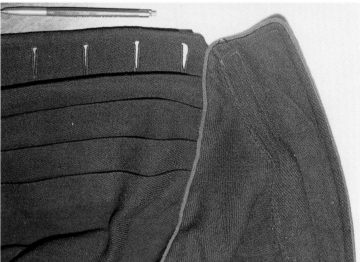

1872-pattern infantry enlisted plaited blouse as adopted. The cord was worsted rather than the silk on the 1868 prototypes. Other differences from the prototypes of the 1868 board included the elimination of cording along the plaits. Sky-blue, as seen here, was for infantry. SI

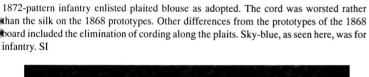

Clockwise from top right, and following two pages: Detail of the yoke, collar, cuff, size label, front, and rear of the 1872-pattern enlisted plaited blouse, in this case for artillery as indicated by the scarlet cord. The cord for other branches was sky-blue (infantry); yellow (cavalry), orange (signalmen), crimson (ordnance), cadet gray for commisary sergeants, and emerald green (hospital stewards). One small button regularly was sewn at the cuff, but photographs also indicate three buttons on each cuff for some blouses. Kurt Cox Photographs. SI

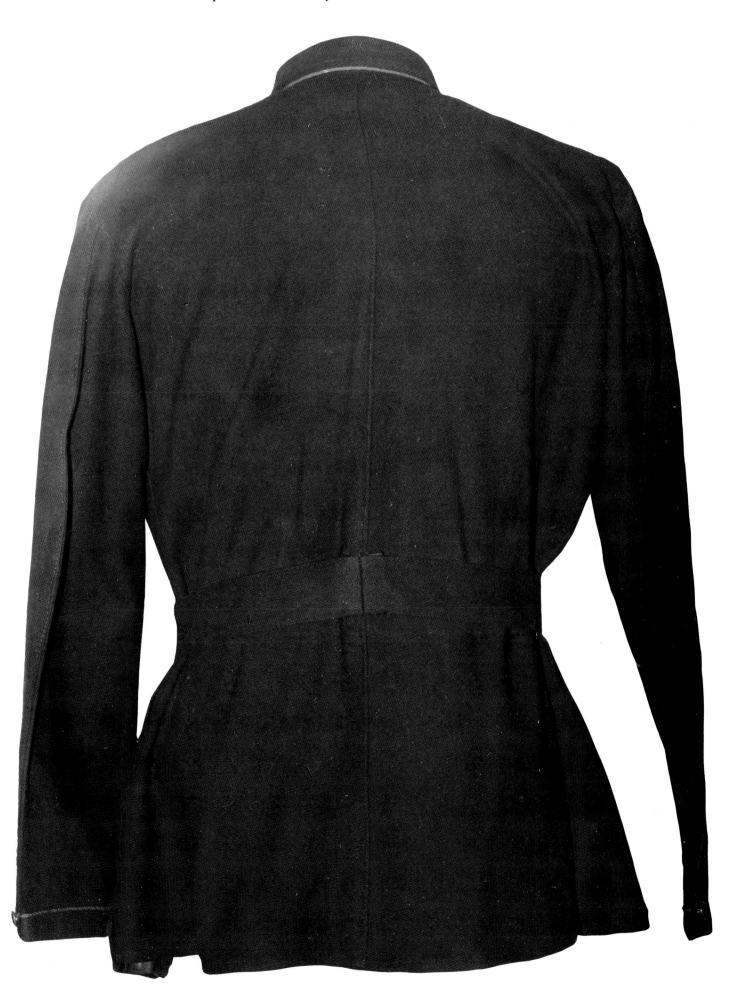

branch color that was worn centered above the chevrons.[74] These three innovations, however, soon were abolished by General Orders No. 92, AGO, July 22, 1870.

Another matter having to do with insignia stemmed from a resolution by the United States Congress that permitted "officers and soldiers to wear the badge of the corps in which they served during the rebellion."[75] This extended to regular army, volunteer, and militia personnel who had been honorably discharged or continued to serve for wear "on occasions of ceremony."

Probably a number of individuals welcomed the ability to display their wartime affiliation. Conversely many sought to discard one of the issue items remaining from the war, the leather neckstock.[76] The "dog collar" regularly was disregarded in many cases, although it constituted a part of the regulation dress.[77] One soldier from the Forty-fifth Infantry Regiment even submitted a proposed replacement for consideration, but was told that while his design was "a decided improvement on the present uniform stock" it seemed that a worsted stock or cravat was being contemplated.[78] This was not be the case. Finally General Orders No. 37, AGO, April 4, 1871, discontinued these uncomfortable accessories that supposedly kept the wearer in a proper soldierly stance. The United States Marine Corps, however, retained them through the mid-1870s as part of the tradition that still can be found in the nickname "leatherneck."

A move to do away with brass shoulder scales, accessories that harkened back to the days of armor, failed to meet with the same resolution. Nonetheless, several units gradually abandoned them without permission.[79]

So, too, did some companies and individuals cease wearing the 1858-pattern hat albeit without approval from on high.[80] One fellow dubbed it an "unsightly abortion" that would be sent "spinning across the parade to the intense disgust of the wearer" by even a slight gust of wind. He went on to call it a "sombrero feo" (ugly hat).[81] Another writer thought the hat was "unwieldy, ill-shaped, and a perpetual nuisance to the wearer, because it is either knocked off, blown off, or out of gear in some way." Further, he condemned it as "bereft of beauty." Another avowed it was "the most ugly, uncomfortable, and unsoldierly covering that a malignant spirit could have devised for the heads of suffering humanity."[82] A third commentator indicated that in his cavalry regiment it "was tabooed even for full dress."[83]

Yet other units wore it, as indicated by the request to have the brim looped up on the right side for both mounted and dismounted troops alike rather than on opposite sides depending on whether the wearer was a cavalryman or a foot soldier, as had been the previous requirement. The change was approved because of the "carry arms" and "right shoulder" arms movements for infantrymen tended to displace the hat when the musket moved passed it for these evolutions.[84]

In this 1873 candid photograph taken at Ft. McPherson, Nebraska, Hospital Steward Charles Hendy (**left**) and a Private Green, who was detailed to assist in hospital, wear the 1872-pattern plaited blouse. Hendy's blouse is piped in emerald green with the emerald green half chevrons worn on the sleeves to indicate his specialty as an enlisted medical man. He also has emerald green trouser stripes made of facing material, which according to the 1872 regulations were to be of 1 1/4-inch. Private Green's blouse probably is trimmed in yellow for cavalry, that branch constituting the main garrison of the post. Also note Green has three buttons on the cuffs of his blouse rather than one as was the pattern. UPM

This slight alteration in regulations may have been ample for some commanders, but in the case of Brigadier General C.C. Augur, men serving under him in the Department of the Platte were allowed to dispense with the hat all together, even for dress occasions. Instead they would wear the forage cap.[85]

There were those, however, who would have disliked Augur's solution. The tall crowned enlisted forage cap was not a thing of beauty in the eyes of many men as a ditty that might have been sung to the tune of *The Star Spangled Banner* (not at the time the national anthem) so indicated. Some of the verses ran:

> O, say have you seen the unique forage cap
> that good Uncle Sam on his Army doth clap?
> Some turn up its visor, and some turn it down,
> still it gives each poor wearer the air of a clown.
> It looks like a scarecrow – good reason why
> the enemy saw it, took fright and did fly.
> But the flag of our Union in triumph shall wave,
> when each cap and contractor shall lie in one grave.[86]

The dissatisfaction with the forage cap's design prompted some officers and enlisted men to procure examples with lower crowns, a style referred to as the chasseur pattern.[87] Other deviations from regulations related to the forage cap had to do with insignia. Officers were to wear their branch or corps device with the regimental numeral, all in embroidery or simulated embroidery, while enlisted men were to display only the brass company letter.[88] In certain instances soldiers added their branch device from the 1858-pattern hat, and in at least one situation troops at a post in Wyoming Territory were told to place their regimental numeral on the crown of their cap and the company letter below. The hunting horns of infantrymen that evidently had been used by many, if not all of the men previously, were to be removed.[89]

Another reference to cap insignia came from San Francisco, where the adjutant of the Second Artillery asked for lyre and harp devices for the regimental band, a request that was denied by the Quartermaster Department as being outside the authorized items of issue.[90] Another query to have twenty-four light artillery caps sent to the Fourth Artillery band at Fort McHenry likewise was turned down, this time because regulations allowed this type of headgear for mounted artillerymen only.[91] When other non-artillery units made similar requisitions for light artillery caps, they also were refused.[92]

While these applications for the artillery cap for bandsmen was denied, a similar type of headgear was allowed for the musicians at the U.S. Military Academy. In fact, in 1867 a prototype uniform of fine white cloth (later to be replaced by linen duck) was made up for the West Point band, with the cost of manufacture and materials being provided by the quartermaster, a practice that deviated from the norm in that funds required to make special purchases for a band usually were borne by the officers and men of the regiment they served.[93] This atypical allowance for the Academy's band was granted because that organization was the only one officially recognized by statute, all other bands of the era existing on a sort of ad hoc status.[94]

Not only bandsmen were regularly outfitted with non-government funds. Winter clothing, at least for extreme cold, was not available through the quartermaster, with the exception for a brief period when woolen mittens were distributed until stocks obtained during the Civil War ran out.[95] For this reason Meigs suggested that troops should obtain protective garb such as wool lined buckskin mittens, buffalo overcoats and overshoes through purchase from the company fund – a small cash account generated by the soldiers themselves from various sources of revenue. This had been the modus operandi "before the war," and because "no authority existed to purchase and issue" this type of gear, it seemed to make sense to continue the practice, or order and issue the special clothing at cost to the enlisted men.[96]

The surgeon general's office took a different approach. Its officers pointed out the need for "those posts where the cold is represented by twenty-five degrees below zero, and lower, in the winter" to be supplied with garments such as buffalo robes that would entirely "envelop the wearers" a convention that was followed "in many places" at cost to the individual, rather than "by the supreme authority" of the government which seemed a more suitable course.[97]

Another 1868 advocate of special gear suggested double-breasted buffalo overcoats, fur-lined buffalo boots or shoes, fur caps, and mittens. He also felt that the army should make these items available to the troops much as certain European powers did for the health and comfort of the men.[98]

Before the government responded to these suggestions, however, the soldier had to make his own arrangements to deal with Jack Frost. During the 1868 winter campaign, some Seventh Cavalry troopers used blankets to line the tails of their overcoats, and even added homemade leggings over boot tops.[99] During the same campaign officers of the regiment, during the "long weary hours of terrible cold and comfortless" buttoned "their huge overcoats closely about them" including their cavalry capes as they awaited for the dawn attack on the Washita.[100]

Field duty was not the only time such requirements came about, as indicated by one typical garrison where the men resorted to a sort of pseudo-havelock to cut the chilling winds that buffeted the head and face. This was a piece of cloth with three button holes to attach it to the rear of the forage cap, and a drawstring at the front bottom to close the appendage as protection for the ears and part of the face, not unlike the flap that had been affixed to some of the 1839-pattern forage caps years earlier.[101]

Using burlap sacks wrapped around issue shoes was another form of improvisation that came about to rectify the lack of government issue for some men stationed along the Bozeman Trail in 1866-67.[102] In other instances men at Fort Buford, Dakota Territory bought bearskin or buffalo coats from sources at hand.[103]

The surgeon at that post discovered another means to provide what Uncle Sam did not. He received a buffalo robe whenever he rendered his professional services to local trappers or Indians. These could be converted into many items of winter dress as he recalled:

> buffalo overshoes – buffalo hide with the hair on, making a shoe about two inches thick all around, thus adding four inches in length and four in breadth to my natural foot; gloves reaching nearly to my shoulders, woolen, and line with deerskin, a shaggy buffalo overcoat, and bearskin leggins [sic]. My cap was made from beaver's skin and is the respectable feature of my outlandish outfit.[104]

Trumpeter Aloys Bohner, Company D, Seventh Cavalry wears the 1872-pattern cavalry trumpeter's uniform with its distinctive yellow "herringbone" trim on the chest that flanks each of the nine buttons of the coat. The gauntlets are privately purchased or a photographer's prop because these accessories were not issued to cavalrymen until 1884. Bohner, who was born in Germany, did not die at the Little Big Horn as many of his comrades would. He remained in the regiment until his discharge in 1879, at which time he was serving the chief musician of the Seventh's band. RBM

On the 1872-pattern cavalry coat the regimental number was to be indicated by stamped sheet brass numerals on each side of the collar. One of the numerals is missing on this coat that was worn by William Williams. Seventh U.S. Cavalry. LBNB

LEFT: Cavalry bandsmen could wear the same uniform as the trumpeters assigned to troops, such as the 1872-pattern coat. Additionally, in 1873, a chevron was authorized for the regiment's chief trumpeter for the first time, being a hunting horn with an arc above and three stripes below in facing cloth, as seen here. As of 1872, chevrons were to made of facing material rather than worsted or silk tape, and had the stripes constructed by means of silk thread chain-stitching. SI

At first the Quartermaster Department indicated the improbability of its procuring "wearing apparel of furs and skins for the use of troops stationed in the colder latitudes."[105] Nevertheless, this stance shifted over time as provisions eventually were made to address the colder climates. This included an 1867 recommendation that 500 buffalo overcoats and 3,000 pairs of overshoes of the same material be procured for the Department of Dakota, with ten coats being allowed for each post in that command.[106] Similarly the acquisition of 2,000 pairs of buffalo overshoes "for issue only in the higher latitudes, where from the severity of the climate they may be absolutely necessary" was sanctioned.[107] This restrictive control continued when in 1868 additional instructions underscored the buffalo overshoes were "not intended for regular issue but . . . only to be provided in cases of emergency." Further, they were not to be "purchased, unless in the opinion of the Departmental Commander, the necessities of the service require them."[108] One such allowance was for active "campaign against Indians," thereby permitting troops at Fort Hays, Kansas to have buffalo overshoes.[109] Mail carriers at Fort Sully, Minnesota, and elsewhere also had the luxury of receiving buffalo overcoats providing the cost was under $10 to make each coat. These would remain government property and not be charged to the soldier unless lost or damaged.[110] Likewise, "those subjected to long continued exposure to the severity of the weather," including express riders and sentinels, temporarily could draw a buffalo coat.[111]

By 1871, the quartermaster general finally obtained funds to provide overshoes and woolen mittens (two pairs annually), but these were to be charged at cost to the men, along with buffalo overcoats, in those circumstances where it could be demonstrated by departmental commanders that these expensive garments were justified. When authorized, these coats remained government property, being issued for the season, then returned them to the local quartermaster thereafter for storage and preservation.[112] The company fund still was to be the source of payment for overshoes, while it was recommended that Congress authorize funds to buy a buffalo overcoat in the first and third year of each soldier's enlistment for those men posted to the Department of Dakota along with all garrison from 42 degrees latitude and above.[113]

During the same year (1871) the use of surplus blankets as linings for mounted overcoats began, a practice that was continued briefly until gray shirting flannel was provided as a substitute.[114] This latter fabric soon was found of insufficient weight. As such new blankets from existing stocks were selected as linings thereafter.[115]

If dealing with the bone-chilling Northern Plains were not enough to tax the quartermaster, the opposite extremes of heat presented another puzzlement. The surgeon general noted that the 1858-pattern hat and the forage cap were found objectionable by many officers, "a light straw hat, during the warm weather, a period that varies with locality," being deemed optimum as a "defense against the direct rays of the sun." Such a hat had been granted to the Fort Monroe garrison prior to the Civil War, and thereafter use of straw hats continued informally out "of necessity of substituting *something* for the uniform [hat or cap], its accessibility, and its low cost."[116]

An unexplained variant of 1872-pattern enlisted collar using worsted cord of the type that ornamented the plaited blouse in lieu of facing material for piping. The numeral is for the Ninth U.S. Cavalry, one of two regiments authorized in 1866 to be manned by black enlisted troopers. RBM

Bands continued to have latitude in their uniform based on the authorization of the regiment's colonel to depart from regulations. Evidently the Second U.S. Cavalry's commanding officer took advantage of this prerogative. JG

Another answer to this problem, according to the surgeon general's office, was: "either a kepi or casque or light brimmed hat, essentially the style of a Malay hat. To be made of some stiff, light material with pearl-colored cover and an air-space of half an inch between the ring and the head."[117] Such a headpiece was not adopted officially, however, for more than a decade.

The same statement was true of yet a second recommendation found in the 1868 report. This was "A light-colored, brimmed felt hat," a piece of headgear generally recommended by those who responded to the survey. It could be either as a simple felt slouch hat, "or looped up on the side for dress." The pattern proposed was the Andrews hat made in the Mexican War and issued for a short period, in the early 1850s, to the Second Dragoons. Thus, "a gray, light felt hat," in the estimation of the report, was "without a doubt, the most serviceable" solution to the problem of dealing with heat as far as the head was concerned.[118]

For the remainder of the uniform as far as the surgeon general was concerned, a "closely milled, light woolen cloth" proved just the thing for uniforms year round.[119] The quartermaster general shared this opinion, advocating absorbent wool over cotton clothing for dealing with the hat.[120] In fact, wool was the universal answer for all climates in Meigs' eyes. He even questioned why something else would be considered for those troops posted to the newly acquired territory of Alaska concluding, "Alaska is not as cold as Minnesota," and as such he could see no need for special trousers to be made up for the soldiers stationed there![121] It seems that waterproof trousers were being asked for in this situation, and at that time the only "rubber suit issued to enlisted men of the U.S. Army" was either the "rubber poncho for mounted men, and the rubber blanket for foot men."[122]

This minimal protection against rain and moisture was the norm for several years to come. Surplus stocks were issued for some time, as were leather and linen leggings, although these latter items soon were exhausted, and replacements not adopted for nearly two decades.[123]

The Quartermaster Department also was willing to furnish mounted clothing, at least to foot troops in the Department of the Pacific if, "the peculiarities of climate, the health and the comfort of troops require it."[124] Additionally, officers were permitted to purchase material to fashion into their own uniforms. Originally this privilege would be extended

In the regimental history of the Second U.S. Cavalry, artist E. Forbes also illustrated special musician's or trumpeter's dress alongside the regulation 1872-pattern dress.

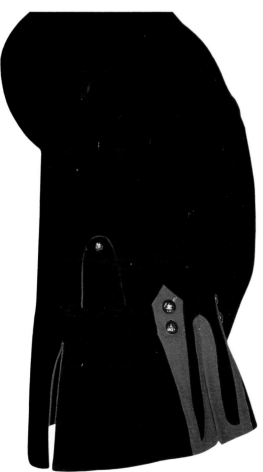

only to those who made application in person, and that the cloth thus ordered would not be sent out so that these would be an expense to the government.[125] A price list was established ranging from .12 1/2¢ a yard for unbleached muslin to $3.50 a yard for blue cloth.[126]

As an extension to offering cloth for sale to officers, there even was a recommendation to furnish those "serving at remote stations on the frontier" with uniform clothing made to order. While Sherman thought the idea had merit, he felt this "semi-official and half private transaction" would cause accounting problems. Additionally, he noted that regulations already provided for enlisted uniforms to be furnished "for officers use whenever and wherever needed. . . ." Therefore, he wanted to continue the past routine rather than institute a new one.[127]

On occasion, though, the norm was reviewed and a different direction considered. One such example that was a portent of things to come arose in 1867, when a prototype of a sergeant's uniform consisting of a coat and trousers was authorized in response to a request from the engineers.[128] Not surprisingly, the coat was to be made in the *chasseur a pied* cut. Unlike previous engineer clothing that had been distinguished by yellow trim, this proposed outfit had a red and white color combination, thereby offering a distinctive scheme that set the engineers apart

Light artillery (mounted batteries) were issued a coat of the same pattern as cavalry except that their facings were scarlet, as seen for this example showing a portion of the tails, a belt loop, and the slash at the hip to facilitate riding. Mounted coats had such slashes and also were piped along the bottom of the skirts, as is evident here, while the coats for foot troops had no slashes and were left with raw edges at the skirt bottoms. SI

A musician (**left**) and a private (**right**) of the Fifth Infantry Regiment stationed at Ft. Leavenworth, Kansas wear the dress coat adopted by General Orders No. 92, 26 October 1872 with its light blue facing on the collar, cuffs, shoulder loops, tails, and matching piping down the front, at the split of the rear skirt, and around a pair of belt loops. Instead of wearing the new dress cap, they have elected to pose in their 1872-pattern forage caps which bore the company letter (in this case an 1858-pattern brass "K") on the front. Not until General Orders No. 67, 25 June 1875, was the badge of the corps and a small company letter called for to be worn with the forage cap for infantry, cavalry, artillery, and engineer troops. FAM not only from cavalry, with whom they shared the same shade, but also from all other organizations who had single color trim. The coat was to have service chevrons indicating one enlistment, as well as chevrons of a sergeant and trouser stripes to indicate this rank.[129] When completed, the jacket resembled the one worn by the 109th Pennsylvania (Curtain Light Guards), a garment that had been produced by the quartermaster at Schuylkill Arsenal late in the Civil War for that volunteer unit.

Following the engineers' lead, the Ordnance Department likewise asked for an outfit of this "new pattern" but with yellow twisted cord (thereby giving the garment a nearly duplicate appearance to the 1860-pattern French model from which it was taken) as opposed to crimson as the branch color, a request that presumed the engineers would be allowed to switch to the new red and white configuration.[130] The idea was to provide a more distinctive look for the enlisted men, while officers were to have a frock coat that bore facings 3-inches back on each side of the collar in the old crimson, this serving as the background for the traditional shell and flame device.[131] Given that the inventory of ordnance enlisted uniforms at the time nearly were depleted, the time for adopting another pattern seemed appropriate. Instead conversion of infantry or artillery frock coats was taken as the course of action.[132]

Nonetheless, the fact that both the proposed engineer and ordnance coats were of the chasseur pattern was noteworthy in that the preeminence of France's military at the time still was evident. Even Meigs noted that the French army had simplified things by adopting only two styles of tunics, "one for mounted men, and another for footmen, and the only differences to distinguish regiments and corps, are in the buttons, which are sewn on at the moment of issue to the troops."[133] The French policy had something to offer to the Americans, as Meigs noted, but this nation was not to be the exclusive source for martial styles in the United States.

Indeed, France's star was on the decline as a dominant martial power in Europe even as Prussia's star was on the rise, reaching new heights when the two countries clashed in one of many struggles for preeminence. Civil War veteran Brigadier General William Hazen was on hand to observe the dueling powers. He was impressed by the Prussian uniform, which he recorded as,"much like that of our own troops" with its prevailing color of blue and its single-breasted cut. He made special note of the helmet with eagle displayed in front, and the visorless forage cap. While he particularly thought the uniform of mounted troops was "very fanciful and beautiful" what seemed to strike him even more was

Infantry bands could have special belts, buckles, and coats depending on the availability of regimental funds and the desires of the commanding colonel. For example, this 1872-pattern infantry coat has three rows of staff officers' buttons rather than a single row of enlisted brass buttons. JG

1872-pattern sergeant major of infantry coat. SI

LEFT: Completely attired in the 1872-pattern infantry enlisted dress this Fifth U.S. Infantry private holds a .50 caliber Springfield rifle, rather than the .45 caliber which began to be issued in 1873 as a replacement for the earlier long arm. The soldier's cap is topped with a white pompon and adorned with brass bugle device. This infantry private appears in the parade uniform that remained regulation through 1881, when a new type of headgear was adopted for dress purposes to replace the cap. Ultimately, a rifle insignia was ushered in for all infantry enlisted personnel with a small number to designate the regiment above the letter of the company, both in brass, per General Orders No. 96, 19 November 1875. Musicians were the exception in that they were to continue to wear the hunting horn with brass company letter only. Later, General Orders No. 21, 20 March 1876 dictated that the company letter was to be placed in the lower angle of the cap badge and the regimental numeral was to be positioned in the upper angle. This private has elected to place the regimental numeral in the center of his horn but displays no company letter, nor does his coat have the correct collar numerals for the regiment. Considerable variations such as this existed even though the new regulations had been drafted in part to overcome this type of departure from established standards. USAMHI

the quality of the garments. He found these to be "of excellent, strong, all-wool cloth, and fit neatly. In addition the men have for drill and fatigue common cotton pantaloons and a short cloth jacket."[134]

One other Prussian practice attracted Hazen's attention. They issued three sets of uniforms for each soldier in the following manner:

> The suit for every day he turns in when he has permission to go to town, and dresses neatly for his holiday. He turns in his common suit on Saturday, and is given the one for Sunday. He has still another, brought out only on great occasions, such as reviews before the king. The clothing is kept by the first sergeant, and although, on the average, a suit lasts only a year, each of the old suits being degraded one degree in importance when a new one is issued, it is not uncommon to find suits in stock that have been in use twenty years.[135]

In all this Hazen seemed impressed with the systematic approach to clothing Prussian troops and the quality of the product. Nonetheless, whether the inspiration was Germanic, Gallic, or otherwise, Meigs still resisted anything but the old Union Army uniform. In a critical letter to

A family portrait? On the right a heavy artillery private wears the 1872-pattern coat and cap—the coat displaying two service stripes and the regimental collar brass. The young man on the left is a musician, perhaps with the regimental band, although his coat does not have the regulation herringbone on the chest, but instead the ornamentation ends in trefoils. RB

Detail of cuff and infantry pioneer brassard of facing material axes sewn to matching cloth of dark blue as used to construct the 1872-pattern enlisted coat. SI

The facings on the tails of the 1872-pattern infantry coat differed from the mounted pattern, those for foot soldiers being more like some British military coats of the era while those for mounted troops were more similar to the French 1860-pattern chasseur jacket. SI

the chief quartermaster of the Department of the Pacific, Meigs' stand on one item of wear typified his point of view which tended to be both sensitive as well as restrained in nature. He wrote:

> The Army trousers are generally of strong cloth, though not all of standard color. This it was not possible to command in all the war contracts and purchases. The supply of trousers on hand is nearly consumed, and new ones are being made of good cloth, of which abundance of excellent quality is still in store from the supply delivered towards the close of the war, when the Department was providing for an army over a million strong.[136]

Meigs concluded with a remonstrance to those who complained about poor quality uniforms and equipment stating that it was not generally the place of officers to pass judgment on articles furnished them by the taxpayer. Moreover, he felt that they should not attack the Quartermaster Department "which during the war clothed and supported and moved one-fifth of the able-bodied men of the loyal states." He also deemed it unjust, "to accuse unknown contractors of fraud, because every yard of so many millions of yards of cloth" was not precisely of "the

same shade of color. . . ." The quartermaster general ended with the pronouncement:

> In the attempt to make the best use of the many millions of dollars worth of military material left in possession of the Department at the close of the war, this office expects to have the aid of its officers. The changing fancies of fashion, the whims of officers not responsible for the use or waste of this costly property, tend to agitation in favor of changes in uniform, both in color and style, and in material. But it is believed that economy, which is our duty, requires no considerable changes to be made in the uniform until the material on hand is consumed, and I believe that the country and the great body of the Army are attached to the Army blue, and will hold to it for many years to come.[137] The quartermaster general opined further that the Civil War uniform had become an icon in the nation in that it stirred "recollection of many a hard-fought field. . . ."[138]

An anonymous writer and veteran who signed his letter to the editor of the *Army and Navy Journal* as "Army Blue" concurred. He decried: "Do not say so much about the gray as a color for troops who have immortalized the blue." Neither the economic argument that gray was less expensive to produce than blue, or the benefit of gray being less conspicuous than blue to the enemy could dissuade the man. In fact, he replied to the former argument with a challenge – why not also adopt the Rebel flag, it being less costly to produce? He also was aghast that brave men wanted to hide from their foe. His conclusion was emphatic. He would "rather be shot in blue . . . than live to a green old age to draw a pension . . . in gray."[139]

Several men opposed those who sanctified blue. One of this group called for a return to the gray garb of the War of 1812 and the voltiguers of the Mexican War, rather than maintain blue as the official color for the uniform.[140] Another federal officer concurred but conceded that those who served the stars and stripes would reject such a notion completely, saying that while gray was "the most serviceable, the least noticeable, the color most agreeable to the eye, a Rebel adoption has effectually damned" its use by the U.S. Army. England's scarlet, Russia's green, Austria's and Spain's white, and Portugal's brown all had been appropriated, too, leaving a blue mix as the best option remaining in the author's opinion.[141] A third promoter of gray sought a double-breasted coat in the shade worn by West Point cadets, with collars and cuffs faced in red.[142] This had been the regulation for the Confederate artillery, thereby posing a difficulty in gaining support for this proposal.[143]

Despite these obstacles, a former Union general turned United States congressman, John Coburn, could support a change from blue, which he found when trimmed with white or light facings could be seen readily by the enemy. Recalling that "the dirty gray or butternut colors of the Rebel enabled him to sufficiently conceal himself when doing outpost duty much better than" the Yankees could because these hues blended with "the ground and barks of trees" as well as with fences, stumps, and other surroundings.

Coburn was savvy enough also to realize that one type of uniform was not sufficient to provide concealment in all situations. For summer Coburn believed gray or butternut would be better replaced by green, "to correspond with the color of leaves." He pointed out that during the

First Lieutenant Daniel M. Taylor's transferred to the Ordnance Department in 1874. He wears a 1872-pattern officer's blouse that exhibits heavier braid than most examples of this jacket, as but one example of numerous differences which existed from one tailor to the next. RBM

Five black mohair trefoils appeared at the end of braid which trimmed the chest of officer's jackets of the 1872-pattern. The same material edged the collar and skirts of the coat and ornamented its back as well as the cuffs. Shoulder straps, which for some unexplained reason are absent here, were to designate rank. The hat is a version of the 1872-pattern which was designed to be worn folded closed or open with a flat brim, depending on weather conditions. The saber is an officer's model adopted in the late 1850s. USAMHI

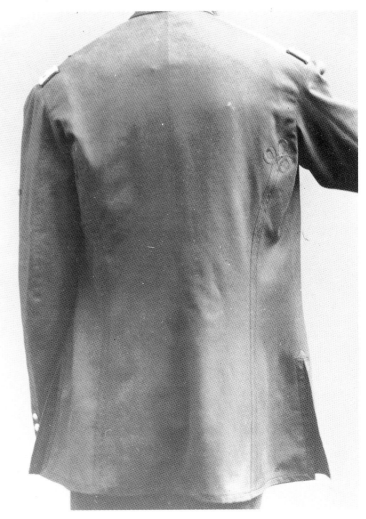

This pattern sample of the 1872 officer's sack coat has a pair of stars attached to the collar. When the jacket was first proposed brevet ranks (given in recognition of merit or valor, most often to Civil War veterans) were considered as an adornment for the collar while the individual's actual serving rank was to be indicated by shoulder straps (in this case a staff colonel). The concept of displaying brevet rank, however, was discarded before the blouse actually was adopted. NA

Rear view of the 1872-pattern officer's blouse which had slashes at the hips. NA

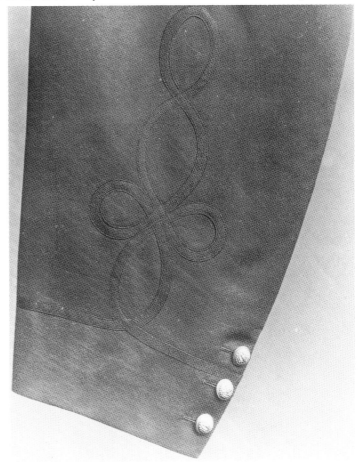

war a Confederate sniper had covered himself with leaves to look like a bush. He managed to wreak havoc among Coburn's men who only discovered their hidden assailant by the telltale smoke from the black powder of his rifle.

Coburn went on to state: "The dead colors enable a secure approach . . . and aid the surprise and sudden advance, or the more deliberate & cautious work of observation." Summarizing, he declared: "The uniform is for use, not show, and the life of one brave, faithful soldier, saved by a carefully selected uniform, will count against all the brilliance of a hundred reviews."[144]

In these few words Coburn set forth the rationale behind those who sought functional attire that was adopted according to environmental conditions and the realities of modern warfare. Not being a career military man Coburn put aside tradition to follow a path dictated by technological changes in armament. Although he was ahead of his times in suggesting different types of camouflage for different environmental conditions – a common application in the twentieth century but novel in the nineteenth – he was but one of many advocates for replacement of old patterns with new. in the air.

RIGHT: Cuff braid of the 1872-pattern officers' blouse. NA

This fairly widespread call for change was known to certain influential officers who convened in response to Special Orders No. 523, GO, December 18, 1867 to consider a revision of all U.S. Army regulations.[145] The trio of men assigned this daunting duty were Brigadier General Christopher C. Augur, Lieutenant General Philip H. Sheridan, and General William T. Sherman, all noted Civil War generals who after the war were among the most senior men in the army. Sherman presided, at least until his departure for the field after January 1868.[146] Before doing so, he submitted a draft of the board's findings up to that point to the adjutant general.[147] After that, Augur and Sheridan continued for several more days. Despite the immense task at hand, and the relatively conservative nature of the three, they still reviewed prototype uniform articles during their sessions. These included a fully trimmed cadet officer's cap, and a lined dark blue flannel blouse specially made up for their consideration.[148] A new hat and various types of trim for it, that included two thistle pompons (green and red), a hair plume for cavalry, plus two cords and tassels (green and red), evidently were reviewed as well.[149] Additionally, there were samples of two uniform coats (probably the ones made up for the engineers late the previous year), a pair of trousers (possibly one of the pairs for the engineer uniform), a cavalry jacket of an unknown type, and a gray blouse.[150] The last mentioned item was of particular note in deference to the prejudice in some circles against that color. The blouse had white trim. Later one with sky-blue trim was produced as well. Both jackets probably were inspired by the British Norfolk (although the 1868 report from the surgeon general referred to this as a "Swiss" garment) that had been used by some Union volunteer units and adopted by certain Yankee and Rebel officers during the Civil War.[151] The pattern had been featured in the 1868 report from the surgeon general.

In fact, Surgeon General J.K. Barnes recommended that the board be given this report as part of the data available for considering new uniforms.[152] This document may have had little influence on the board, though, in that on February 14 it adjourned, soon after the surgeon general suggested he provide a copy for consideration.[153] With this the members of the 1868 board disbanded, as had their 1862 counterparts, without taking any real action relative to the uniform. There was some confusion over the board afterwards, however, with certain military suppliers particularly believing that it actually had issued new directives for replacements of the previous pattern, or portions of the uniform.[154] The contractor who furnished a sample of the Andrews hat based upon the favorable notice for this design in the surgeon general's report, wanted to know about future directions of the uniform, and even offered to produce another sample or samples of the hat "that would combine all the requirements of comfort and utility desired, in a better quality than the

Front and rear view of an 1872-pattern officer's blouse, in this case for a field-grade officer of the Corps of Engineers. Michael McAfee Photograph. WPM

Second Lieutenant Frank Baker, Thirteenth U.S. Infantry wears the 1872-pattern officer's jacket and the 1872-pattern officer's forage cap, a typical combination. The new forage cap was of the chasseur style that had long been popular. RBM

Second Lieutenant Benny Hodgsen also wears the company grade cavalry dress uniform of the 1872-pattern. His shoulder knots have pronounced pads, just one of many variations for officers' uniforms of the period. LBNB

Captain Thomas French of the Seventh Cavalry wears the dark blue wool dress cape with velvet collar over his 1872-pattern dress uniform. This basic style of cape had been in use as early as the 1851 regulations. The helmet has a less sloping visor than many others, this being another variation according to the source the officer selected when purchasing his kit. The saber likewise is not the regulation model, but one of many designs available from U.S. and foreign sources. Trousers display the 1 1/2-inch yellow stripes along the outer seams as designated for line officers in 1872 to replace the 1/8-inch welts of previous regulations. LBNB

1872-pattern company grade cavalry officer's coat so indicated by the two gold lace ornaments on the sleeves and seven buttons in each row, as well as the gold lace saber belt with three stripes of yellow running horizontally. JG

The gold lace on officers' coat was to measure 1/4-inch, but many officers, including Major Marcus Reno, Seventh U.S. Cavalry, selected 1/2-inch lace. Field grade officers had three stripes on their cuffs. WC

previous submission that was made "only to give an idea of <u>shape</u> and <u>appearance</u>.[155]

While the rumors of a new uniform were unfounded, continued calls for change still were in the air. As one example, in 1871, Brevet Major General James A. Hardie, a West Pointer who had taught at the academy and had served in the Mexican War, Indian campaigns, and the Civil War, made a suggestion for a new cap to the adjutant general, declaring: "I dislike our present one, and equally so the French 'kepi' which officers generally wear." What Hardie proposed was "a plain military fashion" that would "attract no condemnation for want of utility or of taste. . . ."[156]

The army's commanding general also felt the time was approaching for a new cap. While William T. Sherman did not "expect soon to see a hat that will be fixed and appropriate for the Army" he did admit, "Fashions change and we must do the same." His preference was for "The old leather gig top" (evidently meaning the 1833-pattern leather forage cap).[157] However, he acknowledged this style "now would be grotesque." What seemed most practical to Sherman was a "round felt hat with a brim – for common wear – with some pompoms to be worn for *dress* parade."[158]

There were a few individuals at least who took a different approach to what constituted the ideal headgear. For instance, some light artillery officers reveled in the glory of their scarlet horsetail bedecked caps, and were the envy of others. Furnishing these coveted caps proved difficult, however, because soon after the Civil War, stocks dwindled, going from 2,886 on June 30, 1866 to none by early 1868.[159] Indeed, when the Third Artillery required 400 of the caps in San Francisco, there were not enough on hand to fill the order.[160] Permission was granted to buy the hats and attaching rings for cords, and Horstmann of Philadelphia was given a contract to make sample caps.[161]

Other artillery units around the country required the caps as well. In Louisiana 200 caps had been sent to the light battery at New Orleans, leaving only 145 on hand. More were needed, and as was authorization to have them produced.[162] A similar situation could be found in Richmond, necessitating an order to make more for the mounted gunners there.[163] This last communique became garbled. This caused the commanding colonel of the Fifth Artillery to think a new uniform was being produced, rather than just orders for replacement caps.[164] Part of this confusion stemmed from the correspondence to both Richmond and Fort Leavenworth stating the depleted stock of caps meant that when caps

Cuffs of the dress coat adopted for officers in 1872 had three gold lace ornaments for field grade officers. The buttons which are shown were prescribed for staff officers, while the lace is the regulation 1/4-inch. There were to be two gold braid stripes on the cuffs of company grade cuffs. NA

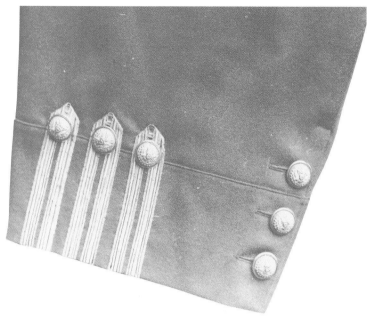

A Corps of Engineer captain's 1872-pattern gold lace belt has three black stripes as did all company grade officers except for cavalry who had yellow, infantry who had medium blue, and artillery who were to wear scarlet. He holds the low profile chapeau de bras introduced in 1872 as regulation for staff officers. The buttons are Corps of Engineers and the shoulder knots have a dark blue or black pad with a silver castle and silver captain's bars to indicate rank and branch. The sword is the M1860 staff and field. RBM were required they were to be ordered in small quantities in that the design might be changed soon "and for that reason also it is not desirable to accumulate any more of the present style."[165] Another letter to the Third Independent Battery of Ohio Volunteer Militia was even more telling as to why some officers and contractors presumed there was a uniform change in the offing. This letter stated: "no changes have yet been made for the United States Army uniforms, though it is contemplated making some after the present stock is exhausted."[166]

Although this was a bit premature certain artillery officers seized upon these rumors, or took the initiative for other reasons to ask for a uniform that would set them apart from the infantry. This was the case with the First Artillery. The argument was made that the regiment had "gained a high reputation during the war as artillerists" but after that conflict it became increasing more difficult "to tell where the infantry man ends, and the artillery man begins. In hope of fostering "pride in profession" the commander of the First sought "a marked and distinctive uniform" that he thought was embodied by the light artillery of his regiment.[167] Sherman looked into the matter. He learned that 120,000 dark blue artillery jackets were in storage, and asked if the acting secretary of war had any objections to these being issued to all artillerymen, not just mounted batteries. Because so few light artillery caps were to be had, Sherman recommended that the 1858-pattern hat be retained.[168] In like manner the Second Artillery was informed that the cap could not be issued to any but mounted batteries, but the secretary of war had concurred that the jackets could be adopted by all mounted and foot or heavy units alike. Again the cautionary statement was made, though that this all was in accordance with the belief that a new uniform might be prescribed.[169] All these comments created a certain degree of continued commotion because for a time Sherman's intentions evidently were misconstrued. For instance, when jackets were ordered for some

dismounted artillery companies the request was disallowed and coats supplied instead.[170]

It seems that all this was sorted out for the artillery, but became a moot point because the long simmering cauldron of change boiled more furiously than ever when Civil War stocks finally were reduced considerably. The time approached when replacements could be contemplated. Perhaps this was one reason why a document providing descriptions of each article of clothing and equipment had been requested for use by the quartermaster general's office on the eve of yet another board being called together.[171] Special Orders No. 260, Headquarters of the Army, July 3, 1871 established another group of officers to again review army regulations, the 1868 effort having never gone into effect. This body was made up of Andrew J. Alexander, Eighth Cavalry; Richard I. Dodge, Third Infantry; Henry J. Hunt, Fifth Artillery; John H. King, Ninth Infantry; and Inspector General of the Army Randolph B. Marcy, the senior member and president of the board.[172]

Marcy seemed an appropriate choice to guide the revision of regulations because the Inspector General's Department served as the watchdog to see that these rules were being obeyed. More to the point, his political connections and enviable personal military record afforded him considerable clout. A West Point graduate, Class of 1832, Marcy had compiled an impressive service record prior to the outbreak of the Civil War. Soon after the war erupted, he became inspector general under his son-in-law, George McClellan (his daughter also had been courted unsuccessfully by A.P. Hill). Marcy recorded much of his long and eventful career in three publications, *Prairie Traveler*, *Thirty Years of Army Life on the Border*, and *Border Reminiscences*, published in 1859, 1860, and 1871, respectively, works that brought him some degree of fame as well as favor.[173] Even after McClellen's star lost its luster, Marcy and Sherman had become close associates, hunting buffalo together and shar-

Detail 1872-pattern company grade officer's dress saber and belt. Note the three horizontal stripes that were in scarlet for the artillery, yellow for the cavalry, medium blue for the infantry, and black for all other officers. NA

Assistant Surgeon Calvin DeWitt poses in the regulation 1872-pattern company grade staff officer's dress uniform, its most noteworthy feature being the chapeau de bras that was to be worn by all officers except those for the artillery, cavalry, and infantry. His gold lace sword belt had three black horizontal stripes. The sword is the M1860 staff and field rather than the prescribed M1840 medical officer's sword. RBM

Assistant Surgeon William Corbusier in the 1872-pattern uniform for medical officers. He holds the M1840 Medical Department sword and his chapeau de bras, one that is slightly different in profile to Lieutenant DeWitt's. AHS

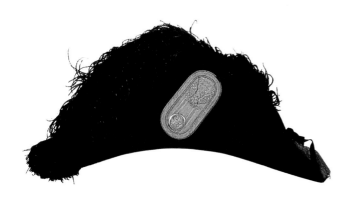

1872-pattern staff officer's chapeau. FWMSH

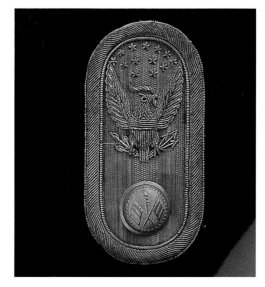

Photo Detail of side piece on an 1872-pattern staff officer's chapeau. JG

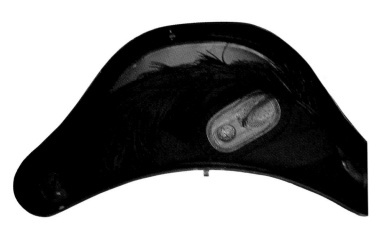

1872-pattern staff officer's chapeau in japanned tin case. FAM

Japanned tin case for the chapeau with lid closed. FAM

ing a certain nostalgia as the years passed for the "golden days" of the Civil War.

Because the various bureaus and departments in Washington of the era enjoyed a great deal of autonomy and reported to the secretary of war rather than the commanding general, having highly placed allies, as Marcy did, afforded him a good deal of power. As such, the inspector general, as head of the 1871 board, and the surgeon general, based upon the 1868 Woodhull report, in effect had taken over the lead from the quartermaster corps when it came to the uniform.

Thus, others besides Meigs and his operatives would dictate future patterns, at least for the early part of the 1870s. Perhaps this is why Meigs had not been in favor of the board when it was called into being, once more taking the stand that the regulation had been adequate during the acid test of the Civil War and need not be changed.[174]

Marcy and his board seemed of a different mind because he had asked whether the board should extend its sitting and if so, should the men make recommendations about any changes in the uniform. To the latter inquiry Marcy asked: "Do you wish that we should bring into [the] new regulations any changes in uniform?" He went on to assert, "We think it can be improved upon and made better for service. At present so much clothing of the old pattern has been sold to citizens that they are found wearing it everywhere. If material changes were made this

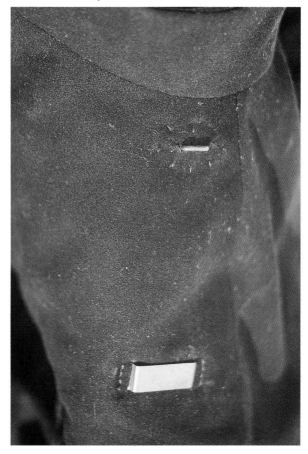

RIGHT: Detail of typical metal fasteners on the 1872-pattern officer's coat that allowed for attachment of shoulder knots. WC

Front view of 1872-pattern field grade staff officer's coat that was double-breasted with nine buttons in each row. This is Colonel Miles' coat. WC

Front and rear of 1872-pattern colonel of staff shoulder knots. These belonged to Nelson A. Miles and may have been worn by him prior to obtaining a proper pair with medium blue background and regimental number. WC

would not be the case. . . ."[175] Although Marcy appears not to have received a reply to this issue, he forged ahead and requested a copy of the 1862 board's actions regarding the same subject.[176]

Perhaps had Sherman not been abroad in Europe at the time this request might have been denied, he being conservative when it came to the uniform. This was not the case, however. With Sherman away, in April 1872, Marcy's comrades were informed that they should delve into the matter the Army's clothing. Reconvening for this purpose, the board deliberated from May though June 21, 1872, then adjourned soon thereafter having fulfilled all their duties.[177] In the process this body ignored Meigs and his department, all the prototypes of uniform components being obtained by them without calling upon the quartermaster or his subordinates for assistance.

This situation probably did not escape Meigs because word soon reached the rest of the army that Marcy was heading the effort to obtain samples of uniforms, and report on new styles that might be adopted, including a hat which was described by the *Army and Navy Journal* as "a sombrero which can be looped up at the sides so as to resemble a chapeau."[178]

This item was the folding hat reviewed by the 1868 board and also featured in the surgeon general's report on clothing in that year. There is no direct evidence to support the fact that the men had a copy of the Woodhull report. The fact that this document had been reprinted years earlier in the *Army and Navy Journal* leaves little doubt that in many cases that they were aware of the study, particularly its illustrations, as well as by what they saw in reviewing the 1862 board's efforts.

These sources and many ideas found elsewhere were evident in the board's decision-making process, a matter that went on behind closed doors for several weeks as indicated by a letter from Meigs that admitted: "the new Regulations will be out before very long. No one but their

Colonel Miles' 1872-pattern knots (probably made circa 1875) with the proper color and insignia. WC

The knots adopted in 1872 were to have dark blue (and oftentimes actually black) backgrounds for staff officers that bore various devices such as an "MD" in silver embroidery for Medical Department. The spread eagle is for a colonel. USA

1872-pattern Quartermaster Department officers knots. The "QD" indicated the branch and a silver bar on each side, indicated a first lieutenant (the silver first lieutenant bars have been removed). SI

framers know what they are."[179] Marcy even remained quiet about the details after they had been submitted to the secretary of war for review.[180] This silence was broken in late July when the secretary of war related that President Ulysses S. Grant had approved the new uniform, and it was to be adopted as of December 1872.[181]

In fact, the board's recommendations as approved and revised by the secretary of war, dated July 29, 1872, as General Orders No. 76, Adjutant General's Office, was printed in the August 3, 1872 issue of the *Army and Navy Journal*.[182] Later the same order was published by the government with color plates featuring headgear, coats, blouses, dress belts, and shoulder knots for officers. After that an identical text, without lithographs, was released as General Orders No. 92, War Department, October 26, 1872.[183]

The illustrations from the earlier version of the orders especially would prove useful for those interested in manufacturing uniform components for officers, as well as for those in the Quartermaster Department required to oversee compliance to the regulations adopted by these orders. These images were based upon photographs taken of the prototypes for the forage cap made by Warnock and the dress helmet fabricated by Horstmann, two changes having been made from the board specimens. One was the removal of braid from the forage cap and the other was the reduction of the helmet braid's diameter by one-third.[184]

Meigs estimated that the first order for helmets should provide for approximately 9,600 cavalry models and 400 light artillery.[185] Inquiries were sent on to prospective suppliers.[186] Horstmann, the firm that had delivered the board sample for $59.60, received the contract to furnish 9,000 helmets (8,700 cavalry and 300 light artillery), at a cost of $5.46 1/2 each complete, being more than sufficient to allow one helmet per eligible soldier for the first and third year of his five year enlistment.[187]

While this helmet took its basic inspiration from European military fashion, its origins cannot be attributed directly to one foreign military power only. It fact, it was very much a hybrid, especially in that the helmets worn in Europe regularly were of leather or metal, or a combination of these two materials, rather than "black felt," as was the one adopted in the United States by General Orders No. 92.[188] Moreover, the helmet cord and bands, that could be traced to as early as 1833 for U.S. dragoons and subsequently to light artillery batteries, were not used in tandem with foreign styles.[189]

A few years later, however, Colonel Hunt, a member of the board recalled "the model was that of the English horseguards."[190] Hunt further commented:

> The helmet is not according to the model selected by the Board . . .
> The visor is unnecessarily large and awkward, and has not the military style of the model, the horse hair plume is unnecessarily large, awkward, heavy and long – one third the amount of horse hair and of shorter length would answer the purpose much better than the present pattern. The model was more erect and the plume sat better than the one actually issued.[191]

Whether quartermaster officials made more changes than just the diameter of the helmet braid, or in fact Hunt's memory was faulty, cannot be determined. The latter case seems somewhat more likely in that Meigs evidently had the Horstmann sample held in Washington until

LEFT: Shoulder knots adopted in 1872 for dress purposes also had a gold aiguillette attached to the right knot for aides de camp, as well as adjutant generals, inspector generals, and regimental adjutants, as seen in this official photograph which also shows stars on the collars to indicate brevet rank. This scheme was abandoned, however, before the final draft of the 1872 uniform regulations was released, and as such never put into place. NA   RIGHT:Rear of the 1872-pattern officer's coat with the skirts ornamented with four buttons. The aiguillette also is visible. NA

Marcy could pass judgement on the proposed pattern.[192] This he did in 1873, writing it "seemed to conform to the requirements of Genl. Order No. 92."[193]

All this not withstanding, production of the helmet moved forward. The quartermaster officer charge with the production even reveled: "It is the most sightly head-gear I have ever seen. . . ."[194]

Despite this praise, he added some short-comings would have to be rectified later. He specifically indicated the fur felt of the shell was "almost too light; the disk on the crown should be broader to bear the strain of the spear, plume, and socket, and the binding should be heavier and broader."[195]

Even before these comments, the color of the plume came into question. Obtaining a uniform shade of yellow posed a difficult problem that even experts had no solution for save leaving the color as natural white.[196] No authority existed to depart from the yellow plume set forth in the general orders. Further, Horstmann assured Meigs that it could produce a permanent yellow dye, although it was understood that over time, exposure to the elements would tend to fade the hue, as it would

do on the facings for the uniform coat. As such, retaining the yellow plume was recommended and approved.[197]

The same fugitive dye problem affected the helmet cords as well, or so Horstmann Brothers contended. For this reason they produced cords that were darker than the sealed samples (they had an orange cast).[198] The company had manufactured some 200 cords by this point, enough to complete the first small lot of helmets that of 228 that were being made.[199] Horstmann defended its actions by stating: "The color used is the same as we have used for the Army since 1851 – and it was adopted on account of it durability, being not likely to fade – and a medium between an orange and a yellow."[200] The firm then concluded with the question as to whether they should produce a lighter color.

The answer was to the affirmative.[201] Horstmann's response was that delivery would be delayed if new ones had to be made up. and the firm would lose money.[202]

While it is unclear what the final outcome was about the color of cords, one other matter related to these adornments would be considered. How were these cord to be worn? The light artillery cap had no such provisions. Surviving photographs depict a number of options. This

Captain William M. Wherry, Sixth U.S. Infantry, has added a gold aiguillette while serving as the adjutant for the U.S. Military Academy. He also wears a field grade officer's belt rather than a company grade belt for some inexplicable reason. His shoulder straps likewise appear under the knots. RBM

First Lieutenant W.W. Cooke was adjutant of the Seventh Cavalry. His right 1872-pattern knot had the aiguillette attached permanently. Gordon Chappell Photograph. CSPM

same latitude was not to continue with the new uniform in that GO No. 67, War Department, Adjutant General's Office, June 25, 1873 read:

> The helmet cords will be attached to the left side of the helmet, and come down to the left shoulder, where they are held together by a slide; one cord then passes to the front and the other to the rear of the neck, crossing upon the right shoulder and passing separately around to the front and rear of the right arm, where they are again united and held together by a slide under the arm; the united cords then cross the breast, and are looped up to the upper button on the left side of the coat.

This prescription essentially coincided with the issuing of the first 194 helmets, but did not address the cumbersome matter of a soldier extracting himself from the tangle of cords when he needed to remove his helmet.[203] In due course, some enterprising individuals cut their cords, often near the tassel on the helmet band, and improvised an attachment scheme, such as a hook and eye or a brass spring clip, much as had been provided for on officers' helmet cords. For the remainder of the decades during which the dress helmet was issued, the government failed to make a similar adjustment, thereafter providing cords of one piece instead of taking this more practical approach.[204]

While mounted troops and officers were set off by the new helmet, foot troops and officers of infantry and heavy artillery were to have a distinctive cap. Once again this piece of headgear drew from a number of European antecedents, including the circa 1840 French 'casquette d'Afriqué. The British adapted a version of the cap from the French.[205] Her Majesty's officers had shakos both of the 1860-1869-pattern and its 1869-1878 replacement, that were much like that of their sometimes rivals from across the Channel.[206] Indeed, military dealers in the United States had carried similar design in the 1860s, while the dress shako

The pencils (so-called because early examples of the aiguillette supposedly served a practical function by having writing implements attached to allow adjutants to take orders) were placed at the end of the aiguillette. CSPM

Shoulder straps could be substituted for knots with the 1872-pattern coat in which case the forage cap could be worn in lieu of the chapeau or other dress headgear as this first lieutenant of the Ordnance Department has done in this portrait taken about 1873. RBM

worn by the U.S. Marine Corps, since 1859, and that of cadets at the U.S. Military Academy, starting prior to the Civil War, were also along comparable lines.[207] Further, the Woodhull report had depicted head-dress that was akin to the 1872-pattern dress cap.

Although not identical to counterparts from across the Atlantic, the cap had a distinctive European flavor. Horstmann Brothers and Allien of New York furnished the prototype officer's cap for the board's review, and at some point made two enlisted samples as well.[208] The main enlisted model for the board, however, was from Warnock, also the maker of the pattern campaign hat.[209]

A stiff fur felt body covered with fine material, trimmed in gold lace was the basic element of the sample officer's cap. Surmounting this was a white cock feather plume and on the front appeared this with an embroidered bugle device for insignia completed the model. The plume was retained for a short period as a sample by the Quartermaster Department, after the officer's and enlisted caps were sent back to Horstmann.[210]

This particular ornament caught Meigs' attention. He wanted to have the color changed. While remembering, "the ballad on the white plume

of Henry of Navarre," he nonetheless was repulsed by the idea of "any officer of the United States Army being made liable to the state joke of `showing the white plume.'"[211] Although he made this point, the white cock feathers remained regulation for infantry officers, while the heavy artillery at least could avoid being the butt of humor with their scarlet versions.

The enlisted cap was analogous to that to be worn by officers, but it was to be trimmed in worsted braid to match facings on the coat, and had a "pear-shaped" (somewhat more like a unopened pine cone) woolen pompon to match, except for infantrymen who had white pompons to coincide with the cock feather plumes of their officers.

Meigs acknowledged an obstacle existed in the production of these caps. He wrote the secretary of war that just as it was impossible-to-obtain regulation ostrich feathers (about 3,000,000) for every man in the Union Army because not that many were available in "the markets of the world, or in the accessible wilds of Africa" so, too, might Warnock face a problem in procuring the right kind of furs to make the cap formula.[212] He seemed confident that the contractors would find a way to deal with this situation when it came time to respond to bids.[213] Evi-

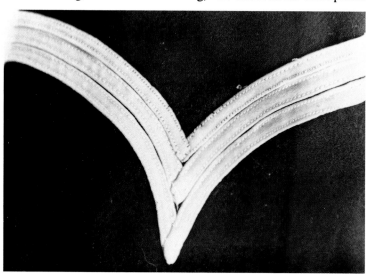

After being promoted to sergeant, William Williams elected to have custom-made chevrons of separately sewn stripes of facing material applied to his 1872-pattern coat. This practice was not uncommon among non-commissioned officers during the 1870s. LBNB

Detail of 1872-pattern infantry first sergeant's chevrons and service stripes on the dress coat of Joseph W. Huntington, a non-commissioned officer of the Fifth U.S. Infantry, Company B. The service stripe bordered in scarlet indicates Huntington's stint during the Civil War with the Second Massachusetts Cavalry, while the peacetime chevron above this is for his completed tour with the Thirty-seventh U.S. Infantry. DCM

This sergeant of Company E, Second U.S. Infantry has followed the new 1872 regulations to perfection, including his service stripes and chevrons. USAMHI

Signal Corps enlisted personnel likewise were to be issued to the mounted coat. Here Signal Private Will C. Barnes poses in his 1872-pattern dress uniform with its distinctive orange trim on the coat and with orange cords and horsehair plume attached to the helmet. The model 1839 foot soldier's belt is worn rather than appropriate mounted saber belt. Perhaps this was a photographer's prop or maybe because signal personnel often were stationed away from military posts Barnes was issued a surplus infantry private's belt rather than a cavalry saber belt as would have been consistent with his mounted style uniform. The signal flags are red with a white center and white with a red center. These went on the left arm only for privates of the second class and on both arms for privates of the first class in the Signal Service. They also went above the orange chevrons for non-commissioned officers. Probably very few of these dress uniforms were issued prior to the early 1880s. Barnes was to become a Medal of Honor recipient for heroism during an 1881 Apache attack in Arizona. NA

dently he was correct, although Warnock did not obtain the order. Bent and Bush were to deliver 18,000 caps complete with trimmings at $2.49 each. These were to be as the sealed samples except that they "should contain two ounces of Double Ring Russia" [a type of fur commonly used by hatters of the era] and one half ounce of Coney [hare] each."[214] In this instance, Meigs' supposition as to some means being found to provide the cap resulted in an allowed change from the original specification.[215]

When finally provided, the cap was "admitted on all sides to be a vast improvement on the old unshapely and unserviceable thing which was dignified with the name of a dress hat."[216] But praise was not universal. An infantry officer soon asked for the chapeau as a substitute.

In his estimation the cap was so small it had the tendency to blow off of the head when officers were mounted. The writer, a lieutenant colonel of infantry, ventured the trowsers should be changed as well. He wrote: "The trowsers are objected to as a matter of taste and on economic grounds. One officer of Cavalry objects to the trousers, because the uniform as it is, makes it difficult at any distance to distinguish the Colonel of a Regiment from a Lieutenant."[217] Perhaps the officer wanted to see the previous practice of having dark blue trousers for field grade officers and light blue trousers for company grade officers, reinstated.

Contrary to an older practice, the 1872 orders called for light blue trousers for all officers who were not part of the staff and for all enlisted men. In the case of generals and general staff or staff officers dark blue

The Signal Corps enlisted device for privates through sergeants was adopted during the Civil War and continued as part of the 1872 regulations. These were sewn on to a patch of dark blue cloth of the type used for coats, and red and white facing material cut out to form the flags that were edged in small, tightly coiled brass wire. The flag staffs were of white embroidered thread. AHS

cloth patterns without stripe or ornamentation, except for military store-keepers who were to have 1 1/2-inch stripes, were prescribed.[218] The trousers, however, universally were to have a higher waistband than those issued during the late war, measuring 3 1/2-inches, closed by two buttons, with a pair of curved top opening front pockets and leg stripes were of different widths than in the past, being 1 1/2 inches for artillery, cavalry, and infantry officers, 1-inch for sergeants, and 1 1/4-inches for ordnance sergeants and hospital stewards, as opposed to the 1/8-inch welt for officers and 1 1/2-inch stripes for all sergeants as was the regulation prior to 1872. Corporals retained their 1/2-inch stripes, while musicians and privates had no leg stripes at all, contrary to popular Hollywood depictions.[219] The colors were to match the facings of the branch, except infantry who had dark blue stripes, once again following earlier practices. The question arose though as to the material the stripes should be made from, the reply being that instead of worsted lace as had been used by the non-commissioned officers, facing cloth should be employed instead in so much as it was "believed that cloth will look better; will cost less; and be more satisfactory to the men, but differ from those of the officers only in width."[220] The secretary of war concurred. Cloth was adopted at that point over lace.[221]

Conversely the secretary of war ultimately disapproved the new higher waistband and pocket arrangement for the trousers once it was learned that these would be more costly than earlier types.[222] Trousers of Civil War pattern, therefore, remained in use for the next several years, the main exception being that a fifth size was added being larger than the previous four.[223] This addition addressed to some extent the complaints about small dimensions supposedly meant that these gar-

ments were now "as nearly as correct as can be made."[224] A further concession came in that one-third of all five sizes of trousers were to be shipped to various garrisons bundled with all the buttons, thread, and necessary items to have them completed by local tailors.[225]

Another pattern that was kept from the earlier issue was the double-breasted sky-blue mounted overcoat, but this time it became universal for all enlisted men. In turn, officers were to replace the old cloak coat with a dark blue wool overcoat and optional detachable cape that resembled the enlisted style, complete with gilt officer's buttons rather than the black frogging of the 1851-pattern. An inquiry came from the field as to proper linings for the officer's model. While Marcy felt this should be left to the individual officer's discretion, as had been previous custom, the secretary of war wanted the linings to match the color of facings for the respective corps and branches.[226]

Although the new order added details previously not included, such as branch-lined capes, combined with earlier patterns, it also dispensed with certain old items. For instance, sashes for officers and senior non-commissioned officers disappeared.[227] Shoulder scales likewise were discontinued, following in the footsteps of neckstocks that had been terminated the prior year, although most other leather accoutrements remained little-changed at first.[228]

In due course, all such materials were reviewed for sale as surplus. Shoulder scales and plumes for light artillery caps were among the first items placed on the open market.[229] Some 60,000 uniform hats, forage caps, sack coats, and enlisted frock coats were to be sold too.[230]

With the machinery set in motion to provide new items and sell old ones, Meigs ordered the Philadelphia Depot to "commence the manufacture of uniforms without delay, and commence shipping to the most distant posts. The supply on the Upper Missouri should be sent first, Arizona next."[231] Thereafter, these remote posts remained the primary goal for supply as far as Meigs was concerned, although some garrisons located elsewhere submitted their requests early on as well.[232]

These actions proved premature because of a bill in Congress "to dispose of the greater part" of the old pattern did not pass. In response Meigs decided to refrain from sales and dictated that purchases of new cloth were not to be made because of the large quantities already in stock and also because adequate appropriations for the new uniform were not forthcoming as supposed.[233]

Under the circumstances the quartermaster general wanted to delay publishing the list for the new issue, especially in light of the fact that his department would run out of funds early in 1873 for making up the items called for in General Orders No. 92.[234] Manufacture would be halted as a result, and the issue of new garments made only to those posts that already had been sent advance supplies. Thereafter, old patterns were to be sent out until the fiscal situation could be solved.[235] This likewise forced Meigs to ask the chairman of the military affairs committee in the Senate to advance a substantial sum of money from the next year's appropriations to rectify the problem.[236] Meigs told the secretary of war as well, indicating that just over $397,000 was required, no mean sum for its day.[237] As another recourse, Meigs called for lists of old stocks to sent in for disposition to be held until issues of new garments were on hand.[238]

At the end of 1872 Meigs summarized his dilemma. Previous appropriations for clothing being almost exhausted, the need to purchase 10,000 campaign hats at $2.80 each, produce 28,969 dress coats each at

$3.50, and 13,019 blouses at a unit cost of $1.50, along with foot and mounted trousers, and dress caps, all of which had been authorized prior to December 2, along with funds for another 25,000 blouses, 5,000 uniform coats, and 50,000 pairs of Berlin gloves would result in the department incurring a tremendous debt. The only recourse was for supplemental funds from Congress to sustain the new uniform procurement through the end of the fiscal year (June 30, 1873).[239]

Meigs went on to conclude:

The Government is granted 30,000 men to defend the frontier, protect settlements, and keep order. They are fully and usefully employed, and it would involve a great responsibility with the demands for protection for frontier settlers, to leave the army unfilled.[240]

Meigs drove home his point. All these defenders of westward expansion required clothing, shelter, and necessities at a considerable expense. Added to this was the unforeseen change in uniform that had not been included in the original budget submissions by the department, which after all had not been part of the process of changing the uniform in the first place.

Thus everything was put on hold until a plan as to how to proceed was developed to avoid giving certain bidders an unfair advantage, as well as finding a resolution to the funding shortfalls.[241] Some would be purchasers complained that blouses and overcoats were not being offered on the market because of this situation, but Meigs held his ground about releasing overcoats and blouses.[242]

The wisdom of this cautious reduction of old stocks became evident in a number of ways, not the least of which arose when the quantities of mounted overcoats began to run low. Originally all troops were to be clothed in this garment.[243] Stocks were so limited, though, that an alternative had to found, there being only 55,300 mounted patterns left versus 181,611 foot overcoats. The military storekeeper at Philadelphia indicated that the foot overcoats could be converted by adding a long cape to give the an outward appearance similar to the mounted one at a cost of $1.50 each, thereby preventing further waste to the government. This was seen as an interim measure, however, as Meigs thought it desirable to begin experiments "on a new pattern overcoat."[244]

Meigs expanded on this view:

The troops occupy some stations in which they are exposed to Arctic temperature and in which they cannot safely be out of doors,

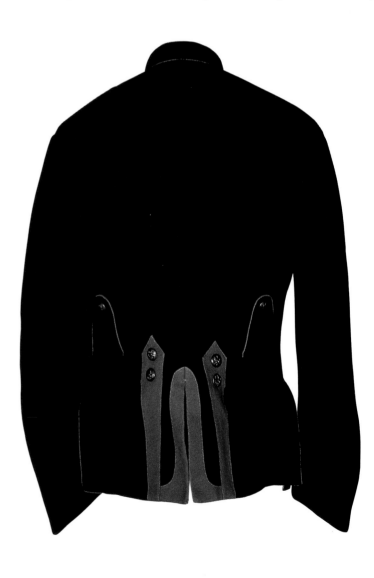

Side and rear views of the 1872-pattern Signal Service enlisted coat with crossed flags device on the sleeves and orange facings. No collar insignia ever were authorized for this coat. SI

unless clothed as Arctic voyagers or as Esquimaux clothe themselves, viz. complete suits of fur. I have heard of an escort of soldiers sent out with an Engineer of the North [sic] Pacific Railroad in pleasant weather, who were caught in a violent snow storm and gale, and the whole party, Engineers and soldiers, were insufficiently clad. . . .[245]

Meigs stated the men narrowly escaped with their lives. It was in some cases that he thought a complete fur outfit should be experimented with because wool did not provide sufficient warmth. Research in the Library of Congress into reports of Arctic expeditions and study of Russian troops or other forces engaged in such hostile environments seemed appropriate.[246]

In the meantime, modification of old pattern woolen dismounted overcoats moved forward, mounted versions being supplied only to cavalry and light artillery troops thereafter. The foot version with new cape then was to be given dismounted troops.[247] Two types were proposed, one with a new, larger cape that could be buttoned to the existing collar, and thus be capable of being removed at will to be worn separately. The other was to be buttoned under the short cape, but also was able to be detached for separate use.[248] In either case, the old short cape was to be retained to add to the comfort of the wearer, and a sample was submitted to Inspector General Randolph Marcy and Secretary of War William Belknap for approval.[249] They concurred, and after June 1873 the converted, double-cape coat was to be issued.[250] The pattern with the larger cape under the smaller prevailed. In addition, beginning in 1871, overcoats that had been lined with blankets to provide extra warmth were retained for mounted troops.[251] It seems, however, the idea of the detachable second cape was abandoned, and that the additional longer cape was sewn on permanently at Philadelphia "so as to match the color of the coats for which they are intended."[252]

As part of efforts to maintain standard colors and quality a quartermaster officer was dispatched to inspect the clothing and cloth to be sold, and in the latter instance to test its strength in case it could be retained for making new uniforms.[253] In one case the cloth was pronounced unsuitable for trousers but adequate for overcoat manufacture. The inspector also found that the cloth treated with the Cowles process

1872-pattern principal musician of infantry coat with herringbone on the chest. The regimental number was supposed to be placed on both sides of the collar in stamped sheet brass. Chevrons were made in pairs and were to have the hunting horn facing forward. SI

The enlisted version of the 1872-pattern campaign hat as issued, open and folded. Gordon Chappell Photograph. USA

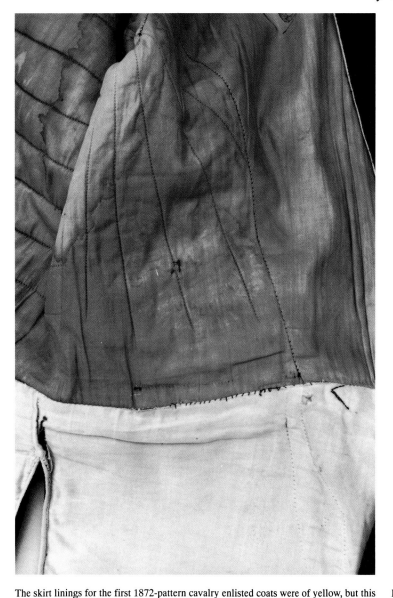

The skirt linings for the first 1872-pattern cavalry enlisted coats were of yellow, but this was changed to black Italian cloth less than a year after production began as one of several changes to the first garments made. KHC

Rear 1872-pattern cavalry enlisted coat after the belt loops had been ordered to be moved further back beginning in 1873. By 1876 a revised cut of the waist also was ordered to provide a better fit for the coat. SI

was stronger when tested, having been contracted by the chemical process. For this reason Meigs approved retaining the material for overcoats.[254]

Another change that occurred soon after the first production 1872-pattern coats for cavalry were issued had to do with the placement of the belt loops. Originally they were sewn in to the waist too far forward, thereby interfering with the saber belt hangers on the left side, as is the case with Sergeant William Williams' coat. Kurt Cox Photograph. RBM

The quartermaster general also looked further into the matter and found that the cloth still had utility. He suggested it was strong enough to be retained. Meigs went on to indicate it was not as coarse as the inspector at Philadelphia had contended. Additionally, Meigs believed it was "not of an unpleasant color to the eye" and well could made into "a hunting suit of the richest man in the land" much less uniforms for soldiers on duty "in the field, in the wilderness and mountains."[255] The secretary of war agreed, directing the material be used for blouses, although not uniform coats.[256]

Dealing with stocks on hand was not the only challenge confronting the quartermaster, however. First, while many old patterns items were issued until new ones could replace them Meigs again wanted to ensure that history was preserved. To this end, he required examples of each the previous woolen garments be moth proofed and retained as specimens for the museum at Schuylkill.[257]

Concurrently a number of articles considered or recommended previously had found their way into the new scheme of things as set forth by Marcy's board. All of these had to have standards established, prices fixed for annual appropriations and issue tables of allowance, requirements determined, then everything either had to be made or procured

Detail of belt loop on Sergeant Williams' 1872-pattern cavalry coat. LBNB

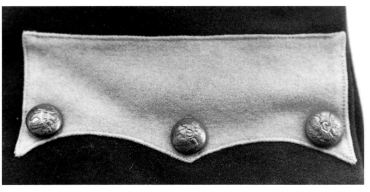

Among the other custom features of Sergeant Williams' 1872-pattern coat were officers' "C" buttons on the cuff flashes in lieu of the standard enlisted button. This practice was not unique to Williams. Other examples exist that demonstrate some non-commissioned officers of the 1870s followed a similar course. LBNB

based upon the accepted patterns.[258] Some of these were minor, such as white Berlin gloves (a knitted glove of Berlin wool) to complete the dress uniform.[259] Others were more notable, not the least of which was the plaited blouse.

The desire to have the new pattern of the blouse bespoke of a powerful backing for replacement of the old patterns, or at least influential champions of specific changes. In as much as the plaited blouse had been singled out by General Sherman, who commented a "hunting or shooting jacket" was "possibly the most convenient for soldiers in service in the Indian country," might have influenced the adoption of this item.[260] More to the point was Sherman's reference to campaign conditions in the West, the major region for U.S. Army field operations during the three decades after the Civil War. Often it seemed those who designed clothing and equipment ignored the extremes of climate faced in that vast, varied region.

Ironically, with the exception of winter gear none of the early boards gave serious thought to borrowing from the rugged buckskin of the Plains Indians. While some individuals, such as George Armstrong Custer, opted to take on the guise of the frontiersman who had seen the wisdom of the ways of the native peoples, an American hunting dress was disregarded for one of more traditional European design. This was somewhat ironic given the precedence to the contrary in the early history of the American military, when during the Revolutionary War some continental forces, such as Butler's Rangers, Hall's Delaware Regiment, and the Sixth Virginia Regiment were among those who donned "hunting" or "rifle" dress.[261]

While the tried and accepted garb of many frontiersmen was not officially sanctioned, the plaited blouse at least had been tested previously in combat conditions as Meigs noted: "Burnside wore this blouse during the early part of the war."[262] Meigs added that he would not relish wearing this "close blouse of three thicknesses of flannel in Washington in summer," much less "in Arizona, or the Rio Grande." As such he doubted the wisdom of adopting this pattern.[263]

Meigs' thoughts aside, the plaited blouse was retained as the new work and campaign garment. Soon a number of contractors offered to make up the blouse, but Meigs responded that piece work given to local women living near the quartermaster arsenals had been employed for this purpose and he urged continuing the seamstress system that gave employment to widows and spouses of Civil War veterans.[264]

Meigs made this observation in reply to a statement by a civilian employee at the Schuylkill Arsenal who faulted the quality of the work

by these seamstresses. This man was F.S. Johnson, who likewise felt he could improve on the blouse and submitted a revised design that he advocated and took "great pride in."[265] Meigs answered that Johnson's blouse was "substantially the same as that adopted by the Board" but his revision was "neater in appearance, simpler and more easily made

In 1873 commissary sergeants were to have white piping and gray facings as the trim on their dress coat. Prior to that time piping and facings were to be gray. Note the crescent on the chevron also is white and is placed points up, despite the fact that regulations called for these devices to be sewn points forward. German silver crescents were to be applied to both sides of the collar as well. SI

German silver crescents were to be worn with points up on the dress cap and forage cap for commissary sergeants. RBM

and it is said, made at less cost." He went on to list the differences from the board's version, which required considerably more pieces of flannel to fashion the body and the skirts; the reduction of the number of internal pockets from seven to two; and the removal of the silk cord from the plaits on the breast, substituting worsted cord that matched the traditional colors of the branch facings. Further, "the plaits turned to the front below as well as above the belt instead of the front above and to the rear below. Finally the skirt hung "closed in front, below the belt" on Johnson's design, rather than was open as was the case with the Board's sample. All these revisions reduced costs by an estimated $.65 per garment, for a projected $39,000 savings to the army, a figure that prompted Meigs to advocate Johnson's prototype![266] Meigs was instructed that Johnson's model would supersede the original and he thus required samples to be sent to his "office to be sealed as the standard, as soon as possible."[267] This transaction took place, although some confusion persisted as to whether the cord for all blouses should be light blue, or rather that color would serve for infantry only, while the other branches would have cord to match the color of their respective facings.[268]

Meigs provided clarification by indicating branch colors were approved, but cautioned: "you will be careful in selecting the light blue cord [for infantry], to use only such as will not be likely to fade."[269] Even then, some of the early pattern had been made up, and Meigs, in the interest of economy, said he wanted them issued. He went on to state that the new model likewise should be lined as it was the intention to have blouses sent out "during the coming winter."[270]

Anxious to have this particular item in production as soon as possible, Meigs previously instructed that the new patterns be sent with an individual skilled in cutting garments to the Jeffersonville Depot in Indiana, where the blouses and trousers were to be made. This workman would have considerable labor ahead because Meigs wanted 30,000 blouses to be produced there![271] One-third of these would be cut and all materials, including thread and needle, packaged and set aside until quartermasters from the various garrisons actually made requisitions for them.[272] His goal was to have the work force mobilized and fabrication undertaken rapidly.[273] He thought that these actions would "better suit present prevailing tastes

Ordnance Sergeant Leodegar Schnyder, as befitted his long years as a staff non-commissioned officer (depicted by his nine service stripes) chose to have a tailor-made ordnance sergeant coat with Ordnance Department officers' buttons, and crimson chevrons and service stripes that were sewn separately rather than of the machine-stitched regulation style. FLNHS

1872-pattern corporal of ordnance. Shell and flame insignia of stamped sheet brass were to be attached to both sides of the collar. All trim and facings originally were to be crimson. SI

In 1873 Inspector General Marcy concurred with a recommendation to change the piping on ordnance sergeant's coats to white as seen here. Stamped brass shell and flame insignia were to be worn on the collars as with the all-crimson trimmed coat. SI

in the army and thus avoid the recutting which it is believed, is a caprice, and not a necessity. . . ."[274]

To expedite the work, and in order to demonstrate that the government was not at the mercy of the professional cloth cutters, Meigs authorized a contract to obtain a cutting machine as an emergency measure that would be abandoned after the "delivery of the uniform now so urgently needed and pressed especially for posts on the Upper Missouri River."[275]

This letter was telling in two ways. First, it indicated the concern for delivery to remote forts that for much of the year could only be reached with some difficulty because of severe weather conditions. In fact, these circumstances prompted Meigs to indicate that "The uniform coat is the principal part of the uniform and in case of necessity be worn with the New, or even with the Old forage cap or hat."[276]

But obtaining this coat proved difficult. First, facing material was not readily available. For this reason Meigs instructed: "Quietly ascertain where you can find a stock of facing cloth and new trimmings, and prepare to purchase on telegraphic instructions to that effect."[277]

While Quartermaster Department personnel sought facing material, some veterans who had lived through the era of the 1851-pattern

uniform expressed a concern that it was not possible to locate color-fast materials based on prior experiences. Meigs responded by ordering tests on samples. The findings indicated scarlet and crimson held up the best to exposure from light and the elements.[278]

Moreover, J.R. Ackerman, the supplier who produced the original pattern for the dress coat adopted in 1872, assured the facings "would stand and not fade."[279] Still Marcy thought the facings submitted for approval were not of the best dye or as brilliant as they could be. The secretary of war seemed less critical. He approved slight variations from the approved sample colors, so long as the color was not fugitive.[280] With this, the Quartermaster Department persisted in its search for adequate facings, although the quest went on for years.[281]

Besides experiencing difficulties with procuring proper material for branch facings, the quartermaster also confronted problems with the work force at the Philadelphia Arsenal, where all these coats were to be produced at first. This meant outside contracts had to be let with firms that cut clothing for civilian manufacturers.[282] While this procedure went against previous practice, the quartermaster general allowed for a change especially in view of the problem that the call to produce new uniforms came during the peak manufacturing period in the local garment industry. Supposedly not enough workers could be found to take on the jobs, thereby forcing the Philadelphia depot to make contracts with Leon & Son and Bradley & Leach, who accomplished their assignment so well and quickly that more orders were made with the latter firm.[283] This decision brought about a letter of protest from local cutters who had been employed at the depot previously.[284]

Another factor in deviating from the past manufacturing system can be traced to the contention by Schuylkill Arsenal's energetic, if not outspoken employee who maintained:

These uniform coats require to be made by persons understanding the business. Not five women in every hundred, who have worked on army clothing ever learned the trade. The old uniform was simply cut and required no great experience to put it together. The new uniform being of an entirely different pattern and properly made in all details will require skilled hands, and such hands are only to be found among men.[285]

Johnson went on to assert: "Coats require not only a knowledge of the business," but also one had to have the strength "to press the parts" properly before putting them together. While he conceded, "certain portions of the coat can no doubt be made by women, but the supervision of men is necessary to watch them and the pressing and finishing must in the end be done by men: that is if the government requires a standard of work equal to the sample uniform. . . ."[286]

Johnson's immediate superior concurred, with certain qualifications. He remarked:

There are a large number of small establishments in this city [Philadelphia], employing men and women conjointly, many of them composed of one family each. They are under the supervision of men, who do the heavier and more difficult portions of the work, and make clothing for dealers in this and other cities. To such establishments, as referred to above, uniform coats might be given, and a good style of work secured. . . ."[287]

While these remarks sound sexist by today's standards, in truth they stemmed from a simple fact. Then, much as now, males dominated the tailor trade. Even though this was a reality of the garment business Meigs persisted in his desire to secure employment for spouses and family members of veterans, the payment for piece work on military clothing being one of the few official means of assistance to this group in the immediate post-Civil War era. For this reason he retorted: "I think that women should be employed, as far as possible, making up the uniform and that while it will not be proper to employ those who are unskillful, it will be equally improper to decide that men only can sew the parts. . . ."[288] He reinforced this directive requiring: "Give a fair and reasonable price to the work women. Demand and secure good work."[289]

While he was "disappointed that the old arsenal system of giving out work" to the spouses of veterans could "not be continued with the new uniform," he nonetheless set aside his own preferences and gave not only approval for contracting firms to cut the uniforms. But he still was anxious to forge ahead, so he had a quantity of infantry and cavalry coats that had been cut out sent to Jeffersonville for assembly to hasten production "by employing the full capacity of both depots at the same time."[290] The coats that caused so much consternation were close approximations of the French line infantry model for mounted troops (light artillery, cavalry, and signal service enlisted men), that had received so much notice in the past, except that the tails were fully faced with material in branch colors unlike the original that had piping on the tails as an outline. Curiously, the cuffs did not have the same type of trim as the French model either, these being similar to the so-called English cuff that had adorned jackets or coats of some volunteer units in the Civil War, including some prominent New York regiments. The coat for dismounted enlisted men (infantry, engineers, heavy artillery, ordnance, and hospital stewards) had different tails, once more being similar to English patterns of the period. Additionally foot soldiers' coats had a longer skirts that were left raw at the bottom edges rather then being edged in facing material as was the case for the mounted coat. In effect, there were only two types of coats now, at least for dress, this being very much in keeping with the French system that Meigs had mentioned previously.

Officers jackets and coats were a bit more somber than those for enlisted men. The latter garments were trimmed in black mohair rather than branch piping, and resembling the former sack coat more than the plaited blouse. One of the main differences was the new jackets had five buttons on the chest and three on the cuffs, whereas the previous pattern had four chest buttons, and there was no specific requirement for sleeve buttons. The black mohair trim decorated the chest and skirts, with frogs emanating from the buttons in a sort of three-leaf clover design. Additional black mohair quatrefoils were sewn on the sleeves and other trim on the rear of the jacket, the "binding braid" being called out at 1/2-inch wide and the "trimming braid" being set as 1/4-inch wide.[291] The prototype of the 1872-pattern officer's jacket also displayed brevet rank on the collars, as did the draft of the new uniform regulation, but this was disallowed in the final version based upon a movement in the U.S. Congress to downplay the confusing brevet system that had arisen in the wake of the Civil War. Dress coat collars for officers, likewise were at first to bear the brevet rank, but again this was overruled and dropped from the official version of the regulation.[292] With an estimated 1,700 brevets to brigadier general or major general being doled out to the Union brass, the reaction to this system and its abandonment soon after the Civil War seemed inevitable.[293]

Another important aspect of the new officer's coat was the fact that all were now double-breasted regardless of rank, the number of buttons being one means of setting field grade and company grade apart from the other (i.e., nine in each row for majors through colonels and seven in each row for second lieutenants through captains). The only exception was for "storekeepers" serving in the Quartermaster Department in various capacities. They were to retain the old style single-breasted coats, a variation that caused Meigs to protest in that he pointed out these officers by statute were to have the same pay and privileges as captains of cavalry.

The quartermaster expressed dismay that his subordinates would be treated differently from their brother officers. Moreover, the Quartermaster Department was listed in the draft regulations as an "administrative service" rather than part of the staff corps. Meigs protested seeing these as a "cruel injustice" that had occurred because only line officers and the inspector general who chaired the board made decisions without representatives of the other staff corps being present.[294]

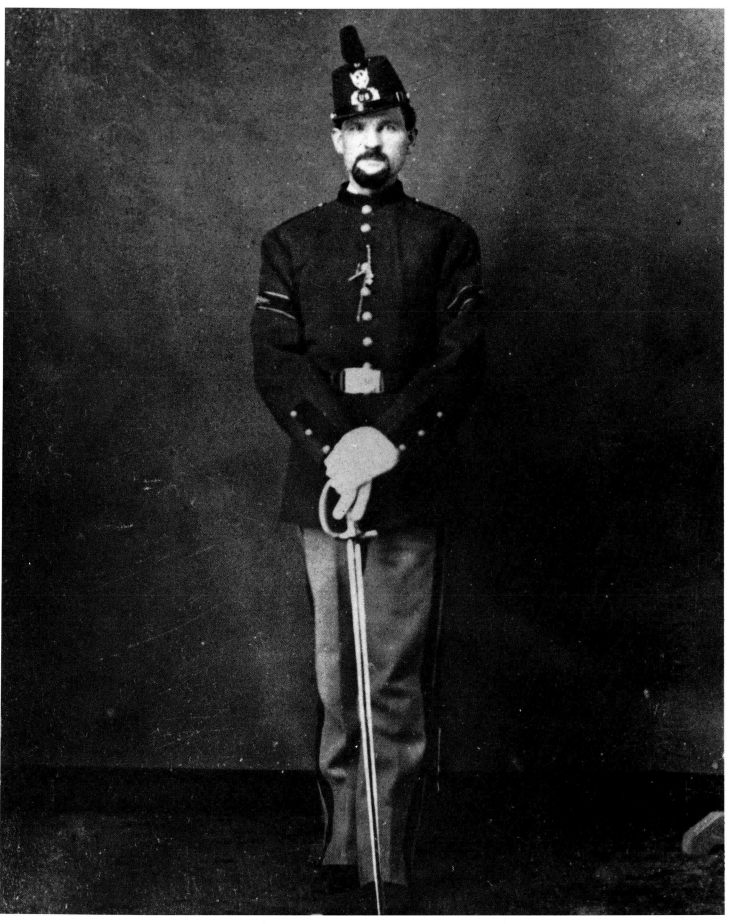

In 1872 emerald green piping and facings were to set off the dark blue basque coat prescribed for hospital stewards as full dress wear, with a cap that had matching green mohair trim around the top and base of the crown and on a vertical at the rear and each side. A green pompon, sheet brass eagle, and a gilt wreath with silver "U.S." also adorned the cap, these details related to cap insignia being clarified shortly after the new regulations were released. Light blue wool trousers had green 1 1/4-inch stripes down the outer seams. It appears that this medical man assigned to Ft. McKeen, Dakota Territory, has attached a civilian watch chain to the front of his coat. FLNHS

Regardless of these issues, at least storekeepers wore shoulder straps of the same style as all other officers to indicate their rank as officers. The straps adopted in 1872 were nearly identical to the previous patterns with some notable exceptions. First, the bars for first lieutenants and captains now were to be silver rather than gold. Additionally, the device for the general-in-chief (Sherman) was new, being a silver arms of the United States flanked by two silver stars that appeared on a dark blue background. The center of straps for all other officers were of the same color cloth except for artillery, cavalry, and infantry who had the traditional scarlet, yellow, and light blue facings. All straps were to be worn with the new blouse, or in certain instances with the dress coat.[295]

Officers' coats often had provisions for easy replacement of straps with epaulets for generals, or for the shoulder knots that had been ushered in with General Orders No. 76. These devices were similar to those adopted for junior officers in the U.S. Navy in 1869.[296] Gold cord over scarlet, yellow, or light blue facings was the standard for artillery, cavalry, and infantry officers, while all other officers were to have dark blue backings (although some extant examples appear black).[297] Rank, regimental numerals, branch devices for certain staff elements, and Old English initials for other staff corps or departments identified the wearer's station and assignment, in keeping with the hierarchical principal.[298] Aiguillettes likewise formed part of the knots worn on the right shoulder by officers of the Adjutant General's and Inspector General's Departments, as well as for aides-de-camp and regimental adjutants. At first these were to be attached permanently to the knots, although this requirement was changed later so that the cords could be detached, so long as they were placed under the knot when worn.[299]

After the board disbanded the matter of enlisted rank devices arose, too.[300] A new style chevron for non-commissioned officers patented by Frank Johnson, the same civilian inspector at Schuylkill Arsenal who had suggested a streamlined blouse pattern, was proposed. These were to be made by labor saving means, using a solid piece of facing material that was then chain-stitched by sewing machine to provide the various insignia. Examples of Johnson's chevrons and old patterns were to be circulated to each board member, who in turn were to contact the quartermaster general with their opinions.[301] Although Meigs was somewhat reluctant to have these patented items considered, fearing the inventor might require high royalties for his design, he nonetheless sent on samples to Marcy even after the board had disbanded so that all the members could examine the old pattern with the proposed replacement and provide their input.[302] The results were favorable and specimens were made up to serve as standard patterns late in the year.[303] Service chevrons ultimately were included, although men who joined the regulars but who had been volunteers during the Civil War probably were disappointed to find out that they were not entitled to display these devices.[304]

All coats and overcoats were to display the chevrons, points down above the elbow, except for hospital stewards. These were to be the emerald green half chevron with yellow trim and caduceus, this time being machine embroidered rather than made by hand. They were to run obliquely downward from the outer seam to the inner seam at approximately a thirty-degree angle, rather than being placed points downward as was the regulation for all other non-commissioned officers. These insignia were already pre-sewn onto the coat, as were the leg stripes when sent from the arsenal.[305]

White piping was authorized for hospital stewards' coats, in 1873, but facings continued to be emerald green. No collar insignia were authorized until 1882 for enlisted medical men. Even then, they may not have been worn. SI

1872-pattern hospital steward's cap. SI

1872-pattern coat for engineer enlisted personnel, in this case for a first sergeant. SI

1872-pattern engineer private's coat. JG

The chevrons on the dress coat applied in this way were seen easily, but capes would obscure those on overcoats. Further, regulations did not mention that chevrons were to be worn on blouses, but wearing chevrons on blouses was the norm. In fact, they actually were to be applied at the depots as noted. By early 1874, the practice of wearing chevrons on the blouse was standard policy.[306]

Another device for enlisted men, in this case of the signal service, also was submitted after the board had disbanded. This insignia resembled the type used during the Civil War and prescribed again in 1868.[307] Some minor adjustments followed that took advantage of similar thread stitching as that proposed by Johnson for chevrons, then these devices were adopted.[308]

Other chevrons were added that had not formed part of earlier regulations or orders. Principal musicians of artillery and infantry regimental bands, for example, were to have a bugle in the branch color over sergeants' chevrons, according to GO No. 92, later seconded by Marcy.[309] Chief trumpeters for cavalry regiments, at first had no chevrons authorized, nor did company saddler sergeants, despite the fact that both were non-commissioned officers. An interim measure allowed the two specialties to be indicated by company sergeants' chevrons, but soon thereafter Marcy was asked to approve a bugle with an arc over

sergeants' chevrons for the former and a saddler's knife over sergeants' chevrons for the latter rank.[310]

One more expansion of non-commissioned specialties required new chevrons and another uniform variation. In 1873, after Congress authorized post commissary sergeants to be added to the regular army, cadet gray was adopted as the color of all facings, and a crescent points front over standard sergeants' chevrons, all in cadet gray, was prescribed. So, too, were white metal cap, hat, and collar badges, also to be worn with the line vertical, although in practice they all seem to be worn horizontally.[311] For headgear several new designs appeared in addition to the new dress cap and helmet. First, the Andrews hat was another example of the 1868 board and surgeon general's report items that were adopted. The prototype adopted by the board was made by R. Warnock & Co., but others bid on the contract to provide the 10,000 hats called for by the quartermaster.[312] In the meantime, Philadelphia hatter P. Herst had furnished Langdon C. Easton, the chief quartermaster officer at the depot in that city, with a sample hat which was then sent along to Meigs. Meigs examined the Warnock and Herst prototypes and pronounced the pattern on hand from the board as "plain" in comparison to the Herst sample which he described as having a "velvet" finish.[313] Nevertheless, Meigs confessed he was not a hat expert., and while he thought the

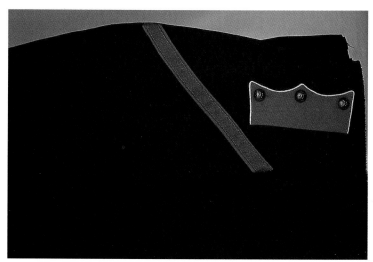

Detail of 1872-pattern engineer enlisted coat with brass castles affixed to collar as decreed by Inspector General R. Marcy in 1873. Originally the letters "CE" were to appear on the cap for Corps of Engineers enlisted men, prior to Marcy's agreement to change to the castle. JG

Cuff facing and service chevron on an 1872-pattern engineer coat. The chevron is edged in scarlet with sky-blue in the center, indicating service in war in the infantry. SI

Herst example was "better finished and likely to keep cleaner than the Board hat, and I think it may be received, so far as appearance goes, as fully equal," he still was not convinced as to "the important question of durability and wear." Consequently he recommended that Easton "get the best expert advice and aid in inspection" before selecting the best choice between the two hats.[314]

Perhaps Easton followed this prescription because a contract was not issued for nearly a month. When it was made, the award went to Herst who bid $2.83 1/2 for each hat with cords and tassels.[315] Just after this agreement, however, the contractor discovered he could not obtain cords on the open market for the hat as supposed, artillery ones being the only ones that had been released as surplus in quantities.[316] This finding was minor in that sufficient quantities were in stock at the depots to make delivery without cords acceptable, although the ones for infantry tended to be very faded, a factor that seemed of little consequence because the hats were "only to be worn on fatigue duty and on campaign or marches."[317] Herst thus received an order for 10,000 hats without cords at $2.80 each.[318]

Even then, Easton's subordinate, J.F. Rodgers, proposed an abbreviated brim. He observed the standard hat, after wear in the field, became very pliable. Then, because of the weight associated with the broad brim it tended to droop "down in an uncomfortable and unsightly manner over the neck and face of the wearer."[319] Easton forwarded an improved sample for Meigs to examine.[320] This was beginning of several years of deliberation on this matter that led to the adoption of a new pattern in 1876.[321]

William O. Tyler, a Seventh Cavalry trooper who had to wear this hat on rugged campaign service summed up the reason why this headpiece ultimately was replaced. Tyler rightly recollected the old black campaign hat had:

> a very wide brim that had hooks and eyes on it, front and rear so
> that it might be made to appear in shape at least like a chapeau of a
> Major General, but the handling that it got and the rain and wind
> gave it an appearance unlike anything I ever saw on the head of a

man. Some of the Companies like L, F, and C, refused to wear them and purchased out of private funds, a hat of much better shape and quality. Owing to the cheap material and its great width the brim of my hat had become separated from the crown for nearly one half

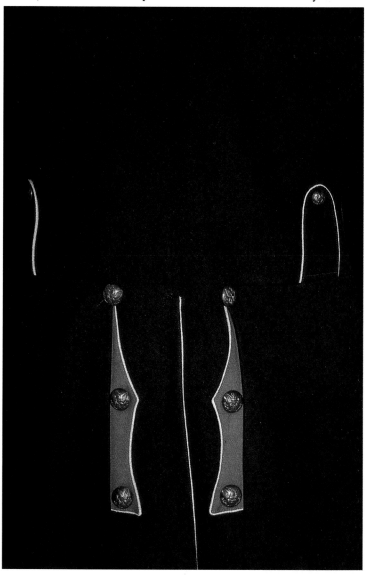

Rear of 1872-pattern engineer coat showing the belt loops and tail facings. SI

the way round, and in consequence I was sometimes looking over the brim and sometimes, under it.[322]

Fewer derogatory comments accompanied the introduction of another of the 1872-pattern pieces of headgear, the low crowned forage cap of the type previously popular with officers and those enlisted personnel inclined to purchase it. Now it was to be worn by everyone. Warnock & Co. also produced the sample for the board. This prototype had braid on it, but that trim was ordered removed for the cap adopted while the first contract went to Bent and Bush of Boston, for 28,000 caps.[323]

Some 30,000 cap covers conforming to the shape of the sloping crown likewise were to be issued to render this headgear more serviceable in foul weather.[324] These were similar to the covers that had been issued with the 1851-cap and provided for earlier forage caps by the Civil War in that black treated material was used as a water repellent. Although the concept was utilitarian, the execution evidently met with little favor. It seems many enlisted men did not draw them at all, and if they did, the covers were disposed of or not used, thereby resulting in their discontinuance as an item of issue by 1877.[325]

Nonetheless, Meigs intended for these covers to be issued by July 1, 1873, along with the new forage caps, dress caps, campaign hats, Berlin gloves, mounted helmets, and dismounted dress caps.[326]

Marcy, as president of the board, must have been pleased with this goal. He had been a major proponent of change stating:

The inspection reports for several years past have shown that the issues from the clothing remaining on hand after the rebellion which as a measure of economy have been considered unavoidable, have caused considerable dissatisfaction among the enlisted men; for the reason that this clothing is made from material inferior in quality and cut so badly that the soldier generally has been obliged, at his own expense, to have his coat and trousers made over again.[327]

Other general officers supported Marcy, at least in terms of the uniform with chapeau, epaulets, and sash that they were to wear for formal occasions.[328] In voicing his opinion to General William T. Sherman, Lieutenant General Philip H. Sheridan added that he would like to see the sash worn over the shoulder, as had been the case in prior times for an officer of the day. He likewise concluded with a less than enthusiastic endorsement: I only favor the above uniform because I do not know what to substitute for it."[329]

Sherman, who according to one biographer had "evidenced little interest in military attire," and tended to don a "daily uniform" that "to the surprise of the impeccably tailored staff officers" who surrounded him "consisted of a combination of the most available items, thrown together with little regard for cleanliness or effect" had his own thoughts on the matter, which he communicated to Sheridan.[330]

For one thing, Sherman contended that aiguillettes were derived from metal tips on cords or thongs that soldiers used "for tying booty, securing prisoners," and other less colorful employment. Sherman concluded: "If I am right in the etymology of this word it would seem inappropriate that a general office should carry a cord to secure plunder and you may reason also that it would neither be becoming a staff officer."[331]

Sherman, a seasoned campaigner, proceeded to larger matters, writing: "Every Army should have three distinct parts" and that "each class should have a distinctive dress that can be recognized-and adopted to active service in the field."[332] Continuing, the general noted:

The present new uniform was invented by Inspector General Marcy and was substantially adopted by the Secretary of War during my absence in Europe and I would not wish to support even a modification as many officers had made purchases under the new dress when I was consulted. I have no serious objection to any part of it but the embroidered belts which will not in my opinion stand the test of time and exposure to wind and bad weather.

If the General officers generally wish to dispense with the epaulet I should not oppose but as to the aiguillette for Generals, my opinion is pretty firm that they should only be worn by Staff Officers proper.[333]

Sherman's stand on this matter was upheld, but he was not the only one to find fault with the new regulations.[334] Some like Sherman wanted to make minor changes, but were told that this could not be done because many officers already had purchased their new outfit.[335]

On a broader level other individuals wanted to halt issuance of the new uniform for the rank and file, alleging that an enlisted man had to outlay as much as fifteen dollars (more than a month's pay for a private) to replace his previous issue with the new outfit, while officers faced the an outlay of hundreds of dollars to obtain the new items.[336] Meigs disagreed, pointing out when uniform costs rose, so too did the allowances for the enlisted men. This fact, coupled with the practice of many men to obtain inspected and condemned items (surplus) at lesser costs than the rate set for issue items, would continue to insure that the common soldier would not suffer.[337]

Others took exception, and still maintained the new prices were unfair, harkening back to earlier problems when rough service and poor quality cloth combined to force soldiers to purchase clothing as replacements for items that had worn out before new annual allotments were authorized.[338] Meigs reply to the complaints of inferior clothing was that when soldiers bought condemned items they saved money but in fact obtained "inferior quality clothing" that had been disposed of by the army. To Meigs, such "extensive use of this cast off and rejected material" was false economy and at the heart of such complaints.[339]

Meigs' views aside, others continued to find fault with the expense incurred by enlisted personnel who had to have the proper alterations performed on their new coats and trousers.[340] The former garment particularly drew criticism because the fit of the collar, length of the sleeves, and chest sizes were pronounced disproportional, making the 1872-pattern coat little better than the style it replaced. Indeed, it seemed the larger the coat, the worse the problem became, inducing the officer who brought this matter to the attention of others to suggest that each major post should be authorized "one competent cutter and sufficient journeymen tailors" to produce the articles required for their garrisons with custom wear.[341] Such an approach might have been cost effective if the contention of another writer were true. He noted it cost at least five dollars for a soldier to have the company tailor or civilian counterpart properly fit the uniform, a figure that approached what the government paid to produce the coat in the first place![342]

Theoretically the 1872-pattern coat would not require this sort of extensive reworking. J.R. Ackerman's sample for the board cost the princely sum of $132 (nearly a year's pay for a private), and was made expertly.[343] This coat provided an excellent pattern for the standard. The Quartermaster Department likewise engaged professional cutters and procured the best materials to produce the coats.

Still, some adjustments were in order, first for cavalry coats. One of the changes had to do with the lining. The military storekeeper at Schuylkill Arsenal sent two specimens, one with a black Italian cloth lining and the other that was yellow lined. He preferred the black although the yellow Italian cloth had been selected as standard. It was difficult to obtain that color, however, whereas black presented no such problem.[344]

Marcy considered the matter and decided the black lining was "preferable to the yellow and orange, and did not conflict with the requirements of the regulations for the new Uniform." Meigs thus ordered that thereafter the dress coats would "be lined with black instead of the colored Italian cloths, as soon as the stock of materials purchased for that purpose shall be exhausted."[345] This meant the underside of the skirts for the first lot of cavalry dress coats would show a flash of color that coincided with their trim. Later examples would not. Here again aesthetics gave way to practical considerations.

The next practical turn related to the mounted dress coat had to do with the loops that were let into the waist so that they could be buttoned over the saber belt to keep it in place. Captain, A.E. Bates, a cavalry officer then serving at West Point, noted a design error. He submitted the loop of the left side was "so placed that the sabre sling and hook come directly over it . . . and prevent its being buttoned over the belt."[346] A reworking of the loop so that the saber sling could pass through it, or relocation of the loop to prevent it from interfering with the sling were two possibilities to rectify the situation in the officer's estimation.

Meigs wanted the necessary alterations carried out on the pattern coat, followed by correction of the problem based on the solution selected on all light artillery and cavalry coats that were to be issued thereafter. He closed with: "all the garments sent out from the arsenal must be perfect."[347]

The reconfiguration of the sample and those issued after the correction was simply a repositioning of the supports so that they would not interfere with the saber strap, thereby correcting Captain Bates' original concern.[348] But that officer later pointed out other faults that had to be remedied. During an inspection of his detachment, he discovered "that the coats & blouses all required alteration for the following reasons: Cavalry coats are all too wide at the neck, breast and waist, even for the largest men & the waist generally too short."[349] The No. 4 coats were at least 3-inches too short in the waist, according to Bates, and the sleeves "rather too short" as well.

Meigs required an investigation into the matter. The reply was: "The waist of the standard No. 4 coat will always fit a well proportioned man" while the collar purposely was "made to fit loosely so that if necessary, it can be made smaller."[350] Additionally he was informed that a No. 1 coat was tried on a man 5'6", the No. 2 on a 5'8" man, the No. 3 on a 5'10" man, and the No. 4 on a 6' man, with the conclusion from this test "in all cases they seemed to be good fit so far as length of waist and length of sleeves are concerned." Further, in two cases the men were stout and the coats fit well. In the other two instances the "men were

light and of slender build and the coats too large around the neck and waist." They would have to be altered, but in general it seemed that the coats as cut would "fit a majority of our enlisted men." Indeed, individuals were so different from each other that it would require many sizes to accommodate everyone. The conventional wisdom relayed to Meigs was that the pattern should be left unchanged until more coats went to the field and additional comments came back for consideration.[351] As it turned out, that process took another three years.[352]

Although not stemming from such practical concerns as size and placement of belt supports, another matter concerning coats was addressed, too. On November 26, 1873, the military storekeeper at Schuylkill Arsenal proposed a slight modification of the dress coats for commissary sergeants, ordnance men, and hospital stewards. He asked that his superiors consider the addition of white piping for these three areas of specialization on the dress coat to accent the branch facings, much as was the case with coats of engineer soldiers. To that time, commissary sergeants had all cadet gray piping, collar, cuff, and tail flashes, while ordnance men had complete crimson facings and hospital stewards had all emerald green trim for the dress coat, along with trouser stripes of 1 1/4-inch emerald green facing material in lieu of the slightly wider crimson worsted versions authorized them in 1858.

In December 1873 Inspector General Marcy thought the idea "a decided improvement" and observing no conflict with the uniform regulations saw "no reason why it should not be adopted for the enlisted men of the Staff Corps."[353] Thereafter white piping was approved and uniform coats were to be made up with white piping as sealed samples for future production reference. This meant that coats made earlier differed slightly from those issued later with the white piping.

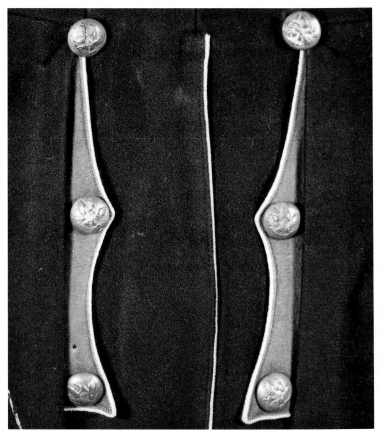

Detail of tail facings for the 1872-pattern engineer coat, and beginning in 1873 for ordnance sergeants, hospital stewards, and commissary sergeants having the white piping added in that year. AHS

This situation characterized the first attempts to make the new uniform available. Other minor areas of adjustment included specifics about the cap for hospital stewards. Was it to have a green pompon and worsted braid of that color? The response from the inspector general through the quartermaster general was in the affirmative.[354] Further, the insignia was to be the same as that worn during the Civil War, to wit, "of white metal, chased: Roman capitals one-half (1/2) inch high, to be placed within the wreath. To have wire loops soldered on the back to fasten to cap." In turn, the wreath was to be, "of dead or unburnished gilt-metal, representing two olive branches, held at the bottom by a loop and a knot, turning upward and bending in an oval shape, approaching each other at the top." The height was given as 1 1/2-inches with the width at the greatest point between the outer edges set at 2 5/8-inches. The branches were five-eighths of an inch and the whole wreath was held by a pair of brass wires on the back.[355]

Marcy also noted in his endorsement that ordnance and engineer soldiers would have the same wreath but white Roman letters "O.D." and "E.C." were to be substituted for the "U.S."[356] Several months later a general order rescinded the ordnance and engineer designs and replaced them with a brass shell and flame device and a brass castle with company letter respectively.[357] Although a number of caps had been made up with the wreath and E.C., they were refitted with the castle before being sent for issue.[358]

On a related subject, the military storekeeper at the Philadelphia Depot thought the ordnance shell and flame device for the collar too small for the cap, while the larger version was too great of a size that the chinstrap covered the lower portion of the insignia.[359] He suggested the wreath be retained, sufficient numbers of these already being on hand from the previous order, and used in tandem with the ordnance smaller bomb.[360] Although this recommendation was not followed, Marcy's concern that the castle for enlisted engineer coat collars was to be smaller than the one shown to him as standard pattern did receive attention.[361] Thus, a second sample was sent for the inspector general to examine and approve, this one being of a lesser size and having a back filed with solder and a loop for attachment on the rear.[362]

The inspector general once again ultimately was contacted because the old 5/8-inch size brass hat numbers were adequate for the regimental designation on the dress coat but too large for dress caps and forage caps. What is more, the larger sizes were being sold as surplus.[363] Marcy concurred that 1/2-inch brass should be procured for caps.[364] Prior to this, Meigs had permitted 1/2-inch numbers to be procured in limited quantities. He further took it upon himself to speculate that the general orders incorrectly had called for the badge of the corps or letter of the company to be worn on caps.[365] Meigs indicated that the wording should have permitted both devices to be used.[366] Marcy thought that the change of adding the company letter rather than a regimental numeral on the forage cap should be adopted for artillery, cavalry, engineer, and infantry troops, but not ordnance, nor would this be necessary for commissary sergeants.[367] No such statement was made in regard to the dress cap, although it seems that a similar method was employed regularly, with the company letter and badge being used together, in the case of infantry and artillery troops at least. It would take another four years for this arrangement finally to be spelled out in detail.[368]

These were not the only insignia issues that raised questions and required further explanation. For instance, Meigs wondered whether brass letters and numbers on hand from the Civil War would suffice for the new uniform.[369]

These were but a few points of fine tuning that were to take place for the new pattern pieces over the ensuing period after the new uniforms was adopted. After the many details and oversights had been addressed though, it should have followed that everyone would be satisfied with the uniform as adopted by Marcy's board and modified shortly thereafter.

This was not to prove the case. Once again, the *Army and Navy Journal* became a forum for the unsatisfied. One of the earliest tirades signed as "Revilo" reviled: "The fiat has at last gone forth. The board which has been in session almost ever since the war has at last decided to dress us in the gorgeous apparel of the drum-major."[370]

While "Revilo" exaggerated the duration of the board's sitting, the fact that several bodies had wrestled with the question intermittently for years, nearly a decade, was true. So, too, were the concerns of many junior officers who had to buy a new expensive uniform. He asked, where would the $200 come from to procure the kit, Congress? What if one could not afford to pay this princely sum, would they "Be tried for 'disobedience of order'" or to avoid this if they secured the new items but did not pay for them, would they be charged with "conduct unbecoming an officer and a gentlemen?"

He also pondered what he and his comrades below the rank of brigadier general were to do with their epaulets. Should they present them as gifts to those who wore stars, "have a grand raffle," he suggested, "or sell out to the circus bands?" Various metropolitan police departments might benefit from such sales as well, with all the single-breasted company grade frock coats being made available by the new order. Now, though, a lieutenant might be mistaken for a major or colonel because everyone was to have double-breasted frocks.

The disappearance of the sash likewise was a concern. How would one tell the officer of the day, once indicated by the wearing the sash scarf-fashion? Perhaps one would have to chalk the letters "O.D." on his back. Alluding to the traditional hierarchical division between officers and non-commissioned officers, "Revilo" asked why not have the former wear trousers of half blue and half red because the new leg stripes were so wide any way compared to the old 1/8-inch welts? Failing this, the difference between the 1-inch NCO leg stripes and the 1 1/2-inch stripes for line officers seemed so inconsequential, he quipped: "Why couldn't the sergeants stripes be placed on the *inside* seam. . . ?"[371]

As for the gold sleeve lace on coats, was it there to keep officers from "wiping their noses" on the cuffs? The gold lace belts seemed out of place to him, too. Maybe it would be less expensive to wear the ones used by somewhat gaudy outfitted fraternal organizations of the era, such as the Knights Templers. The one practical comment he had to make was having each military department furnish the new uniform to the officers in its jurisdiction by contract. He wryly suggested: "The contract could be given to the lowest bidder, provided he is a responsible party and has no relation in Congress."[372]

In the same issue of the journal a more serious letter headed as "THE CHANGE OF UNIFORM" pointed out the great increase in cost to enlisted men over the coming years with the required adoption of the uniform by all in the ranks on or before December 1, 1872. The writer, who signed as "Oglethorpe Barracks," summed up: "Now, Mr. Editor, who will be benefitted by this change in uniform. Certainly not the soldier. The present clothing has been found both serviceable and comfortable at all seasons of the year during the war, and for seven years has answered every purpose during peace. No complaints whatever have been made against it by the rank and file."[373] Here the periodical's editor interjected in disagreement printing parenthetically, "On the contrary, we have had a constant stream of complaints from the rank and file, some of which we have published, but more have not been published. . . ."[374]

Underscoring this dissatisfaction, a reader stationed in New Orleans reproved: "The old outfit never had much to recommend it at best, and six months' service on the seaboard would make it the shabbiest apology for a uniform that ever disgraced the back of an officer."[375] The worse part was the 1858-pattern hat that he damned as being "invented by a dealer in felt, intended as a Sop for Cerberus; a groveling tribute to the civic and Congressional jealously out of that much-abused body – the Army."[376] he did share "Revilo's" regard for the sash, however, which he saw as "the only pretty item in the whole outfit," that was "When of a handsome, fresh color, and properly worn. . . ."[377] Another point where the two concurred was what was to be done with the old uniform that had been so costly? To illuminate the matter he noted that just recently he had to buy a new officers' overcoat at $125. Now, after only seven wearings, it was to be cast aside and for another expensive replacement, along with many other new costly articles.

Enlisted men encountered a like problem in "that no provision has been made to reimburse the soldier for the clothing or old uniform remaining on hand." The men had not only paid for these, but also bore the expense of having them altered in many cases. It seemed proper, according to the correspondent who signed as "Old Soldier," for the government to issue the first new uniform set free of charge. Beyond this he challenged there still was no provision in the new issue "for cool or comfortable clothing."[378] What he counseled was "a dark linen suit, which would have the advantage of being comfortable and more easily kept clean than the white linen in summer." This lightweight outfit could replace the woolen trousers and flannel blouses when temperatures dictated and meant that men on duty or off would be better able to cope with the sweltering sun. In fact, they would not have to go to town on pass to relieve the heat with alchohol "that which only makes them hotter."[379] Here the dual purposes othe uniform in maintaining morale and protecting the wearer were seen as one.

With an open mind another respondent stated all his comrades were "more or less anxious to see whether the new uniform is an improvement over the old."[380] He continued:

The old uniform manufactured during the last years of the war is certainly – to use a mild expression, 'a sham.' Scarcely any two garments are the same color, especially with reference to uniform coats, pants and blouses. In a lot of one hundred pairs of pants there are often found all shades from a deep to a pale muddy blue, while uniform coats and blouses range from gray-green to black.[381]

He spoke for many when he recapitulated: "It is to be hoped that the new uniform will be an improvement on the old, as regards color and material . . ." Beyond this, the plea was that the uniform would "be in a condition to be worn when issued, or the government will make the allowance sufficient to enable the soldier to have it refitted by a tailor at a cost not exceeding the value of the articles drawn."[382] These few words summed up two decades of debate.

Would that these good wishes had come to pass. For one thing, the first uniforms were made available later than Meigs' originally had hoped.[383] Once they did begin to be delivered, an anonymous correspondent early impression was printed in the *Army and Navy Journal*. The review was mixed: "On Sunday last the troops composing the garrison of this post made their first appearance in the new uniform, and the event created quite a little excitement."[384] Continuing he recorded: "Opinions among officers, enlisted men, and outsiders, are various as to the benefits of change. Some parts of the new uniform are highly spoken of, while other parts, excite unqualified disapproval."

According to this informal survey, "the new coat" was among the well-received items, "Being so cut that a man with any pretensions of figure can secure a good fit without alteration, and being substantially made throughout." The unit being infantry, the writer thought the light blue facings gave "a very pleasing effect" although "not so good as was that of the old coat; the light blue facings not being very distinguishable on the dark blue background. . . ." To the contrary, the scarlet and yellow of the artillery and cavalry were "visible at a long distance."

Enlisted 1872-pattern forage cap, in this instance for an Ordnance Deapartment soldier. RB

Side view of 1872-pattern enlisted forage cap. JG

Chapter 3: Continually Wear the Blues, 1866-1873

Turning to the campaign hat, early comments before actual field trials were positive. Supposedly: "It was made of first class material, and its proportions are so generous that, when unhooked and let down it altogether dispenses with the necessity of an umbrella, and enables its happy possessor to utterly defy and spit upon 'Old Sol.'" The conclusion was : "To cavalry especially the campaign hat will prove an inestimable blessing, and many a poor trooper, sitting wearily on his horse in the blinding sun of Colorado or New Mexico will from his heart thank the man who invented the hat."

This was not so for the inventor of the "ruffled blouse" that was "an object of utter disgust and loathing." Upon drawing their blouses many of the men had the pleats sewn flat and "squelched" the voluminous folds. The cost of this alteration again was decried and the result condemned as "rather ugly-looking, nondescript, half blouse and half dress coat." The old four-button sack, when it had been tailored, seemed better than the new converted "shapeless mass" that "when the unsuspecting votary of Mars is inducted into it" lost "all resemblance to anything either in nature or art, and so transmogrifying him that his own mother would fail to recognize him."

This was not the sort of reaction that usually provoked a rebuttal from Meigs, but in this case the quartermaster general agreed. He was no proponent of the blouse either, although his department took pride in the production and eventual issue of the uniform as it trickled out to various posts and commands between July through December 1873.[385]

So it was that in the face of many fiscal constraints and other obstacles, during that period, much of the army received the 1872-pattern items. While a few articles of clothing required more development, including the dress helmet, the department warranted most others items, such as the uniform coat, were "in quality, appearance, and workmanship, vastly superior to the old. None but good cloth has been used, and prices paid for making it have been sufficient to insure good work."[386]

While not perfect, and subsequently subject to negative comments, at this stage the outfit of Uncle Sam's regulars had evolved considerably since 1848. By 1873, even though foreign influences and cultivated fashion concerns remained, practical considerations had gained considerable ground since the 1850s, when a grassroots call for change had been considered but displaced in the face of larger national issues. Despite the continued tension between tradition and coping with environmental challenges, especially as found in the American West, and although still cast in conservative "Army Blue," a distinctly U.S. military garb had taken root.

NOTES

1   For more on the impact of the Crimean War in Great Britain see Howard Bailes, "The Patterns of Thought in the Late Victorian Army," IV *Journal of Strategic Studies* No. 1 (March 1981): 29-45.

2   Coffman, *The Old Army*, and Jack D. Foner, *The United States Soldier Between Two Wars: Army Life and Reforms, 1865-1898* (New York: Humanities Press, 1970), both provide excellent background to understand the climate of change after the American Civil War. Other noteworthy studies in this field include: Stephen E. Ambrose, *Upton and the Army* (Baton Rouge: Louisiana State University Press, 1964); Thomas E. Greiss, "Dennis Hart Mahan: West Point Professor and Advocate of Military Professionalism, 1830-1871" (unpublished Ph.D. dissertation, Duke University, 1968); Thomas C. Leonard, *Above the Battle: War-Making in America from Appomattox to Versailles* (New York: Oxford University Press, 1978); Allen R. Millett, *Military Professionalism and Officerships in America* (Columbus: Ohio State University, 1977); James E. Sefton, *The United States Army and Reconstruction* (Baton Rouge: Louisiana State University Press, 1967); Earl F. Stover, *Up from Handymen: The United States Army Chaplaincy, 1865-1920* (Washington, DC: Office of the Chief of Chaplains, 1977); Donna M.E. Thomas, "Army Reform in America: The Crucial Years, 1876-1881" (unpublished Ph.D. dissertation, University of Florida, 1980); Robert M. Utley, *Frontier Regulars: The United States Army and the Indian, 1866-1891* (New York: Macmillian, 1978); Russell F. Weigley, *Towards an American Army: Military Thought from Washington to Marshall* (New York: Columbia University Press, 1962), and Weigley, *The American Way of War: A History of United States Military Strategy and Policy*; and T. Harry Williams, *Americans at War: The Development of the American Military System* (Baton Rouge: Louisiana State University Press, 1960).

3   *Regular Army O!* Words by Edward Harrigan, published in 1875 and popularized by the vaudeville team of Harrigan and Hart. Became a favorite with troops who improvised many versions of their own as "respectable or unprintable as *Mademoiselle from Armentières* of World War I." Don Rickey, *Forty Miles A Day On Beans and Hay* (Norman: University of Oklahoma, 1966), 189.

4   See, Weigley, *Quartermaster General of the Union Army*, for insights into Meigs' personality and influence.

5   Innis Palmer to Lewis Merrill, February 7, 1867, Fort Laramie LS, Jan. 1-Dec. 31, 1867, U.S. Army Commands, RG393, NA. See also, A.J. Perry to D.H. Rucker, November 7, 1867, LS, C&E Br., Vol. 31, OQMG, RG92, NA.

6   M.C. Meigs to Adjutant General, January 16,, 1869, ibid. In another instance Meigs responded that knit goods, shirts, and drawers that the enlisted men refused to draw, if they could avoid it. were to be inspected and condemned to remove them from the system. M.C. Meigs to W.T Howell, June 30, 1872, Pt. 1, 1872, ibid.

7   Ibid. When a report was received that a large lot of trousers appeared to be on hand at Philadelphia "which the authorities" there considered "unfit for issue" because they were of heavy and coarse material, an inspection was to be made and the items condemned if the findings supported this contention. J.D. Bingham to S. Van Vliet,

February 2, 1871, ibid.

8   M.C. Meigs to C. Powell, January 13, 1869, Vol. 31, ibid. A general order prohibited the drawing of larger sizes in order to have them altered to fit smaller men. GO No. 72, WD, AGO, August 7, 1866, Decision and Circulars Book, 1863-67, OQMG, RG92, NA.

9   A.J. Perry to F. Myers, May 31, 1869, LS, C&E Br., Vol. 31, ibid.

10   M.C. Meigs to Adjutant General, endorsement, March 2, 1869, ibid. Also see, A.J. Perry to D.H. Rucker, November 7, 1868, Vol. 31, ibid.

11   A.J. Perry to E.D. Townsend, November 29, 1867, Vol. 30, ibid; and January 9 and January 10, 1868, ibid. M.C. Meigs to C.S. Roberts, September 5, 1871, CCF "Reports," Box 894, ibid, conveys similar complaints about Civil War stocks and Meigs' response to a Seventeenth Infantry officer about this matter. A similar exchange is found between M.C. Meigs and C.E. Campbell, July 1, 1871, Box 895, ibid. The latter report came from Fort Larned, Kansas. *A&NJ*, December 29, 1866, 298, carried an article that made several of the same points, charging the clothing was of such poor quality that it would not last from one issue period to the next, forcing soldiers to buy replacements from their paltry pay. Supposedly this particularly was the case for the infantry who "moved around constantly" as opposed to the artillery who could "get along" with their supply because of a more stable duty environment.

12   The song "Private Blow" was the work of a H.H. McConnell who later set down this and other memories of life in the Sixth Cavalry as *Five Years a Cavalryman: Or, Sketches of Regular Army Life on the Texas Frontier, Twenty Years Ago* (Jacksboro, NC: J.N. Rogers Co., 1889), 133-4.

13   Letter Book, LS, C&E Br., Vol. 30, OQMG, RG92, NA, contains numerous references to the requisitioning of large sizes from field commands and challenges from the Quartermaster Department for those who made such requests.

14   *A&NJ*, December 11, 1869, 258.

15   McConnell, *Five Years A Cavalryman*, 230.

16   *A&NJ*, August 10, 1867, 809; June 28, 1873, 734; and July 19, 1873, 782.

17   Ibid., October 5, 1867, 106.

18   Ibid., October 19, 1872, 154.

19   Ibid.

20   Innis Palmer to Montgomery Meigs, April 4, 1867, Fort Laramie, LS, US Army Commands, RG393, NA.

21   A.J. Perry to G.H. Crosman, June 13, 1866, LS, C&E Br., Vol. 28, OQMG, RG92, NA. According to ibid., December 14, 1866, another soldier, this time from Company C, First Artillery, stationed at Fort LaFayette, New York, required a 45-inch chest and a 40-inch waist with 45-inch hips and outer seam of 46-inches. This individual was considered "a man of unusual size."

22   Several letters to the *A&NJ* remarked about the lack of uniformity when it came to dye lots as indicated by examples on September 14, 1867, 58; November 6, 1869, 179; December 11, 1869, 258; and October 19, 1872.

23   J.D. Bingham to S. Van Vliet, January 6, 1871, LS, C&S Br., 1871, OQMG, RG92, NA.

24 *A&NJ*, August 12, 1871, 827.

25 J.D. Bingham to C.H. Hoyt, January 6, 1871, LS, C&S Br., 1871, OQMG, RG92, NA.

26 A.J. Perry to S. Van Vliet, January 5, 1870, Vol. 32, ibid. The same letter provided for purchase, "when <u>absolutely</u> necessary, hats of smaller sizes." Two years later, a recommendation was made to have a contract let for 2,000 pairs of sizes 3 and 4 trousers because the depot at Philadelphia could not provide these in as rapid a fashion as required. The suggestion was approved. Endorsement J.D. Bingham to S. Van Vliet, January 13, 1872, ibid., Vol. 1, 1872, and R. Allen to S. Van Vliet January 18, 1872, ibid. There was no need to produce smaller sizes, however, "There being a surplus of No. 1 and No. 2 Trousers <u>Foot</u> and No. 1 <u>Trousers mounted</u> on hand" at the Philadelphia Depot. Military Storekeeper Philadelphia to J.F. Rodgers, October 25, 1872, Box 1170, CCF, OQMG, RG92, NA.

27 M.C. Meigs to S. Van Vliet, August 7, 1871, LS, C&S Br., 1871, OQMG, RG92, NA.

28 J.D. Bingham to W.S. Worth, January 14, 1871, ibid.

29 R. Allen to O. Howard, March 18, 1871, ibid. According to M.C. Meigs to S. Van Vliet, May 18, 1871, ibid., some 7,000 suspender buttons were to be provided from Jeffersonville to ensure that the new trouser production could be accomplished.

30 M.C. Meigs to I.N. Palmer, April 24, 1869, Vol. 102, ibid.

31 Ibid.

32 M.C. Meigs to General of the Army, June 9, 1869, Vol. 31, ibid.

33 *ARSW*, 1866, Vol. I, 102-3.

34 M.C. Meigs to General of the Army, June 9, 1869, LS, C&E Br., Vol. 31, OQMG, RG92, NA.

35 (New Orleans) *True Delta*, November 13, 1864.

36 For a treatment of this important publication and its extraordinary founding editor see, David Nevis Biegloe, *William Conant Church and the Army Navy Journal* (New York: Columbia University Press, 1952). Gordon Chappell, *Search For The Well-Dressed Soldier 1865-1890* (Tucson: Arizona Historical Society, 1972), 1-25, should be read for additional insight into the continued debate about uniforms and equipment in the immediate post Civil War era. Likewise see, Douglas McChristian, *The U.S. Army in the West, 1870-1880: Uniforms, Weapons, and Equipment* (Norman: University of Oklahoma Press, 1995), 9-77. Also of importance is Donald E. Kloster, "Uniforms of the Army Prior and Subsequent to 1872, Part 1," XIV *Military Collector and Historian* No. 4 (Winter 1962): 103-12; and "Uniforms of the Army Prior and Subsequent to 1872, Part 2" XV *Military Collector and Historian* No. 1 (Spring 1963): 6-14.

37 *A&NJ*, May 6, 1865, 583.

38 Ibid., January 19, 1867, 345.

39 Ibid., September 9, 1865, 39; February 1, 1868, 377; January 9, 1869, 326; and T.H Neill to E.D. Townsend, July 27, 1868, LR, A723, Box 1279, File 9, AGO, RG94, NA, who also advocated a change in regulations that would allow all "General Officers whether by Brevet or otherwise," as well as Officers of the General Staff and Staff Corps" to wear a light French chapeau.

40 *A&NJ*, September 23, 1865, 71.

41 Ibid.

42 Ibid., December 23, 1865, 282; and March 28, 1868, 506, respectively.

43 Ibid. A disciplinarian who betrayed his prejudice toward the other ranks had a suggestion to prevent this denigration of esprit. He wanted to reintroduce white leather belts to the regulations because these accoutrements required frequent cleaning and thereby occupied the time of enlisted men giving them less opportunity for "getting drunk." Ibid., September 28, 1867, 90.

44 Above all else uniforms tend to fulfill one of the basic requirements of clothing, "to proclaim (or disguise) our identities" so as "to depict the place in the scheme of things or the pecking order." Lurie, *The Language of Clothes*, 27.

45 *A&NJ*, September 9, 1865, 39. Here the writer alluded to another purpose of clothing, "to attract erotic attention." Lurie, *The Language of Clothes*, 27. It also should be noted that during the decade prior to the Civil War the army attempted to make one basic pattern serve for field and garrison duties. This likewise seemed the case with civilian fashion in the United States at the time, if a foreign commentator of the 1850s was accurate in his assessment that, "shabby broadcloth" outfits pervaded the period. By the last quarter of the nineteenth-century, however, "Work clothing had a special purpose, and once this had been served, it could be removed so that workers could emerge at the end of the day ..." to don another type of dress. Kidwell and Christman, *Suiting Everyone: The Democratization of Clothing in America* (Washington, DC: The Smithsonian Institution Press, 1972), 129.

46 *A&NJ*, December 29, 1866, 298.

47 Ibid., January 25, 1868, 363.

48 Ibid., May 23, 1868, 630.

49 "Woodhull Report," 4.

50 Ibid., 25.

51 *A&NJ*, September 23, 1865, 70. The writer, who signed his name "Anchor," was an artillery officer who claimed he had introduced Secretary of War Jefferson Davis to Austrian uniforms, including rank devices, in 1852, thereby taking credit for the adoption of these patterns as the official dress of the Confederacy some years later. This man also was enamored with the Russian dress helmet. Todd, *American Military Equipage*, 34-5, offers more on the discussion of the basic color for uniforms for the 1840s through the 1860s.

52 *A&NJ*, April 18, 1868, 554.

53 Ibid., January 18, 1868, 345.

54 A.J. Perry to M.C. Meigs, February 5, 1869, Vol. 31, LS, C&E Br., OQMG, RG92, NA.

55 M.C. Meigs to C.P. Kingsbury, January 9, 1869, ibid.

56 Endorsement M.C. Meigs to Adjutant General, November 26, 1869, Vol. 32, ibid.

57 A.J. Perry to G.H. Crosman, January 4, 1867, Vol. 28, ibid. The quartermaster department likewise closed or consolidated some depots, such as St. Louis, which had its stores sold or sent to Leavenworth. M.C. Meigs to A.J. Perry, October 15, 1868, ibid.

58 M.C. Meigs to S. Van Vliet, June 17, 1871, ibid. For further details on this experiment consult a January 1873 report relative to George A. Cowles Company's contract to protect woolen items through chemical treatment of the cloth or clothing, see M.C. Meigs to O.E. Michaelis, September 11, 1872, LS, C&S Br., Pt. 1, 1872, ibid.; Secretary of War to Quartermaster General, July 10, 1872, Abstract from Register of War Office, 1872, even numbers, Office of the Secretary of War, RG107, NA; and Micro film Collections, Heraldry, Box 83, U.S. Army Military History Institute, Carlisle Barracks, PA. *ARSW*, 1873, Vol.I, 121, noted $350,000 had been appropriated and "expended for the treatment of woolen and cotton material in store...,in order to render it proof against moth and mildew." An additional $100,000 was being sought to complete the process.

59 J.D. Bingham to S. Van Vliet, January 13, 1872, Register of Letters Sent, 1872, 89, OQMG, RG92, NA. Another precaution considered for woolen goods involved "a vacuum deprived of air and oxygen, and with the pressure of the atmosphere removed" for from fifteen to twenty minutes the moths and other vermin were to be killed M.C. Meigs to A. Faber du Four, September 3, 1872, LS, C&S Br., Pt. 1, 1872, ibid.

60 A.J. Perry to M.C. Meigs, August 29, 1866, Vol. 28; A.J.Perry to H.W. Jones, November 11, 1867, Vol.30; and A.J. Perry to G.F. Morgan, December 7, 1867, Vol. 30, ibid.

61 A.J. Perry to C.S. Smith, November 24, 1869, Vol. 32, ibid.

62 56.A.J. Perry to T. Pitcher, January 4, 1867, Vol. 30, ibid.

63 A.J. Perry to G.H. Crosman, August 22, 1866, Vol. 28; and A. Terry to D.H. Vinton, October 17, 1866, Vol. 28, ibid.

64 A.J. Perry to T. Pitcher, Vol. 30, ibid.

65 Edgar M. Howell, *Uniform Regulations for the Army of the United States 1861* (Washington, DC: Smithsonian Institution, 1961).

66 A.J. Perry to G.H. Crosman, January 4, 1867; January 23, 1867; and February 2, 1867, LS, C&E Br., Vol. 28, OQMG, RG92, NA.

67 J.D. Bingham to R.O. Tyler, May 27, 1870, Vol. 32, ibid; and Endorsement from M.C. Meigs to Adjutant General, July 24, 1868, Vol. 30, ibid., are examples of correspondence requesting such gloves prior to the adoption of this item. When the gloves did become regulation the quartermaster general set out to procure 30,000 pairs, the first to come from the open market, and called for a contract to have 30,000 more manufactured based on the style bought from stocks dealers had on hand. Those purchased first were to go to the garrisons on the Upper Missouri and Upper Lakes because winter weather precluded delivery of supplies to these posts after the water froze and cut off steamship access. M.C. Meigs to E.A. Easton, August 26, 1872, Pt. 1, 1872, ibid.

68 A.J. Perry to George Deas, December 18, 1867, Vol. 30, ibid.

69 J.D. Bingham to Moses Palmer, April 30, 1870, Vol. 32, ibid.

70 M.C. Meigs to J.D. Bacon, November 21, 1871; M.C. Meigs to S. Van Vliet, November 29, 1871; and M.C. Meigs to R. Ingalls, December 15, 1871, ibid.

71 GO No. 75, AGO, September 5, 1866.

72 GO No. 100, AGO, December 31, 1866. The order underscored that regimental quartermaster sergeants would have three ties above their chevrons.

73 A.J. Perry to D.G. Thomas, March 27, 1867, Vol. 28, LS, C&E Br., OQMG, RG92, NA, noted 135 pairs had been made. Emerson, *Chevrons*, 50-1, states at least 300 pairs were made in all, with half this number being sent to New Orleans.

74 GO No. 40, AGO, April 9, 1867. GO No. 88, AGO, October 22, 1868, also restated the Signal Corps crossed flag devices were worn with cavalry chevrons for non-commissioned officers on cavalry uniforms. This essentially was a repetition of the 1864 general order that created the rank devices for signalmen. One individual also questioned what the proper symbol for a chief musician was to be, this being the only regimental non-commissioned officer not prescribed a chevron by that time. The answer was: "There are no chevrons prescribed for Chief Musicians, but that it has been customary to issue Sergeant's chevrons of the Arm of the Service to which the musicians for whom they are intended are attached." A.J. Perry to H.C. Ransom, May 20, 1868, LS, C&E Br., Vol. 30, OQMG, RG92, NA.

75 GO No. 68, AGO, August 14, 1868.

76 William Emerson, "Leather Stocks in the U.S. Army," XIX *Military Collector and Historian* No. 2 (Summer 1977): 62-3, provides a brief history of this accessory.

77 *A&NJ*, December 11, 1869, 258.

78 A.J. Perry to D.B. Sacket, November 4, 1868, LS, C&E Br., Vol. 31, OQMG, RG92, NA.

79 *A&NJ*, March 28, 1868, 506; and Anson Mills, *My Story* (Washington, DC: Published by the Author, 1918), 87-9. Mills had suggested the replacement of scales by "a sky blue worsted knot in three loops of three cords each 1/6-inch in diameter. He also concluded a straight bugle, or "two bayonets, crossed, shanks down and turned in; for Officers number in Cross below, for enlisted men same with letter in Cross above" was a preferred insignia for infantry. Mills felt that all cap or hat insignia of enlisted men should be of white metal at least 1/8-inch in thickness. A. Mills to Headquarters, Fort Fetterman, W.T., February 26, 1868, LR, A723, 1866, Box 1279, File 9, AGO, RG94, NA.

80 *A&NJ*, September 28, 1867, 90; March 7, 1868, 458; and March 28, 1868, 506.

81 Ibid., February 1, 1867, 377.

82 Ibid., August 31, 1872, 42.

83 Ibid., September 7, 1872, 55.

84 J. Schindel to Adjutant General, March 7, 1872, LR, AGO, RG94, NA.

85 Circular No. 2, Department of the Platte, December 20, 1869, Circulars and Orders, Fort Fetterman, Wyoming Territory Records, Microfilm Copy, Wyoming State Museum, Cheyenne.

86 *A&NJ*, March 2, 1872, 54.

87 Chappell, *Search For the Well Dressed Soldier*, n51, 45.

88 *Revised Regulations* 1863, paragraph 1521, set forth this requirement as pointed out in A.J. Perry to G.V. Henry, December 31, 1867, Vol. 30, LS, C&E Br., OQMG, RG92, NA.

89 GO No. 35, August 1, 1870, Headquarters Fort Fred Steele, W.T., General Orders, 1870, Fort Fred Steele, Records of U.S. Army Commands, RG393, NA.

90 A.J. Perry to J.F. Calef, Vol. 30, LS, C&E Br., OQMG, RG92, NA.

91 J.C. McPherson to E.A. Bancroft, October 15, 1867, ibid; and A.J. Perry to H. Brooks, October 29, 1867, ibid.

92 A.J. Perry to R.S Stranger, November 10, 1868, Vol. 31, ibid; J.J. Dana to A.R. Eddy, June 22, 1869, ibid; and M.C. Meigs to G. Sykes, August 5, 1870, Vol. 32, ibid. The last letter noted approximately 500 light artillery caps remained in stock, and these had to be kept for the mounted batteries. This careful attention to restricting the artillery cap also can be seen in a request for sizes of the men in Battery I, First Artillery and Battery F, Fifth Artillery stationed at Fort Riley, Kansas and Washington, DC respectively, to provide a list of sizes for the gunners in case new ones had to be made. A.J. Perry to S. Van Vliet, January 5, 1870, ibid.

93 A.J. Perry to G.H. Crosman, April 12, 1867, Vol. 29; A.J. Perry to E. Schriver, February 9, 1869, Vol, 31: J.D. Bingham to T. McCrea, May 19, 1870, Vol. 32; and J.D. Bingham to E. Schriver, May 26, 1870, Vol. 31, ibid. The uniform adopted consisted of a white coatee with collar, cuffs, lace on the chest, breast cords, and worsted shoulder knots, all of scarlet. Double scarlet leg stripes along with Austrian knots accented the white trousers. The drum major had a scarlet coat trimmed with white, a bearskin, a baldric, and gold epaulets. Frederick P. Todd, *Cadet Gray* (New York: Sterling Publishing Co., Inc., 1955), 32.

94 Railsback and Langellier, *The Drums Would Roll*, 15-6.

95 A.J. Perry to B.C. Card, November 30, 1867, Vol. 31, LS, C&E Br., RG92, NA; and A.J. Perry to J.L. Donaldson, January 19, 1869, ibid. Card was serving with the Quartermaster Department at Fort Leavenworth, Kansas, the forward depot for supplying the remote posts on the Upper Missouri River, while Donaldson was with the St. Louis Depot which had been responsible for considerable supply in the West during the Civil War. Also see two letters from, A.J. Perry to D.H. Rucker, both dated January 7, 1870, Vol. 30, ibid., indicating no woolen mittens were in stock nor were these items of issue. However, twelve buffalo overcoats were authorized in this correspondence for Fort Snelling, not to be charged to the enlisted men, and Fort Sully was to receive 400 pairs of overshoes that were to be sold to the troops. A third letter on this date from Perry to Rucker permitted twenty buffalo coats for Fort Totten, Dakota Territory, at no charge to the men, but disallowed a request from that post for 300 pairs of buffalo mittens.

96 M.C. Meigs to W.T. Sherman, September 23, 1870, Vol. 32, ibid.

97 ''Woodhull Report,'' 23.

98 *A&NJ*, March 7, 1868, 485.

99 John Ryan, *Ten Years With General Custer among the American Indians* (Bryan, TX: J.M. Carroll, 1980), 47.

100 George A. Custer, *My Life on the Plains* (Norman: University of Oklahoma Press, 1962), 325. Also see, George A. Arms, *Ups and Downs of an Army Officer* (Washington, DC: n.p., 1900), 194-5.

101 ''Woodhull Report,'' 6-7. Ibid. 5-6, also noted the Scottish Glengarry cap as a good option for winter by being ''pulled down over the ears and back of the neck....'' Likewise, a bag cap (the precursor to the overseas or service cap) used by French and Austrian troops had ''side flaps'' that could be turned down against the cold, but unfortunately was ''not suited for exposure to sun in hot climates.'' This drawback pointed out the difficulty of furnishing clothing that would meet the diverse needs of the American soldier.

102 Rickey, *Forty Miles A Day On Beans and Hay*, 123.

103 Michael D. Hill and Ben Innis, eds., ''The Fort Buford Diary of Private Sanford, 1876-1877'' LII *North Dakota History* No. 3 (Summer 1985): 28.

104 Maria Brace Kimball, *A Soldier-Doctor of Our Army James P. Kimball* (New York: Houghton Mifflin Company, 1917), 46. Similarly Second Cavalry officers Edward Spaulding and Henry Noyes were described as ''in fur from head to foot,'' when stationed at Fort Reno, Dakota Territory in 1867. ''Reminiscences of Elizabeth Burt,'' (Typescript, Fort Laramie National Historic Site, c. 1912).

105 A.J. Perry to M.J. Asch, January 18, 1868, LS, C&E Br., Vol. 30, OQMG, RG92, NA. Asch was a partner in Asch & Seeley, a New York firm that was interested in providing furs for clothing to the army.

106 A.J. Perry to S.B. Holabird, November 6, 1867, ibid.

107 A.J. Perry to J.L. Donaldson, November 14, 1867, ibid. For a time, this strict guidance was followed even when a garrison experienced cold weather frequently but was located outside of the northern latitudes, such as Fort Riley, Kansas, where the issue of buffalo overshoes was denied despite the extreme weather conditions experienced there. A.J. Perry to J.L. Donaldson, January 9, 1868, Vol. 31, ibid. In a second letter that day from Perry to Donaldson Forts Harker, Larned, and Zarah, were denied

the issuance of overshoes, and Fort Harker's request for buffalo mittens also was turned down, although wool ones were sent instead.

108 A.J. Perry to B.C. Card, November 17, 1868, Vol. 31, ibid.

109 A.J. Perry to L.C. Easton, November 6, 1868, ibid.

110 A.J. Perry to D.L. Stanley, November 5, 1867, Vol. 30, ibid.

111 A.J. Perry to J.L. Donaldson, March 19, 1868, ibid.

112 GO No. 9, AGO, February 8, 1871. See also, T.J. Sperry, ''Winter Clothing of the North Plains,'' XLIV *Military Collector and Historian* No. 3 (Fall 1992): 116-20.

113 J.D. Bingham to D.L. Rucker, January 4, 1871, LS, C&S Br., 1871, OQMG, RG92, NA; and M.C. Meigs to Secretary of War, February 3, 1871, ibid. J.D. Bingham to D.H. Rucker, February 21, 1872, No. 1, 1872, ibid., indicated that strict controls still remained in place, in this instance Fort Union, New Mexico Territory, could not receive mittens as requested because the post was not in the proper region, being too far south. Also, the requisition for gaiters or leggings for this garrison was denied, these items not being ''articles of issue'' nor would they be until the late 1880s.

114 McChristian, *The U.S. Army in the West*, 69-70.

115 R. Allen to S. Van Vliet, February 28, 1872, LS, C&S Br., No. 1, 1872, OQMG, RG92, NA.

116 ''Woodhull Report,'' 5.

117 Ibid., 7.

118 Ibid., 7-9.

119 Ibid., 11.

120 M.C. Meigs to A.J. Perry, January 11, 1866, LS, C&E Br., Vol. 89, OQMG, RG92, NA; and A.J. Perry to M.C. Meigs, April 18, 1866, Vol. 91, ibid.

121 M.C. Meigs to R. Allen, April 27, 1869, Vol. 31, ibid. This was but one example of Meigs' staunch views that one uniform would answer all circumstances. In another case he condemned officers in the Department of the Pacific who deemed government issue as unsuitable for their region. Meigs retorted in characteristic form that the blankets and shoes which had been perfectly satisfactory in the field during the rebellion and which ''troops east of the Rocky Mountains find warm, strong, comfortable, and lasting'' should be no less adequate for other areas. Here, as elsewhere, he seemed not to grasp the tremendous differences in environment faced by the U.S. soldier of the era.

122 J.D. Bingham to Schuyler, Hartley, and Graham, May 16, 1870, Vol. 32, ibid.

123 A.J. Perry to D.H. Vinton, January 14, 1867, Vol. 28, ibid.; A.J. Perry to D.A. Thomas, March 18, 1868, and March 28, 1868, Vol. 30, ibid.

124 A.J. Perry to R. Allen, July 1, 1868, Vol. 30, ibid. Allen was the quartermaster in San Francisco, but another officer serving in Texas at nearly the same time was told that despite the fact, ''Certain men of your command, not attached to the mounted arm of the service, but who sometimes were in charge of horses and mules and were sometimes sent on scouts after Indians'' could not be issued boots. Army regulations required shoes for foot soldiers, not boots. A.J. Perry to P. Stevens, November 19, 1868, Vol. 31, ibid.

125 A.J. Perry to G.H. Crosman, November 11, 1867, Vol. 30, ibid.

126 A.J. Perry to R.N. Batchelder, November 5, 1867, ibid. At the time Batchelder headed up the Jeffersonville Depot.

127 A.J. Perry to D.H. Rucker, January 31, 1868, ibid.

128 A.J. Perry to G.H. Crosman, November 21, 1867, Vol 30, ibid.

129 Endorsement, Engineer Department, Memorandum relating to uniforms for enlisted men of Engineers, April 13, 1868, Vol. 30, ibid. Apparently a pompon was included as well, although there is no mention of a new cap or hat on which to mount the piece. A.J. Perry to T.L. Casey, April 28, 1868, ibid. Later Perry wrote D. Thomas on May 13, 1868, ibid., and indicated that red facings should be placed on the skirts of the jacket.

130 A.J. Perry to J.C. McFerran, June 20, 1868, ibid., directed: ''have the coat which accompanies this communication altered in conformity with the written description, and made into one for a sergeant of Ordnance.'' See also, A.J. Perry to G.H. Crosman, June 16, 1868, and June 25, 1868, ibid.

131 A.B. Dyer to L. Thomas, July 9, 1868, LR, Microcopy M-619, Reel 449, AGO, RG94, NA. This request came about as a result of the new draft 1868 regulations discussed later in this chapter, but never adopted.

132 A.J. Perry to S. Van Vliet, February 15, 1870, Vol. 32, LS, C&E Br., OQMG, RG92, NA, called for the conversion of 1,000 infantry or artillery coats to ordnance, a relatively simple task requiring only the removal of the piping of these branches from collars and cuffs and replacement with the proper crimson welt. A similar process was involved for hat cords that began to run low for ordnance enlisted personnel. About 2,000 artillery cords were to be dyed to convert them to the proper crimson. A.J. Perry to G.H. Crosman, February 10, 1868, Vol. 30, ibid.

133 M.C. Meigs to General of the Army, June 9, 1869, Vol. 31, ibid.

134 W.B. Hazen, *The School of the Army in Germany and France* (New York: Harper & Brothers, Publishers, 1872), 87.

135 Ibid., 89.

136 *A&NJ*, August 12, 1871, 827. This was a reprint of a letter from Meigs to Lieutenant Colonel R.O. Tyler, who was a deputy quartermaster serving with the Department of the Pacific headquartered in San Francisco.

137 Ibid.

138 *ARSW*, 1870, Vol. I, 149.

139 *AN&J*, August 22, 1868, 6.

140 Ibid., May 23, 1868, 631. Ironically, the U.S. Army adopted gray for certain regiments during the War of 1812 simply because of a lack of availability of blue cloth. The same issue of *AN&J* also carried a portion of the Woodhull Report, a study that

advocated gray. See, ibid., 630. Other portions of the report were printed in ibid., May 16, 1868, 613; and May 30, 1868, 647.

141 Ibid., September 23, 1865, 70.

142 Ibid., November 9, 1867, 186. Likewise see, ibid., August 8, 1868, 810; and February 13, 1869, 406, for additional comments supporting gray over blue.

143 See Todd, *American Military Equipage*, 426 and 434.and Elting, *Military Uniforms in America*, Vol. III, 114-5, for brief information on Confederate artillery garb.

144 J. Coburn to E. D. Townsend, January 19, 1869, Microcopy 619, Roll 450, AGO, RG94, NA. Coburn, an attorney and judge before the war, rallied to the Union cause as colonel of the Thirty-third Indiana. His war record was diverse and brought him a number of brigades to command. After the war he was elected to the U.S. House of Representatives, became a judge, and eventually went on to be a supreme court justice in Montana.

145 SO No. 523, HQ of the Army, December 18, 1867.

146 W.T. Sherman to Adjutant General, January 28, 1868, LR, AGO, RG94, NA; and U.S. Grant to Secretary of War, January 29, 1868, LS, HQ of the Army, RG108, NA.

147 W.T. Sherman, P.H. Sheridan, and C.C. Augur to E.D. Townsend, February 3, 1868, LR, A723, 1866, Box 1279, Pt. 8, AGO, RG94, NA.

148 A.J. Perry to P.H. Sheridan, February 10, 1868, Vol. 30, LS, C&E Br., OQMG, RG92, NA, and A.J. Perry to D.G. Thomas, February 5, 1868, ibid.

149 A.J. Perry to E.D. Townsend, January 18, 1868. ibid.

150 P.H. Sheridan to Quartermaster General, February 14, 1868, Register LS, HQ of the Army, RG108, NA. According to a March 7, 1866 entry in the Subject Index, Letters Written, 1865-69, OQMG, RG92, NA, the three generals also were furnished patterns of uniforms made for the 1850 board.

151 "Yet another version of the lounge coat to appear in the early 1860s was the Norfolk jacket, at first called the Norfolk blouse, cut with box pleats on either side of the centre front and at the centre back, with a belt at the waist." These jackets "appeared at the time of the formation of the Volunteer Movement in 1859-60; They were adopted by many of the Rifle Corps and were subsequently adapted to shooting costume in general." Byrde, *Nineteenth Century Fashion*, 104.
This Volunteer movement arose from the threat of war with France in 1859, when "the Volunteers were revived with great gusto" in England. For the most part, the uniforms of the British volunteers of this time were "less showy and more practical than those of the regular army. Grey, or various shades of brown or drab were often worn...." R. Money Barnes, *Military Uniforms of the Empire 1742 to Present* (London: Seeley Service and Co. Limited, 1960), 150. The Norfolk was in evidence in Great Britain as part of this movement, as well as Canada. Laver, *British Military Uniforms*, 36.

152 Surgeon General to General in Chief, February 1, 1868, LS, Surgeon General, RG112, NA; Surgeon General to Headquarters of the Army, Register LR, HQ of the Army, RG108, NA.

153 February 14, 1868 P.H. Sheridan and C.C. Augur to Adjutant General, LR, AGO, RG94, NA, asked for additional instructions having completed their work as required by SO 523. Also see, LR, A723, 1866, Box 1279, Pt. 18, ibid., which contains the "Original Draft of Regulations and Articles of War proposed by Gen. Townsend." These did not go into effect, but some of the draft is of interest such as the description of trousers as being sky-blue mixture with a "full peg top, waistband three and a-half inches wide, to button with two buttons in front with, pocket in seam, and ornamented with white worsted cord" for enlisted infantrymen and a 1 1/2-inch stripe for sergeants. The artillery was to have identical trousers. Both the cord or stripe were to be scarlet. Light artillerymen were to have reinforcing, and a 1 1/2-inch stripe in scarlet for sergeants and a 5/8-inch stripe of the same color was designated for all other enlisted men. The trousers for cavalry were the same as for artillery but the color of stripes was to be yellow in lieu of scarlet.

154 Examples include, A.J. Perry to Stiehl and McBride, September 2, 1868, LS, C&E Br., Vol. 30, OQMG, RG92, NA; Perry to Shannon, Miller, and Crane, September 3, 1868, ibid.; and Perry to Horstmann, November 11, 1868, Vol. 31, ibid.

155 W.R. Cole to L. Thomas, June 6, 1868, LR, A 723, 1866, Box 1279, File 8, AGO, RG94, NA. The writer of the letter was the proprietor of Wm. R. Cole and Co., Fur Wool and Straw Hats, No. 30 Sharp Street, Baltimore, MD.

156 J. A. Hardie to Adjutant General, March 27, 1871, LR, 1871, AG0, RG94, NA. At the time Hardie was the inspector general for the Military Division of the Missouri.

157 W.T. Sherman to Adjutant General, March 28, 1871, ibid. A sketch of a cap with a visor and round top similar to that worn by U.S. Navy officers and civilian sailing men, as well as railroad conductors and some police forces, was included in this piece, and was not unlike the cap ultimately adopted in 1895 for the army at large.

158 Ibid.

159 Howell, *United States Army Headgear, 1855-1902*, 27. As further indication of the depletion of stocks, by early 1867 the New York supplies had been reduced to only eight tulips to hold plumes, twelve plumes, and twelve pairs of rings. A.J. Perry to G.H. Crosman, November 11, 1867, Vol. 30, Letter Book, LS, C&E Br., OQMG, RG92, NA.

160 A.J. Perry to G.H. Crosman, December 11, 1867, ibid. The order also included 500 cap rings to suspend the scarlet cords from the artillery cap, 2,000 neck stocks, 2,000 ponchos, 20,000 forage caps, 500 cavalry hats cords, 5000 for artillery, 500 ordnance, and 800 for infantry, as well as 5,000 stable frocks, 50 pairs of sergeants major of cavalry chevrons, 50 pairs of regimental quartermaster chevrons, 200 first sergeants, and 50 quartermaster sergeants. Like numbers of artillery sergeants major, regimental quartermasters, and first sergeants, were called for, along with

500 pairs of chevrons for artillery sergeants and corporals each, 10,000 untrimmed 1858-pattern hats, 5,000 castles for the engineers stationed at Goat Island, 5,000 sabers for cavalry troops in the command, and 10,000 bugles for the infantry, with that many ostrich feathers, too. Finally, 50 sets of artillery bugle cords, a regimental color for artillery and two cavalry regimental standards were to be shipped from the best stock by sailing ship around Cape Horn.
Previously 25 artillery caps had been sent to Philadelphia from New York, as part of a transfer of material that also included 1,000 oilcloth forage cap covers, and 1,000 pairs of sergeants major chevrons. At the same time, New York supplied another 1,000 cap covers to Fort Monroe, Virginia. A.J. Perry to D.H. Vinton, February 26, 1867, Vol. 30, ibid.

161 A.J. Perry to G.H. Crosman, December 16, 1868: and D.H. Rucker to A.J. Perry, December 16, 1867, ibid.

162 A.J. Perry to R.N. Batchelder, April 3, 1868, Vol. 30, ibid.

163 A.J. Perry to J.M. Moore, May 11, 1868, ibid.

164 A.J. Perry to J.A. Moore, July 9, 1868, ibid.

165 A.J. Perry to B.C. Card, May, 9, 1868, ibid. This letter further related purchases should be made "from time to time only as they are actually required for issue and not to provide a surplus of them for any of the depots."

166 A.J. Perry to J.S. Totten, July 9, 1868, ibid.

167 Commanding Officer, First Artillery to Commanding General Department of the East, December 13, 1869, Microcopy 619, Roll 760, LR, AGO, RG94, NA.

168 Ibid. With but 1,200 caps on hand as of January 25, 1870, this made sense. Ibid.

169 E.D. Townsend to Commanding General Military Division of the Pacific, February 16, 1871, ibid.

170 A.J. Perry to B.K. Roberts, January 3, 1870: A.J. Perry to E. Rupell, January 5, 1870; and A.J. Perry to R. Ingalls, January 7, 1870, Vol. 32, LS, C&E Br., OQMG, RG92, NA. As another related matter, when GO No. 6, AGO, February 18, 1869, reduced the number of light batteries from two to one per artillery regiment. Additional turmoil resulted in at least one instance according to an inspector general who found Battery I, First Artillery continuing to wear the light artillery uniform despite the fact it had been dismounted. The same report also noted another discrepancy in that Battery G of that regiment appeared on parade with the brass US plate on their cartridge boxes, while Battery M did not. While a minor matter, this represents just one of many instances of the lack of uniformity that existed at that time. D.B. Sacket to E.D. Townsend, October 16, 1871, LR, Microcopy 619, Roll 760, AGO, RG94, NA. For complete details on this incident see: H.B. Reed to R. Arnold September 25, 1869 and February 11, 1870; R. Randal to Adjutant General, April 11, 1871; E.D. Townsend to Commanding General Department of the Atlantic, October 23, 1871; Second Endorsement I. McDowell to Commanding Officer First Artillery, November 9, 1871; R. Arnold to C. McKeever, November 11, 1871; and Acting Quartermaster General to E.D. Townsend, January 31, 1872, ibid.

171 J.D. Bingham to S. Van Vliet, June 14, 1871, LS, C&S Br., 1871, OQMG, RG92, NA.

172 Alexander began his career on July 26, 1861 as an officer with the mounted rifles, then moved his way steadily upward to brigadier general of volunteers. Among other appointments, he served on McClellan's staff and Wilson's Cavalry Corps. Hunt was a Mexican War veteran who had been breveted for his participation in that conflict in which he had been twice wounded. Subsequently, in 1856, he served on a board to revise light artillery tactics. Five years later, during the Civil War he saw considerable service at such places as Gettysburg, Rapidian, and Petersburg, raising to the rank of major general during the conflict. He may have been the officer who signed himself as "Anchor" in the *AN&J*, who advocated a change in the color of the uniform. King's career started in 1837 as an infantry officer in Florida, then in the West, and through the Mexican War. He was a major when the Civil War began, and rose to the rank of major general of volunteers by the war's end. Boatner, *The Civil War Dictionary*, 6, 418, and 463.

173 Ibid., 512.

174 M.C. Meigs to J.M. Schofield, August 7, 1876, Series V, Subject File, Arguments-Army, Schofield Papers, Library of Congress.

175 R.B. Marcy to Secretary of War, September 14, 1871, Office of the Secretary of War, RG 107, NA.

176 Howell, *United States Army Headgear, 1855-1902*, 33.

177 Adjutant General to R.B. Marcy, April 25, 1872, LR, AG, RG94, NA; Secretary of War to Adjutant General, June 26, 1872, ibid; and M.C. Meigs to Secretary of War, July 29, 1872, ibid.

178 *A&NJ*, June 22, 1872, 720. The article also noted Colonel Henry B. Clitz was to assist Marcy in "obtaining the samples and reporting upon the new styles to be adopted." ibid. This officer graduated with the Class of 1845. After West Point, he joined an infantry regiment as a second lieutenant. He later saw service in the Mexican War, for which he was breveted, then returned to the U.S. Military Academy to teach infantry tactics, "before going to the frontier." Soon after the Civil War began he rose to the rank of major of the Twelfth Infantry, participated in a number of engagements, was captured and held at Libby Prison, then paroled to return to the banks of the Hudson as commandant of cadets. His Civil War service brought him a brevet as brigadier general in the U.S. Army. He retired in 1885 as the colonel of the Tenth Infantry. Boatner, *The Civil War Dictionary*, 159.

179 M.C. Meigs to R.N. Scott, July 15, 1872, LS, General and Miscellaneous, 1872A, OQMG, RG92, NA. In response to an inquiry from the field the adjutant general's office also confessed a lack of particulars as to what the new outfit would be

responding: "the report of the Board on the uniform has not yet been made and no information on the subject is possessed by the Adjutant General." J.P. Brown to E.D. Townsend, May 30, 1872, LR, AGO, RG92, NA.

180 See H.L. Barnes to Adjutant General, June 15, 1872, ibid.

181 Secretary of War to E.D. Townsend, July 29, 1872, ibid.

182 M.C. Meigs to T.R. Davis, August 17, 1872, LS, C&S Br., Pt. 1 1872, OQMG, RG92, NA; and J.B. Bingham to L.C. Easton, August 28, 1872, ibid. See also Brooks Brothers to Secretary of War, July 30, 1872, Register of LR, War Department, RG108, NA; Adjutant General to J.D. Bingham, August 10, 1872, ibid.

183 144.See Appendix D for a complete version of the document as found in General Orders No. 92.

184 J.M. Lee to Quartermaster General, April 5, 1872, CCF, Box 1170, OQMG, RG92, NA, requested photographs to be taken of the articles the board was considering so that they might be used to illustrate the report expected to be made at the end of the deliberations. See also M.C. Meigs to L.C. Easton, August 15, 1872, LS, C&S Br., Pt. 1, 1872, ibid., called for photographs of the cap and helmet and the changes required to bring them to final standards.

185 M.C. Meigs to L.C. Easton, August 13, 1872, ibid.

186 M.C. Meigs to Warnock, August 12, 1872, ibid.; and Horstmann Brothers & Co. to L.C. Easton, August 3, 1872, CCF, Box 1170, ibid., in which Horstmann originally estimated a cost of $4.50 to $5.00 per complete helmet.

187 M.C. Meigs to R.B. Marcy, June 28, 1872, LS, C&S Br., Pt. 1, 1872; M.C. Meigs to R.B. Marcy, July 16, 1872; ibid; M.C. Meigs to L.C. Easton, August 9, 1872, ibid; M.C. Meigs to L.C. Easton, August 15, 1872, ibid.; M.C. Meigs to W.B. Baker, October 24, 1872, ibid.; and Contract in Branch E, Regular Supplies, Contracts, ibid., GO No. 73, WD, July 10, 1872; and GO No. 138, WD, March 20, 1873.

188 One notable exception to this was the dark felt helmet with blue *paggri* worn by British officers in the Second Punjab Cavalry (Probyn's Horse). In the late 1840s, these helmets were used in India for parade, in which case they had white plumes, while in the field "a brass spike was substituted." Christopher Wilkinson-Latham, *The Indian Mutiny* (London: Osprey Publishing, 1991), 33 and Figure B1. Probably this helmet was unknown in the United States, however, and if anything was more a precursor to the 1878-pattern British home service helmet, examples of which appear in Rankin, *Military Headdress*, 76 and 81.
The exact composition of the body for the U.S. 1872-pattern would be published as Specification No. 1, May 31, 1876, and represented another step in the evolution of the Quartermaster Department's efforts at standardization. The opening paragraph of this document read in part: "To be made of felt composed of one part each of Russia, best coney-back, muskrat, extra coney, and a half part of wash-blow." This meant a combination of furs from muskrats, hares, and other animals would be combined with suitable fillers to produce the felt.

189 Gordon Chappell, *Brass Spikes and Horsetail Plumes: A History of U.S. Army Dress Helmets, 1872-1904* (Gettysburg: Thomas Publications, 1997), 5-6, makes several insightful comments on the various European models that presaged the American helmet. In his reprint of *Regulations and Notes for the Uniform of the United States Army 1857* (Staten Island: Manor Publishing, 1973), Jacques Noel Jacobsen, Jr. includes circa 1860 advertisements from Robert Weir, a Boston military costumer, and from Horstmann Brothers & Allien, John A. Baker, and Schuyler, Hartley & Graham, a trio of military outfitters. All four firms depict a Prussian "Pickle Haube" of leather as available for purchase, thus indicating the Germanic influence that began to influence martial wear in the U.S. military even before the Franco Prussian War.

190 H.J. Hunt, to Adjutant General, March 13, 1875, LR, AGO, RG94, NA. For examples of British helmets that were in vogue at the time see Rankin, *Military Headdress*, 61, 65 and 67; and Wilkinson-Latham, *Collecting Militaria*, plates 5 and 7.

191 H.J. Hunt to Adjutant General, March 13, 1875, LR, AGO, RG94,, NA.

192 M.C. Meigs to Horstmann Brother & Co., October 1, 1872, LS, C&S Br., Pt. 1, 1872, OQMG, 92, NA.

193 M.C. Meigs to L.S. Easton, February 13, 1873, Book A, 1873, ibid.

194 *ARSW*, 1873, Vol. I, 152.

195 Ibid.

196 Endorsement M.C Meigs to Secretary of War, August 26, 1872, Pt. 1, 1872, OQMG, RG92, NA.

197 M.C. Meigs to Secretary of War, September 12, 1872, ibid.; M.C. Meigs to L.C. Easton, September 21, 1872, ibid; Horstmann & Brothers to M.C. Meigs, September 28, 1872, CCF, Box 1170, ibid.

198 M.C. Meigs to L.C Easton, December 10, 1872, LS, C&S Br., Pt. 2, 1872, ibid.

199 J.D. Bingham to M.C. Meigs, December 17, 1872, CCF, Box 1170, ibid.; and *ARSW*, 1873, Vol. I, 60.

200 Horstmann & Brothers to L.C. Easton, December 12, 1872, Letter Book, LS, C&E Br., Pt. 2, 1872, OQMG, RG92, NA.

201 R.B. Marcy to Secretary of War, December 16, 1872, ibid.; and M.C. Meigs to L.C. Easton, January 2, 1873, Book A, 1873, ibid.

202 Horstmann & Brothers to M.C. Meigs, December 23, 1872, Pt. 2, 1872, ibid.

203 *ARSW*, 1873, Vol. I, 60.

204 The author has examined a dozen signal corp examples, however, that had uniformly been made as separate breast cords with snap devices for attachment and which evidenced no cutting. Rather they were made as a single cord. No informa-

tion as to why this batch was made or for whom, has been found, however.

205 Mollo, *Military Fashion*, 160

206 W.Y. Carmen, *British Military Uniforms from Contemporary Pictures, Henry VII to the Present Day* (London: Leonard Hill, Ltd., 1957), 141. For comparative images see, Rankin, *Military Headdress*, 38, 60, and 61.

207 *A&NJ*, February 20, 1869, and January 1, 1870, 316, carried advertisements from Bent and Bush for a hat of nearly identical appearance. Evidently the Boston firm offered these caps for sales to militia units.

208 J.D. Bingham (for Meigs) to Horstmann Bros. and Allien, November 29, 1872, LS, C&S Br., Pt. 2, 1872, OQMG, RG92, NA.

209 M.C. Meigs to L.C. Easton, August 9, 1872, Pt. 1, 1872, ibid. Evidently this cap survives and is in the collections of Museum of American History, Smithsonian Institution. Howell, *United States Army Headgear*, 1855-1902, 37.

210 J.D. Bingham to Horstmann Brothers and Allien, November 29, 1872, LS, C&S Br., Pt. 2, 1872, OQMG, RG92, NA. Earlier the firm had been told that some of the samples they supplied had to be held for a time for Marcy's review. M.C. Meigs to Horstmann, October 1, 1872, ibid.

211 M.C. Meigs to the Secretary of War, August 2, 1872, Pt. 1, 1872, ibid.

212 Endorsement M.C. Meigs to Secretary of War, September 14, 1872, ibid.

213 M.C. Meigs to L.C. Easton, September 21, 1872, ibid.

214 Executive Document #159, House, 43rd Cong., lst Sess.; October 30, 1872 Contract with Bent & Bush, QM Contracts, OQMG, RG92, NA; and M.C. Meigs to W.B. Baker, October 24, 1872, LS, C&S Br., Pt. 1, 1872, ibid. Horstmann had estimated about $2.25 per cap, but that figure was not firm, and the company must have found it cost more to produce the headgear as evidenced by the fact that they did not receive the contract. Horstmann and Brothers to L.C. Easton, August 3, 1873, CCF, Box 1170, ibid. J.D. Bingham (for Meigs) to L.C. Easton, December 4, 1872, LS, C&S Br., Pt. 2, 1872, ibid., indicated thirty-seven caps were sent to Fort Sullivan, Maine for Battery K, Fifth Artillery. This appears to be one of the first issuances of the headpiece. Later, GO No. 38, AGO, March 20, 1873, set the price of issuance to the enlisted men as $2.50 each with trimmings and brass ornaments. GO No. 73, AGO, July 10, 1873, set the allowance at one cap for each year of enlistment.

215 The composition of the fur felt bodies ultimately was essentially that of the helmet. See Specification Number 3, May 31, 1876, War Department, Quartermaster General's Office.

216 *A&NJ*, October 4, 1873, 122.

217 J. Van Voast to Adjutant General, October 1, 1872, LR, AGO, RG92, NA.

218 Plain black trousers were designated for chaplains. R.B. Marcy to W.W. Belknap, June 21, 1872, LR, AGO, RG94, NA.

219 There seems to have been some confusion about trouser stripes being worn by musicians because the Quartermaster Department had to clarify this fact at one point in correspondence. J.D. Bingham to I. Quinby, February 26, 1874, LS, C&S Br., Book A, 1874, OQMG, RG92, NA.

220 Quartermaster General to Adjutant General, August 6, 1872, Vol. I, 1872, ibid.

221 Adjutant General to Quartermaster General, August 10, 1872, CCF, Box 1170, ibid.

222 J.D. Bingham endorsement to Adjutant General and Inspector General, January 2, 1874; and H.B. Morse, January 3, 1874, ibid. This negated an earlier but not acted upon order from Meigs to make up 8,000 pairs of dismounted trousers and 15,600 pairs of mounted trousers in accordance with the new specifications. M.C. Meigs to Schuylkill Arsenal, June 25, 1872, Register of Letters Received, C&S Br., ibid. Nevertheless, five pairs of mounted and five pairs of dismounted trousers were made from the pattern as a test to be tried at Fort Hamilton, New York and Fort McHenry, Maryland for mounted types and in the Philadelphia area for dismounted types. These were to be accompanied by "letters describing the differences between the trousers cut from the new pattern and those cut from the old, and the advantages and improvements in those made from the new." M.C. Meigs to S. Van Vliet, May 31, 1872, LS, C&S Br., Pt. 1, 1872, ibid. Ultimately twenty pairs of the new pattern were produced and treated with moth repellant for trial at Forts Hamilton and McHenry. January 10, 1872, ibid. Despite this effort, no others were made for general issue after the experiment, for nearly four years. A letter to the officer in charge of Philadelphia shed light on the reason, quoting the secretary of war's words: "'In view of the great increase in the cost of the trousers with the new pattern pockets, the Secretary of War directs that the side seam pockets be continued.'" J.D. Bingham to L.C. Easton, January 3, 1874, LR, Philadelphia Depot, Box 78, ibid.

223 M.C. Meigs to L.C. Easton, August 2, 1872, LS, C&S Br., Pt. 1, 1872, ibid.

224 M.C. Meigs to J. Chandler, October 15, 1872, ibid.

225 M.C. Meigs to L.C. Easton, August 2, 1872, Pt. 1, 1872, ibid.

226 R.B. Marcy to E.D. Townsend, January 22, 1873, LR, AGO, RG94, NA. The secretary of war also was unclear whether the new officers' overcoats were to be "sack or close-fit" in cut, having been referred to as a cloak coat in earlier regulations, but not specified in the draft of the new ones. E.D. Townsend to R.B. Marcy, August 5, 1872, ibid. J.M. King to Adjutant General, November 26, 1872, ibid., raised a related question as to the wearing of the sword belt with the overcoat for officers. He asked whether it was to be worn over or under the coat. The reply was that all officers below the grade of brigadier general would wear the sword-belt outside the overcoat. GO No. 107, AGO, December 14, 1872.

227 M.C. Meigs to C.H. Hoyt, September 9, 1872, LS, C&S Br., Pt. 1, 1872, OQMG, RG92. NA, directed the sale of ostrich feathers and non-commissioned officers' sashes, but called for the retention of 1858-pattern hat cords.

228 For instance, improved footgear was considered to raise the standards, including a trial issue of brass screwed soles versus sewed soles of boots and bootees, and additional stitching on the body of the footwear as well. M.C. Meigs to Secretary of War, April 19, 1872, ibid.; M.C. Meigs to E.A. Bancroft, April 22, 1872, ibid.; Endorsement M.C. Meigs to Adjutant General, May 31, 1873, Book A, 1873, ibid; M.C. Meigs to Inspector General, June 17, 1873, ibid.; M.C. Meigs to L.C. Easton, July 9, 1873, ibid.; M.C. Meigs to L.C. Easton, June 4, 1873, ibid.; and M.C. Meigs to L.C. Easton, June 6, 1873, ibid. A proposal for issuing moccasins, however, was not endorsed. M.C. Meigs to W.W. Robinson, LS, General & Misc., Book A, 1872, ibid.; M.C. Meigs to L.C. Easton, April 9, 1873, LR, Philadelphia Depot, Box 69, indicated John Mundell & Co., manufactured the boots and bootees that were adopted as standards, and directed that specifications be drawn up based on these. That same firm was given a contract for 20,0000 solid brass screwed boots, at $4.20 per pair, and for 80,000 solid brass screwed bootees. M.C. Meigs to L.C. Easton, June 6, 1873, Box 76, ibid.

For more on footgear read Sidney B. Brinckerhoff, *Boots and Shoes of the Frontier Soldier* (Tucson: Arizona Historical Society, 1976). This monograph offers comparative information on footwear, another area of responsibility of the Quartermaster Department. Because this topic is not treated in *Army Blue*, Brinckerhoff's monograph especially is important for further reading.

In regard to accoutrements, the Quartermaster Department no longer had responsibility for any of the equipage previously under its charge as of 1871, the Ordnance Department assuming all responsibilities for knapsacks and other items. Risch, *Quartermaster Support of the Army*, 502. Suffice it to say that this was a fluid area for change during the time with many weapons being looked at and various accoutrements being experimented with or adopted, such as the over-the-shoulder sword belt for non-commissioned officer that began to be replaced by a waist-belt-mounted frog starting in 1868, as the one of several changes of accoutrements that was to follow after the 1872 uniform regulations came into being. McChristian, *The U.S. Army in the West*, 91. Belt mounted cartridge boxes and locally-made cartridge belts also came unto the scene during this evolutionary stage. See, ibid., 78-98, for a concise overview of other changes taking place in the area of equipage that paralleled uniform evolution in the late 1860s through 1872.

229 M.C. Meigs to Secretary of War, April 9, 1873, LS, C&S Br., Book A, 1873, OQMG, RG92, NA.

230 M.C. Meigs to C.H. Hoyt, August 16, 1872, Pt. 1, 1872, ibid.

231 M.C. Meigs to L.C. Easton, August 13, 1872, ibid. In this effort Forts Sully, Buford, Stevenson, McKeever, and Rice were to be supplied with the new uniform along with the troops at the Grand River, Cheyenne, and Lower Brule Agencies. M.C. Meigs to Easton, August 27, 1872, and August 28, 1872, ibid. The execution did not move forward as planned, however, Meigs noting that delivery to Sioux City for distribution to the Dakota Territory posts was not going according to schedule, thus prompting him to ask whether old patterns should be sent instead. M.C. Meigs to D.H. Rucker, September 18, 1872, ibid. Nevertheless, he persisted, directing that the orders should be sent in time to make the last steamer setting sail from Sioux City in mid-October before the weather prohibited further movement until the spring thaw. M.C. Meigs to L.C. Easton, September 18, 1872, ibid.

232 Texas posts, including Forts Bliss, Concho, Davis, Duncan, McKavitt, Quitman, Stockton, as well as Austin and San Antonio placed orders according to M.C. Meigs to D.H. Rucker, October 7, 1872, ibid. These installations were to be given priority along with those in the Department of the Missouri over the Recruiting Service. M.C. Meigs to J.C. Davis, October 9, 1872, ibid. Later, all orders for recruits continued on hold, when appropriations were not forthcoming. M.C. Meigs to Secretary of War, March 20, 1873, LR, Office of the Secretary of War, RG107. In the meantime, the Fourth Infantry at Taylor Barracks, Kentucky was anxious to obtain their new uniforms as soon as possible, too. General of the Army to W.H. Bisbee, December 26, 1872, LS, C&S Br., Pt. 1, 1872, OQMG, RG92, NA. Similar requests went out from Colonel E.V. Sumner in New York, who was told "The new uniform was not yet ready for issue." J.D. Bingham to E.V. Sumner, August 17, 1872, Pt. 1, 1872, ibid. Requests for the new uniform followed from the chief of engineers for troops under his command at Willets' Point, New York, and the secretary of war himself wanted issue to commence at Forts Monroe, McHenry, Delaware, Foote, Whipple, and the harbor defense posts around New York. Chief of Engineers to Secretary of War, April 22, 1873, ibid.; and M.C. Meigs to L.C. Easton, January 4, 1873, Book A, 1873, ibid. Other early efforts to secure the new uniform came from such diverse commands as Custer's Seventh Cavalry and the national guard of Minnesota. Circular No. 74, Headquarters Detachment 7th Cavalry, June 18, 1873, General and Special Orders and Circulars Issued by General Custer's Detachment, April 1873-September 1873, Vol. 2, Records of U.S. Army Mobile Units, RG 391, NA; and Adjutant General State of Minnesota to Quartermaster General, January 5, 1873, LR, Secretary of War, RG 107, NA.

233 M.C. Meigs to Secretary of War, October 1, 1872, LS, C&S Br., Pt. 1, 1872, OQMG, RG92, NA.

234 M.C. Meigs to Secretary of War, October 8, 1872, ibid.

235 M.C. Meigs to L.C. Easton, January 3, 1873, LS, C&S Br., Book A, 1873, OQMG, RG92, NA; M.C. Meigs to J.A. Eakin, January 3, 1873, ibid.; and M.C. Meigs to D.H. Rucker, January 4, 1873, ibid.

236 M.C. Meigs to John Logan, Book A, 1873, ibid.

237 M.C. Meigs to Secretary of War, February 25, 1873, ibid.

238 M.C. Meigs to A.J. Perry, September 19, 1872, ibid.

239 M.C. Meigs to Secretary of War, December 31, 1872, LS, Gen., & Misc., Vol. B, 1872, ibid.

240 Ibid.

241 M.C. Meigs to J.S. Holden September 6, 1872, LS, C&S Br., Pt. 1, 1872, ibid.

242 Endorsement M.C. Meigs to Secretary of War August 27, 1872, Pt. 1, 1872, ibid.; M.C. Meigs to Secretary of War, August 30, 1872, ibid.; M.C. Meigs to J.C. Collins, September 7, 1872. ibid.; M.C. Meigs to Doughten, Renshaw & Wilkins, September 7, 1872, ibid.; See also, LR Index, January 20, 1872 (entry 580); February 3, 1872 (entry 1048); August 7, 1872 (entry 7028); August 30, 1872(entry 7568); and September 17, 1872 (entry 7836), Letters transmitted from the Quartermaster General to Secretary of War, Register of LR, Office of the Secretary of War, RG107, NA.

243 For instance GO NO. 92 called for this practice, and recruits were to receive mounted overcoats as part of their first uniform issue. W.D. Whipple to Superintendent General, Recruiting Service, October 19, 1872, CCF, Box 1170, OQMG, RG92, NA.

244 M.C. Meigs to A. Baird, January 30, 1873, LS, C&S Br., Book A, 1873, ibid.

245 Endorsement M.C. Meigs to Adjutant General, March 11, 1873, ibid.

246 Ibid.

247 M.C. Meigs to R. Allen, April 30, 1873, ibid.

248 M.C. Meigs to L.C. Easton, May 14, 1873, ibid. Also, J.F. Rodgers to L.C. Easton, May 26, 1873, LR, Philadelphia Depot, Box 76, ibid., noted an infantry overcoat was altered to have "the new mounted cape button to the collar over the short one already on the coat."

249 M.C. Meigs to R.B. Marcy, May 26, 1873, LS, C&S Br., Book A, 1873, ibid.

250 GO No. 67, AGO, June 25, 1873; and *ARSW*, 1873, Vol. I, 151-2.

251 McChristian, *The U.S. Army in the West*, 69-70; and J.D. Bingham to L.C. Easton, November 10, 1873, LR, Philadelphia Depot, Box 58, OQMG, RG92, NA.

252 Endorsement J.D. Bingham to Chief Quartermaster Officer Division of the Pacific, January 6, 1874, LS, C&S Br., Book A, 1874, ibid.

253 M.C. Meigs to L.C. Easton, August 16, 1872, Pt. 1, 1872, ibid.

254 M.C. Meigs to L.C. Easton, September 3, 1872, CCF, Box 1170, ibid., and M.C. Meigs to L.C. Easton, September 21, 1872, ibid.

255 M.C. Meigs to Secretary of War, August 21, 1872, LS, C&S Br., Pt. 1, 1872, ibid.

256 M.C. Meigs to Secretary of War, August 25, 1872; and August 30, 1872, LR, Office of the Secretary of War, RG 107, NA. The first letter caused the secretary to respond that one of the samples was "a sort of dahlia hue" and as such was rejected because it was thought the cloth "will change color on exposure to sun and rain." Another letter sent by Meigs on August 30, 1872, (Letter 7566) contained a list of cloth and material on hand that the quartermaster general did believe should be sold as surplus. He received approval from the secretary of war to do so. Previously, Meigs had directed to use light shade for overcoats and darker shade cloth for trouser production, while also ordering that no trousers be sold as surplus "unless clearly out of color as to be absolutely unfit for use." M.C. Meigs to C.H. Hoyt, August 27, 1872, LS, Pt. 1, 1872, OQMG, RG92, and M.C. Meigs to L.C. Easton, August 27, 1872, ibid.

257 M.C. Meigs to J.B. Easton, August 29, 1872, ibid.

258 M.C. Meigs to Secretary of War, July 23, 1872, Pt. 1, 1872, ibid.; M.C. Meigs to L.C. Easton, August 12, 1872, ibid.; M.C. Meigs to D.H Rucker, August 13, 1872, ibid.; M.C. Meigs to L.C. Easton, August 13, 1873, ibid.; M.C. Meigs to R.O. Tyler, August 14, 1872, ibid.; M.C. Meigs to Dr. Woodward, August 16, 1872, ibid.; M.C. Meigs to J.L. Meredith, August 16, 1872; M.C. Meigs to L.C. Easton, August 22, 1872, ibid.; M.C. Meigs to L.C. Easton, October 24, 1872; M.C. Meigs to J.L. Hays, October 25, 1872, ibid.; and M.C. Meigs to L.C. Easton, June 13, 1873, Book A, 1873, ibid. The last letter noted that the official pattern stable frock and overalls had not been accompanied by correspondence. In the future, Meigs also stated in this letter that he wanted clips of all sample materials adopted as standard to be supplied if possible.

259 M.C. Meigs to A.K. Eddy, September 9, 1872, Pt. 1, 1872, ibid., indicated that the pattern was to be adhered to strictly by those officers purchasing the gloves for troops. Several months later 180,000 pairs were ordered at $2.17 per dozen from J.H. Wilson of Philadelphia. M.C. Meigs to W.H. Baker, October 24, 1872, ibid.; and M.C. Meigs to L.C. Easton, June 6, 1873, LR, Philadelphia Depot, Box 76, ibid.

260 M.C. Meigs to R.B. Marcy, November 18, 1871, LS, C&S Br., ibid. In this brief letter Meigs "expressed no opinion in regard to the fitness and beauty of the Coat," at least at that time. In general though, Sherman was not an ardent supporter of changing the uniform. His absence in Europe at the time Marcy's board met may have precluded him from acting to halt the process had he been in Washington.

261 John R. Elting, ed., *Military Uniforms in America The Era of the American Revolution*, 1755-1795 (San Rafael, CA: Presidio Press, 1974), 48, 80, and 90, respectively.

262 M.C. Meigs to Secretary of War, August 2, 1872, LS, C&S Br., Pt. 1, 1872, OQMG, 92, NA.

263 Ibid.

264 Jacob Reed to L.C. Easton, July 30, 1872, Box 1170, CCF, RG92, bid $2.52 per blouse and $3.35 per dress coat and stated the firm could deliver 30,000 in five months. Rockhill & Wilson to J.D. Easton, July 31, 1872, ibid., gave a six month delivery time at a cost of $1.50 each. Neale Campbell to L.C. Easton, July 31, 1872, ibid., also could provide the blouse in six month, and bid $1.25 each,

providing they were the sole source for all dress coat and trousers as well. John Wanamaker & Co. to L.C. Easton, August 5, 1872, ibid., stated blouses could be made at $1.35 each exclusive of cloth.

[265] L.C. Easton to Quartermaster General, September 2, 1872, ibid.

[266] M.C. Meigs to Secretary of War, September 3, 1872, LS, C&S Br., Pt. 1, 1872, OQMG, RG92, NA.

[267] M.C. Meigs to L.C. Easton, September 10, 1872, ibid.

[268] J.D. Bingham to C.H. Hoyt, September 16, 1872, ibid.; and L.C. Easton toQuartermaster General, September 23, 1872, ibid.

[269] M.C. Meigs to L.C. Easton, September 25, 1872, ibid.

[270] M.C. Meigs to J.A. Eakin, October 10, 1872, ibid. The material used for lining the original blouses is unknown, although later specifications were clear and may give some indication of the first garments made.

[271] M.C. Meigs to L.C. Easton, August 26, 1872, ibid. For more on this facility read: W.T. Williams, "History of Jeffersonville Quartermaster Intermediate Depot," V *Quartermaster Review* No. 4 (January-February 1926): 10-20; and C.S. Hamilton, "Jeffersonville Quartermaster Intermediate Depot History and Functions," VII *Quartermaster Review* No. 1 (July-August 1927: 3-9.

[272] M.C. Meigs to C.H. Hoyt, August 26, 1872, LS, C&S Br., Pt. 1, 1872, OQMG, RG92, NA.

[273] M.C. Meigs to D.H. Rucker, August 13, 1872, ibid.

[274] M.C. Meigs to E.A. Goodwin, August 7, 1872, LS, General & Misc., Vol. A, 1872, ibid.

[275] M.C. Meigs to L.C. Easton, September 10, 1872, LS, C&S Br., Pt. 1, 1872, ibid.

[276] M.C. Meigs to L.C. Easton, September 5, 1872, ibid.

[277] M.C. Meigs to Secretary of War, August 28, 1872, ibid., expressed the concern that "The facing cloth is to be found in this country only in small quantities, and all that was found on inquiry has been purchased and the rest of the cloth necessary to complete 30,000 uniforms has been ordered from Messrs Horstmann Bros. as the quickest way of procuring it from abroad." This meant it was highly unlikely that supply of the new uniform could be made by December 1, 1872, but efforts would be made to supply as many of the remote posts as possible by then. Previously Meigs had contacted a military supplier to ascertain whether the firm could provide facing cloth in scarlet, white, crimson, sky-blue, yellow, red, and emerald green, requesting that samples be provided. M.C. Meigs to Shannon, Miller and Crane, August 12, 1872, ibid. Also see, M.C. Meigs to L.C. Easton, August 2, 1872, ibid.; M.C Meigs to W.B. Baker, October 24, 1872, ibid.; and L.C. Easton to Quarter master General, October 29, 1872, LR, AGO, RG94, for more on the problem of facing material supply. Here Easton had obtained trim for only 1,000 cavalry coats and 600 artillery from Horstmann. A bit more was expected in a week.

[278] M.C. Meigs to Secretary of War, March 19, 1873, LS, C&S Br., Book A, 1873, OQMG, RG92, NA.

[279] M.C. Meigs to L.C. Easton, April 7, 1873, ibid.

[280] Ibid. Later Ackerman amended his declaration. He indicated that only the sky-blue facing material was color-fast. M.C. Meigs to R.B. Marcy, April 12, 1873, ibid.

[281] M.C. Meigs to Secretary of War, June 19, 1873, ibid., forwarded samples to the secretary of war with the confession that a fast dye could not be found on the market. Meigs interjected that under the circumstances he thought the dyes used by his department were as good as any available.

[282] M.C. Meigs to L.C. Easton, August 29, 1872, ibid.; M.C. Meigs to L.C. Easton, September 10, 1872, ibid.; and M.C. Meigs to L.C. Easton, September 16, 1872, ibid.

[283] J.F. Rodgers to L.C. Easton, November 28, 1873, CCF, Box 1170, ibid.

[284] J. Thalford to W.W. Belknap, November 15, 1873, ibid. Thalford represented the cutters and Belknap was the secretary of war under Grant who ultimately would leave his post under a cloud of scandal that tainted the administration.

[285] F.S. Johnson to C.A. Alligood, August 15, 1872, ibid.

[286] Ibid. Of additional interest were allegations that Johnson was sympathetic to local trade unions in a labor dispute that was ongoing at the time, and had let contracts or made bargains with them to assist their cause. M.C. Meigs to L.C. Easton, September 20, 1872, LS, C&S Br., Pt. 1, 1872, ibid.; and M.C. Meigs to L.C. Easton, September 30, 1872, ibid.

[287] C.A. Alligood to L.C. Easton, August 13, 1872, ibid.

[288] M.C. Meigs to Secretary of War, August 27, 1872, ibid.

[289] M.C. Meigs to L.C. Easton, August 2, 1872, ibid.

[290] M.C. Meigs to L.C. Easton, September 18, 1872, ibid; and M.C. Meigs to L.C. Easton, August 21, 1872, ibid. In the September letter Meigs also noted his sensitivity to sending items to Indiana stating he had "no intention of throwing people out of work" in Pennsylvania but simply wanted to relieve pressure on Philadelphia while also making room there for coat manufacturing. Perhaps as a means to offset this he instructed that 15,000 blouses should be made up at Schuylkill and half the number of trousers required to fill orders for the year as well.

[291] M.C. Meigs to Daulin & Company, September 10, 1872, ibid.

[292] M.C. Meigs to Secretary of War, August 2, 1872, ibid., noted that while the quartermaster general prized his brevet rank and felt Congress treated officers poorly in prohibiting the wear of the uniform of their brevet rank, he nonetheless thought the collar insignia violated Section 16, Chapter 294, Statute 16, p. 319, and wanted the secretary of war's reading on the matter. In reply, W.D. Whipple to Quartermaster General, October 4, 1872, ibid., stated: "The Secretary of War has decided that the wearing of insignia of Brevet rank on the coat collar, by the Advisory Board, would be contrary to the 16th Section of the Act approved July 15, 1870, forbidding any officer to wear while conducting any duty, any uniform other than that of his actual rank. "It should be noted that R.B. Marcy to W.W. Belknap, June 21, 1872, LR, AGO, RG94, NA, contains two printed copies of the original proposed uniform regulations, both of which had the brevet rank sections stricken out, as were new buttons bearing Old English letters for the Pay Department, Quartermaster's Department, Subsistence Department, Judge Advocates, Signal Services, and military professors at West Point.

[293] Boatner, *The Civil War Dictionary*, 84.

[294] M.C. Meigs to Secretary of War, July 29, 1872, LS, C&S Br., Vol. 1, 1872, OQMG, RG92, NA; M.C. Meigs to Secretary of War, August 2, 1872, ibid; and M.C. Meigs to J.F. Rodgers, December 20, 1872, ibid., indicating that Meigs' objections were noted but somehow not published. E.D. Townsend to R.B. Marcy, August 5, 1872, LS, AGO, RG94, clearly stated that the secretary of war, "ordered the regulations for military storekeepers uniform to be stricken out, because they are now commissioned officers," and further noted that the Commissary and Quartermaster Departments considered themselves general staff whereas the Ordnance, Medical, and Pay Departments as well as the Corps of Engineers, were seen as staff corps, fine distinctions but important ones considering the constant ebb and flow between the various elements that made up the U.S. Army's high command at the time.

[295] GO No. 67, AGO, June 25, 1873, permitted shoulder straps to be worn on the dress coat when officers were "not on armed duty."

[296] James C. Tily, *The Uniforms of the United States Navy* (New York: Thomas Yoseloff, Publisher, 1964), 198-9, indicates lieutenants and officers of lesser rank were to wear knots rather than epaulets as of 1869. This lasted only a short period.

[297] Originally the August 3, 1872 issue of *A&NJ* had reported the backing to be black. This was not to be the case as indicated in a letter from J.D. Bingham to Horstmann Bros., November 21, 1872, LS, C&S Br., Pt. 2, 1872, OQMG, RG92, NA. Endorsement M.C. Meigs to Secretary of War, August 2, 1872, Pt. 1, 1872, ibid., further underscored cap badges would be fashioned on velvet backgrounds but the backgrounds of shoulder knots were to be of facing material. The same letter recommended that GO No. 92 be modified slightly when referring to the "tails" of the uniform coat. Meigs thought this word should be replaced by "skirts" as more intelligible.

[298] GO No. 107, AGO, December 14, 1872, changed this scheme slightly in that a solid silver shield, a silver castle, and a silver embroidered shell and flame were adopted for officers of the Adjutant General's Department, Corps of Engineers, and Ordnance Department, respectively. One military supplier submitted a smaller silver shield for consideration on the knots for officers of the Adjutant General's Department, suggesting that the sample on the pattern was too large. Shannon, Miller and Crane to E.D. Townsend, February 11, 1873, LR, AGO, RG94, NA. The cap badge for adjutants general likewise changed from the Old English "U.S." in a wreath to a silver shield in the gold wreath.

[299] GO No. 67, AGO, June 25, 1873.

[300] R.B. Marcy to E.D. Townsend, May 8, 1872, LR, AGO, RG94, NA.

[301] M.C. Meigs to R.B. Marcy, June 5, 1872, LS, C&S Br., Pt. 1, 1872, OQMG, RG92, NA.

[302] M.C. Meigs to Secretary of War, May 9, 1872; M.C. Meigs to R.B. Marcy, June 5, 1872; and M.C. Meigs to Adjutant General, June 6, 1872, ibid. Later the inventor was instructed to report to Marcy to discuss the topic. Telegram M.C. Meigs to L.C. Easton, July 20, 1872, ibid.

[303] M.C. Meigs to L.C. Easton, October 5, 1872, ibid.

[304] J.W. Powell to Adjutant General, December 16, 1872, LR, AGO, RG94, NA. Red was to border service chevrons for war service in all but the case of artillerymen who were to have white borders on their chevrons. Additionally, GO No. 92, AGO, September 15, 1873, stipulated that the chevrons themselves were to "conform in color to the arms of the service in which the solider served," and went on to state "If he has served more than one enlistment, in different arms, the Service Chevron will be of different colors to correspond."

[305] J.D. Bingham to O.O. Howard, November 19, 1872, Letter Book, LS, C&S Br., Pt. 2, 1872, OQMG, RG92, NA.

[306] J.D. Bingham to A.E. Millimore, January 19, 1874, Book A, 1874, ibid. Later GO No. 21, AGO, March 29, 1876 reiterated: "Chevrons, similar to those prescribed for the uniform-coat, will be worn by non-commissioned officers upon both sleeves of their blouses."

[307] L.C. Easton to Quartermaster General, November 18, 1872, CCF, Box 1170, OQMG, RG92, NA; C.A. Alligood to L.C. Easton, November 20, 1872, ibid.; and J.D. Bingham to Quartermaster General, December 11, 1872, LS, C&S Br., Pt. 1, 1872, ibid.

[308] M.C. Meigs to L.C. Easton, January 3, 1873, ibid.; and L.C. Easton to J.D. Bingham, November 7, 1872, CCF, Box 1170, ibid. J.D. Bingham to T. Moore, November 6, 1872, LS, C&S Br., Pt. 1, 1872, ibid., stated: "You will issue the Observer Sergeant of Signal Corps at Cheyenne such clothing as he may require for his use." Evidently, this man was to be one of the first to receive the new pattern insignia, and possibly the new uniform as well. The chief signal officer approved the patterns for his enlisted men in early 1873 according to M.C. Meigs to L.C. Easton, January 8, 1873, Book A, 1873, ibid. Again, the chevrons or devices for first and second class privates of the signal service were sewn to the blouses and coats at the depot, as were leg stripes on trousers. J.D. Bingham to E.B Grimes, June 18, 1873, ibid.

309 M.C. Meigs to L.C. Easton, February 13, 1873, ibid.; and M.C. Meigs to L.C. Easton, February 21, 1873, ibid.

310 M.C. Meigs to L.C. Easton, April 21, 1873, ibid.; and M.C. Meigs to L.C. Easton, May 7, 1873, ibid. See also GO No. 67, AGO, June 25, 1873. Chief musicians, however, still had no rank indication assigned, but were to wear a uniform prescribed by the regimental commander according to GO No. 107, AGO December 14, 1872. This same order noted that the white uniform trimmed in scarlet, that was worn by the West Point Band, was to remain in use.

311 GO No. 38, AGO, March 20, 1873.

312 M.C. Meigs to L.C. Easton, August 9, 1872, and M.C. Meigs to D.H. Rucker, August 13, 1872, LS, C&S Br., Pt. 1, 1872, OQMG, RG92, NA; Horstmann Brothers & Co. to L.C Easton, August 3, 1872, and P. Herst to L.C. Easton, August 5, 1872, CCF, Box 1170, ibid.

313 L.C. Easton to M.C. Meigs, September 16, 1872, ibid., and Endorsement M.C. Meigs, September 17, 1872, to ibid.

314 M.C. Meigs to L.C. Easton, September 18, 1872, LS, C&S Br., Pt 1, 1872, ibid.

315 Contract with P. Herst, Phila., October 19, 1872, QM Contracts, ibid.

316 P. Herst to L.C. Easton, October 24, 1872, CCF, Box 1170, ibid.

317 L.C. Easton to Quartermaster General, November 1, 1872, ibid.; and J.D. Bingham to L.C. Easton, November 23, 1872, LS, C&S Br., Pt. 2, 1872, ibid.

318 P. Herst to L.C. Easton, November 7, 1872, CCF, Box 1170, ibid.; and R. Allen to L.C. Easton,November 22, 1872, LS, C&S Br., Pt. 2 1872, ibid.

319 J.F. Rodgers to L.C. Easton, November 12, 1872, LR, Philadelphia Depot, Box 56, ibid.

320 Endorsement 1, L.C. Easton to ibid., November 14, 1873.

321 James S. Hutchins, "The Army Campaign Hat of 1872," XVI *Military Collector and Historian* No. 3 (Fall 1964): 65-73, offers additional information on the hat's promises, pitfalls, and uses.

322 William O. Tyler, *With Custer on the Little Bighorn* (New York: Viking, 1996), 155. Previous to this time, however, Tyler's commanding officer, George Custer, ordered: "Felt hats differing in color or materially in shape from the regulation campaign hat, will not be worn by officers or men of this command." Circular No. 52, Headquarters Detachment 7th Cavalry, May 22, 1873, General and Special Orders and Circulars Issued by General Custer's Detachment, April 1873- September 1873, Vol. 2, Records of U.S. Army Mobile Units, 1821-1942, RG 391, NA. This order was ignored by many, including Custer himself! Custer also dictated guard mount was to be performed in full dress, and without overcoats, while white berlin gloves or light colored gauntlets could be worn. Conversely, he prohibited top boots for officers and men on dismounted duty. Special Order No. 76, Headquarters Battalion 7th Cavalry, November 19, 1873, ibid.

323 M.C. Meigs to L.C. Easton, August 15, 1872, LS, C&S Br., Pt. 1, 1872, OQMG, RG92, NA; and Exec. Doc. No. 159, House, 43rd Congress, lst Session.

324 J.D. Bingham (for Meigs) to L.C. Easton, February 3, 1873, and M.C. Meigs to L.C. Easton, July 12, 1873, Book A, 1873, OQMG, RG92, NA.

325 Howell, *United States Army Headgear, 1855-1902*, 52.

326 M.C. Meigs to D.H. Rucker, LS, C&S Br., Book A, 1873, OQMG, 92, NA.

327 R.B. Marcy to E.D. Townsend, October 10, 1872, LS, Office of the Inspector General, RG 159, NA.

328 Telegrams from C.C. Augur, P.H. Sheridan, and G. Meade to W.T. Sherman, October 5, 1872, LR, AGO, RG94.

329 P.H. Sheridan to W.T. Sherman, October 5, 1872, ibid.

330 Richard Allen Andrews, "Years of Frustration:William T. Sherman, The Army and Reform, 1869-1883," (MA Thesis, Northwestern University, 1968), 35-6. Additionally, during Grant's second inauguration in March 1873, his old comrade in arms, Sherman recorded: "certain civilian officials opposed having military officers in the capital, for the politicians are most jealous of the military, and seem actually to hate the sight of the uniform." In protest Sherman supposedly considered attending in civilian garb and to suggest that other officers follow suit. After considerable persuasion, he relented and appeared in uniform, albeit one that was rumpled and "accented by a pair of bright yellow non regulation gloves. Ibid., 101.

331 W.T. Sherman to P.H. Sheridan, March 11, 1873, Autograph Letters, Sherman to Sheridan, Vol. 1, LC.

332 Ibid.

333 Ibid.

334 In addition to the comments cited from the *A&NJ* in the foregoing text, additional reactions are found in Promulgation of Special Orders No. 76, 1872, File 3028, LR, AGO, RG94, NA.

335 W. Whipple to J. Van Voast, October 16, 1872, CCF, Box 1170, OQMG, RG92, NA.

336 *A&NJ*, August 17, 1872, 10.

337 M.C. Meigs to Editor *Army and Navy Journal*, August 21, 1872, LS, C&S Br., Pt. 1, 1872, OQMG, RG92, NA. See also M.C. Meigs to Adjutant General, August 21, 1872, ibid., in which Meigs noted the old less expensive uniform prices remained in effect until January 1, meaning the men would get the new uniform at reduced cost for the first year, thereby also reliving the troops from hardships during the transition period. This meant there really was no need to increase the clothing allowance from $6 to $16, as one officer had advocated.

One of Meigs' operatives reinforced this sentiment, telling his superior: "I do not think it necessary to do any more for the interests of the soldier than has been done." The reason for this was that the helmet for mounted men, dress cap for foot troops, and forage cap for all personnel represented the only major changes in the clothing tables. For all purposes he claimed, "The other articles of uniform remain unchanged." J.D. Bingham to Quartermaster General, August 30, 1872, CCF, Box 1170, ibid.

338 *A&NJ*, December 29, 1866, 298; December 29, 1867, 58; November 6, 1869, 179; and October 8, 1870, 122.

339 M.C. Meigs to Editor, *Army and Navy Journal*, August 21, 1872, LS, C&S Br., Pt. 1, 1872, OQMG, RG92, NA.

340 *A&NJ*, October 5, 1867, 106 and October 18, 1872, 154; McConnell, *Five Years A Cavalryman*, 230.

341 *A&NJ*, June 28, 1873, 734.

342 Ibid., July 19, 1873, 782.

343 M.C. Meigs to R.B Marcy, April 12, 1872 and June 20, 1872, LS, C&S Br., Pt. 1, 1872, OQMG, RG92, NA.

344 J.F. Rodgers to L.C. Easton, April 4, 1873, LR, Philadelphia Depot, Box 85, ibid.

345 M.C. Meigs to L.C. Easton, April, 12, 1873, Box 69, ibid.

346 A.E. Bates to Quartermaster General, April 29, 1873, Box 76, ibid. Local commanders also were to see to it that the linings of uniforms were to be marked so that they could be identified as to ownership by a combination of numbers and letters generated from stencil sets. M.C. Meigs to L.C. Easton, April 12, 1873, Box 69, ibid. Specifically all light colored linings were to be marked in black and all dark colored linings in white "until a better method" was determined. M.C. Meigs to Adjutant General, March 3, 1873, LS, C&S Br., Book A, 1873, ibid.

347 Endorsement M.C. Meigs to L.C. Easton, May 13, 1873, ibid.; and M.C. Meigs to L.C. Easton, May 27, 1873, LR, Philadelphia Depot, Box 69, ibid.

348 J.F. Rodgers to L.C. Easton, May 22, 1873, ibid.

349 S.M. Mills to Quartermaster General, July 18, 1873, Box 55, ibid.

350 3rd Endorsement J.F. Rodgers to L.C. Easton, August 9, 1873, ibid.

351 4th Endorsement L.C. Easton to Quartermaster General, August 10, 1873, ibid.

352 Special Orders No. 75, WD, December 27, 1875, called for a board to convene for the expressed purpose of remedying a number of problems related to the uniform. Among other recommendations they called for the lengthening of uniform coat waists "from three-eighths of an inch to three-quarters of an inch according to size." *ARSW*, 1876, Vol. I, 204-5. Ultimately additional coat sizes were added as well.

353 J.D. Bingham to L.C. Easton, December 6, 1873, LR, Philadelphia Depot, Box 78,OQMG, RG92, NA.

354 L.C. Easton to Quartermaster General, November 25, 1872, and L.C Easton to Quartermaster General, December 9, 1872, CCF, Box 1170, ibid; First Endorsement, M.C. Meigs, December 6, 1872, ibid.; and Second Endorsement, R.B. Marcy,

December 10, 1872, which also noted the brass wreath and Roman "U.S." as proper insignia. See also, J.D. Bingham to M.C. Meigs, December 17, 1872, Letter Book, LS, C&S Br., Pt. 2, 1872, ibid.

[355] GO No. 107, AGO, December 14, 1872. Also see, *ARSW*, 1877, 266-7, for the first published specifications for this cap insignia.

[356] Second Endorsement, R.B. Marcy, December 10, 1872, CCF, Box 1170, OQMG, RG92, NA; and GO No. 67, AGO, June 25, 1873. Originally GO No. 92, AGO, October 26, 1872, had called for a castle, but GO No. 107, WD, December 14, 1872, had changed this to "C.E."

[357] GO NO. 76, AGO, June 25, 1873. Even before this it had been noted that the old shell and flame insignia were too large for the dress cap adopted in 1872, and as such new, smaller versions would have to be designed and procured. Memoranda, J.D. Bingham, November 23, 1872, CCF, Box 1170, OQMG, RG92, NA; and L.C. Easton to Quartermaster General, November 23, 1872, Box 1172, ibid. M.C. Meigs to L.C. Easton, March 6, 1873, Letter Book, LS, Book A, 1873, ibid., noted Marcy approved the castle as a replacement for the letters "EC". J.D. Bingham to Chief Quartermaster Department of the South, January 12, 1874, Book A, 1874, ibid., indicated that enlisted ordnance men now were to have the new shell and flame on their caps.

[358] J.F. Rodgers to L.C. Easton, April 5, 1873, LR, Philadelphia Depot, Box 85, ibid.

[359] Previously, the quartermaster general had inquired as to whether any of the old pattern uniform hat ornaments were on hand that might be used for the new caps. It seems that their size made this impractical. M.C. Meigs to L.C. Easton, August 12, 1872, LS, C&E Br., Pt. 1, 1872, ibid.

[360] J.F. Rodgers to L.C. Easton, September 6, 1873, LR, Philadelphia Depot, Box 76, ibid.

[361] M.C. Meigs to L.C. Easton, March 31, 1873, Letter Book, LS, C&S Br., Book A, 1873, ibid.

[362] M.C. Meigs to Inspector General, April 8, 1873, Book, A, 1873, ibid.; and M.C. Meigs to L.C. Easton, June 10, 1873, ibid.

[363] L.C. Easton to Quartermaster General, September 11, 1872; L.C. Easton to M.C. Meigs, September 19, 1872; L.C. Easton to Quartermaster General, December 21, 1872, CCF, Box 1170, ibid.

[364] M.C. Meigs to L.C. Easton, March 31, 1873, LS, C&S Br., Book A, 1873, ibid.

[365] M.C. Meigs to L.C. Easton, September 21, 1872, Pt. 1, 1872, ibid.

[366] M.C. Meigs endorsement to Adjutant General, January 3, 1873, ibid. Adjutant General to Quartermaster General, January 15, 1873, CCF, Box 1170, ibid.

[367] M.C. Meigs to R.B. Marcy, June 6, 1873, Letter Book, LS, C&S Br., Book A, 1873, ibid., M.C. Meigs to L.C. Easton, June 19, 1873, ibid; and Endorsement to D.H.

Brotherton to Adjutant General, November 23, 1873, LR, Office of the Secretary of War, RG107, NA. M.C. Meigs to L.C. Easton, June 3, 1873, Book A, 1873, LS, C&S Br., OQMG, RG92, NA, indicated Marcy had been sent cavalry crossed saber insignia and the commissary and ordnance insignia for his approval as well. Also see, GO No. 67, AGO, June 25, 1873, for the company letter and badge combination being generally called for on the forage cap of enlisted men except for the ordnance department.

[368] GO No. 8, AGO, February 8, 1877, rendered a concise requirement for how the various forage cap and dress cap insignia was to be worn.

[369] M.C. Meigs to L.C. Easton, August 22, 1872, LS, C&S Br., Pt. 1, 1872, OQMG, RG92, NA.

[370] *AN&J*, August 17, 1872, 10.

[371] Ibid.

[372] Ibid.

[373] Ibid.

[374] Ibid.

[375] Ibid., September 7, 172, 55.

[376] Ibid.

[377] Ibid.

[378] Ibid., September 28, 1872, 106.

[379] Ibid.

[380] Ibid., October 19, 1872, 154.

[381] Ibid.

[382] Ibid.

[383] M.C. Meigs to D.H. Rucker, April 9, 1873, LS, C&S Br., Book A, 1873, OQMG, RG92, NA, indicated that after several obstacles, Meigs had not been able to meet the December 1, 1872 issuance of the uniform, but intended to begin issue by July 1, 1873, at the start of the new fiscal year. The idea was that all men would receive the cavalry and artillery helmets, dress caps, forage caps, and cap covers, Berlin gloves, trousers, and coats with stripes attached, and troops in the West also would have their campaign hats. This goal was met according to *ARSW*, 1873, Vol. I, 120.

[384] *AN&J*, October 4, 1873, 122. Unless otherwise indicated, the following quotations were taken from this same source.

[385] Even before the issue began, one of Meigs' officers asserted acceptance of the new uniform was widespread, and, according to one member of the Inspector General's Department, would have a beneficial effect on the army, even to the point that it should lessen desertions. L.C. Easton to Quartermaster General, October 29, 1872, LR, AGO, RG94, NA.

[386] ARSW, 1873, Vol. I, 152. Also see, ibid., 120-1, for a recap on the new issue as well as continued moth and mildew proofing efforts through the Cowles process.

APPENDIX A:
Uniform Regulations, 1847

UNIFORM AND DRESS OF THE ARMY OF THE UNITED STATES, 1847.
THE MAJOR-GENERAL COMMANDING THE ARMY.

Dress.

Coat – dark blue, double-breasted; two rows of buttons, eight in each row, at equal distances; the distance between the rows, four inches at top, and three at bottom; stand up collar, to meet and hook in front, and no higher than the chin; cuffs two and a half inches deep, to go around the sleeve, parallel with the lower edge, and to button with three small buttons at the under seam; pointed cross flaps to the skirts, with four buttons equally distributed; the skirts to reach to the bend of the knee, with buff kersimere turnbacks; the bottom of the skirts not less than three and a half, nor more than five inches broad, with a gold embroidered star on buff cloth three and a half inches diameter by three inches, the longest point perpendicular at the connecting point of the buff on each skirt; two hip buttons, to range with the lower buttons on the breast: collar, cuffs, and facings, of buff cloth or kersimere; lining buff. The cuffs, collar, and cross flaps may, at the option of the General, be embroidered with the oak leaf in gold, in which case the collar and cuffs will be of blue cloth instead of buff.

Epaulettes – gold, with solid crescent; device, three silver embroidered stars, one 1 1/2 inch in diameter, one 1 1/4 inch, one 1 1/8 inch, placed on the strap, in a row longitudinally, and equi-distant; the largest star in the centre of the crescent, the smallest at the top; dead and bright gold bullion.

Buttons – gilt, convex, with spread eagle and stars, and plain border.

Hat – cocked without binding fan or back part not more than eleven inches, nor less than nine inches; the front or cock not more than nine inches, nor less than eight inches; each corner six inches; black ribbons on the front sides.

Loop and Cockade – black silk cockade; loop gold. eleven inches long, ornamented with a silver spread eagle; gold rays emanating from the eagle 2 1/2 inches, computing from the centre, terminating in 24 silver stars, plain or set with brilliants.

Tassels – gold, with worked hangers.

Plume – yellow swan feathers, drooping from an upright stem, feathered to the length of eight inches.

Cravat or stock – black silk.

Trousers – from the 1st of October to the 30th of April, dark blue cloth, with a buff or gold lace stripe down the outer seam, one and a half inch wide and welted at the edges; from the 1st of May to the 30th of September, plain white linen or cotton.

Boots – ankle or Jefferson.

Spurs – yellow metal or gilt.

Sword and scabbard – straight sword, gilt hilt, silver grip, brass or steel scabbard.

Sword-knot – gold cord with acorn end.

Sword-belt – Russian leather, with three stripes of gold embroidery; the carriages to be embroidered on both sides; the belt to be worn over the coat.

Plate – gilt, having the letters 𝖀.𝕾. and a sprig of laurel on each side in silver.

Sash – buff, silk net, with silk bullion fringe ends; sash to go twice around the waist and to tie on thy left hip. The sash may be made of silk and gold mixed, at the option of the General.

Gloves – buff or white.

Undress.

Coat – plain, dark blue, standing collar, buttons same as full dress, with two in the centre and one at the termination of each fold; without the buff and turnbacks.

Epaulettes, buttons, hat, loop and cockade, tassels, plume, cravat or stock, boots, spurs, sword, scabbard, sword-knot, belt, (black patent leather,) *plate, sash and gloves,* the same as in DRESS uniform.

Trousers – The same as in DRESS uniform, but without the stripe.

Forage Cap – according to pattern in Clothing bureau.

Appendix A: Uniform Regulations, 1847

....ALL OTHER MAJORS-GENERAL.

Dress and Undress.

The same as for the *Major-General commanding the Army*, excepting that the nine buttons in each row on the breast of the coat are to be placed by threes.

Epaulettes – the same, excepting that there shall be two stars on the straps, instead of three.

Plume – the same form and materials, excepting that it will be black and white; the black at top, half the length of the plume.

...A BRIGADIER-GENERAL.

Dress and Undress.

The same as for a *Major-General*, excepting that the coat is to have eight buttons in each row on the breast, in pairs.

Epaulettes – the same, excepting that there shall be one star on the straps, instead of two.

Plume – the same as to materials and form, excepting that it will be white and red, the white tip half the length.

Frock coat for general officers – blue cloth; two rows of buttons, placed according to rank, as on the dress coat; stand-up collar of dark blue velvet; cuffs also of blue velvet; lining, black silk, or blue cloth; pockets in the folds of the skirt, with one button at the hip and one at the end of each pocket; making only four buttons on the back and skirts of the coat.

... OFFICERS OF THE GENERAL STAFF.

Dress.

Officers of the general staff, having rank as such, and below the rank of Generals, will wear a uniform coat corresponding with that of the Generals, excepting that it will be single breasted, with a row of eight to ten buttons placed at equal distances, according to the length of the waist; the collar to be part buff; the buff to extend four inches on each side from the front; the rest of the collar blue; the cuff also blue.

Epaulettes – according to rank, as hereafter described.

Buttons – gilt, convex, same as General officers.

Hat – cocked, the same as that for General officers.

Loop and cockade – same as that for Generals, omitting the rays and stars; the eagle to be gilt instead of silver.

Tassels – gold.

Plume – swan feathers, the same as the General officers, with the distinction of colors to designate the departments of the staff, as hereafter described.

Sword-knot – gold lace strap, with gold bullion tassel.

Cravat or stock, trousers, boots, spurs, sword, steel scabbard, plate, gloves, and sash (red silk net work, silk bullion fringe ends) the same as for General Officers.

Sword-belt – black leather, with two stripes of gold embroidery; carriages embroidered on one side only.

Undress.

Coat – as prescribed for DRESS; but without the buff, and turnbacks.

Trousers – as prescribed for DRESS; but Without the stripe.

Epaulettes, buttons, hats, loop and cockade, tassels, plume, cravat or stock, boots, spurs, sword, scabbard, sword-knot, belt, (black patent leather,) *plate and gloves,* the same as in DRESS uniform.

Forage-cap – according to pattern in Clothing bureau.

Frock-coat for Staff Officers under the rank of General officer – dark blue cloth, single-breasted, with stand-up cloth collar, cloth cuffs, regulation-button, one row of eight buttons on the breast, lining and buttons on the skirt same as General officers.

Cloak for General and Staff officers – blue cloth, lined with buff or blue.

PLUMES FOR THE DIFFERENT DEPARTMENTS OF THE STAFF

Adjutant-General's – white.

Inspector-General's – green .

Quartermaster's – light blue.

Subsistence – light blue and white, blue at top, half the length of the plume.

Aides-de-camp, and officers attached to Generals, the same plume as worn by their Generals, only an inch shorter. These plumes to be of the same material and form as prescribed for the General commanding the army.

AIDES-DE-CAMP

May wear the uniform of the General Staff, according to rank, or that of their corps, at their option, the plume being the distinctive mark.

... CORPS OF ENGINEERS.

Coat – dark blue, single-breasted, one row of nine buttons, placed at equal distances; standing, Prussian collar of black velvet, meeting in front; bold embroidered wreath on each side near the front, of laurel and palm, crossing each other at the bottom, encircling a star of gold embroidery; cuffs of black velvet, without indentation, three inches deep; slashed flap on the sleeve, of black velvet embroidered with gold; for a Field-Officer, the flap to be six inches long, with four coat buttons; for a Captain, four and a half inches long, with three buttons; for a Subaltern, three inches long, with two buttons; the width of the flap, in each case, to be two and three-fourths inches at the points, and two and one-eighth inches at the narrowest part of the curve; against each button, united in gold embroidered sprigs of palm and laurel; the opening of the sleeve to be closed with hooks and eyes; skirt to extend to within three and a half inches of the bend of the knee; bottom of the shirts not less than three, nor more than five inches broad; turn-backs of the same cloth as the coat; at the bottom of the skirt, a gold embroidered wreath of palm and laurel encircling a star, on a diamond-shaped piece of black velvet, whose diagonals are two and three-fifths inches, and one and four-fifths inch, with embroidered edging; two large buttons at the hip.

Trousers – from the 1st of October to the 30th of April, dark blue cloth, with a black velvet stripe down the outer seam, one and a half inch wide; from the 1st of May to the 30th of September, white linen or cotton, plain.

Epaulettes – gold, according to rank, as hereafter described: within the crescent, a turretted castle of silver.

Buttons – gilt, nine-tenths of an inch exterior diameter, slightly convex; a raised bright rim, one-thirtieth of an inch wide; device, an eagle holding in his beak a scroll, with the word

"Essayons, " a bastion with embrasures in the distance, surrounded by water, and a rising sun; the figures to be of dead gold upon a bright field. To be made after the design in the Engineer office. Small buttons of the same form and device, and fifty-five hundredths of an inch exterior diameter.

Hat – same as for General officers, except that the corners are to be four and a half inches long, instead of six.

Loop – plain gold strap, two inches wide, raised embroidered edge; ornamented with gilt spread eagle and scroll.

Cockade – same as for General Staff.

Tassels – same as for General Staff.

Plume – three black ostrich feathers.

Cravat or Stock – black silks or bombazine.

Boots – same as for General Staff.

Spurs – yellow metal or gilt, straight shank, made to unscrew; to be fastened with straps and buckles; to be made after the design in the Engineer office.

Sword and scabbard – light rapier, with shell and guard; hilt gilt, no sword knot; scabbard, metal, covered with black leather; gilt mounting, according to patterns in Engineer office.

Sword-belt – plain frog belt of black, smooth, glossy leather, (patent,) one and seven-eighths inch wide for service; for dress occasions, black velvet, with gold embroidered sprigs of laurel and palm, may be used.

Belt-plate – rectangular, dead gold field with a bright gold double rim; a wreath of laurel and palm, enveloping a turretted castle, raised in silver; according to design in Engineer office.

Frock coat and cloak – same as for General Staff; buttons of the corps; cloak lined with blue.

Forage cap – according to pattern in Clothing bureau; black velvet band with a gold embroidered wreath of laurel and palm, encircling a silver turretted castle, in front.

N.B. All the embroidery is to be according to designs in the Engineer office.

ENGINEER SOLDIERS.

Sergeant's coat – dark blue, single breasted, one row of nine buttons at equal distances; a small pocket covered by a flap on the right side for carrying percussion caps; the collar of black cotton velvet, with a single button and loop on each side, three and one-eighth inches long, of one and three-eighths inch yellow Prussian binding allowing the black facing to show through; cuff of black cotton velvet, to have three buttons or loops on the slash sleeve, conforming in pattern to that of a Captain; yellow Prussian binding; in all other respects the coat to be after the pattern of an Artillery Sergeant's.

Two Epaulettes – corresponding in pattern with those of a Captain, of silk bullion, with solid metallic crescent.

Trousers – light blue mixture like those of Artillery and Infantry, with black cotton velvet stripe, one and one-half inches wide on the outer seam.

Plume – black upright hackle, twelve inches long. First Sergeants to wear a red sash.

Corporal's coat – same as Sergeant's, excepting that there will be two buttons and loops on the slash sleeve, conforming to the pattern of sleeve for the subalterns.

Trousers – blue mixture with a black welt in the outer seam.

Two Epaulettes of the pattern of subalterns, and same material as Sergeants'.

Privates – same as Corporals, except that instead of epaulettes, a shoulder strap, of the pattern of the Artillery, will be worn on each shoulder.

Musicians – same as privates, excepting that the coat will be of red cloth lined with white.

Pompon – black worsted, spherical, three inches diameter; tulip, like that of the Artillery.

Schako – same pattern as that of the Artillery, bearing a yellow eagle over a castle like that worn by the Cadets.

Shell jacket – dark blue, with collar and buttons like those of the uniform coat; a pocket for percussion caps, covered by a flap on the right side; in other respects to conform to the Artillery pattern.

White cotton shell jacket – like that of the Artillery, with the button of the Engineer soldiers, and with a percussion cap pocket as in the woollen shell jacket.

Woollen trousers – light blue mixture with black welt in outer seam.

White trousers for summer like those of the other corps. Canvass overalls to be drawn over the other trousers for working in.

Forage cap – band of black cotton velvet with a yellow castle in front, according to drawing and pattern in Clothing bureau.

Great coat – Artillery pattern with the button of the Engineer soldiers.

Button – yellow metal, convex; devices a castle and river in relief – bright, on a ground deadened by parallel lines, according to drawing and pattern in Clothing bureau.

Two sizes – large – diameter 75-100 inch,
smaller " 6-10 inch.

. . . CORPS OF TOPOGRAPHICAL ENGINEERS

Coat – dark blue cloth, double-breasted, two parallel rows of buttons, ten in each row, at equal distances; the distance between the rows four inches throughout, measuring from the centres or eyes of the buttons; standing collar, to meet with hooks and eyes, and to rise no higher than to permit the chin to turn freely over it; square cuff, three and one-fourth inches deep; slashed flap on the skirt, of dark blue cloth, seven and one-fourth inches long, and three and one-tenth inches wide at the upper and lower edges, with three large buttons, one at each point; two large buttons at the waist; the skirt to extend within three and a half inches of the bend of the knee; the collar, cuffs, and skirt-facings, or turnbacks, to be of dark blue velvet; the collar, cuffs, and slashed skirt-flaps to be embroidered in gold, with oak-leaves and acorns, according to the designs in the Topographical bureau.

Epaulettes – according to rank, as described hereafter. Within the crescent, which will be solid and bright, a shield embroidered in gold, and below it the letters T.E. [print in old English] in old English characters; the letters to be of silver for all grades, except the *Majors*, who will wear yellow letters to form the contrast with their epaulette-straps of silver lace. The spread-eagle, of silver, to be worn by the *Colonel* only, is to be placed upon the epaulette-strap above the shield.

Buttons – gilt, seven-eighths of an inch diameter in the extreme, convex, and solid; device, the shield of the United States, occupying one-half the diameter, and the letters T.E. [old English characters here] in old English characters, occupying the other half; small buttons one-half inch diameter, device and form the same.

Hat, loop and cockade, tassels, stock or cravat, sword-knot, boots, gloves – the same as for officers of the General Staff, except that the button in front of the hat will be that of the corps.

Plume – black, of the same form and materials as for the General Staff.

Sash – crimson silk-net, with silk bullion fringe ends, to go twice round the waist, and to be tied on the right hip; the pendant part to extend uniformly one foot two inches below the tie.

Spurs – yellow metal, straight shanks to correspond with the design in the Topographical bureau.

Trousers – from the first of October to the 30th of April, dark blue cloth, with a gold stripe down the outer seam for full dress, one and three-fourth inches wide, to correspond with the pattern in the Topographical bureau; from the first of May until the 30th of September, white linen or cotton, plain.

Saber – the same form as that prescribed for the dragoons; fishskin gripe, bound with yellow wire; gilt hilt, of half basket form; bright steel scabbard, to correspond with the pattern to be deposited in the Topographical bureau.

Waist-belt – black, one and a half inch wide, like that of the dragoons.

Plate – gilt, elliptical, two inches in the shortest diameter; device, the eagle and shield of the United States, and the letters U.S. [old English characters here] in old English characters underneath, with the words CORPS OF TOPOGRAPHICAL ENGINEERS, in small Roman capitals, around the edge of the plate.

Frock coat – same as for the General Staff, except that the buttons will be those of the corps, and ten in front. With the frock coat, or for undress, the stripes on the trousers will be of black silk and worsted lace, with oak leaf and acorn figure, and one and three-fourths inch wide.

Forage-cap – according to pattern in Clothing bureau.

Cloak – same as for the General Staff, except the button; lining blue.

. . . ORDNANCE DEPARTMENT.

Coat – of the same pattern as the artillery; to be of dark blue cloth throughout; no red; lace the same as the artillery.

Buttons – gilt, convex, plain border, cross cannons and bomb-shell.

Epaulettes – according to rank and pattern, as hereafter described.

Hat – cocked, and ornaments the same as the General Staff.

Plume – the same as the artillery.

Trousers – of dark blue cloth, with stripe one and a half inch wide, of the same material and color, welted at the edges; plain white linen or cotton for summer.

Boots, spurs for mounted officers, swords and scabbard, waist-belt, plate – same as for the artillery, except that the sword belt will be of black patent leather, and worn round the waist.

Sword-knot, sash, stock, gloves, frock coat, and cloak, the same as for the artillery, except that the sword-belt will be of black patent leathers and worn round the waist.

Forage cap – according to pattern in Clothing bureau.

Ordnance-Sergeants to wear the uniform of the Sergeant-Major of artillery, except the aiguillette; the stripe of the cloth pantaloons will be dark blue instead of red. Ordnance men the same as the artillery, except that the shoulder-straps will be red; the overalls and jackets will be made of dark blue cloth; the yellow lace on the jacket will be replaced by a scarlet welt inserted in the collar seam, and a similar welt will be inserted in the outer seam of the overalls.

. . . DRAGOONS.

Coat – dark blue cloth, double-breasted, two rows of buttons, ten in each row, at equal distances, after the fashion of the coat described for the infantry; the lace gold; the collar, cuffs, and turnbacks, yellow; the skirt to be ornamented with a star, instead of a bugle, and the length of the skirt to be what is called three quarters; the slash-flap on the skirt and sleeve to correspond with that of the infantry; the slash on the sleeve to designate rank in the same manner; the collar to be framed with lace, two loops on each side of the collar, with small uniform buttons at the back end of the loops.

Epaulettes – according to the established rule, where the button is yellow, and according to rank.

Button – gilt, convex; device, a spread-eagle, with the letter D on the shield.

Trousers – for the company officers, blue grey mixture, of the same color as that for the infantry, with two stripes of yellow cloth, three-fourths of an inch wide up each outward seam, leaving a light of one-fourth inch between.

For the Colonel, Lieutenant-Colonel, Major, and Adjutant, dark blue cloth, with two stripes of gold lace up each outward seam, three-fourths of an inch wide, leaving a light between. For the summer all officers to wear plain white drilling.

Cap – of the same material as that for the infantry, but according to a pattern furnished; to be ornamented with a gilt star, silver eagle, and gold cord; the star to be worn in front, with a drooping white horse-hair pompon; the field officers to have a small strip of red hair to show in front of their pompons.

Boots – ankle.

Spurs – yellow metal.

Sabre – browned steel scabbard, half basket hilt, gilt, with two fluted bars on the outside, fish-skin gripe, bound with silver wire, and of the pattern deposited with the Ordnance department.

Sword-knot – gold cord, with acorn end.

Waist-belt – black patent leather, one and a half inch wide, with slings, hooks, and plate, like those of the General Staff, omitting on the plate the letters U.S. [old English characters here] and inserting the letter D within the wreath.

Sash – silk net, deep orange color, and like that of the infantry as to shape and size; to be tied on the right hip; to be worn only when in full dress, and with the frock coat.

Stock – black silk.

Gloves – white.

Frock coat – dark blue cloth, cut after the fashion of that described for the artillery. Officers upon ordinary stable duty, marches, or active service, will be permitted to wear a shell, or stable jacket, corresponding with that of the men, with gold lace trimmings.

Great coat – blue grey mixture, like that furnished the men, double-breasted, with sleeves, stand-up collar, cape to meet, and button all the way in front, and reach down to the upper edge of the cuff of the coat.

Forage cap – according to pattern in Clothing bureau.

NON-COMMISSIONED OFFICERS, BUGLERS, AND PRIVATES.

Coat – dark blue cloth short coat, double-breasted, with yellow collar, cuffs, turnbacks, and brass shoulder-knots, of the exact cut and fashion of the one furnished the Clothing bureau. Sergeants to wear chevrons of three bars, points towards the cuffs, on each sleeve, above the elbow; corporals, two bars. The collar of the chief musicians' and sergeants' coats to be trimmed with yellow worsted binding after the style of the officers. Musicians coats to be of red cloth, yellow turnbacks and cuffs, yellow buttons.

Trousers – same material as for other corps, but cut and made after the style and fashion of a pair furnished the Clothing bureau. Sergeants to have two yellow stripes three-fourths of an inch wide up each outward seam, leaving a light of one-fourth of an inch between. Corporals and privates one yellow stripe up each outward seam. The stripes to be in advance of the seam.

Jacket – blue cloth for winter, white cotton for summer; stand-up collar, trimmed with yellow worsted binding, like a sergeant's coat; single-breasted, one row of buttons in front. These jackets are to be made of cloth of the quality used for the old uniform coats.

Cap – same materials as for other corps; but the pattern, ornaments, and trimming, like the one furnished the Clothing bureau; drooping white horse-hair pompon.

Great coat – same materials as for other corps; stand-up collar, double-breasted, cape to reach down to the cuff of the coat, and to button all the way up.

Boots – ankle.

Spurs – yellow metal.

The non-commissioned staff to wear aiguillettes on the left shoulder, like those for the artillery. Non-commissioned staff and first sergeants of companies wear yellow worsted sashes.

Forage-cap – according to pattern in Clothing bureau.

... REGIMENT OF MOUNTED RIFLEMEN.

The " Undress" shall, for the present, be the same as that for the dragoons – except,

1st. That the button, and waist-belt plate, shall bear the letter R, instead of the letter D.

2d. The trousers of dark blue cloth, with a stripe of black cloth down the outer seam, edged with yellow cord.

3d. The forage-cap to be ornamented with a gold embroidered spread-eagle, with the letter R in silver on the shield.

4th. The sash to be crimson silk.

5th. Wings for coat according to pattern to be provided.

ARTILLERY.

Coat – dark blue cloth, double-breasted, two rows of buttons, ten in each row, at equal distances; the distance between the rows four inches at top, and two inches at bottom, measuring from the centres or eyes of the buttons; standing collar, to meet in front with hooks and eyes, and rise no higher than to permit the free turning of the chin over it; two loops, four and a half inches long, on each side of the collar, with one small uniform button at the end of each loop; the collar edged all round with red; plain round cuff, three inches deep; slashed flap on the sleeve, six and a half inches long and two and two-eighths of an inch wide at the points, and two inches wide at the narrowest part of the curve; four loops and four small buttons on the slashed flap on the sleeve for field officers; for captains, a sleeve of the same pattern, but the slash only four and a half inches long, with three loops and three small buttons; and for subalterns, a slash sleeve of three and a half inches long, with two loops and two small buttons; loops to be placed at equal distances; slashed flap on the skirt, with four loops and large buttons; the slashed flaps on the sleeves and skirt to be edged with red on the ends and indented edge; two large buttons at the waist; skirt to extend to within three and a half inches of the bend of the knee; red kerseymere turnbacks and skirt linings; gold embroidered shell and flame at the bottom of the skirt; loops on the collar and flaps to be of gold lace, half an inch wide, and the entire loop not to exceed one and a quarter inch in breadth; the coat to be lined with red.

Epaulettes – according to rank and pattern, as hereafter described.

Buttons – gilt, convex; seven-eighths of an inch in diameter; device, a spread eagle with shield, bearing the letter A.

Cap – black beaver, seven and a half inches deep, with lackered sunk tip seven and a half inches diameter, with a band of black patent leather to encircle the bottom of the cap; black patent leather peak, gilt eagle, and cross cannons and number of regiment; a strap or black patent leather, fastened to each side of the cap, to be worn under the chin.

Plume – red cock feathers, falling from an upright stem, eight inches long, with a gilt socket. Officers of the horse artillery will be allowed to wear a red horsehair plume, instead of a cock-feather.

Trousers – from the 1st of October to the 30th of April, white and light blue mixture cloth, producing the effect of a sky-blue, to come well down over the boots, and made perfectly plain, except a red stripe down the outer seam, one and a half inch wide, and welted at the edges; from the 1st of May to the 30th of September, white linen or cotton, without the stripe.

Boots – ankle or Jefferson.

Spurs – (for mounted officers) yellow metal or gilt.

Sword and scabbard – according to pattern furnished by the Ordnance department.

Sword-knot – crimson and gold, with bullion tassel.

Shoulder-belt – white leather, two and a half inches wide, with frog; to be worn over the coat, with a breast-plate, according to pattern to be furnished by the Ordnance department. The Colonel, Lieutenant-Colonel, Major, Adjutant, an(l Quartermaster of a regiment, will wear a *waist-belt* of the pattern now used.

Sash – crimson silk net, with silk bullion fringe ends; sash to go twice round the waist, and to be tied on the left hip; the pendant part to be uniformly one foot in length from the tie.

Stock – black silk.

Gloves – white.

Frock coat – dark blue cloth, single-breasted, with not less than eight nor more than ten (depending on the size of the officer) large regimental buttons down the front at equal distances, and two small regimental buttons at the fastening of the cuff; plain stand-up collar; two large buttons at each pocket in the skirt, one of which at the hip, and the other at the bottom of the fold of the pocket, making four buttons behind; lining of the coat, blue.

Cloak – blue, lined with scarlet shalloon; walking length; clasp ornaments at bottom of collar, gilt eagle, with chain.

Forage-cap – according to pattern in Clothing bureau.

NON-COMMISSIONED OFFICERS, MUSICIANS, ARTIFICERS AND PRIVATES.

Sergeant-Major – the same as established for the field officers, excepting that binding will be substituted for gold lace; the epaulettes to be of the same pattern as that of the subalterns, excepting that worsted bullion will be substituted for gold bullion; *plume*, red upright hackle, twelve inches long; *aiguillette* on the left shoulders of yellow worsted with gilt tabs.

Quartermaster-Sergeant – the same as the *Sergeant-Major*, excepting that the plume will be of light blue.

Chief Musician – the same as *Quartermaster-Sergeant*, excepting that the coat will be of red cloth, with white linings and turnbacks; plume, white.

Sergeants – coat to be of dark blue, single-breasted, with one row of nine buttons, placed at equal distances; the skirts to extend within seven inches of the bend of the knee; the coat to conform to the pattern of the officers' coats in other respects, excepting that the cuff shall have three buttons and loops on the slash sleeve, to conform to that designated for a Captain; the lace to be of worsted; two worsted epaulettes, corresponding in pattern with those of a Captain; First Sergeant of companies to wear a red worsted sash; all Sergeants to wear the red stripe on the blue mixture trousers, as designated for officers; same for the non-commissioned staff.

Corporals – same as Sergeants, excepting that there will be but two buttons on the slash sleeve conforming to the pattern of the sleeve for the subalterns; *trousers* some as Sergeants, *without the stripe*; two epaulettes of the pattern for the subalterns, of the same materials as those of the Sergeants.

Privates – the same as the Corporals, except in that instead of epaulettes a strap will be worn on each shoulder, composed of the same materials and form of the epaulettes of the Corporals, with pad, and half fringe.

Musicians – the same as the privates, excepting that the coat will be of red cloth, lined with white, turnbacks white; white plume, upright hackle ten inches long.

The cap of the non-commissioned officers, musicians, and privates, to be of the same pattern as that designated for the officers.

The plumes of the sergeants, corporals, and privates, red worsted, eight inches long.

. . . INFANTRY.

Coat – the same pattern as that of the artillery; to be of dark blue cloth, lined with white serge; edged with white kerseymere where the artillery coat is edged with red; turnbacks and skirt lining of white kerseymere; skirt ornament, silver embroidered bugle; the lace to be silver.

Epaulettes – according to rank and pattern, as hereafter described.

Buttons – same as at present worn.

Cap – same as the artillery, except the ornaments, which are a silver bugle, number of regiment, surmounted by a gilt eagle, as at present worn.

Plume – white cock-feathers, falling from an upright stem, eight inches long with a gilt socket.

Trousers – the same as the artillery, except that the stripe on the mixture trousers to be of white kerseymere.

Boots, spurs for mounted officers, sword, scabbard, sword-knot, shoulder belt and plate, sash, stock and gloves the same as for the Artillery.

Frock-coat – same as for the Artillery, except the button, which will be the regimental button.

Cloak – same as for the Artillery, except the lining which will be white shalloon.

Forage-cap – according to pattern in Clothing bureau.

NON-COMMISSIONED OFFICERS, MUSICIANS, AND PRIVATES.

The same as for the Artillery, excepting the facings and trimmings, which will be white; *plume*, white.

. . . VOLTIGEURS, OR FOOT RIFLEMEN.

Undress.

Frock coat – dark grey cloth, single-breasted, with nine large regimental buttons down the front, at equal distances; in other respects conforming to the prescribed frock coat for the Artillery.

Scales – or counter straps for the shoulder, in lieu of epaulettes, with the usual insignia designating the rank of the officer.

Buttons – gilt, same as for the Mounted Riflemen, except that they shall bear the letter V.

Trousers – dark grey cloth, (from the 1st of October to the 30th of April,) with a stripe, of the same color, down the outer seam, edged with yellow cord; from the 1st of May to the 30th September, white linen or cotton, without stripe.

Sword and scabbard – same as for the Infantry.

Shoulder belt – black patent leather – in other respects conforming to the pattern prescribed for the Infantry.

All other military equipments, necessary for service in the field will conform to those established for the Infantry, except as to color; the letter V being substituted where necessary.

NON-COMMISSIONED OFFICERS, MUSICIANS, AND PRIVATES.

Coat and trousers – dark grey cloth – in other respects the same as the Infantry.

. . . BANDS

A band will wear the uniform of the regiment or corps to which it belongs. The commanding officer may, at the expense of the corps, sanctioned by the Council of Administration, make such additions in ornaments as he may judge proper.

MEDICAL DEPARTMENT.

Coat – dark blue cloth, double breasted; two rows of buttons, ten buttons in each row; the rows to commence at the collar and to run in right lines to the bottom of the lapels, four inches apart at the top, and two and a half inches at the bottom; the buttons in each row to be equidistant; standing collar, and cuffs of black velvet; the collar to meet with hooks and eyes, and to rise no higher than to permit the chin to turn freely over it; to be embroidered at each end with a bold laurel branch five inches long; the outer edges to be embroidered with a gold vine of laurel leaves. The cuffs to be three inches deep, and to have a laurel branch and vine similar to that on the collar. The skirts to be made after the fashion of a citizen's coat lined with blue cloth, with a button at each hip, one at the end of each fold, and one intermediate in each fold.

Epaulettes – gold, with solid bright crescent. The bullion of the Surgeon-General will be half an inch in diameter, and three and a half inches long; that of the Surgeons, half an inch in diameter, and three and a half inches long; that of Assistant Surgeons over five years one-fourth inch diameters and two and a half inches long; and of Assistant Surgeons under five years one-eighth inch diameter, and two and a half inches long. Within the crescent, a laurel wreath embroidered in gold and the letters **M.S.** in old English characters within the wreath. The straps to be gold lace for all grades except the Surgeons, which will be silver lace; the letters to be silver where the lace is gold, and gold where the lace is silver. A spread eagle of solid silver metal to be worn by the Surgeon-General only, is to be placed upon the Epaulette strap above the wreath.

Buttons – gilt, convex, with spread eagle and stars, and plain border.

Hat – cocked, with black silk binding fan on back part not more than eleven inches, nor less than nine inches; the front or cock not more than nine inches nor less than eight; each corner, six inches, black button and black silk gimp loop, ornamented with a cockade and gilt spread eagle; tassels gold.

Cravat or stock – black silk.

Trousers – from the 1st of October to the 30th of April, dark blue cloth, with black mohair lace down the outer seam one and one-half inch wide, having a laurel vine with satin face. From the 1st of May to the 30th of September, plain white linen or cotton.

Boots – ankle or Jefferson.

Spurs – yellow metal or gilt.

Sword – small sword and scabbard, according to pattern in Surgeon-General's office.

Sword-knot – gold lace strap with gold bullion tassels.

Waist-belt – black patent leather, one and a half inch wide, with slings and hooks.

Plate – gilt, having the letters U. S. and a sprig of laurel on each side in silver.

Gloves – white.

Undress.

Frock coat – dark blue cloth, single breasted, with stand-up collar cloth cuffs; regulation buttons; one row of eight buttons on the breast lining black silk or blue cloth; pockets in the folds of the skirts, with one button at the hip and one at the end of each pocket, making only four buttons on the back and skirts of the coat; shoulder straps according to grade.

Cloak – blue cloth, lined with blue.

Forage cap – according to pattern.

Appendix A: Uniform Regulations, 1847

... PAY DEPARTMENT.

The uniform of the Paymaster-General will be the same as that of the Surgeon-General; and the uniform of Paymasters the same as that of Surgeons, except that the collar and cuffs of the Pay department will be of the same material as that of the coat; the letters 𝔓.𝔇. (in old English characters) will be placed within the crescent of tile epaulettes.

... MILITARY ACADEMY.

The uniform of the Professors, Teachers, and their assistants, not in the line of the Army, including the Sword-master, shall be a citizen's blue cloth dress coat, with buttons of the Corps of Engineers; round black hat; pantaloons and vest plain, of same color and material as for officers of Engineers; stock, black. The uniform of the Chaplain shall be the dress usually worn by the clergy.

... UNIFORM OF THE CORPS OF CADETS.

One gray cloth coatee, single-breasted; three rows of eight gilt bullet buttons in front; and button holes of black silk cord in the herringbone form, with a festoon turned at the back end; a standing collar, trimmed with black silk lace, to fit the neck, and hook in front; the cuffs four inches wide; the bottom of the breast and the hip buttons to range; on the collar, one blind button hole of cord, formed like that of the breast, four inches long with a button on each side; cord holes in the like form, to proceed from three buttons placed lengthwise on the skirts, with three buttons down the plaits; the cuffs to be indented, with three buttons, and cord holes likewise on each sleeve, corresponding, with the indentation of the cuff, in the centre of which is to be inserted the lower button.

One surtout coat of gray cloth, single-breasted, to reach to within four inches of the ankle joint, with a stand and fall collar rising to the tip of the ear, and hooked in front; buttons gilt, cupped, three quarters of an inch in diameter, and stamped across the face with the Word "Cadet;" one button on each side of the collar, with a blind button hole of black silk braid, four inches long; five buttons down the front, and three in each plait behind; a cape of the same material as the coat, to descend two-thirds of the length of the waist; the coat to have cross flaps at the hips, two and a half inches wide, and to be lined, cape, skirts, and sleeves, with black rattinet.

One gray cloth vest for winter; single breasted; gilt buttons; trimmed with black silk lace.

Two white vests for summer. The vest is not an indispensable part of the uniform; it may be worn or not at the option of the Cadets but when worn, must be of the prescribed uniform; and when not worn, the coat must be buttoned whenever out of quarters or tent.

Two pairs of gray cloth trousers for winter, with a black stripe an inch wide down the outer seam.

Six pairs of plain white drilling trousers for summer.

One fatigue jacket; to be made of unbleached drilling; single-breasted, with a stand and fall collar; one gilt button half an inch in diameter on each side of the collar, and ten buttons of the same pattern down the breast.

One black cap, round crown, seven inches high, or more, in proportion to the size of the Cadet, with a circular visor in front; black worsted pompon, eight inches long set in a yellow metal socket; cap plate worn on front of the cap; the whole according to pattern deposited with the Quartermaster at West Point.

One forage cap, according to pattern deposited with the Quartermaster at West Point.

... CIVIL STAFF.

MILITARY STOREKEEPERS, ORDNANCE STOREKEEPERS.

Coat – plain, of blue cloth.

Button – of the department to which the officers respectively belong; if to no particular arm, the General Staff button.

Trousers – plain blue cloth for winter, and plain white linen or cotton for summer.

Round Hat, black cockade, and yellow eagle.

Sword and belt – same as for Pay department.

Forage cap – same as worn by officers of the department.

Frock coat – same as the General Staff; single breasted; button of department; without straps.

BADGES TO DISTINGUISH RANK.

Epaulettes.

Of General officers – as above described.

Of a Colonel – bright bullion, half an inch diameter, three inches and a half long; plain lace strap, ornamented with an embroidered spread eagle; the number of the regiment to be embroidered within the crescent; crescent solid; eagle and number to be silver where the bullion is gold, and gold where the bullion is silver.

Of a Lieutenant-Colonel – the same as the Colonel, omitting the eagle.

Of a Major – the same as a Lieutenant-Colonel as to shape and size; the strap to be of silver lace where the bullion is gold, and of gold lace where the bullion is silver; the number on the strap to correspond in color with the bullion, the border of the strap the same color of the bullion.

Of a Captain – plain lace straps and solid crescent; bullion one fourth inch diameter and two and a half inches deep; regimental number on the strap to be gold embroidered where the bullion is silver, and to be silver embroidered where the bullion is gold.

Of a Lieutenant – the same as for a Captain, except that the bullion is one-eighth inch in diameter.

The bullion of all epaulettes to correspond in color with the button of the coat.

All officers having military rank, to wear one epaulette on each shoulder.

The number on the strap of the epaulette being intended to denote the regiment, will be worn by regimental officers only.

Epaulettes may be worn either with pads or boxes.

Aiguillettes.

Staff officers, general as well as regimental, except the engineers, topographical engineers, and ordnance, will be distinguished by *aiguillettes*.

Aiguillettes of General Staff officers – twisted gold cord, with gilt engraved tags, worn on the right shoulder, under the epaulette. The General Staff is to include –

The officers of the Adjutant-General's department.
The Inspectors-General.
The Aides-decamp.
The officers of the Quartermaster's department.
The officers of the Subsistence department.
The officers of the Pay department.
The officers of the Medical department.

Aiguillettes of Regimental Staff officers – twisted gold and silver cords with gilt tags, worn under the epaulettes of the right shoulder.

Shoulder-straps.

To be worn on the frock coats of General, General Staff, Artillery, and Infantry officers.

The Major-General commanding the Army – strap of blue cloth, one inch in breadth, and not less than three and a half inches, nor more than four inches in length; bordered with an embroidery of gold a quarter of an inch wide; three silver embroidered stars of five rays, one star on the centre of the strap, and one on each side, equi-distant between the centre and outer edge of the strap. The centre star to be the largest; where these stars would come in contact with the embroidery of the strap, there must be described an arc of a circle, (having the centre of the star for its centre, and the radius of the star for its radius,) taking out a sufficient quantity of the embroidery to admit them.

A Major-General – the same as the Major-General commanding the army, except that there will be trio stars instead of three; the centre of each star to be one inch from the outer ed e of the gold embroidery on the ends of the strap; both stars of the same size.

A Brigadier-General – the same as a Major-General except that there will be one star instead of two; the centre of the star to be equi-distant from the outer edge of the embroidery on the ends of the strap.

A Colonel – strap of the same size as above; the embroidery on the border to be one-half the width (i.e. one-eighth of an inch;) an embroidered spread eagle on the centre of the strap, two inches between the tips of the wings, having, in the right talon an olive branch, and in the left a bundle of arrows; an escutcheon on the breast as represented in the arms of the United States; the embroidery of the eagle to be of silver where the border is gold, and of gold where the border is silver.

A Lieutenant-Colonel – the same as for a Colonel, omitting the eagle, and introducing a leaf at each end, each leaf extending seven-eighths of an inch from the end border of the strap; the embroidered leaf of the same color with the border.

A Major – the same as that for a Lieutenant-Colonel, except that the leaves will be of silver where the border is of gold, and of gold where the border is of silver.

A Captain – the same as that for a Major, except that two embroidered bars will be substituted for each leaf, of the same width and color as the border; to be placed parallel to the ends of the strap; the distance between them and from the border equal to the width of the border.

A First Lieutenant – the same as for a Captain, excepting that there will be one bar at each end, instead of two.

A Second Lieutenant – the same as for a First Lieutenant, omitting the bars.

Note – The embroidery of the borders of the straps is, in every instance, to correspond in color to the button of the coat.

Shoulder-straps of Dragoons.

Formed like the strap of the epaulette, and made of blue cloth, edged with gold lace like an epaulette; solid gilt crescent, with the number of regiment embroidered within. The strap of the Colonel to have on it a silver embroidered eagle; that of the Lieutenant-Colonel two gold leaves at the points, where the crescent joins it; that of the Major, two silver

Chevrons.

As a badge of distinction when in *fatigue dress*, non-commissioned officers are permitted to wear upon the sleeves of their undress jackets, above the elbow, chevrons of lace corresponding to their uniform, after the following description:

For a Sergeant-Major, *three bars, and an arc.*

For a Quartermaster-Sergeant, *three bars, and a tie.*

For a First-Sergeant, *three bars, and a lozenge.*

For a Sergeant, *three bars.*

For a Corporal, *two bars.*

Non-commissioned officers and privates, as well as musicians, who shall have served faithfully for the term of five years, shall be permitted to wear a chevron on the sleeves of their *uniform* coats, above the elbow, points up; and an additional chevron on each arm for every additional five years of faithful service. And those who have served in war, shall have a red stripe on each side of the chevron.

Chevrons adopted for the field in 1847.

leaves; that of the Captain, two gold bars; that of the First Lieutenant, one bar; that of the Second Lieutenant, plain.

Chevrons.

As a badge of distinction when in fatigue dress, non-commissioned officers are permitted to wear upon the sleeves of their undress jackets, above the elbow, chevrons of lace corresponding to their uniform, after the following description:

For a Sergeant-Major, *three bars, and an arc.*
For a Quartermaster-Sergeant, *three bars, and a tie.*
For a First-Sergeant, *three bars, and a lozenge.*
For a Sergeant, *three bars.*
For a Corporal, *two bars.*

Noncommissioned officers and privates, as well as musicians, who shall have served faithfully for the term of five years, shall be permitted to wear a chevron on the sleeves of their uniform coats, above the elbow, points up; and an additional chevron on each arm for every additional five years of faithful service. And those who have served in war, shall have a red stripe on each side of the chevron.

... GENERAL REMARKS.

General and General Staff Officers.

The DRESS uniform of Generals and General Staff officers is to be worn at dress reviews, and on extraordinary occasions.

The UNDRESS is for general use, and may be worn on all occasions not specified above.

The blue frock coat may be worn by General officers on common occasions off parade, and when the troops are ordered to wear their great-coats upon a march; to be worn buttoned, and hooked at the collar.

Officers of the Staff may wear, under the same circumstances, the blue frock coat prescribed for them.

The sword-belt to be worn over the frock coat.

The sash to be worn by General and Staff officers, when in full dress, and on all occasions when serving with the troops, whether in undress or frock coat.

Officers of Dragoons, Artillery, Infantry, &c.

Colonels of regiments or corps, having the brevet rank of Generals, may wear the uniform of their respective regiments or corps, or that of General officers according to their brevet rank, with the exception of the plume, which is to be worn only when commanding according to their brevets. They will wear the plume of their respective corps.

All other brevet officers will wear the epaulettes distinctive of their highest rank according to their arm.

The sash is to be worn on all occasions where the officer in full dress.

The frock coat may be worn as common morning dress in quarters and on certain duties of parade, to wit: at drills – inspections of barracks and hospital courts of inquiry and boards – inspections of articles and necessaries – working parties and fatigue duties – and upon the march; on all such occasions to be buttoned, and hooked at the collar.

The sword-belt is to be worn over the frock coat, and when the officer is engaged on duty of any description, except that of the stable, the sash is to be worn.

The sword of mounted officers will be suspended from the belt, by slings of the same materials as the belt, with a hook attached to the belt, to suspend the sword more conveniently when on foot.

Officers of regiments and posts will be provided with *Shell jackets*, to be worn in summer, during the extreme heat of the season; the *Shell jacket* to be of the following pattern: – white cotton or linen, with standing collar; cuffs two and a half inches deep round the wrist, to open at the lower seam; where they will be buttoned with two small uniform buttons. A row of nine small uniform buttons down the front at equal distances; the front and rear of the jacket to come down in a peak. A similar jacket of light blue cloth may be worn in campaign, or on fatigue duty.

The commanding officer will determine in orders, when the *Shell Jacket* is to be worn by the officers and men, according to the state of the weather. On duty, the sash will be worn with the *Shell jacket*.

APPENDIX B:
Uniform Regulations, 1851

UNIFORM AND DRESS OF THE ARMY UNITED STATES, 1851.

COAT.

For Commissioned Officers.

1. All officers shall wear a frock-coat of dark blue cloth, the skirt to extend from two-third to three-fourths of the distance from the top of the hip to the bend of the knee; single-breasted for Captains and Lieutenants; double-breasted for all other grades.

2. *For a Major General* – two rows of buttons on the breast, nine in each row, phased by threes; the distance between each row, five and one-half inches at top, and three and one-half inches at bottom; stand-up collar, to rise no higher than to permit the chin to turn freely over it, to hook in front at the bottom, and slope thence up and backward at an angle of thirty degrees on each side, making the total opening in front an angle of sixty degrees; cuffs two and one-half inches deep, to go around the sleeves parallel with the lower edge, and to button with three small buttons at the under seam; pockets in the folds of the skirts, with one button at the hip, and one at the end of each pocket, making four buttons on the back and skirt of the coat, the hip button to range with the lowest buttons on the breast; collar and cuffs to be of dark blue velvet; lining of the coat black.

3. *For a Brigadier General* – the same as for a Major General, (par. 2,) except that there will be only eight buttons in each row on the breast, placed in pairs.

4. *For a Colonel* – the same as for a Major General, (2,) except that there will be only seven buttons in each row on the breast, placed at equal diztaneces; collar and cuffs of the same color and material as the coat.

5. *For a Lieutenant Colonel* – the same as for a Colonel, (4.)

For a Major – the same as for a Colonel, (4.)

For a Captain – the same as for a Colonel, (4,) except that there will be only one row of nine buttons on the breast, placed at equal distances.

For a First Lieutenant – the same as for a Captain, (7.)

For Second Lieutenant – the same as for a Captain, (7.)

For a Brevet Second Lieutenant – the same as for a Captain, (7.)

For Enlisted Men.

11. The uniform coat for all enlisted men shall be a single-breasted frock of dark blue cloth, with a skirt extending one-half the distance from the top of the hip to the bend of the knee.

12. *For a Sergeant Major and Quartermaster Sergeant of Artillery* – one row of nine buttons on the breast, placed at equal distances; stand-up collar, to rise no higher than to permit the chin to turn freely over it, to hook in front at the bottom and slope thence up and backward at an angle of thirty degrees on each side, making the total opening in front an angle of sixty degrees; cuffs pointed according to pattern, and to button with two small buttons at the outer seam; collar and cuffs of scarlet cloth; on both sides of the collar, near the front, the number of the regiment in yellow metal one inch long; on each shoulder a scarlet worsted epaulette according to pattern; narrow lining for skirt of the coat of same material and color as the coat; pockets in the folds of the skirts with one button at the hip to range with the lowest buttons on the breast; no buttons at the ends of the pockets.

13. *For a Sergeant Major and Quartermaster Sergeant of Infantry* – the same as for Artillery, (19,) except that the collar and cuffs will be of light or Saxony blue cloth; and the epaulettes of light or Saxony blue worsted.

14. *For a Sergeant-Major and Quartermaster Sergeant of Riflemen.* – the same as for Artillery, (12,) except that the collar and cuffs will be of medium or emerald green cloth; and the epaulettes of medium or emerald green worsted.

15. *For a Sergeant Major and Quartermaster Sergeant of Dragoons* – the same as for Artillery, (12,) except that the collar and cuffs will be of orange colored cloth; and that, instead of worsted epaulettes, brass shoulder-knots of the pattern now prescribed, will be worn.

16. *For a Sergeant of Artillery, Infantry, Riflemen and Dragoons –* the same as for the Sergeant Major of those corps respectively, (12, 13, 14, 15,) except that the worsted bullion of the epaulettes will be according to pattern.

17. *For a Sergeant of Light Artillery –* the same as for a sergeant of Artillery, (16,) except that brass shoulder knots (as for Dragoons) will be substituted for worsted epaulettes.

13. *For a Sergeant of Engineer soldiers –* the same as for a sergeant of Artillery, (16,) except that the collar and cuffs will be of the same material and color as the coat, but edged all around with a yellow welt inserted in the seam; on both sides of the collar, near the front, a castle of yellow metal one and five-eighths inches, by one and one-fourth inches high; epaulettes of yellow worsted, of the same size and form as for a sergeant of Artillery, (16.)

19. *For an Ordnance Sergeant –* the same as for a sergeant of Engineer soldiers, (18,) except that the collar and cuffs will

be edged with crimson instead of yellow, and that on the collar, on both sides near the front, there will be a shell and flame of yellow metal, two inches long; epaulettes crimson, the same size and pattern as for a Sergeant Major of Artillery, (12.)

20. *For a Corporal of Artillery, Infantry, Riflemen, Dragoons, Light Artillery and Engineer soldiers –* the same as for a sergeant of those corps respectively, (l0, 17, 18,) except that the worsted bullion of the epaulettes will be according to pattern.

21. *For a Private of Artillery, Infantry, Dragoons, Light Artillery and Engineer Soldiers –* the same as for a corporal of those arms respectively (20).

22. *For the enlisted men of Ordnance –* the same as for Ordnance Sergeants, (19,) except the epaulettes, which will be crimson, the same size and pattern as for a private of Artillery, (21.)

23. *For a Musician of Artillery, Infantry, Riflemen, Dragoons, Light Artillery and Engineer Soldiers –* the same ad for a private of those corps respectively, (21,) with the addition of a facing according to pattern, and corresponding in color with the collar and cuffs.

24. *For a Principal or Chief Musician –* the same as for a musician of his regiment, (23,) with epaulettes or shoulder knots, as for a Sergeant Major, (13, 14, 15.)

25. *For a Chief Bugler –* the same as for a Principal or Chief Musician, (24.)

26. On all occasions of duty, except fatigue, and when out of quarters, the coat shall be buttoned and hooked at the collar.

BUTTONS.

97. *For General Officers and Officers of the General Staff –* gilt, convex, with spread eagle and stars and plain border; large size, seven-eighths of an inch in exterior diameter; small size, one-half inch.

98. *For Officers of the Corps of Engineers –* gilt, nine-tenths of an inch in exterior diameter, slightly convex; a raised bright rim, one-thirtieth of an inch wide; device, an eagle holding in his beak a scroll, with the word "Eassayons," a bastion with embrasures in the distance surrounded by water, with a rising sun; the figures to be of dead gold upon a bright field. Small buttons of the same form and device, and fifty-five-hundredths of an inch in exterior diameter

99. *For Officers of the Corps of Topographical Engineers –* gilt, seven-eighths of an inch exterior diameter, convex and solid; device, the shield of the United States, occupying one-half the diameter, Old the letters T.E. [old English character here] in old English characters the other half; small buttons one-half inch diameter, device and form the same.

30. *For Officers of the Ordnance Department –* gilt, convex, plain border, cross cannon and bombshell, with a circular scroll over and across the cannon, containing the words "Ordnance Corps;" large size, seven-eighths of an inch in exterior diameter; small size, one-half inch.

31. *For Officers of the Artillery, Infantry, Riflemen, and Dragoons –* gilt, convex; device a spread eagle with the letter A, for Artillery – I, for Infantry – R, for Riflemen, D for Dragoons, on the shield; large size, seven-eighths of an inch in exterior diameter; small size, one-half inch.

32. *Aides-de-camp* may wear the button of the General Staff, or of their regiment or corps, at their option.

33. *For all enlisted men –* yellow, to correspond with those for the officers of their respective corps, (28, 30, 31;) large size, three-fourths of an inch in exterior diameter; small size, fifty-five-hundredths of an inch.

TROUSERS.

34. The uniform trousers for both officers and enlisted men, will be of cloth throughout the year; made loose, and to spread well over the boot; of white and light blue mixed, commonly called sky blue mixture for regimental officers and enlisted men; and of dark blue cloth for all other officers; reinforced for all enlisted mounted men.

35. *For General Officers –* plain, without stripe, welt or cord, down the outer seam.

36. *For Officers of the General Staff and staff Corps –* with a buff welt, one-eighth of an inch in diameter, let into the outer seam.

37. *For Regimental Officers –* with a welt let into the outer seam, one-eighth of an inch in diameter, of the following colors: for Artillery, scarlet – Infantry, dark blue – Riflemen, medium or emerald green – Dragoons, orange.

38. *For all enlisted men –* with a cord, one-eighth of an inch in diameter, down the outer seam, of the following colors: for Artillery, scarlet – Infantry, dark blue – Riflemen, medium or emerald green – Dragoons, orange – Engineers, yellow – Ordnance, crimson.

CAP.

39. *For all officers and enlisted men –* dark blue cloth, according to pattern; crown of four upright pieces, height in front from five and three-fourths to six and one-fourth inches along the front seam; length behind, from seven and one-fourth to seven and three-fourths inches along the back seam; tip from five and one-half to six inches in diameter, and inclining downward slightly from rear to front when the cap is worn, (the dimensions given to vary with the circumference of the head ;) vizor of strong neat's leather, two and one-fourth inches wide at the middle, black on the upper and green on the under sides, to be put on at right angles to the front of the cap, or in other words, to be horizontal

when the cap is worn; strap of strong black leather fastening under the chin by a yellow metal buckle and leather slide; band two inches wide from the lower edge of the cap, and pointed in front according to pattern, of material, color, and with ornament as follows:

40. *For General Officers* – band of dark blue velvet; with a gold embroidered wreath in front, encircling the letters U.S. [old English characters here] in old English characters, in silver.

41. *For Officers of the Adjutant General's, Inspector General's, Quartermaster's, Subsistence, Medical and Pay Departments, and the Judge Advocate of the Army* – band of the same material and color as the cap, welted at the edges; the same ornament in front as for General officers, (40.)

42. *For Officers of the Corps of Engineers* – the same as for the General Staff, (41,) except the ornament in front, which will be a gold embroidered wreath of laurel and palm encircling a silver turretted castle.

43. *For Officers of the Corps of Topographical Engineers* – the same as for the General Staff; (41,) except the ornament in front, which will be a gold embroidered wreath of oak leaves encircling a gold embroidered shield.

44. *For Officers of the Ordnance Department* – the same as for the General Staff, (41,) except the ornament in front, which will be a gold embroidered shell and flame.

45. *For Officers of Artillery* – the same as for the General Staff, (41,) except the ornament in front, which will be gold embroidered cross cannon, with the number of the regiment in silver, above their intersection.

46. *For Officers of Infantry* – the same as for the General Staff, (41,) except the ornament in front, which will be a gold embroidered bugle, with the number of the regiment in silver, within the bend.

47. *For Officers of Riflemen* – the same as for the General Staff, (41,) except the ornament in front, which will be a trumpet, perpendicular, embroidered in gold, with the number of the regiment in silver, within the bend.

48. *For Officers of Dragoons* – the same as for the General Staff, (41,) except the ornament in front, which will be two sabres crossed, (edges upward,) embroidered in gold, with the number of the regiment in silver, in the upper angle.

49. *For enlisted men of Artillery, Infantry, Riflemen and Dragoons* – bands of scarlet, light or Saxony blue, medium or emerald green, and orange colored cloth, respectively, with the letter of the company in front, of yellow metal one inch long. *For Engineer soldiers* – band of the same material and color as the cap, but edged with yellow, with a turretted castle in yellow metal, in front. *For enlisted men of Ordnance* – band of the same material and color as the cap, but edged with crimson; a shell and flame in yellow metal, in front.

CAP COVER.

50. *For officers and men* – (to be worn in bad weather) black, of suitable water proof material, with a cape extending below the cap ten inches, coming well forward, and tying under the chin; according to pattern.

POMPON.

51. The pompon will be worn by all officers whenever the epaulettes are worn, and by the enlisted men, on all duty under arms; except when the cap cover, (50,) is put on.

52. *For General Officers* – a gold embroidered net acorn, three inches long, with a gold embroidered spread eagle, one and three-fourths inches between the tips of the wings, and so attached to the base of the pompon as to show in front of the cap below its top.

53. *For all other officers, and for all enlisted men* – spherical, two and one-fourth inches in diameter, and as follows:

For Commissioned Officers.

54. Of worsted, permanently attached at the base to a gold netted circular ring two-thirds of an inch in diameter, by one-third deep, with gold embroidered spread eagle, as for General Officers, (52;) and of the following colors:

55. *For the Adjutant Generals Department* – lower two thirds buff, upper third white.

56. *For the Inspector General's Department* – lower two-thirds buff, upper third scarlet.

57. *For the Judge Advocate* – white.

58. *For the Quartermaster's Department* – lower two-thirds buff, upper third light or Saxony blue.

59. *For the Subsistence Department* – lower two thirds buff, upper third royal or ultra marine blue.

60. *For the Medical Department* – lower two-thirds buff, upper third medium or emerald green.

61. *For the Pay Department* – lower two-thirds buff, upper third dark olive green.

62. *For the Corps of Engineers and Topographical Engineers* – lower two-thirds buff, upper third black.

63. *For the Ordnance Department* – lower two-thirds buff, upper third crimson.

64. *For the Artillery* – scarlet.

65. *For the Infantry* – light or Saxony blue.

66. *For the Riflemen* – medium or emerald green.

67. *For the Dragoons* – orange.

68. *For Aides-de-camp* – buff.

69. *For Adjutants of Regiments* – same as for the Adjutant General's Department, (55.)

70. *For Regimental Quartermasters* – same as for the Quartermaster's Department, (58.)

For Enlisted Men.

71. Permanently attached at the base to a yellow metal circular ring, two-thirds of an inch in diameter, by one-third deep, with yellow metal spread eagle, one and three-fourths inches between the tips of the wings, and so attached to the base of the pompon as to show in front of the cap below its top; according to pattern; and of the following colors: for *Ar-*

tillery, scarlet – *Infantry*, light or Saxony blue – *Riflemen*, medium or emerald green – *Dragoons*, orange – *Engineers*, yellow – *Ordnance*, crimson.

CRAVAT OR STOCK.

72. *For all officers* – black; when a cravat is worn, the tie not to be visible at the opening of the collar.

73. *For all enlisted men* – black leather, according to pattern.

Boots.

74. *For all officers* – ankle or Jefferson.

75. *For enlisted men of Riflemen, Dragoons and Light Artillery* – ankle and Jefferson, rights and lefts, according to pattern, and in the proportion as now for the Light Artillery.

76. *For enlisted men of Artillery, Infantry, Engineers and Ordnance* – Jefferson, rights and lefts, according to pattern.

SPURS.

77. *For all mounted officers* – yellow metal, or gilt.

78. *For all enlisted mounted men* – yellow metal, according to pattern.

GLOVES.

79. *For General Officers and officers of the General Staff and Staff Corps* – buff or white.

80. *For Officers of Artillery, Infantry, Dragoons and Riflemen* – white.

SASH.

81. *For General Officers* – buff, silk net, with silk bullion fringe ends; sash to go twice around the waist, and to tie behind the left hip, pendant part not to extend more than eighteen inches below the tie.

82. *For Officers of the Adjutant General's, Inspector General's, Quartermaster's, and Subsistence Departments, the Corps of Engineers, Topographical Engineers, Ordnance, Artillery, Infantry, Riflemen and Dragoon, and the Judge Advocate of the Army* – crimson silk net; for Officers of the Medical Department – medium or emerald green silk net; with silk bullion fringe ends; to go around the waist and tie as for General Officers, (81.)

83. *For all Sergeant Majors, Quartermaster Sergeants, Ordnance Sergeants, First Sergeants, Principal or Chief Musicians and Chief Buglers* – red worsted sash, with worsted bullion fringe ends; to go twice around the waist and to tie behind the left hip, pendant part not to extend more than eighteen inches below the tie.

84. The sash will be worn (over the coat) on all occasions of duty of every description, except stable and fatigue.

85. The sash will be worn by "Officers of the day," across the body, scarf fashion, from the right shoulder to the left side, instead of around the waist, tying behind the left hip as prescribed (81.)

SWORD BELT.

86. *For all officers* – a waist belt not less than one and one-half inches, nor more than two inches wide; to be worn over the sash; the sword to be suspended from it by slings of the same material as the belt, with a hook attached to the belt upon which the sword may be hung, (97.)

87. *For General Officers* – Russian leather, with three stripes of gold embroidery; the slings embroidered on both sides.

88. *For all other officers* – black leather, plain.

89. *For all non-commissioned officers* – black leather, plain.

SWORD BELT-PLATE.

90. *For all officers and enlisted men* – gilt, rectangular, two inches wide, with a raised bright rim; a silver wreath of laurel encircling the "Arms of the United States;" eagle, shield, scroll, edge of cloud and rays bright. The motto, "E PLURIBUS UNUM," in silver letters, upon the scroll; stars also of silver; according to pattern.

SWORD AND SCABBARD.

91. *For General Officers* – straight sword, gilt hilt, silver grip, brass or steel scabbard.

92. *For Officers of the Adjutant General's, Inspector General's, Quartermaster's, and Subsistence Departments, Corps of Engineers, Topographical Engineers, Ordnance, the Judge Advocate of the Army, Aides-de-Camp, Field Officers of Artillery, Infantry, and Foot Riflemen, and for the Light Artillery* – the sword of the pattern adopted by the War Department, April 9, 1850.

93. *For the Medical and Pay Departments* – small sword and scabbard, according to pattern in the Surgeon General's office.

94. *For Cavalry Officers* – sabre and scabbard now in use, according to pattern in the Ordnance Department.

95. *For the Artillery, Infantry and Foot Riflemen* – except the field officer(92) – the sword of the pattern adopted by the War Department April 9, 1851.

96. The sword and sword belt will be worn upon all occasions of duty, without exception.

97. When on foot the sabre will be suspended from the hook attached to the belt, (86.)

98. When not on military duty, officers may wear swords of honor, or the prescribed sword, with a scabbard, gilt, or of leather with gilt mountings.

SWORD-KNOT.

99. *For General Officers* – gold cord with acorn end.

100. *For all other officers* – gold lace strap with gold bullion tassel.

BADGES TO DISTINGUISH RANK.

Epaulettes.

101. *For the Major General Commanding the Army* – gold, with solid crescent; device, three silver embroidered stars, one, one and a half inches in diameter, one, one and one-fourth inches in diameter, and one, one and one-fourth inches in diameter, placed on the strap in a row, longitudinally, and equidistant, the largest star in the centre of the crescent, the smallest at the top; dead and bright gold bullion one-half inch in diameter and three and one-half inches long.

102. *For all other Major Generals* – the same as for the Major General Commanding the Army (101) except that there will be two stars on the strap instead of three, omitting the smallest.

103. *For a Brigadier General* – the same as for a Major General, (101,) except that, instead of two, there shall be one star, (omitting the smallest) placed upon the strap, and not within the crescent.

104. *For a Colonel* – the same as for a Brigadier General, (103,) substituting a silver embroidered spread eagle for the star upon the strap; and within the crescent for the *Medical Department* – a laurel wreath embroidered in gold, and the letters, **M.S.** in old English characters, in silver, within the wreath; *Pay Department* – same as the Medical Department, with the letters, **P.D.** in old English characters; *Corps of Engineers* – a turretted castle of silver; *Corps of Topographical Engineers* – a shield embroidered in gold, and below it the letters **T.E.**, in old English characters in silver; *Ordnance Department* – shell and flame in silver embroidery; *Regimental Officers* – the number of the regiment embroidered in gold, within a circlet of embroidered silver, one and three-fourths inches in diameter, upon cloth of the following colors: *for Artillery* – scarlet; *Infantry* – light or Saxony blue; *Riflemen* – medium or emerald green; *Dragoons* – orange.

105. *For a Lieutenant Colonel* – the same as for a Colonel, (104,) according to corps, but substituting for the eagle, a silver embroidered leaf.

106. *For a Major* – the same as for a Colonel, (104,) according to corps, omitting the eagle.

107. *For a Captain* – the same as for a Colonel, (104,) according to corps, except that the bullion will be only one-fourth of an inch in diameter, and two and one-half inches long; and substituting for the eagle two silver embroidered bars.

108. *For a First Lieutenant* – the same as for a Colonel, (104,) according to corps, except that the bullion will be only one-eighth of an inch in diameter, and two and one-half inches long; and substituting for the eagle one silver embroidered bar.

109. *For a Second Lieutenant* – the same as for a First Lieutenant, (108,) omitting the bar.

110. *For a Brevet Second Lieutenant* – the same as for a Second Lieutenant, (109.)

111. All officers having military rank will wear one epaulette on each shoulder.

112. The epaulette may be dispensed with when not on duty, and on certain duties off parade, to wit: at drills, at inspections of barracks and hospitals, on Courts of Inquiry and Boards, at inspections of articles and necessaries, on working parties and fatigue duties, and upon the march, except when in war there is immediate expectation of meeting the enemy; and also when the overcoat is worn.

Shoulder Straps.

113. *For the Major General Commanding the Army* – dark blue cloth, one and three-eighths inches wide by four inches long; bordered with an embroidery of gold one-fourth of an inch wide; three silver embroidered stars of five rays, one star on the centre of the strap, and one on each side equidistant between the centre and the outer edge of the strap; the centre star to be the largest.

114. *For all other Major Generals* – the same as for the Major General Commanding the Army, (113,) except that there will be two stars, instead of three; the centre of each star to be one inch from the outer edge of the gold embroidery on the ends of the strap; both stars of the same size.

115. *For a Brigadier General* – the same as for a Major General (114,) except that there will be one star instead of two; the centre of the star to be equidistant from the outer edge of the embroidery on the ends of the strap.

116. *For a Colonel* – the same size as for a Major General, (114,) and bordered in like manner with an embroidery of gold; a silver embroidered spread eagle on the centre of the strap, two inches between the tips of the wings, having in the right talon an olive branch, and in the left a bundle of arrows; an escutcheon on the breast as represented in the arms of the United States; cloth of the strap as follows: for the *General Staff and Staff Corps* – dark blue; *Artillery* – scarlet; *Infantry* – light or Saxony blue; *Riflemen* – medium or emerald green; *Dragoons* – orange.

117. *For a Lieutenant Colonel* – the same as for a Colonel, (116,) according to corps, omitting the eagle, and introducing a silver embroidered leaf at each end, each leaf extending seven-eighths of an inch from the end border of the strap.

118. *For a Major* – the same as for a Colonel, (116,) according to corps, omitting the eagle, and introducing a gold embroidered leaf at each end, each leaf extending seven-eighths of an inch from the end border of the strap.

119. *For a Captain* – the same as for a Colonel, (116), according to corps, omitting the eagle, and introducing at each end two gold embroidered bars of the same width as the border, placed parallel to the ends of the strap; the distance between them and from the border equal to the width of the border.

190. *For a First Lieutenant* – the same as for a Colonel, (116,) according to corps, omitting the eagle and introducing at each end one gold embroidered bar of the same width as the border, placed parallel to the ends of the strap, at a distance from the border equal to its width.

121. *For a Second Lieutenant* – the same as for a Colonel, (116,) according to corps, omitting the eagle.

122. *For a Brevet Second Lieutenant* – the same as for a Second Lieutenant, (121.)

123. The shoulder strap will be worn whenever the epaulette is not.

Chevrons.

124. The rank of non-commissioned officers will be marked by chevrons upon both sleeves of the uniform coat and overcoat, above the elbow, of silk or worsted binding one-half an inch wide, same color as the cord on the pantaloons, except for infantry, which will be of light or Saxony blue; points down; as follows:

125. *For a Sergeant Major* – three bars and an arc, in silk.

126. *For a Quartermaster Sergeant* – three bars and a tie, in silk.

127. *For an Ordnance Sergeant* – three bars and a star, in silk.

128. *For a First Sergeant* – three bars and a lozenge, in worsted.

129. *For a Sergeant* – three bars, in worsted.

130. *For a Corporal* – two bars, in worsted.

131. *To indicate service* – all non-commissioned officers, musicians and privates v ho have served faithfully for the term l of five years, will wear, as a mark of distinction, upon both sleeves of the uniform coat, below the elbow, a diagonal half chevron, one-half an inch wide, extending from seam to seam, the front end nearest the cuff, and one-half an inch above the point of the cuff, to be of the same color as the cord on the trousers, except for Infantry, for which light or Saxony blue will be substituted. In like manner an additional half chevron, above and parallel to the first, for every subsequent five years of faithful service; distance between each chevron, one-fourth of an inch. Service in war will be indicated by a light or Saxony blue stripe on each side of the chevron for Artillery, and a red stripe for all other corps, the stripe to he one-eighth of an inch wide.

OVERCOAT.

For Commissioned Officers.

132. A *"cloak coat"* of dark blue cloth, closing by means of four frog buttons of black silk and loops of black silk cord down the breast, and at the throat by a long loop *à echelle*, without tassel or plate, on the left side, and a black silk frog button on the right; cord for the loops fifteen-hundredths of an inch in diameter; back, a single piece, slit up from the bottom, from fifteen to seventeen inches according to the height of the wearer, and closing at will, by buttons, and button holes cut in a concealed flap; collar of the same color and material as the coat, rounded at the edges, and to stand or fall; when standing to be about five inches high; sleeves loose, of a single piece, and round at the bottom, without cuff or slit; lining, woolen; around the front and lower border, the edges of the pockets, the edges of the sleeves, collar and slit in the back, a flat braid of black silk one-half an inch wide; and around each frog button on the breast, a knot two and one-quarter inches in diameter of black silk cord, seven-hundredths of an inch in diameter, arranged according to drawing; cape of the same color and material as the coat, removable at the pleasure of the wearer, and reaching to the cuff of the coat sleeve when the arm is extended; coat to extend down the leg from six to eight inches below the knee, according to height. *To indicate rank*, there will be on both sleeves, near the lower edge, a knot of flat black silk braid not exceeding one-eighth of an inch in width, arranged according to drawing, and composed as follows:

133. *For a General* – of five braids, double knot.

134. *For a Colonel* – of five braids, single knot.

135. *For a Lieutenant Colonel* – of four braids, single knot. 136. *For a Major* – of three braids, single knot.

137. *For a Captain* – of two braids, single knot

138. *For a First Lieutenant* – of one braid, single knot.

139. *For a Second Lieutenant, and Brevet 2d Lieutenant* – a plain sleeve, without knot or ornament.

For Enlisted Men.

140. *Of Cavalry and the Light Artillery* – of blue grey mixture; stand-up collar; double breasted; cape to reach down to the cuff of the coat when the arm is extended, and to button all the way up; buttons of the regiment or corps.

141. *All offer enlisted men* – of blue grey mixture; stand-up collar; single-breasted; cape to reach down to the elbows, when the arm is extended, and to button all the way up; buttons of the regiment or corps.

OTHER ARTICLES OF CLOTHING AND EQUIPMENT.

142. *Flannel shirt, drawers, stockings and stable frock* – the same as now furnished.

143. *Blanket* – woolen, grey, with letters U. S. in black, four inches long, in the centre; to be seven feet long, and five and a half feet wide, and to weigh five pounds.

144. *Canvass overalls for Engineer soldiers* – of white cotton; one garment to cover the whole of the body below the waist, the breast, the shoulders and the arms; sleeves loose, to allow a free play of the arms, with narrow wristband buttoning with one button; overalls to fasten at the neck behind with two buttons, and at the waist behind with buckle and tongue.

145. *Belts of all enlisted men* – black leather.

146. *Cartridge box* – according to pattern in the Ordnance Department.

147. *Drum sling* – white webbing; to be provided with a brass drum-stick carriage, according to pattern.

148. *Knapsack* – according to pattern in the Quartermaster's Department. The great coat, when carried, to be neatly folded, not rolled, and covered by the outer flap of the knapsack.

149. *Haversack* – of gutta percha, tin, or other material, and of pattern to be prepared by the Quartermaster's Department, after making the requisite experiments.

150. *Canteen* – of pattern, to be prepared by the Quartermaster's Department.

151. *Tent* – French bell-tent, according to pattern in the Quartermasters Department – for all enlisted men.

(Paragraphs 152 through 191 having to do with horse equipage eliminated here)

MILITARY ACADEMY.

192. The uniform of the Professors, Teachers, and their assistants not in the line of the army, including the Sword and Riding Masters, shall be a citizen's blue cloth dress-coat, with buttons of the Corps of Engineers, (28;) round black hat; pantaloons and vest plain, white, or dark blue; cravat or stock, black. The uniform of the Chaplain shall be the dress usually worn by the clergy.

For Cadets.

193. *Coat* – a grey cloth coatee, single breasted; three rows of eight gilt bullet-buttons in front; and button holes of black silk cord in the herring bone form, with a festoon turned at

the back end; stand up collar, trimmed with black silk lace, to fit the neck and hook in front; cuffs four inches wide; buttons on the hip to range with the lower buttons on the breast; on the collar one blind button hole of cord, formed like that of the breast,' four inches long, with a button on each side; cord holes in the like form, to proceed from three buttons, placed lengthwise on the skirts, with three buttons down the plaits; cuffs to be indented, with three buttons and cord holes likewise on each sleeve, corresponding with the indentation of the cuff, in the centre of which is to be inserted the lower button.

194. *Riding jacket* – grey cloth, single breasted; stand-up collar, trimmed with black silk lace; to fit the neck, and hook in front; one gilt button, (195,) one-half an inch in diameter on each side of the collar, and eight gilt buttons, (195,) seven-eighths of an inch in diameter down the breast; small pocket covered by a flap, on the right side, for carrying percussion caps.

195. *Overcoat* – grey kersey, double breasted; to reach two inches below the knee; stand and fall collar, rising to the tip of the ear, and hooked in front; buttons, gilt, seven-eighths of an inch in diameter; device, a spread eagle, with shield, and having the word "CADET" near the margin at top, and the letters "U.S.M.A." at bottom; six buttons down the front on each side; two buttons at the hip, and one at the bottom of each plait behind; cape of the same material as the coat, sixteen and one-half inches in length, to button in front; coat, cape, and skirts lined with woolen, sleeves with twilled muslin.

196. *Fatigue jacket* – brown linen drilling; single breasted, with a stand and fall collar; one gilt button half an inch in diameter (195) on each side of the collar, and ten buttons of the same-size and device down the breast.

197. *Vest* – for *winter*, grey cloth; single breasted; gilt buttons; (195;) trimmed with black silk lace. For *summer*, white. The vest is not an indispensable part of the uniform; it may be worn or not at the option of the cadet, but when worn, must be of the prescribed uniform; when it is not worn, the coat must be buttoned whenever out of quarters or tent.

198. *Trousers* – for *winter*, grey cloth, with a black stripe, one inch wide, down the outer seam. For *summer*, white drilling. For riding, grey kersey; reinforced on the inside; black stripe one inch wide down the outer seam; faced at bottom with black leather for the space of eight inches; outer seam slashed at bottom the same length.

199. *Cap* – black; round crown; seven inches high, or more, in proportion to the size of the cadet; with a circular vizor in front; black

worsted pompon, eight inches long, set in a yellow metal socket; cap plate worn on front of cap. The whole according to pattern deposited with the Quartermaster at West Point.

200. *Forage Cap* – according to pattern deposited with the Quartermaster at West Point.

For the Band.

Dress.

201. *Frock coat* – dark blue cloth; single breasted, standing collar, hooked in front; collar part red, the red to extend four inches on each side from the front; ten engineer soldier buttons down the front; cuffs red, two inches and one-half deep, pointed on the outside, making whole depth five inches; skirt reaching to within two inches of knee; hip and flap buttons.

203. *Trousers* – light blue mixed; two red stripes down the outside of each leg, each three-fourths of an inch wide, and one-eighth f an inch apart.

204. *Epaulettes* – red worsted, as at present worn.

205. *Pouch and pouch belt* – as at present worn.

206. *Sword and belt* – as present worn.

207. *Sword belt plate* – as described, (90.)

208. *Gloves* – white.

Undress.

209. *Jacket* – dark blue cloth; single breasted, stand-up collar; trimmed along the top and front edges of the collar, with red worsted binding; two small buttons, with loops of same binding, on each side of collar; blue cloth shoulder strap, bound with red worsted, buttoned to the collar on each side, and reaching to the shoulder seam; one row of nine small buttons on front.

210. *Trousers* – same as dress, (202.)

211. *Forage cap* – as present worn.

Military Storekeepers.

212. A citizen's frock coat of blue cloth, with buttons of the department to which they are attached; round black hat; pantaloons and vest, white or dark blue; cravat or stock, black.

Miscellaneous.

213. General officers and Colones having the brevet rank of General Officers may, on occasions of ceremony, and when not serving with troops, were the "dress" and "undress" prescribed by existing regulations.

214. Officers below the grade of Colonel having brevet rank may wear the epaulettes and shoulder-straps distinctive of their army rank. In all other respects, their uniform and dress will be that of their respective regiments, corps, or departments, and according to their commissions in the same. Officers above the grade of Lieutenant Colonel by

Left to right 1851-pattern uniforms for majors of the Adjutant General's Department; captains Corps of Engineers; engineer privates and engineer musicians.

ordinary commission, having brevet rank, may wear the uniform of their respective regiments or corps, or that of General Officers, according to their brevet rank.

215. Officers are permitted to wear a plain dark blue body coat, with the button depicting their respective corps, regiments, or departments, without any other rank or ornament upon it. Such a coat, however, is not to be considered as dress for any military purpose.

216. In the like manner as at 215) officers are permitted to wear a buff, white or blue vest, with the small button of their respective corps, regiment or department.

217. Officers serving with mounted troops are allowed to wear for stable duty, a plain dark blue cloth jacket, with one, or two rows of buttons down the front, according to rank(1); stand-up collar, sloped in front as that of the uniform coat; shoulder straps according to rank, but no other ornament.

218. The hair to be short, or what is generally termed *cropped; the whiskers not to extend below the lower tip of the ear., and a line thence with the curve of the mouth; moustaches will not be worn except by cavalry regiments, by officers or men on any pretense whatever.*

A band – will wear the uniform of the regiment, or corps to which it belongs. The commanding officer may, at the expense of the corps, sanctioned by the Council of Administration, make such additions and ornaments as he may judge proper.

Left to right 1851-pattern uniforms for colonels, sergeants major, and musicians of dragoons.

Left to right 1851-pattern uniforms for light artillery captains and first sergeants and heavy artillery first sergeants and musicians. The chief difference in terms of uniform between light and heavy artillery enlisted personnel were the brass shoulder scales for mounted troops and reinforced trousers versus scarlet worsted epaulets for foot artillery whose trousers also were without reinforcing.

Left to right 1851-pattern uniforms for captains, first sergeants, and musicians of infantry.

Left to right 1851-pattern uniforms for captains, first sergeants, and musicians of foot riflemen (actually for the regiment of Mounted Rifles), and for a colonel of the Ordnance Department and ordnance sergeants. Ordnance and engineer enlisted personnel had welts of crimson and yellow respective on their caps, collars, and cuffs, as opposed to the fully faced versions in branch colors for other enlisted men.

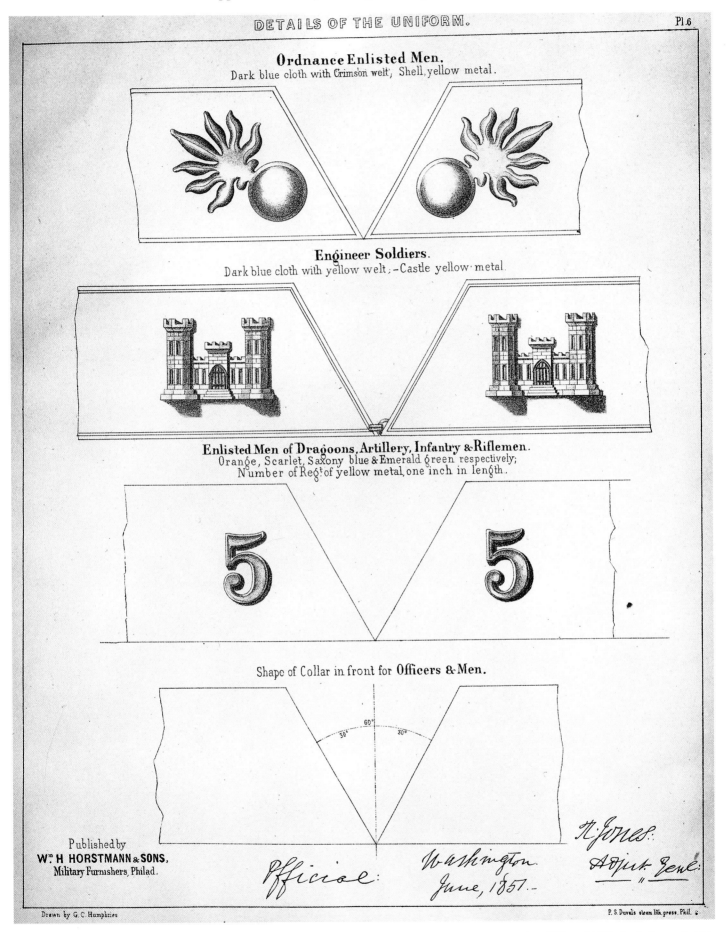

DETAILS OF THE UNIFORM.　Pl.6

Ordnance Enlisted Men.
Dark blue cloth with Crimson welt; Shell, yellow metal.

Engineer Soldiers.
Dark blue cloth with yellow welt; - Castle yellow metal.

Enlisted Men of Dragoons, Artillery, Infantry & Riflemen.
Orange, Scarlet, Saxony blue & Emerald green respectively;
Number of Reg.t of yellow metal, one inch in length.

Shape of Collar in front for **Officers & Men.**

60°　30°　30°

Published by
W.m H HORSTMANN & SONS,
Military Furnishers, Philad.

Official:

Washington.
June, 1851. -

N. Jones.
Adjut. Gen.l
"

Drawn by G. C. Humphries
P. S. Duvals steam lith. press, Phil.

The collars for 1851-pattern coats, both officers and enlisted, were to be cut at a thirty-degree angle unlike the uniforms of the 1830s and 1840s that had uncomfortable collars that were to close completely. Engineer and ordnance enlisted personnel had welts in yellow or crimson respectively on their collars while artillery, dragoon, infantry, and riflemen had collars and cuffs covered in branch colors of facings material. Stamped brass insignia (castles for engineers, shell and flame for ordnance, and regimental numerals for all others also were prescribed for enlisted men. The collars for all officers were plain, without welts, facing, or insignia, except for generals who were to have black velvet collars and cuffs.

Army Blue

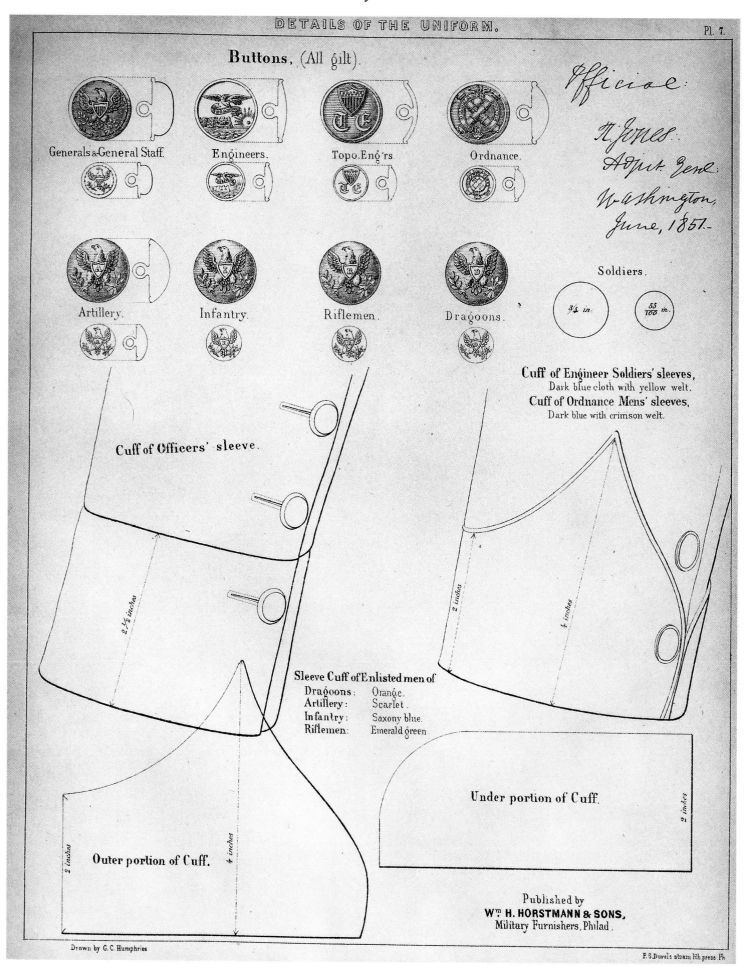

Pl. 7.

Buttons, (All gilt).

Generals & General Staff.

Engineers.

Topo. Eng'rs.

Ordnance.

Officiae:
N. Jones.
Adjut. Genl.
Washington,
June, 1851.

Artillery.

Infantry.

Riflemen.

Dragoons.

Soldiers.

¾ in.

$\frac{55}{100}$ in.

Cuff of Officers' sleeve.

Cuff of Engineer Soldiers' sleeves,
Dark blue cloth with yellow welt.
Cuff of Ordnance Mens' sleeves,
Dark blue with crimson welt.

2½ inches

2 inches

4 inches

Sleeve Cuff of Enlisted men of
Dragoons: Orange.
Artillery: Scarlet.
Infantry: Saxony blue.
Riflemen: Emerald green.

Under portion of Cuff.

2 inches

2 inches

4 inches

Outer portion of Cuff.

Drawn by G.C. Humphries

Published by
Wm H. HORSTMANN & SONS,
Military Furnishers, Philad.

P.S.Duvals steam lith press Ph

Officers and enlisted men wore the same buttons according to the corps or branch as one method of unit identity found in the 1851 uniform regulations. Cuffs of the frock coats differed, however, in that enlisted men had welts or facing cloth in branch colors and wore two rather than the three buttons that were sewn at the cuffs for officers.

EPAULETTES.

General in Chief, Major General & Brigadier General. Gold with Silver embroidered Stars: Bullion 3½ inches long, & ½ inch. in diam.   Pl. 8.

Major Generals.

Brigadier Generals.

General in Chief.

Published by
Wᵐ. H. HORSTMANN & SONS,
Military Furnishers, Philad.

Drawn by G.C. Humphries.

P.S.Duval's steam lith press Ph.

Epaulets for general according to the 1851-pattern essentially were the same as prescribed in previous regulations being gold with silver embroidered stars.

ORNAMENTS ON STRAPS OF EPAULETTES (OFFICERS) DESIGNATING RANK.

Pl. 9

Major.
Gold lace strap, without ornament.

Lieut. Colonel.
Gold lace strap, with silver embroidered leaf.

Colonel.
Gold lace strap, with silver embroidered eagle.

2d Lieut & Bvt. 2d Lieut.
Gold lace strap, without ornament.

1st Lieutenant.
Gold lace strap, with silver embroidered bar.

Captain.
Gold lace strap, with silver embroidered bars.

Note:
The bullion on Epaulettes of Colonel, Lieut.
Colonel & Major, same length & size as for
General Officers.

The bullion of
Captain's epaulettes,
1st Lieut, 2d Lieut,
& Bvt. 2d Lieut.

2½ in. long, ½ in. diam.

2½ in. long, ⅛ in. diam.

Washington
June, 1857.—

Published by
Wm H. HORSTMANN & SONS.
Military Furnishers.—Philada

P.S.Duval's steam lith.press Phil

Drawn

All epaulets of the 1851-pattern were gold. The same devices as previously adopted for shoulder straps now were to indicate rank on the epaulets as well.

ORNAMENTS WITHIN CRESCENTS OF EPAULETTES (OFFICERS), DESIGNATING REGIMENTS OR CORPS. Pl 10.

Topo.Engineers.
Gold embroidered Shield, metallic Silver letters.

Medical Staff.
Gold embroidered wreath with Silver embroidered letters.

Engineers.
Silver metal Castle.

Ordnance.
Silver embroidered Shell & Flame.

Published by
Wm H. HORSTMANN & SONS,
Military Furnishers. Philad.^a

Drawn by G.C.Humphreys.

1851-pattern insignia for epaulets of Corps of Engineers, Topographical Engineers, Ordnance Department, and Medical Staff officers.

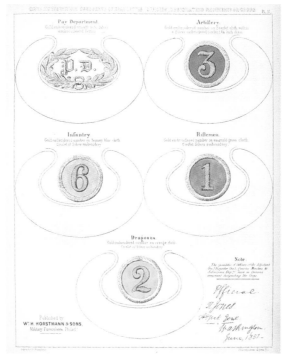

1851-pattern insignia for epaulets of the Pay Department along with line units.

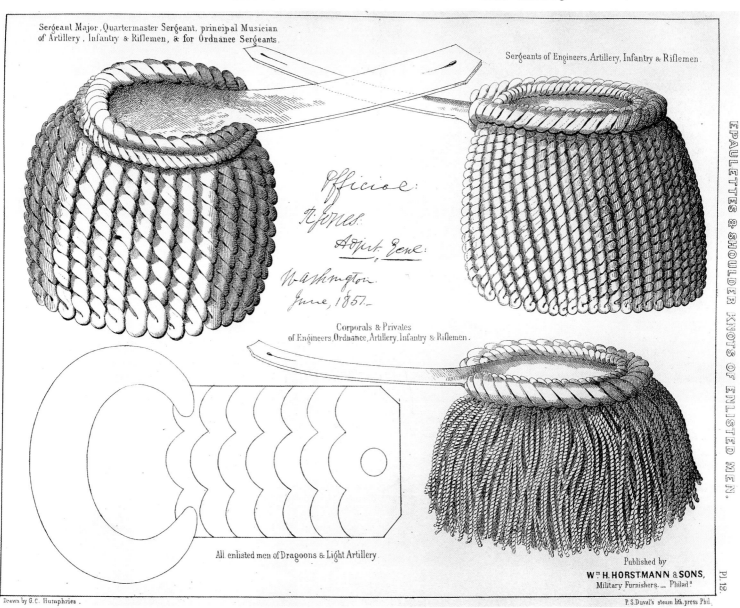

EPAULETTES & SHOULDER KNOTS OF ENLISTED MEN.

Worsted epaulets of the 1851-pattern for enlisted men followed a similar scheme in terms of fringe size to differentiate gradations in the rank structure. So, too, did the three types of shoulder scales issued to mounted troops which distinguished privates and corporals, sergeants, and the regimental non-commissioned staff.

CAP FOR OFFICERS & ENLISTED MEN.

Pl. 13.

Dimensions:

Height in front . . . . 5¾ to 6¼ inches.
Height behind . . . . 7¼ to 7¾ in.
Width of Visor . . . . 2¼ inches.
Diameter of tip . . . . 5½ to 6 in.
Width of band . . . . 2 inches.
Width of band in front . . . 3⅛ inches.

Width of chin strap . . . . ¾ inch.

Cap-Cover, black, extending down upon
the shoulders 10 inches below the lower edge of cap.

Official.
N. Jones.
Adjut. Gene.
Washington,
June, 1851.

Published by
Wᵐ H. HORSTMANN & SONS,
Military Furnishers, Philad.

Drawn by G. C. Humphries.

P. S. Duval's steam lith. press Phil.

1851-pattern caps were provided with covers for foul weather.

ORNAMENTS FOR CAP BANDS OF OFFICERS AND ENLISTED MEN.

PL. 14.

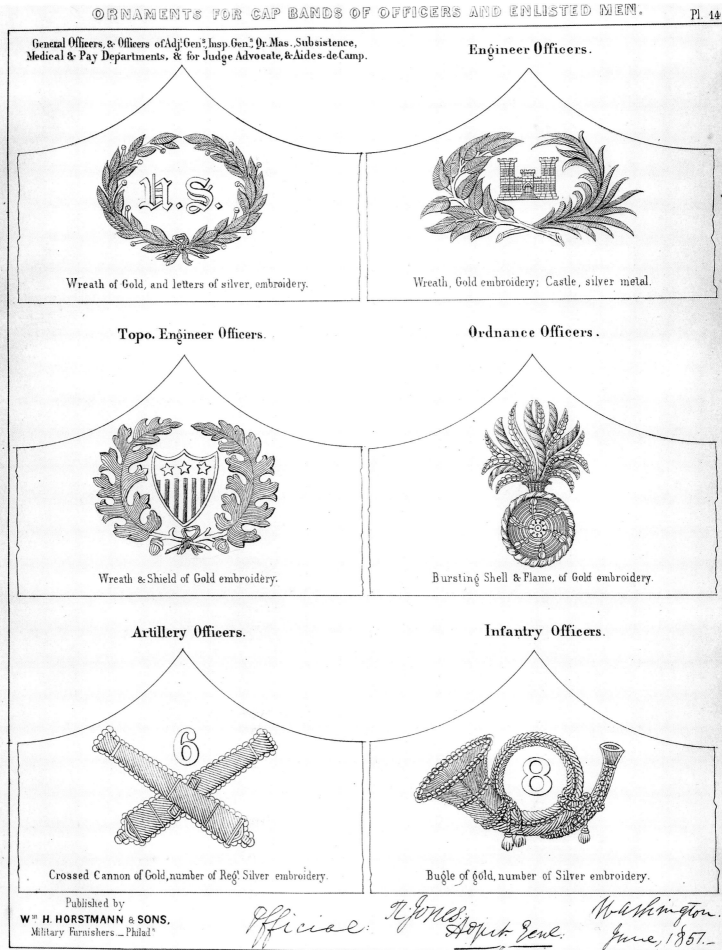

General Officers, & Officers of Adj! Gen.s, Insp. Gen.s, Qr. Mas., Subsistence, Medical & Pay Departments, & for Judge Advocate, & Aides-de-Camp.

Wreath of Gold, and letters of silver, embroidery.

Engineer Officers.

Wreath, Gold embroidery; Castle, silver metal.

Topo. Engineer Officers.

Wreath & Shield of Gold embroidery.

Ordnance Officers.

Bursting Shell & Flame, of Gold embroidery.

Artillery Officers.

Crossed Cannon of Gold, number of Reg! Silver embroidery.

Infantry Officers.

Bugle of gold, number of Silver embroidery.

Published by
W.ᵐ H. HORSTMANN & SONS,
Military Furnishers.— Philad.ᵃ

Official: N. Jones, Adjut. Genl. Washington June, 1851.

Drawn by G.C.Humphries.

P.S.Duval's steam lith.press.Phil

Embroidered insignia for officers' 1851-pattern caps.

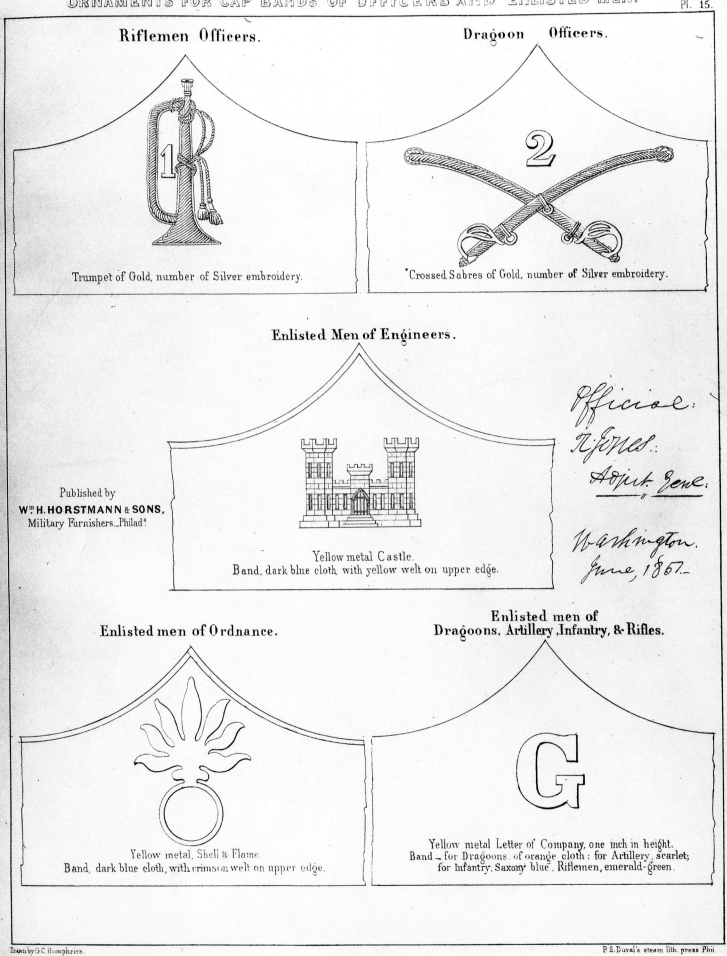

ORNAMENTS FOR CAP BANDS OF OFFICERS AND ENLISTED MEN.

PL. 15.

Riflemen Officers.

Dragoon Officers.

Trumpet of Gold, number of Silver embroidery.

Crossed Sabres of Gold, number of Silver embroidery.

Enlisted Men of Engineers.

Published by
W.ᵐ H. HORSTMANN & SONS,
Military Furnishers. Philad.ᵃ

Yellow metal Castle.
Band, dark blue cloth, with yellow welt on upper edge.

Official:
T. Jones.
Adjut. Genl.

Washington.
June, 1851.

Enlisted men of Ordnance.

Enlisted men of
Dragoons, Artillery, Infantry, & Rifles.

Yellow metal, Shell & Flame.
Band, dark blue cloth, with crimson welt on upper edge.

Yellow metal Letter of Company, one inch in height.
Band – for Dragoons, of orange cloth ; for Artillery, scarlet;
for Infantry, Saxony blue ; Riflemen, emerald-green.

Drawn by G.C. Humphries.

P.S. Duval's steam lith. press Phil.

Mounted rifle and dragoon officers' cap insignia and enlisted cap insignia. Note the welt for engineer and ordnance enlisted men versus the full band of facing cloth for line troops.

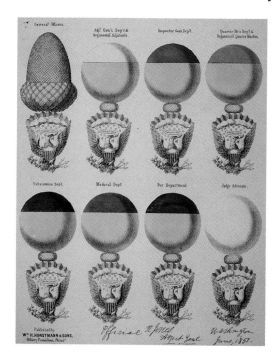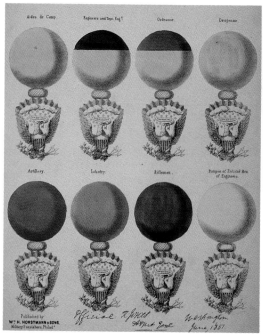

1851-pattern pompons for officers and enlisted men.

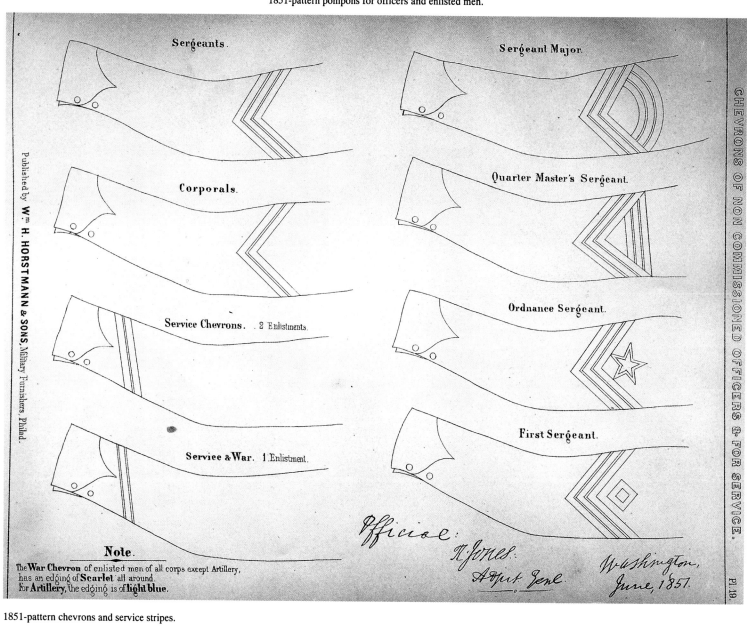

1851-pattern chevrons and service stripes.

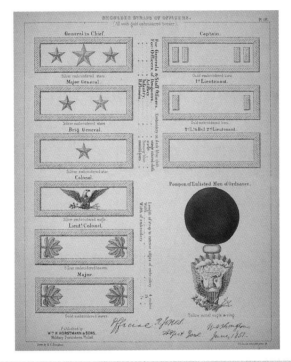

1851-pattern officers' shoulder straps and the pompon for ordnance enlisted men.

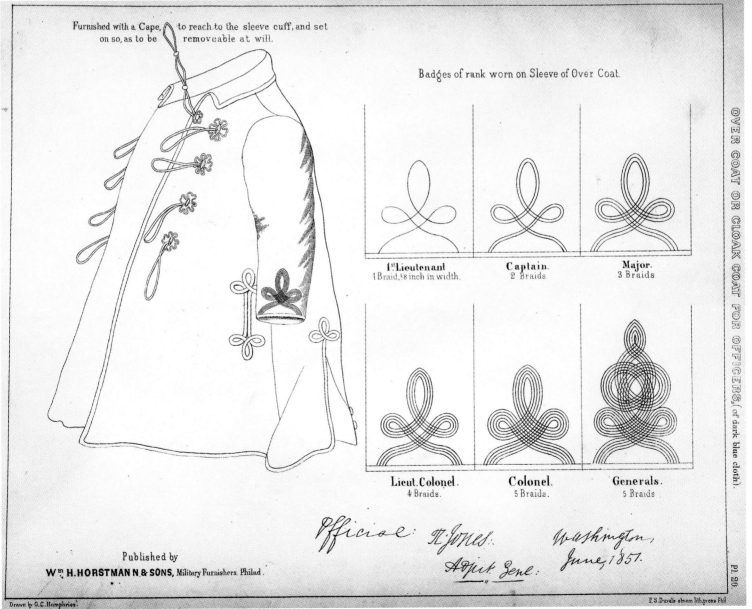

1851-pattern officer's overcoat or cloak coat with sleeve braid to indicate rank.

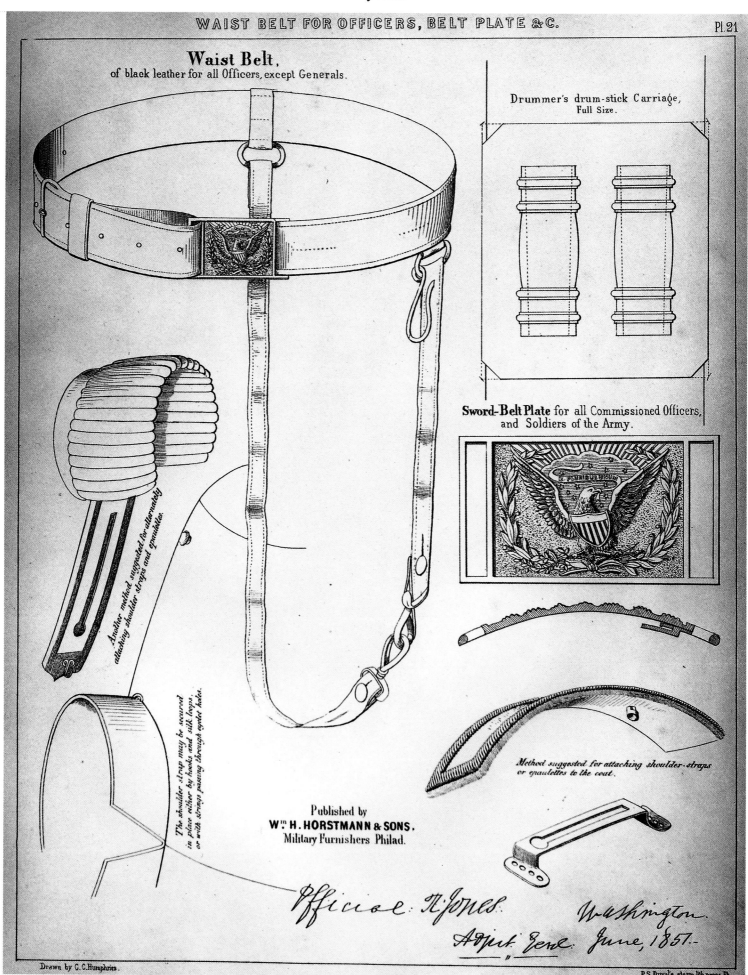

Waist Belt,
of black leather for all Officers, except Generals.

Drummer's drum-stick Carriage, Full Size.

Sword-Belt Plate for all Commissioned Officers, and Soldiers of the Army.

Another method suggested for alternately attaching shoulder straps and epaulets.

The shoulder strap may be secured in place either by hooks and silk loops, or with straps passing through eyelet holes.

Method suggested for attaching shoulder-straps or epaulettes to the coat.

Published by
W. H. HORSTMANN & SONS.
Military Furnishers Philad.

Officiae N. Jones
Adjut. Genl.

Washington.
June, 1851.

Drawn by C. C. Humphries.

P. S. Duval's steam lith press Ph.

1851-pattern belts, belt plate, and varied means of attaching officers' epaulets and shoulder straps to the coat.

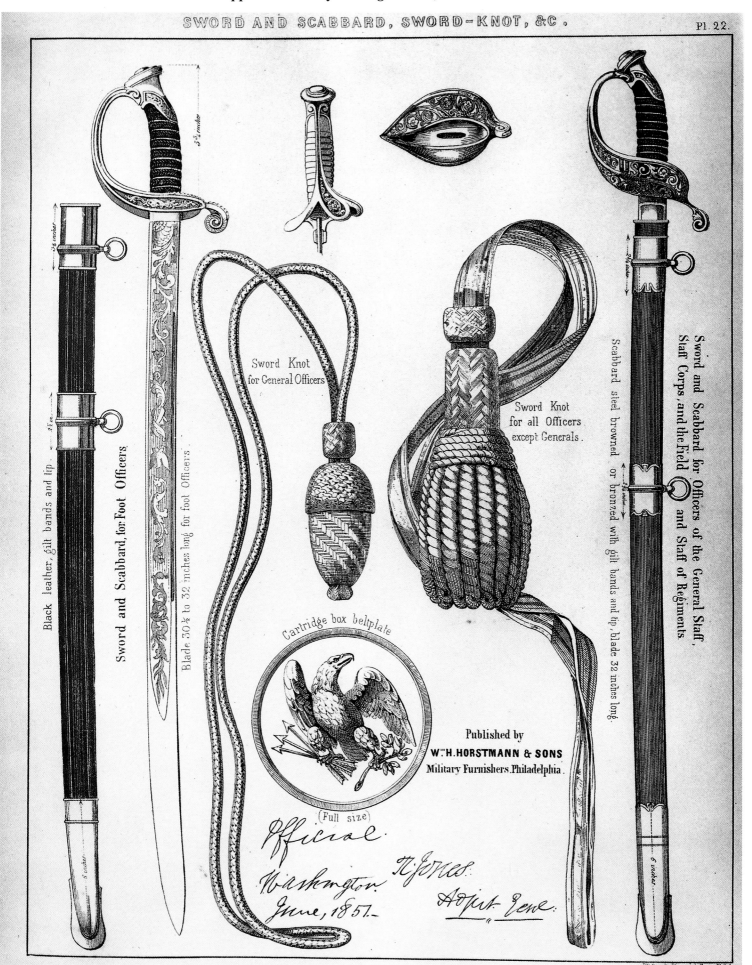

M1850 officer's swords with gold sword knots and enlisted cartridge cross strap plate worn on the chest.

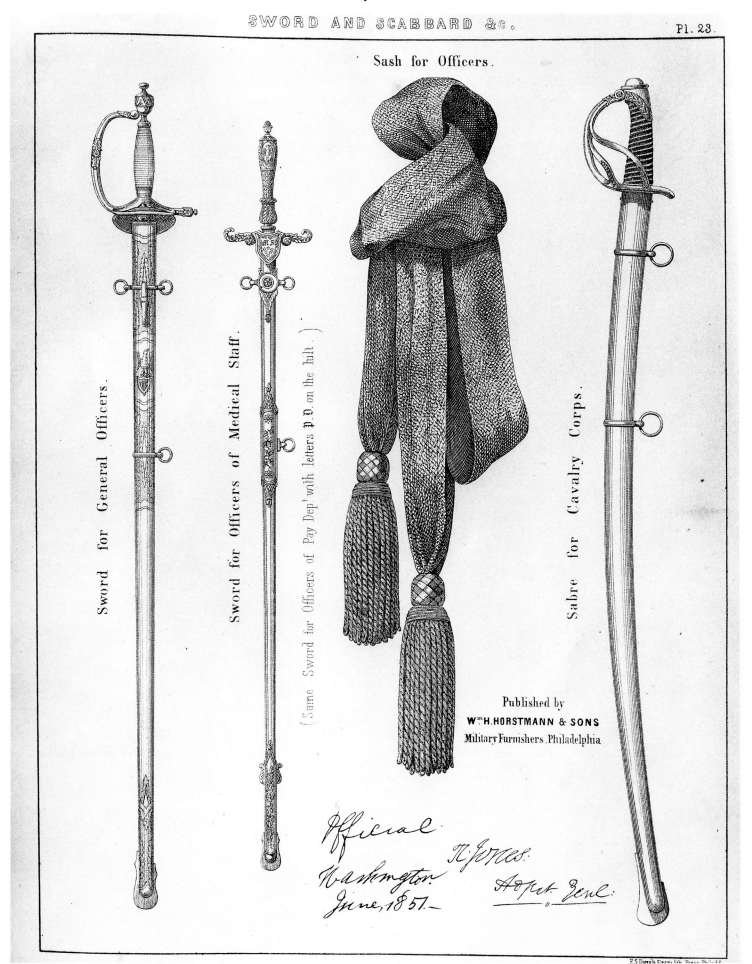

Sash for Officers.

Sword for General Officers.

Sword for Officers of Medical Staff.

(Same Sword for Officers of Pay Dep.t with letters P.D. on the hilt.)

Sabre for Cavalry Corps.

Published by
Wm H. HORSTMANN & SONS
Military Furnishers, Philadelphia

Official
Washington.
June, 1851.—

N. Jones.
Adjt. Genl:

Silk sashes for officers of the 1851-pattern were yellow or buff for generals, green for surgeons, and crimson for all others. Also illustrated is the M1840 heavy cavalry or dragoon saber, M1840 medical and pay officer's sword, and a general officer's sword, one of many varieties available for purchase from military suppliers.

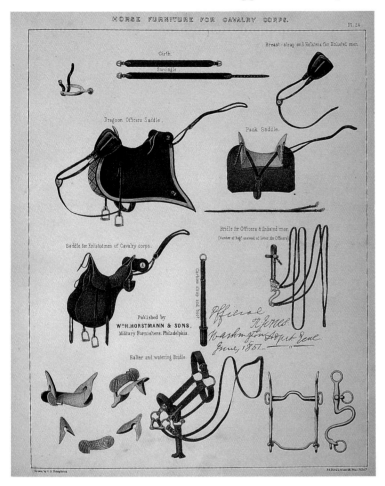

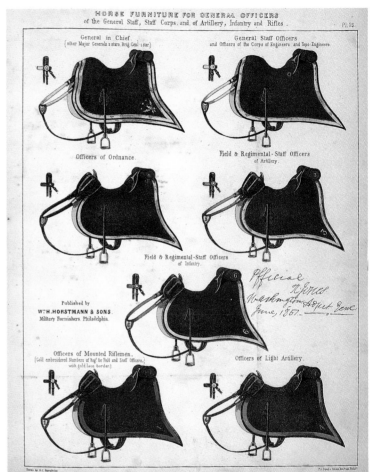

Horse equipage for mounted troops as published in the 1851 uniform regulations.

Horse equipage for generals and other officers as published in the 1851 uniform regulations.

APPENDIX C:
Uniform Regulations, 1861

UNIFORM AND DRESS OF THE ARMY OF THE UNITED STATES, 1861

GENERAL ORDERS, No. 6 WAR DEPARTMENT,
ADJUTANT GENERALS OFFICE
Washington, March 13, 1861.

The UNIFORM, DRESS AND HORSE EQUIPMENTS OF THE ARMY having been changed in many respects since the "General Regulations" of 1857, the following description of them is published for the information of all concerned:

COAT.

For Commissioned Officers.

l. All officers shall wear a frock coat of dark blue cloth, the skirt to extend from two-thirds to three-fourths of the distance from the top of the hip to the bend of the knee; single-breasted for Captains and Lieutenants; double-breasted for all other grades.

2. *For a Major General* – two rows of buttons on the breast, nine in each row, placed by threes; the distance between each row, five and one-half inches at top, and three and one-half inches at bottom; standup collar, to rise no higher than to permit the chin to turn freely over it, to hook in front at the bottom, and slope thence up and backward at an angle of thirty degrees on each side; cuffs two and one half inches deep to go around the sleeves parallel with the lower edge, and to button with three small buttons at the under seam; pockets in the folds of the skirts, with one button at the hip, and one at the end of each pocket, making four buttons on the back and skirt of the coat, the hip button to range with the lowest buttons on the breast; collar and cuffs to be of dark blue velvet; lining of the coat black.

3. *For a Brigadier General* – the same as for a Major General, except that there will be only eight buttons in each row on the breast, placed In pairs.

4. *For a Colonel* – the same as for n Major General, except that there will be only seven buttons in each row on the breast, placed at equal distances; collar and cuffs of the same color and material as the coat.

5. *For a Lieutenant Colonel* – the same as for a Colonel.

6. *For a Major* – the same as for a Colonel.

7. *For a Captain* – the same as for a Colonel, except that there will be only one row of nine buttons on the breast, placed at equal distances.

8. *For a First Lieutenant* – the same as for a Captain.

9. *For a Second Lieutenant* – the same as for a Captain.

10. *For a Brevet Second Lieutenant* – the same as for a Captain.

11. A round jacket, according to pattern, of dark blue cloth, trimmed with scarlet, with the Russian shoulder-knot, the prescribed insignia of rank to be work in silver in the centre of the knot, may be worn on undress duty by officers of the light artillery.

12. The uniform coat for all enlisted *foot* men, shall be a single-breasted frock coat of dark blue cloth, made without plaits, with skirt extending one-half the distance from the top of the hip to the bend of the knee; one row of nine buttons on the breast placed at equal distances; stand-up collar to rise no higher than to permit the chin to turn freely over it, to hook in front at the bottom and then to slope up and backward at an angle of thirty degrees on each side; cuffs pointed according to pattern, and to button with two small buttons at the under seam; collar and cuffs edged with a cord or welt of cloth as follows, to wit: Scarlet *for Artillery*; sky-blue *for Infantry*; yellow *for Engineers*; crimson *for Ordnance* and *Hospital stewards*. On each shoulder a metallic scale according to pattern; narrow lining for skirt of the coat of the same color and material as the coat; pockets in the folds of the skirt with one button at each hip to range with the lowest buttons on the breast; no buttons at the end of pockets.

13. *All Enlisted Men of Dragoons, Cavalry, Mounted Rifles, and Light Artillery*, shall wear a uniform jacket of dark blue cloth, with one row of twelve small buttons on the breast placed equal distances; stand-up collar to rise no higher that to permit the chin to turn freely over it, to hook in front at the bottom, and to slope the same as the coat collar; on the collar, on each side, two blind buttons holes of lace, three-eighths of

an inch wide, and a strip of the same extending down the front and around the whole lower edge of the jacket; the back seam laced with same, and on the cuff a point of the same shape as that on the coat, but formed of the lace; jacket to extend to the waist, and to be lined with white flannel; two small buttons at the under seam of the cuff, as on the coat cuff; one hook and eye at the bottom of the collar; color of lace, (worsted,) orange for *Dragoons*, yellow for *Cavalry*, green for *Riflemen*, and scarlet for *Light Artillery*.

14. *For all Musicians* – the same as for other enlisted men of their respective corps, with the addition of a facing of lace three-eighths of an inch wide on the front of the coat or jackets made in the following manner: bars of three-eighths of an inch worsted lace placed on a line with each button six and one-half inches wide at the bottom, and thence gradually expanding upwards to the last button, counting from the waist up, and contracting from thence to the bottom of the collar, where it will be six and one-half inches wide, with a strip of the same lace following the bars at their outer extremity – the whole presenting something of what is called the herring-bone form; the color of the lace facing to correspond with the color of the trimming of the corps.

15. *For Fatigue Purposes* – a sack coat of dark blue flannel extending half way down the thigh, and made loose, without sleeve or body lining, falling collar, inside pocket on the left side, four coat buttons down the front.

16. *For Recruits* – the sack coat will be made with sleeve and body lining, the latter of flannel.

17. On all occasions of duty, except fatigue, and when out of quarters, the coat or jacket shall be buttoned and hooked at the collar.

BUTTONS.

18. *For General Officers and Officers of the General Staff* – gilt, convex, with spread eagle and stars, and plain border; large size, seven-eighths of an inch in exterior diameter; small size one-half inch.

19. *For Officers of the Corps of Engineers* – gilt, nine-tenths of an inch in exterior diameter, slightly convex; a raised bright rim, one-thirtieth of an inch wide; device, an eagle holding in his beak a scroll, with the word "Essayons," a bastion with embrasures in the distance surrounded by water, with a rising sun – the figures to be of dead gold upon a bright field. Small buttons of the same form and device, and fifty-five hundredths of an inch in exterior diameter.

20. *For Officers of the Corps of Topographical Engineers* – gilt, seven-eighths of an inch exterior diameter, convex and solid; device, the shield of the United States, occupying one-half the diameter, and the letters **T.E.** in old English characters the other half; small buttons, one-half inch diameter, device and form the same.

21. *For Officers of the Ordnance Department* – gilt, convex, plain border, cross cannon and bombshell, with a circular scroll over and across the cannon, containing the words "Ordnance Corps;" large size, seven-eighths of an inch in exterior diameter; small size, one-half inch.

22. *For Officers of Artillery, Infantry, Riflemen, Cavalry, and Dragoons* – gilt, convex; device, a spread eagle with the letter A, for Artillery – I, for Infantry – R, for Riflemen – C, for Cavalry – D, for Dragoons, on the shield; large size, seven-eighths of an inch in exterior diameter; small size, one-half inch.

23. *Aides-de-camp* may wear the button of the General Staff, or of their regiment or corps, at their option.

24. *For all Enlisted Men* – yellow, the same as is used by the Artillery, &c., omitting the letter in the shield.

1851-through 1871 mounted enlisted overcoat. The sabers are attached to the forage cap incorrectly in that they are upside down. USAQM

TROUSERS.

25. *For General Officers and Officers of the Ordnance Department* – of dark blue cloth, plain, without stripe, welt, or cord down the outer seam.

26. *For Officers of the General Staff and Staff Corps*, except the Ordnance – dark blue cloth, with a gold cord, one-eighth of an inch diameter, along the outer seam.

27. *For all Regimental Officers* – dark blue cloth, with a welt let into the outer seam, one-eighth of an inch in diameter, of colors corresponding to the facings of the respective regiments, viz: *Dragoons*, orange; *Cavalry*, yellow; *Riflemen*, emerald green; *Artillery*, scarlet; *Infantry*, sky-blue.

28. *For Enlisted Men*, except companies of Light Artillery – dark blue cloth; sergeants with a stripe one and one-half inch wide; corporals with a stripe one-half inch wide, of worsted lace, down and over the outer seam, of the color of the facings of the respective corps.

29. *Ordnance Sergeants and Hospital Stewards* – stripe of crimson lace one and one-half inch wide.

30. *Privates* – plain, without stripe or welt.

31. *For Companies of artillery equipped as Light Artillery* – sky-blue cloth.

In an effort to take advantage of a large stock of surplus single-breasted foot over-coats on hand from the Civil War the quartermaster general ordered an additional longer cape affixed to these sky-blue wool garments, thus adding a degree of warmth as well as creating a look similar to some civilian overcoats of the Victorian era. This expedient proved short-lived after its original 1871 conception, although a general order in 1872 required its continued use until stocks were exhausted. The soldier shown here is an infantryman or heavy artillerymen because of the bayonet and M1839 foot soldier's belt. USAQM

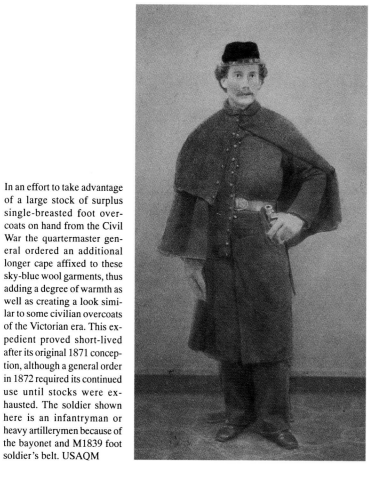

1861 through 1872 regulation light artillery private's uniform. Note the service stripes on the jacket. The saber is not correct. It is the proper edged weapon for cavalry troops, not artillery. USAQM

1861 through 1872 regulation infantry uniform with the hat brim pinned on the left, the prescribed method until changed to the right in 1868, although photographs of the period depict examples both on the right and left, as well as not secured to the body at all. USAQM

1861 through 1872 heavy artillery regulation uniform, once more with the hat brim pinned on the left, the prescribed method until changed to the right in 1868. The model holds the cavalry saber which was not the correct edged weapon for this branch either, bayonets being correct for junior enlisted and the M1833 short sword was prescribed for non-commissioned officers, although the M1840 NCO sword also was used in certain cases. USAQM

1861 through 1872 regulation cavalry uniform, once more with the hat brim pinned on the left, although this incorrect in that the brims of cavalry troopers were to be looped up on the right. USAQM

The regulation field and fatigue uniform of the 1861 through 1872 period, although surplus Civil War era four button sack coats continued to be worn for several more years. Trousers of the 1861-pattern likewise remained standard until a new design was adopted in 1876. Even then, considerable time passed before the new patterns were issued. USAQM

All trowsers to be made loose, without plaits, and to spread well over the boot; to be re-enforced for all enlisted mounted men.

HAT.

32. *For Officers*: Of best black felt. Tile dimensions of medium size to be as follows:
Width of brim, 3 1/4 inches,
Height of crown, 6 1/4 inches.
Oval of tip, 1/2 inch,
Taper of crown, 3/4 inch,
Curve of head, 3/8 inch.
The binding to be 2 inch deep, of best black ribbed silk.

33. *For Enlisted Men*: Of black felt, same shape and size as for officers, with double row of stitching, instead of binding, around the edge. To agree in quality with the pattern deposited in the clothing arsenal.

Trimmings.

34. *For General Officers.* – Gold cord, with acorn-shaped ends. The brine of the hat looped up on the right side, and fastened with an eagle attached to the side of the hat; three black ostrich feathers on the left side; a gold embroidered wreath in front, on black velvet ground, encircling the letters U. S. in silver, old English characters.

35. *For Officers of the Adjutant General's, Inspector General's, Quartermaster's, Subsistence, Medical and Pay Departments, and the Judge Advocate, above the rank of Captain*: The same as for General Officers, except the cord which will be of black silk and gold.

36. *For the same Departments, below the rank of Field Officers*: The same as for Field Officers, except that there will be but two feathers.

37. *For Officers of the Corps of Engineers*: The same as for the General Staff, except the ornament in front, which will be a gold embroidered wreath of laurel and palm, encircling a silver turreted castle on black velvet ground.

38. *For Officers of the Topographical Engineers*: The same as for the General Staff, except the ornament in front, which will be a gold embroidered wreath of oak leaves, encircling a gold embroidered shield, on black velvet ground.

39. *For Officers of the Ordnance Department*: The same as for the General Staff, except the ornament in front, which will be a gold embroidered shell and flame, on black velvet ground.

40. *For Officers of Dragoons*: The same as for the General Staff, except the ornament in front, which will be two gold embroidered sabres crossed, edges upward, on black velvet ground, with the number of the regiment in silver in the upper angle.

41. *For Officers of Cavalry*: The same as for the Dragoons, except that the number of the regiment will be in the lower angle.

42. *For Officers of Mounted Riflemen*: The same as for the General Staff, except the ornament in front, which will be a gold embroidered trumpet, perpendicular, on black velvet ground.

43. *For Officers of Artillery*: The same as for the General Staff, except the ornament in front, which will be gold embroidered cross-cannon, on black velvet ground, with the number of the regiment in silver at the intersection of the cross-cannon.

44. *For Officers of Infantry*: The same as for Artillery, except the ornament in front, which will be a gold embroidered bugle, on black velvet ground, with the number of the regiment in silver within the bend.

45. *For Enlisted Men*, except companies of Light Artillery: The same as for Officers of the respective corps, except that there will be but one feather, the cord will be of worsted, of the same color as that of the facing of the corps, three-sixteenths of an inch in diameter, running three times through a slide of the same material, and terminating with two tassels, not less than two inches long, on the side of the hat opposite the feather. For Hospital Stewards the cord will be of bluff and green mixed. The insignia of corps, in brass, in front of the hat, corresponding with those prescribed for Officers, with the number of regiment, five-eighths of an inch long, in brass, and letter of company, one inch, in brass, arranged over insignia. Brim to be looped up to side of hat faith a brass eagle, having a hook attached to the bottom to secure the brim – on the right side for mounted men and left side for foot men. The feather to be worn on the side opposite the loop.

46. All the trimmings of the hat are to be made so that they can be detached; but the eagle, badge of corps, and letter of company, are to be always worn.

47. For companies of Artillery equipped as Light Artillery, the old pattern uniform cap, with red horse-hair plume, cord and tassel.

48. Officers of the General Staff, and Staff Corps, may wear, at their option, a light French chapeau, either stiff crown or flat, according to the pattern deposited in the Adjutant General's Office. Officers below the rank of Field Officers to wear but two feathers.

FORAGE CAPS.

49. For fatigue purposes, forage caps, of pattern in the Quartermaster General's Office: Dark blue cloth, with a welt of the same around the crown, and yellow metal letters in front to designate companies.

50. Commissioned Officers may wear forage caps of the same pattern, with the distinctive ornament of the corps and regiment in front.

CRAVAT OR STOCK.

51. *For all Officers* – black; when a cravat is worn, the tie not to be visible at the opening of the collar.

52. *For all Enlisted Men* – black leather, according to pattern.

BOOTS.

53. *For all Officers* – ankle or Jefferson.

54. *For Enlisted Men of Riflemen, Dragoons, Cavalry, and Light Artillery* – ankle and Jefferson, rights and lefts, according to pattern.

55. *For Enlisted Men of Artillery, Infantry, Engineers, and Ordnance* – Jefferson, rights and lefts, according to pattern.

Above pre-1872-pattern sewn shoes are illustrated along with the new 1872-pattern boots that featured brass screws to hold the soles in place. USAQM

In turn, the new 1872-pattern brass screwed shoes were photographed along with the pre-1872 issue boot. USAQM

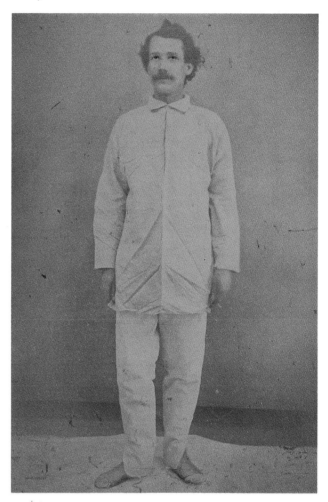

Buffalo overshoes began to be purchased for troops in extreme climates as early as 1862 of the type shown above, while a new design was adopted in 1872 with higher tops as seen below. USAQM

Pre-1872 shirt, drawers, and stockings. USAQM

SPURS.

56. *For all Mounted Officers* – yellow metal, or gilt.

57. *For all Enlisted Mounted Men* – yellow metal, according to pattern. (See No. 174.)

GLOVES.

58. *For General Officers and Officers of the General Staff and Staff Corps* – buff or white.

59. *For Officers of Artillery, Infantry, Cavalry, Dragoons, and Riflemen* – white.

SASH.

60. *For General Officers* – buff, silk net, with silk bullion fringe ends; sash to go twice around the waist, and to tie behind the left hip, pendent part not to extend more than eighteen inches below the tie.

Pre-1872 shirt, drawers, stockings, and shoes with the undershirt shirt, drawers, and stockings. USAQM

61. *For officers of the Adjutant General's, Inspector General's, Quartermaster's, and Subsistence Departments, Corps of Engineers, Topographical Engineers, Ordnance, Artillery, Infantry, Cavalry, Riflemen, and Dragoons, and the Judge Advocate of the Army* – crimson silk net; *for Officers of the Medical Department* – medium or emerald green silk net, with silk bullion fringe ends; to go around the waist and tie as for General Officers.

62. *For all Sergeant Majors, Quartermaster Sergeants, Ordnance Sergeants, First Sergeants, Principal or Chief Musicians and Chief Buglers* – red worsted sash, with worsted bullion fringe ends; to go twice around the waist, and to tie behind the left hip, pendent part not to extend more than eighteen inches below the tie.

63. The sash will be worn (over the coat) on all occasions of duty of every description, except stable and fatigue.

64. The sash will be worn by *"Officers of the Day"* across the body, scarf fashion, from the right shoulder to the left side, instead of around the waist, tying behind the left hip as prescribed.

SWORD BELT.

65. *For all Officers* – a waist belt not less than one and one-half inch, nor more than two inches wide; to be worn over the sash; the sword to be suspended from it by slings of the same material as the belt, with a hook attached to the belt upon which the sword may be hung.

66. *For General Officers* – Russian leather, with three stripes of gold embroidery; the slings embroidered on both sides.

67. *For all other Officers* – black leather, plain.

68. *For all Non-commissioned Officers* – black leather, plain.

SWORD-BELT PLATE.

69. *For all Officers and Enlisted Men* – gilt, rectangular, two inches wide, with a raised bright rim; a silver wreath of laurel encircling the "Arms of the United States;" eagle, shield, scroll, edge of cloud and rays bright. The motto, "E PLURIBUS UNUM," in silver letters, upon the scroll; stars also of silver; According to pattern.

SWORD AND SCABBARD.

70. *For General Officers* – straight sword, gilt hilt, silver grip), brass or steel scabbard.

71. *For Officers of the Adjutant General's, Inspector General 's, Quartermaster's, and Subsistence Departments, Corps of Engineers, Topographical Engineers, Ordnance, the Judge Advocate of the Army, Aides-de-Camp, Field Officers of Artillery, Infantry, and Foot Riflemen, and for the Light Artillery* – the sword of the pattern adopted by the War Department, April 9, 1850; or the one described in G.O. No. 21, of August 28, 1860, for officers therein designated.

72. *For the Medical and Pay Departments* – small sword and scabbard, according to pattern in the Surgeon General's office.

73. *For Officers of Dragoons, Cavalry, and Mounted Riflemen* – sabre and scabbard now in use, according to pattern in the Ordnance Department.

74. *For the Artillery, Infantry, and Foot Riflemen*, except the field officers – the sword of the pattern adopted by the War Department, April 9, 1850.

75. The sword and sword belt will be worn upon all occasions of duty, without exception.

76. When on foot, the sabre will be suspended from the hook attached to the belt.

77. When not on military duty, officers may wear swords of honor, or the prescribed sword, with a scabbard, gilt, or of leather with gilt mountings .

SWORDKNOT.

78. *For General Officers* – gold cord with acorn end.

79. *For all other officers* – gold lace strap with gold bullion tassel.

BADGES TO DISTINGUISH RANK.

Epaulettes.

80. *For the Major General Commanding the Army* – gold, with solid crescent; device, three silver-embroidered stars, one, one and a half inches in diameter, one, one and one-fourth inches in diameter, and one, one and one-eighth inches in diameter, placed on the strap in a row, longitudinally, and equidistant, the largest star in the centre of the crescent, the smallest at the top; dead and bright gold bullion, one-half inch in diameter and three and one-half inches long.

81. *For all other Major Generals* – the same as for the Major General Commanding the Army, except that there will be two stars on the strap instead of three, omitting the smallest.

82. *For a Brigadier General* – the same as for a Major General, except that, instead of two, there shall be one, star (omitting the smallest,) placed upon the strap, and not within the crescent.

83. *For a Colonel* – the same as for a Brigadier General, substituting a silver-embroidered spread eagle for the star upon the strap; and within the crescent for the *Medical Department* – a laurel wreath embroidered in gold, and the letters **M.S.**, in old English characters, in silver, within the wreath; *Pay Department* – same as the Medical Department, with the letters **P.D.** in old English characters; *Corps of Engineers* – a turreted castle of silver; *Corps of Topographical Engineers* – a shield embroidered in gold, and below it the letters **T.E.**, in old English characters, in silver; *Ordnance Department* – shell and flame in silver embroidery; *Regimental Officers* – the number of the regiment embroidered in gold, within a circlet of embroidered silver, one and three-fourths inches in diameter, upon cloth of the following colors: *for Artillery* – scarlet; *Infantry* – light or sky blue; *Riflemen* – medium or emerald green; *Dragoons* – orange; *Cavalry* – yellow.

84. *For a Lieutenant Colonel* – the same as for a Colonel, according to corps, but substituting for the eagle a silver-embroidered leaf.

85. *For a Major* – the same as for a Colonel, according to corps, omitting the eagle.

86. *For a Captain* – the same as for a Colonel, according to corps, except that the bullion will be only one-fourth of an inch in diameter, and two and one-half inches long, and substituting for the eagle two silver-embroidered bars.

87. *For a First Lieutenant* – the same as for a Colonel, according to corps, except that the bullion will be only one-eighth of an inch in diameter, and two and one-half inches long, and substituting for the eagle one silver embroidered bar.

88. *For a Second Lieutenant* – the same as for a First Lieutenant, omitting the bar.

89. *For a Brevet Second Lieutenant* – the same as for a Second Lieutenant.

90. All officers having military rank will wear an epaulette on each shoulder.

91. The epaulette may be dispensed with when not on duty, and on certain duties off parade, to wit: at drills, at inspections of barracks and hospitals, on Courts of Inquiry and Boards, at inspections of articles and necessaries, on working parties and fatigue duties, and upon the march, except when, in war, there is immediate expectation of meeting the enemy, and also when the overcoat is worn.

Shoulder Straps.

92. *For the Major General Commanding the Army* – dark blue cloth, one and three-eighths inches wide by four inches long; bordered with on embroidery of gold one-fourth of an inch wide; three silver-embroidered stars of five rays, one star on the centre of the strap, and one on each side equidistant between the centre and the outer edge of the strap; the centre star to be the largest,

93. *For all other Major Generals* – the same as for the Major General Commanding the Army, except that there will be two stars instead of three; the centre of each star to be one inch from the outer edge of the gold embroidery on the ends of the strap; both stars of the same size.

94. *For a Brigadier General* – the same as for a Major General, except that there will be one star instead of two; the centre of the star to be equidistant from the outer edge of the embroidery on the ends of the strap.

95. *For a Colonel* – the same size as for a Major General, and bordered in like manner with an embroidery of gold; a silver-embroidered spread eagle on the centre of the strap, two inches between the tips of the wings, having in the right talon an olive branch, and in the left a bundle of arrows; an escutcheon on the breast, as represented in the arms of the United States; cloth of the strap as follows: for the *General Staff and Staff Corps* – dark blue; *Artillery* – scarlet; *Infantry* – light or sky-blue; *Riflemen* – medium or emerald green; *Dragoons* – orange; *Cavalry* – yellow.

96. *For a Lieutenant Colonel* – the same as for a Colonel, according to corps, omitting the eagle, and introducing a silver-embroidered leaf at each end, each leaf extending seven-eighths of an inch from the end border of the strap.

97. *For a Major* – the same as for a Colonel, according to corps, omitting the eagle, and introducing a gold-embroidered leaf at each end, each leaf extending seven-eighths of an inch from the end border of the strap.

98. *For a Captain* – the same as for a Colonel, according to corps, omitting the eagle, and introducing at each end two gold-embroidered bars of the same width as the border, placed parallel to the ends of the strap; the distance between them and from the border equal to the width of the border.

99. *For a First Lieutenant* – the same as for a Colonel, according to corps, omitting the eagle, and introducing at each end one gold-embroidered bar of the same width as the border, placed parallel to the ends of the strap, at a distance from the border equal to its width.

100. *For a Second Lieutenant* – the same as for a Colonel, according to corps, omitting the eagle.

101. *For a Brevet Second Lieutenant* – the same as for a Second Lieutenant.

102. The shoulder strap will be worn whenever the epaulette is not.

103. The rank of non-commissioned officers will be marked by chevrons upon both sleeves of the uniform coat and overcoat, above the elbow, of silk worsted binding one half an inch wide, same color as the edging on the coat, points down, as follows:

104. *For a Sergeant Major* – three bars and an arc, in silk.

105. *For a Quartermaster Sergeant* – three bars and a tie, in silk.

106. *For an Ordnance Sergeant* – three bars and a star, in silk.

107. *For a Hospital Steward* – a caduceus two inches long, embroidered with yellow silk on each arm above the elbow, in the place indicated for a chevron, the head toward the outer seam of the sleeve.

108. *For a First Sergeant* – three bars and a lozenge, in worsted.

109. *For a Sergeant* – three bars, in worsted.

110. *For a Corporal* – two bars, in worsted.

111. *For a Pioneer* – two crossed hatchets of cloth, same color and material as the edging of the collar, to be sewed on each arm above the elbow in the place indicated for a chevron, (those of a corporal to be just above and resting on the chevron,) the head of the hatchet upward, its edges outward, of he following dimensions, viz.: *Handle* – four and one half inches long, one-fourth to one-third of an inch wide. *Hatchet* – two inches long, one inch at the edge.

112. *To indicate service* – all non-commissioned officers, musicians, and privates, who have served faithfully for the term of five years, will wear, as a mark of distinction, upon both sleeves of the uniform coat, below the elbow, a diagonal half chevron, one-half an inch wide, extending from seam to seam, the front end nearest the cuff, and one-half an inch above the point of the cuff, to be of the same color as the edging of the coat. In like manner, an additional half chevron, above and parallel to the first, for every subsequent five years of faithful service: distance between each chevron one-fourth of an inch. Service in war will be indicated by a light or sky-blue stripe on each side of the chevron for Artillery, and a red stripe for all other corps, the stripe to be one-eight of an inch wide.

OVERCOAT.

For Commissioned Officers

113. A *"cloak coat"* of dark blue cloth, closing by means of four frog buttons of black silk and loops of black silk cord down the breast, and at the throat by a long loop *a echelle*, without tassel or plate, on the left side, and a black silk frog button on the right; cord for the loops fifteen-hundredths of an inch in diameter; back, a single piece, slit up from the bottom, from fifteen to seventeen inches, according to the height of the wearer, and closing at will, by buttons, and button-holes cut in a concealed flap; collar of the same color and material as the coat, rounded at the edges, and to stand or fall; when standing, to be about five inches high; sleeves loose, of a single piece, and round at the bottom, without cuff or slit; lining, woolen; around the front and lower border, the edges of the pockets, the edges of the sleeves, collar, and slit in the back, a flat braid of black silk one-half an inch wide; and around each frog button on the breast, a knot two and one-quarter inches in diameter of black silk cord, seven-hundredths of an inch in diameter, arranged according to drawing; cape of the same color and material as the coat, removable at the pleasure of the wearer, and reaching to the cuff of the coat-sleeve when the arm is extended; coat to extend down the leg from six to eight inches below the knee, according to height. *To indicate rank*, there will be on both sleeves, near the lower edge, a knot of flat black silk braid not exceeding one-eighth of an inch in width, arranged according to drawing, and composed as follows:

114. *For a General* – of five braids, double knot.

115. *For a Colonel* – of five braids, single knot.

116. *For a Lieutenant Colonel* – of four braids, single knot.

117. *For a Major* – of three braids, single knot.

118. *For a Captain* – of two braids, single knot.

119. *For a First Lieutenant* – of one braid, single knot.

120. *For a Second Lieutenant and Brevet Second Lieutenant* – a plain sleeve, without knot or ornament.

For Enlisted Men.

121. *For all Mounted Corps.* – of sky-blue cloth; stand and fall collar: double breasted; cape to reach down to the cuff of the coat when the arm is extended, and to button all the way up; buttons (24.)

122. *All other enlisted men* – of sky-blue cloth; stand-up collar; single-breasted; cape to reach down to the elbows when the arm is extended, and to button all the way up; buttons (24.)

123. *For Dragoons, Cavalry, and Mounted Riflemen* – a gutta percha talma, or cloak extending to the knee, with long sleeves.

OTHER ARTICLES OF CLOTHING AND EQUIPMENT.

124. *Flannel shirt, drawers, stockings, and stable frock* – the same as now furnished.

125. *Blanket* – woolen, gray, with letters U.S. in black, four inches long, in the centre; to be seven feet long, and five and a half feet wide, and to weigh five pounds.

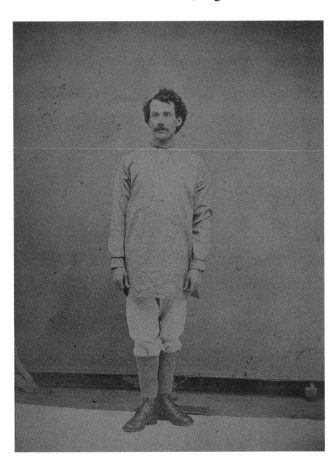

1872-pattern shirt, drawers, shoes, and stockings. USAQM

1872-pattern shirt, drawers, and stockings with shirt tucked into drawers. USAQM

126. *Canvas overalls for Engineer soldiers* – of white cotton; one garment to cover the whole of the body below the waist, the breast, the shoulders, and the arms; sleeves loose, to allow a free play of the arms, with narrow wristband buttoning with one button; overalls to fasten at the neck behind with two buttons, and at the waist behind with buckle and tongue.

127. *Belts of all Enlisted Men* – black leather.

128. *Cartridge box* – according to pattern in the Ordnance Department.

129. *Drum sling* – white webbing to be provided with a brass drumstick carriage, according to pattern.

130. *Knapsack* – of painted canvas, according to pattern now issued by the Quartermaster's Department; the great coat, when carried, to be neatly folded, not rolled, and covered by the outer flap of the knapsack.

131. *Haversack* – of painted canvas, with an inside sack unpainted, according to the pattern now issued by the Quartermaster's Department.

132. *Canteen* – of tin, covered with woolen cloth, of the pattern now issued by the Quartermaster's Department.

Paragraphs 133 through 173 omitted.

174. SPURS, (brass) – 2 spurs, 2 rowels, 2 rivets, 2 spur straps, 19 inches long, 2 roller buckles, 0.625 inch, 2 standing loops.

Length of heel for No. 1, 3 1/2 inches; for No. 2, 3 1/4 inches – inside meas.

Width of heel " 3 1/4 " " 3 "

Length of shank to centre of rowel, 1 inch.

Diameter of rowel, 0.85 inch.

Paragraphs 175 through 180 omitted

MILITARY STOREKEEPERS.

181. A citizen's frock coat of blue cloth, with buttons of the department to which they are attached; round black hat; pantaloons and vest, plain, white or dark blue; cravat or stock, black.

MISCELLANEOUS.

182. General Officers, and Colonels having the brevet rank of General Officers, may, on occasions of ceremony, and when not serving with troops, wear the " dress" and "undress" prescribed by existing regulations .

183. Officers below the grade of Colonel having brevet rank, will wear the epaulettes and shoulder straps distinctive of their army rank. In all other respects, their uniform and dress will be that of their respective regiments, corps, or departments, and according to their commissions in the same. Officers above the grade of Lieutenant Colonel by ordinary commission, having brevet rank, may wear the uniform of their respective regiments or corps, or that of General Officers, according to their brevet rank.

184. Officers are permitted to wear a plain dark blue body coat, with the button designating their respective corps, regiments, or departments, without any other mark or ornament upon it. Such a coat, however, is not to be considered as a dress for any military purpose.

185. In like manner, officers are permitted to wear a buff, white, or blue vest, with the small button of their corps, regiment, or department.

186. Officers serving with mounted troops are allowed to wear, for stable duty, a plain dark blue cloth jacket, with one or two rows of buttons down the front, according to rank; stand-up collar, sloped in front as that of the uniform coat; shoulder straps according to rank, but no other ornament.

187. The hair to be short; the beard to be worn at the pleasure of the individual; but when worn, to be kept short and neatly trimmed.

188. *A Band* will wear the uniform of the regiment or corps to which it belongs. The commanding officer may, at the expense of the corps, sanctioned by the Council of Administration, make such additions in ornaments as he may judge proper.

Arctic overshoes likewise were adopted in 1872. USAQM

APPENDIX D:
Uniform Regulations, 1872

REGULATIONS FOR THE UNIFORM AND DRESS OF THE ARMY OF THE UNITED STATES JULY, 1872

UNIFORM, DRESS, EQUIPMENTS, &c.

No officer or soldier of the Army shall wear any other than the prescribed uniform, when on duty.

COAT.

FULL DRESS FOR OFFICERS.

All officers shall wear a double-breasted frock coat of dark blue cloth, the skirt to extend from one-half to three-fourths the distance from the hip joint to the bend of the knee.

For a General: Two rows of buttons on the breast twelve in each row; placed by fours; the distance between each row five and one-half inches at top and three and one-half inches at bottom; stand-up collar, not less than one nor more than two inches in height, to hook in front at the bottom and slope thence up and backward at an angle of thirty degrees on each side, corners rounded; cuffs three inches deep, to go around the sleeves parallel to the lower edge, and with three small buttons at the under seam; pockets in the folds of the skirts, with two buttons at the hip and one at the lower end of each side-edge, making four buttons on the back and skirt of the coat; collar and cuffs to be of dark blue velvet; lining of the coat black.

For a Lieutenant General: The same as for a General, except that there will be ten buttons in each row, on the breast, the upper and lower groups by threes, and the middle groups by fours.

For a Major General: The same as for a General, except that there will be nine buttons in each row, on the breast, placed by threes.

For a Brigadier General: The same as for a General, except that there will be eight buttons in each rows on the breast, placed by pairs.

For a Colonel, Lieutenant Colonel, and Major: The same as for a General, except that there will be nine buttons in each row, on the breast,

placed at equal distances; collars and cuffs of the same color and material as the coat. The upper half of the cuffs to be ornamented with three double stripes of gold braid running the length of the cuff, pointed at the upper ends, and with a small button below the point of each stripe, according to pattern.

For a Captain, 1st lieutenant, 2d lieutenant, and Additional 2d lieutenant: The same as for a Colonel, except that there will be seven buttons in each row, on the breast, and two stripes on the cuffs.

For all Storekeepers: A single-breasted coat, as lately worn by Captains of the staff, with staff shoulder-straps to indicate rank.

This coat shall be worn on all dress occasions, such as reviews, inspections, dress parades, guards, and courts-martial. It will be habitually worn at battalion drills, except in hot weather, or when otherwise exceptionally directed by the commanding officer.

UNDRESS FOR OFFICERS.

For fatigues, marches, squad and company drills, and other drills when authorized by the commanding officer, and for ordinary wear: A sack coat of dark blue cloth or serge; falling collar; single breasted, with five buttons in front, same as those worn on the dress coat; with black braid, one-fourth of an inch wide, extending from each button and button-hole back six inches and terminating in "herring-bone" loops.

The skirt to extend from one-third to two-thirds the distance from the hip joint to the bend of the knee, and to be slashed at the hip on each side; a knot of black braid, one-fourth of an inch wide, on the upper part of the cuff; according to pattern.

The shoulder-straps will always be worn with it. Black braid binding one-half of an inch wide, around edge of coat.

For storekeepers: Of pattern above described, but without braid.

For Chaplain: Plain black frock coat with standing collar; one row of nine black buttons on the breast, with "herring-bone" of black braid around the buttons and button-holes.

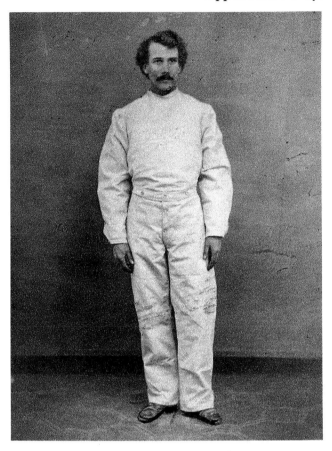

Engineer overalls of the pattern adopted in 1872. USAQM

This pattern of the long single-breasted white canvas stable-frock closed with three buttons. It was adopted as early as the 1850s. These garments were issued to mounted troops (cavalry and light artillery) to keep their more expensive wool uniforms from being soiled. The canvas likewise could be washed easily, a necessary requirement because the color undoubtedly showed the dirt attendant with grooming of horses, cleaning stalls, and the other chores associated with maintaining a mount. USAQM

COATS

FOR ENLISTED MEN.

For Infantry: Single-breasted, dark blue basque, according to pattern deposited in Quartermaster General's Office, piped with sky blue; collar same height as for officers' coat, faced with sly-blue cloth four inches back on each side, cut square to hook up close in front; number of regiment or badge of corps in yellows metal in middle of sky blue facing of collar on each side; skirt of coat on each side of opening behind to be faced with sky-blue cloth, ornamented with four buttons, as per pattern. Two straps of dark blue cloth, piped with the same color as the facings, let into the waist-seam on each side the coat and buttoning above the hip to sustain the waist-belt; shoulder-straps of cloth the color of the facings let into the shoulder-seam and to button over the shoulder-belts at the collar-seam with one button; shoulder-straps for Engineer soldiers to be scarlet, piped with white.

For Enlisted Men of Artillery, Engineers, and Ordnance: Same as for Infantry except that the facings shall be scarlet for Artillery, scarlet and white for Engineers, and crimson for Ordnance.

For Cavalry and Light Artillery: Same as for Infantry, excepting that it is shorter in the skirt, and the facing upon the skirt put on differently, according to pattern in the Quartermaster General's Office; facings for Cavalry yellow, and for Light Artillery red.

Coats for Musicians: Ornamented on the breast with braid same color as the facings, running from the button as now worn, the outer extremities terminating in "herring-bones" and the braid returning back to the buttons.

Coats for Hospital Stewards: Same as for Infantry, except the facing to be of emerald green.

Coats for Ordnance Sergeants: Same as for enlisted men of Ordnance.

Whenever the dress coat is worn by enlisted men, it will invariably be buttoned up and hooked at the collar.

For fatigue purposes, for general wear, and on field service: A dark blue blouse of navy flannel, according to the pattern deposited in the Quartermaster General's Office.

Blouses for winter wear to be lined.

BUTTONS.

The same as now worn for all Officers and enlisted men. *Storekeepers*: General Staff button.

TROWSERS.

For General Officers, Offices of the General Staff, and Staff Corps: Dark blue cloth, plain, without stripe, welt, or cord.

For all Regimental Officers of Cavalry, Artillery, and Infantry. Light blue cloth, same shade of color as for enlisted, with stripe one and one-half inches wide, welted at the edges; color, that of facings of their respective arms, except infantry, which will be dark blue.

Storekeepers: Dark blue cloth, with black stripe one and one-half inches wide.

For Chaplains: Plain black.

*For Enlisted Men of all Arms and of the Ordnance Depart*ment: Sky blue mixture, pattern now worn; waistband three and a half inches wide, to button with two buttons in front; pockets in front, opening at top.

Sergeants to wear a stripe one inch wide, color of facings; and Corporals to wear a stripe one-half inch wide, color of facings, except Infantry, which will be dark blue.

For Engineers: According to pattern in the Quartermaster General's Office.

For Ordnance Sergeants: Crimson stripe, one inch and one-quarter wide.

For Hospital Stewards: Emerald green stripe, one inch and one-quarter wide.

All stripes to be of cloth.

One-third of the trowsers of enlisted men issued on requisition shall be sent to posts cut out but not made up. The material of each pair of trowsers, with the buttons, thread, needles, and all necessary trimmings, shall be rolled up in a bundle, securely fastened and marked with the size of the trowsers.

Trowsers for all mounted men to be reenforced.

There shall be a 5th size, larger than No- 4.

CRAVATS

For all Officers: Black; the tie not to be visible at the opening of the collar. Neither cravats nor stocks will be worn by enlisted men on duty.

BOOTS AND SHOES.

For all Officers: Shall be of black leather and come above the ankle.

For Enlisted Men of Cavalry and Light Artillery: Boots, to come above the swell of the calf of the leg; shoes, Jefferson rights and lefts, according to pattern.

For Enlisted Men of Artillery, Infantry, Engineers, and Ordnance, and other Enlisted Men: Jefferson rights and lefts, according to pattern.

Top-boots only be worn by mounted men.

HAT OR CAP (FULL DRESS).

For General Officers, Officers of the General Staff and Staff Corps: Chapeau, according to pattern.

For Officers of Light Artillery and Cavalry: Black felt helmet, with gold cords and tassels, and gilt trimmings, according to pattern.

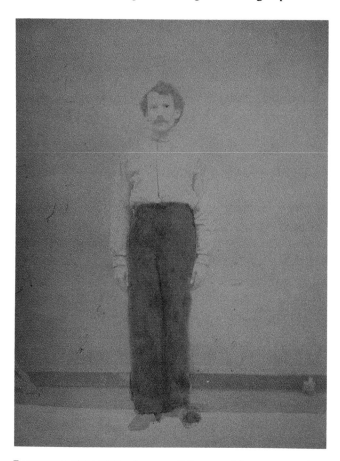

Overalls of this pattern were worn under the stable-frock for cavalry and light artillery troops as of 1872. USAQM

Foot trousers of the 1872-pattern essentially were of the same cut as those worn during the Civil War. USAQM

The collar, cuffs, and yoke piping on the 1872-pattern plaited blouse is evident on this image of an infantry private (piping was sky-blue for infantry at this time) with the new smaller sheet brass hunting horn device adopted in that same year for the dress cap and eventually authorized for the forage cap. The over-the-shoulder strap for the cartridge box was outmoded by this time and was depicted in error during this 1875 photography session for the Quartermaster Department. The same incorrect accoutrements were shown in several of the other pictures taken of 1872-pattern uniforms for this project to document the uniform changes from the 1860s to the early 1870s. This is not surprising in that equipments and weapons were changing significantly during this period as well. USAQM

The 1872-pattern engineer had scarlet facings trimmed in white from the beginning, although the castle insignia on the hat was not called for until 1873, at which time this device was to replace the "CE" originally prescribed in the new uniform regulations. The scarlet and white pompon was unique to engineers, all other enlisted men having pompons of a single color. USAQM

For all Storekeepers: Forage Cap of dark blue cloth, without braid; badge same as for General Officers.

For all other Officers: Of dark blue cloth, ornamented with gold braid and trimmings, according to pattern.

For Enlisted Men of Light Artillery and Cavalry: Black-felt helmets same pattern as for officers, with cords and tassels of mohair – red for Light Artillery and yellow for Cavalry. Helmet, ornamented with yellow metal trimmings, as per pattern.

For all other Enlisted Men: Of blue cloth, same pattern as for officers, ornamented with mohair braid of the same color as facings of the coat; trimmings of yellows metal according to pattern.

FORAGE CAP.

For General Officers: Of dark blue cloth, chasseur pattern, with black velvet band and badge in front.

For all other Commissioned Officers: Of dark blue cloth, chasseur pattern, with badge of corps or regiment in front, top of badge to be even with top of cap, and according to pattern in Quartermaster General's Office.

For all Enlisted Men: Of plain blue cloth, same pattern as for officers, with badge of corps or letter of company of yellow metal worn in front as for officers.

FORAGE CAP BADGES.

For General Officers: A gold embroidered wreath on dark blue cloth ground, encircling the letters U.S. in silver, old English characters.

For Officers of General Staff, and Staff Corps: Same as General Officers, with the exception of those for Ordnance Officers, which will have a gold embroidered shell and flame on dark blue cloth ground.

For Officers of Engineers: A gold embroidered wreath of laurel and palm encircling a silver turreted castle on dark blue cloth ground.

For Officers of Cavalry: Two gold embroidered sabers, crossed, edges upward, on dark blue cloth ground, with number of regiment in silver in upper angle.

For Officers of Artillery: Two gold embroidered cannons, crossed, on dark blue cloth ground, with number of the regiment in silver at the intersection of the cross-cannon.

For Officers of Infantry: A gold embroidered bugle, on dark blue cloth ground, with number of the regiment in silver within bend.

FATIGUE.

For Officers and Enlisted Men: Of black felt, according to pattern, to be worn only on fatigue duty and on marches or campaigns.

PLUMES FOR OFFICERS.

For General-in-Chief: Three black ostrich feathers.

For other General Officers, for Officers of the General Staff, and Staff Corps: Two black ostrich feathers.

For Regimental Officers of Foot Artillery and Infantry: Of cocks' feathers, to rise five inches above the top of the cap, front feathers to reach the vizor, rear feathers to reach the top of the cap, with gilt ball and socket: color of plume to be red for Artillery and white for Infantry.

For Officers of Light Artillery and Cavalry: Horse-hair plume; gilt ball and socket, plume to be long enough to reach the front edge of the vizor of the helmet: color of the plume to be red for Light Artillery and yellow for Cavalry.

PLUMES AND POMPONS FOR ENLISTED MEN.

For Artillery: Red pompon, pattern shape; ball and socket of yellow metal.

For Infantry: White pompon, same shape and with same ball and socket as for Artillery.

For Ordnance: Crimson pompon, same ball and socket as for Artillery.

For Engineer Troops: Red pompon, with white top; same ball and socket as for Artillery.

For Light Artillery: Red; and for Cavalry, yellow horsehair plume, same size and length as for officers; socket according to pattern.

Post ordnance sergeants wore a dress uniform that resembled the issue for engineers as of the 1872 regulation change except that originally the trim was to be crimson. In 1873 this was changed to crimson facing accented by white piping as seen here. Also in 1873 the flaming bomb insignia was adopted in lieu of the letters "OD" that first had been prescribed. A pair of small brass flaming bombs affixed one on each side of the collar. Crimson chevrons consisting of a five-pointed star surmounting three stripes worn points down indicated rank as did 1 1/4-inch leg stripes on the outer seams of the light blue trousers which remained the same as the 1861-pattern. The belt was to have the rectangular brass plate with eagle and silver wreath although the photographer's model in this 1875 image erroneously wears the 1839 pattern infantry belt and the over-the-shoulder cartridge box sling that also is incorrect. USAQM

The 1872-pattern hospital stewards coat was to be trimmed in emerald green with matching facings. In 1873, however, white piping was to be authorized. The cap had an emerald green pompon and mohair trim with the letters "US" centered in a wreath. The trousers were to have a 1 1/4-inch leg stripe on each of the outer seams of facing cloth. The sword and belt shown in this 1875 photograph were not correct, the M1840 NCO sword being the right edged weapon worn on a leather frog suspended from the M1851 non-commissioned officer's belt with eagle plate. USAQM

After the rank of post commissary sergeants was authorized, General Orders No. 38, 20 March 1873 called for a dress uniform much like post ordnance sergeants except that all trim was cadet gray (until 1873 when white piping was to edge the collar, cuff flashes, tail flashes, shoulder tabs, and the front edge as well as split of the skirt at the rear for all non-commissioned staff officers thereafter, i.e. hospital stewards and ordnance personnel). German silver devices were affixed to the collar with points up and a larger version of the insignia went on the dress cap as well as the forage cap. A gray crescent appeared above the gray chevrons which had three stripes worn points down. Around 1880 the crescent was changed to white facing material over gray stripes and remained so through 1885, although some extent examples display gray crescents. The crescent was selected because it had been an ancient symbol of plenty. USAQM

1872-pattern infantry dress uniform. Once more, the cartridge box strap was outmoded by this time. Brass regimental numerals were to be affixed to each side of the collar. USAQM

SPURS.

For all Mounted Officers: Yellow metal or gilt.
For all Mounted Men: Of yellow metal, plain surface.

GLOVES.

For General Officers, Officers of the General Staff; and Staff Corps: Buff or white gauntlets or gloves.
For Field Officers of Artillery, Cavalry, and Infantry; for Officers Light Artillery and Cavalry: White gauntlets or gloves. All other Officers, white gloves.
For all Enlisted Men: Of white Berlin, to be issued as clothing.

SASH.

For General Officers: Buff silk net, with silk bullion fringe ends; sash to go twice around the waist and to tie behind the left hip, pendent plait not to extend more than eighteen inches below the tie.

SWORD-BELT.

For all Officers: A waist-belt, not less than one and one-half nor more than two inches wide, with slings of the same material as the belt, with a hook attached to the belt on which to hang the sword.
The belt to be worn outside the full dress coat and underneath the undress sack.
For General Officers: Of red Russia leather, with three stripes of gold embroidery, as per pattern now worn.
For all Field Officers: One broad stripe of gold lace on black enameled leather, according to pattern.
For all Officers of the General Staff, and Staff Corps, below the rank of Field Officers: Four stripes of gold, interwoven with black silk, lined with black enameled leather, according to pattern.
For Company Officers of Cavalry, Artillery and Infantry: Four stripes of gold lace, interwoven with silk of the same color as the facings of their arms of service, and lined with black enameled leather.
For all Storekeepers: Of black enameled leather, of patterns lately worn.

On undress duty, marches, and campaigns, officers may wear a plain black leather belt.

For all Non-Commissioned Officers: Plain black leather.

SWORD-BELT PLATE.

For all Officers and Enlisted Men: Gilt, rectangular, two inches wide, with a raised bright rim; a silver wreath of laurel encircling the "Arms of the United States;" eagle, shield, scroll, edge of cloud and rays bright. The motto "E pluribus unum" upon the scroll; stars also of silver, according to pattern.

SWORD AND SCABBARD.

General Officers: Straight sword, gilt hilt, silver grip; brass or steel scabbard, same as now worn.

For Officers of Light Artillery and Cavalry: Sabre and scabbard as now worn, and according to pattern in Ordnance Department.

For Officers of the Pay and Medical Departments: Small sword and scabbard, according to pattern in the Surgeon General's Office, as now worn.

For all other Officers: Same as the small, straight sword now worn by the officers of the General Staff, and according to pattern in the Ordnance Department.

The sword and sword-belt will be worn upon all occasions of duty, except stable and fatigue.

When not on military duty, officers may wear swords of honor, or the prescribed sword, with a scabbard, gilt, or of leather with gilt mountings.

SWORD-KNOT.

For General Officers: Gold cord, with acorn end.

For all other Officers: Gold lace strap, with gold bullion tassel, as now worn.

EPAULETTES.

For the General of the Army: Of gold, with solid crescent; device – two silver embroidered stars, with five rays each, one and one-half inches in diameter, and the "Arms of the United States" embroidered in gold placed between them.

For a Lieutenant General: Three Silver embroidered stars of five rays each, respectively, one and one-half, one and one-quarter, one and one-eighth inches in diameter. The largest placed in the centre of the crescent; the others, placed longitudinally on the strap and equidistant, ranking in order of size from the crescent.

For Major General: Same as for Lieutenant General, omitting smallest star, and the smaller of time two remaining stars placed in the centre of the strap.

For a Brigadier General: Same as for a Lieutenant General, omitting the largest star.

1872-pattern cavalry enlisted dress uniform. The saber belt is the type adopted in 1851 and used into the early 1870s. USAQM

1872-pattern light artillery enlisted dress uniform. The saber is a cavalry model and not the correct M1840 artillery saber. USAQM

The 1874-pattern five button blouse gradually replaced the unpopular 1872-pattern plaited blouse. Collar and cuffs continued to have worsted cord in branch colors on the 1874 blouse, however. Once more, the belt and the cartridge box strap illustrated with an infantry private's uniform were not correct for the period. USAQM

SHOULDER-KNOTS.

*For Officers of the Adjutant General's and Inspector General's Departments, and for Aides-de-Camp to General Officers:** Of gold cord, Russian pattern, on dark blue cloth ground; insignia of rank and letters of corps or designation of regiment embroidered on the cloth ground, according to pattern; an aiguillette of gold cord to be worn with the right shoulder- knot and permanently attached thereto, according to pattern.

For Officers of other Staff Corps: Same as above described, without the aiguillette.

For Officers of Cavalry, Artillery, and Infantry: Of the same pattern as for the Staff Corps, but on cloth of the same color as the facings of their arm, with insignia of rank and number of regiment embroidered on the cloth ground, according to pattern.

For Regimental Adjutants: Of the same pattern as for other officers of their arm, but with aiguillettes attached.

* See Miscellaneous.

INSIGNIA OF RANK ON SHOULDER-KNOTS.

For a Colonel: A silver embroidered eagle at the centre of the pad.

For a Lieutenant Colonel: Two silver embroidered leaves, one at each end of pad.

For a Major: Two gold embroidered leaves, one at each end of pad.

For a Captain: Two silver embroidered bars at each end of pad.

For a 1st Lieutenant: One silver embroidered bar at each end of pad.

For a 2d Lieutenant: Plain.

For an Additional 2d Lieutenant: Same as 2d Lieutenant.

The above insignia to be the same as prescribed for the shoulder-straps.

SHOULDER-STRAPS.

For the General of the Army: Dark blue cloth, one and three-eighths inches wide by four inches long, bordered with an embroidery of gold

Hilt of the M1833 heavy artillery short sword.

one-fourth of an inch wide; two silver embroidered stars of five rays each, and gold embroidered "Arms of the United States" between them.

For a Lieutenant General: The same as for the General, except that there will be three silver embroidered stars of five rays, one star on the centre of the strap, and one on each side, equidistant between the centre and outer edge of the strap, the centre star to be the largest.

For all Major Generals: The same as for the Lieutenant General except that there will be two stars instead of three; the centre of each star to be one inch from the outer edge of the gold embroidery on the ends of the strap; both stars of the same size.

For a Brigadier General: The same as for a Major General, except that there still be one star instead of two; the centre of the star to lye equidistant from the outer edge of the embroidery on the ends of the strap.

For a Colonel: The same size as for a Major General, and bordered in like manner with an embroidery of gold; a silver embroidered spread eagle on the centre of the strap, two inches between the tips of the wings, having in the right talon an olive branch, and in the left a bundle of arrows; an escutcheon on the breast, as represented in the "Arms of the United States." Cloth of the strap as follows: for the General Staff and

Hilt of the M1840 light artillery sword.

Staff Corps, dark blue; Artillery, scarlet; Infantry, sky blue; Cavalry, yellow.

For a Lieutenant Colonel: The same as for Colonel, according to corps omitting the eagle, and introducing a silver embroidered leaf at each end, each leaf extending seven-eighths of an inch from the end border of the strap.

For a Major: The same as for a Colonel, according to corps, omitting the eagles and introducing a gold embroidered leaf at each end, each leaf extending seven-eighths of an inch from the end border of the strap.

For a Captain: The same as for a Colonel, according to corps, omitting the eagle, and introducing at each end two silver embroidered bars of the same width as the border, placed parallel to the ends of the strap, at a distance between them and from the border equal to the width of the border.

For a 1st Lieutenant: The same as for a Colonel, according to corps, omitting the eagle, and introducing at each end one silver embroidered bar of the same width as the border, placed parallel to the ends of the strap, at a distance from the border equal to its width.

For a 2d Lieutenant: The same as for a Colonel, according to corps, omitting the eagle.

For an Additional 2d Lieutenant: The same as for a 2d Lieutenant.

Officers serving in the field may dispense with the prescribed insignia of rank on their horse equipments, and may wear overcoats of the same color and shape as those of the enlisted men of their commands, and omit epaulettes, shoulder-knots, or other prominent marks likely to, attract the fire of sharpshooters; but all officers must wear the prescribed buttons, stripes, and shoulder-straps to indicate their corps and rank.

The shoulder-strap will worn whenever the epaulette or shoulder-knot is not.

CHEVRONS.

The rank of non-commissioned officers will be marked by chevrons upon both sleeves of the uniform coat and overcoat, above the elbow; of cloth of the same color as the facings of the uniform coat, divided into bars a half inch wide by black silk stitching, except for Engineers, which will be white stitching and piped with white, points down, according to new patterns in Quartermaster General's Office, as follows:

For a Sergeant Major: Three bars and an arc.

For a Quartermaster Sergeant: Three bars and a tie of three bars.

For a Principal Musician: Three bars and a bugle.

For an Ordnance Sergeant: Three bars and a star.

For a Hospital Steward: A half chevron of emerald green cloth one and three-fourths inches wide, piped with yellow cloth, running obliquely downward from the outer to the inner seam of the sleeve, and at an angle of about thirty degrees with a horizontal, and in the centre a "caduceus" two inches long, the head toward the outer seam of the sleeve.

For a 1st Sergeant: Three bars and a lozenge.

For a Battalion or Company Quartermaster Sergeant: Three bars and a tie of one bar.

For a Sergeant: Three bars.

For a Corporal: Two bars.

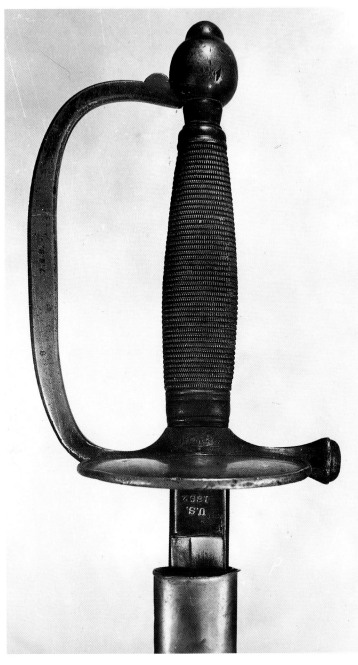

Hilt of the M1840 NCO sword.

For a Pioneer: Two crossed hatchets, of cloth, same color and material as the facings of the uniform coat, to be sewed on each sleeve, above the elbow, in the place indicated for a chevron (those of a corporal to be just above and resting on the chevron), the head of the hatchet upward, its edge outward, of the following dimensions, viz:

Handle, four and one-half inches long, one-fourth to one-third of a inch wide.

Hatchet, two inches long,, one inch wide at the edge.

To indicate service: All non-commissioned officers, musicians, and privates, who have served faithfully for one term of enlistment, will wear as a mark of distinction upon both sleeves of the uniform coat, below the elbow, a diagonal half chevron, one-half inch wide, extending from seam to seam, the front end nearest the cuff; and one-half inch above the point of the cuff, to be of the same color as the edging of the coat.

In like manner an additional half chevron, above and parallel to the first, for every subsequent term of enlistment and faithful service. Distance between each chevron one-fourth of an inch.

Service in war will be indicated by a white stripe on each side of the chevron for Artillery, and a red stripe for all other corps, the stripe to be one-eighth of an inch wide.

OVERCOAT.

For General Officers: Of dark blue cloth, closing by means of four frog buttons of black silk; and loops of black silk cord; cord down the breast, and at the throat by a long loop "à echelle," without tassel or plate, on the left side, and a black silk frog button on the right; cord for the loops fifteen hundredths of an inch in diameter; back, a single piece, slit up from the bottom from fifteen to seventeen inches, according to the height of the wearer, and closing at will by buttons, and button-holes cut in a concealed flap; collar of the same color and material as the coat, rounded at the edges, and to stand or fall; when standing to be about five inches high; sleeves loose, of a single piece and round at the bottom, without cuff or slit; lining woolen; around the front and lower borders, the edges of the pockets, the edges of the sleeves, collar, and slit in the back, a flat braid of black silk one-half an inch wide; and around each frog button on the breast a knot two and one-quarter inches in diameter, of black silk cord, seven hundredths of an inch in diameter, cape of the same color and material as the coat, removable at the pleasure of the wearer, and reaching to the cuff of the coat sleeve when the arm is extended; coat to extend down the leg from six to eight inches below the knee, according to height.

To indicate rank: There will be on both sleeves, near the lower edge, a knot of flat black silk braid, not exceeding one-eighth of an inch in width, and composed of five braids, double knot.

For all other Officers: Dark blue close fitting double-breasted surtout coat, with a cape made to detach from the coat and fall to the tips of the fingers when the arm and hand are extended; the skirt of the coat for mounted officers to reach half way between the knee and the sole of the foot; for dismounted officers, three inches below the knee.

The coat to have seven buttons on each breast of the same pattern as those on the uniform coat. The insignia of rank on the sleeve, as follows, viz:

Colonel, five braids, single knot.
Lieutenant Colonel, four braids, single knot.
Major, three braids, single knot.
Captain, two braids, single knot.
1st Lieutenant, one braid, single knot.
2d Lieutenant and Additional 2d Lieutenant, without braid. Military Storekeepers and Chaplains, without braid.
On the frontier and campaign, officers may wear the soldier's overcoat, with insignia of rank on the sleeve.

For Enlisted Men of all arms: Of sky blue cloth of the pattern now used in the mounted services

OTHER ARTICLES OF CLOTHING AND EQUIPMENTS

Flannel shirt drawers, stockings, and stable-frock: The same as now furnished.

Stable-frocks for Mounted Men: Of white cotton, made loose and extending well down to the knee, without sleeve or body lining; to button in front.

Blanket: Woolen, gray, with letters U.S. in black, four inches long, in the centre; to be seven feet long and five and a half feet wide, and to weigh at least five pounds; to be made of wool; the blanket now issued to troops in California to be the standard.

Canvass overalls for Engineer Soldiers: Of white cotton; one garment to cover the whole of the body above the waist – the breast, the shoulders, and the arms; sleeves loose, to allow free play of the arms, with a narrow wristband buttoning with one button; overalls to fasten at the neck behind with two buttons, and at the waist behind with buckle and tongue.

For Cavalry and Light Artillery: White cotton overalls, to cover only the waist. These overalls are to be worn at all stable duties.

Sets of stencil plates of letters and numbers of two sizes (inch and half inch), for marking equipments, &c., shall be furnished lay the Quartermaster's Department to each company commander and regimental adjutant.

SIGNAL SERVICE

For the Chief Signal Officer: The same uniform as for the Adjutant General's Department, without the a aiguillettes.

The uniform of the Enlisted Men of the Signal Service shall be as follows:

The Cavalry uniform, except that the trimmings and facings be orange instead of yellow, bearing a device on the sleeve of the coat, as follows: crossed signal flags, red and white, on dark blue cloth; size of flags three-fourths of an inch square; length of staff three inches, after the pattern in the office of the Chief Signal Officer of the Army. This device to be worn by the non-commissioned officers above the chevrons; by privates of the first class on both arms; and by privates of the second class on the left arm only, in the same position as the chevron of non-commissioned officers.

MILITARY ACADEMY.

The uniform of the Professors and Sword Master at the West Point Military Academy shall be the same as now worn, excepting they will be permitted to wear the dark blue sack coat prescribed for Army officers, with the buttons of the General Staff to be worn on both coats.

FOR CADETS.

The same uniform as now worn.

MISCELLANEOUS

Aides-de-Camp and the Military Secretary, who have *increased* rank, will were the aiguillette with the uniform of the General Staff.

Aide-de-Camp to major and Brigadier Generals will wear the aiguillette with the uniforms of their Regiments and Corps.

Whenever the full dress coat is worn by officers on duty the prescribed epaulettes or shoulder-knots will be attached. Letters to be embroidered on shoulder-knots in old English:

A.D.	Adjutant General's Department
I.D.	Inspector General's Department
J.A.	Bureau of Military Justice
S.S.	Signal Service
Q.D.	Quartermaster Department
S.D.	Subsistence Department
M.D.	Medical Department
P.D.	Pay Department
E.C.	Engineer Corps
O.D.	Ordnance Department

Sashes will no longer be worn by officers below the grade of Brigadier General, or by non-commissioned officers.

Officers when not on duty are permitted to wear a buff, white, or blue vest, with the small button prescribed for them.

When trowsers and flannel shirts now in store shall have been issued or otherwise disposed of, the troops serving in warm climates will upon requisitions approved by commanding officers, be supplied with those articles of a lighter texture, but of the same material, cut, and color as those furnished the other troops of the Army.

Bands will wear the uniform of their Regiments or Corps. Commanding officers may at the expense of the Corps, sanctioned by the Councils of Administration, make such additions of ornaments as they may judge proper.

NOTE. – Swords of prescribed patterns will be furnished to arsenals as soon as manufactured, for sale to officers. A reasonable time after December 1 will be allowed to officers at remote stations to enable them to procure swords from the Ordnance Department.

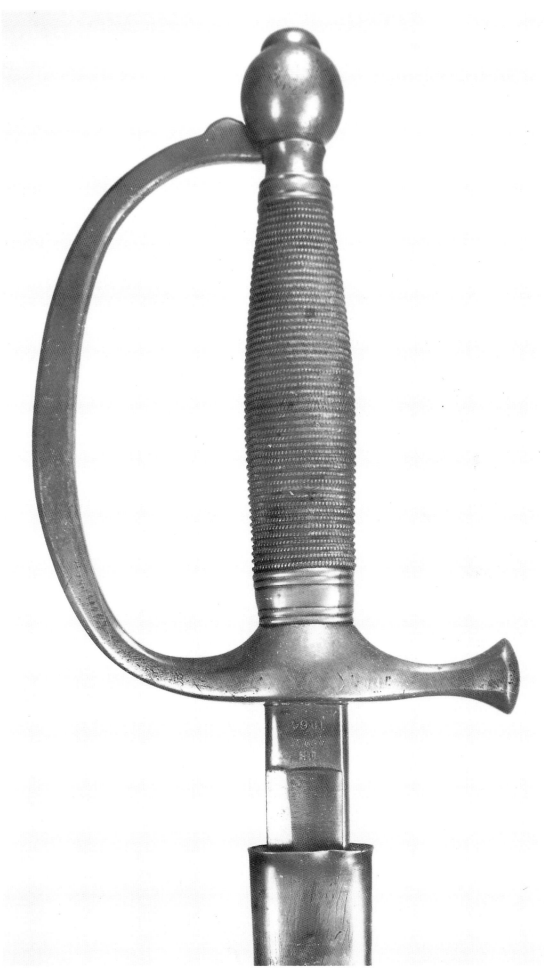

Hilt of the M1840 musician's sword.

GLOSSARY

Accoutrements: Belts, cartridge boxes, canteens, and other personal equipment of the soldier not forming part of the uniform proper, or armament.

Aiguillette: Plaited cord with small needles, points, or aglets at the end worn from the shoulder to set off certain types of officers and enlisted men such as regimental non-commissioned staff or aides de camp.

Austrian knot: Special knot in braid, usually consisting of several loops and worn on the lower sleeves of certain uniform jackets and coats not only in Austria, but in the United States and Europe as well. Some uniform trousers were decorated in this manner as well, but not for the Regular Army in the period under study.

Baldric: Belt worn from one shoulder to the hip.

Basque: Jacket or coat with a short extension of the body, to flare over the hips.

Bearskin: Tall hat made of the fur of that animal, sometimes worn by drum majors in the U.S. Army, as well as certain militia units.

Bicorn, bicorne: Hat with two corners.

Blanco: Compound developed around 1835 to replace whiting to preserve and clean white belts.

Bombasine/bombazeen/bombazin/bombazine: Twilled material of silk and worsted, cotton and worsted, or worsted alone.

Bootees: Another name for brogan, or high topped shoes used in lieu of boots. Also known as Jefferson boots.

Boxed epaulets: Around 1830 the idea of fastening the loose bullion fringe of epaulets came into existence, the term for such a practice of fixing the fringe in place being known as "boxing."

Braid: Woven material sewn to uniform, usually in a contrasting color; also referred to as lace.

Brassard: From the French *bras*, for a band worn on the arm to designate an enlisted specialty.

Breast plate: Metal plate worn on the cross belts that held foot soldiers swords, bayonets, and cartridge boxes.

Broadcloth: Fine-quality woolen cloth, closely woven and with a raised nap. By the nineteenth century it was made from merino wool.

Brogans: Stout shoes with a tongue that falls over the instep, after the term "Brogues"—shoes originally worn by both the Scots and the Irish.

Buff: Oil-tanned leather with the grain layer removed. Prior to 1851 belts made of this material were white. After 1851 they began to be dyed black.

Bugler: Musician serving in a dismounted unit who played a bugle.

Bullion: Gold or silver wire made into a continuous spiral to form the fringe or epaulets, or into lace as trim for music pouches, chevrons, and similar uses.

Bummer's cap: Nickname for the 1861-pattern forage cap, so-called after William Sherman's forces who wore this headgear on the march through Georgia.

Burnside hat: Black slouch hat variant of the 1858-pattern regulation hat that looped on the side, but had a lower crown than the official headgear.

Cadet gray: Shade of gray adopted in the early 1800s for uniforms of cadets at the U.S. Military Academy, West Point.

Canvas: Strong unbleached cloth of flax or hemp.

Cap: Headgear that usually has a bill or visor as opposed to a hat, that has a brim all around.

Cape: Cloak that either attached to an overcoat or was worn separately.

Cap-lines: Cords or lines worn with a cap.

Carbine: Short firearm carried by cavalry and dragoon troops equivalent to the longer rifle of the foot soldier and mounted rifles.

Carbine sling: Leather over-the-shoulder belt with a metal snap swivel that was used by mounted troops to retain their carbine at hand.

Cartridge belt: Belt of leather, canvas, or other materials worn to hold ammunition, chiefly for longarms. In the United States it normally was worn around the waist.

Cartridge box: Pouch, usually with a leather body, used to hold cartridges. It could be worn on an over-the-shoulder belt, or after the Civil War more commonly was attached to a waist belt.

Chapeau de bras. Bicorne type hat that could be folded flat.

Chasseurs: Light infantry from the French *chasseurs à pied*.

Chevrons: "V" shaped device adopted by the United States Army from heraldry principally to designate non-commissioned officers, sometimes called "stripes." "Half chevrons" were used for hospital stewards and service stripes.

Glossary

Cloth: Term used to describe any type of fabric, but in the period under consideration it generally referred to closely woven material of fine-quality wool.

Clothing: Garments worn by the rank and file.

Coat: Outer, upper garment, often with skirts.

Coatee: Outer, upper garment closed in front and cut across the waist, leaving only tails.

Cockade: Badge or cloth device worn on certain types of headgear.

Cocked hat: Another term for a fore and aft *chapeau de bras*.

Cocks'feathers: Curled feathers worn on certain types of headgear.

Collar: Portion of a coat, jacket, or blouse that went around the neck, or the shirt.

Company grade officers. Lieutenants and captains.

Cravat: Cloth worn about the neck starting in the late 1600s; necktie.

Crescent: Large metal end of shoulder scales or epaulets, or a device worn as an insignia.

Cross-belt: Belts worn on each shoulder and crossing at the chest to the opposite hip to secure cartridge boxes, bayonets, and other accoutrements or weapons.

Cuff: Lower end of the sleeve at the wrist. These developed from long sleeves that reached to the knuckles, then turned back to reveal contrasting cloth linings. Cuffs that came to a point had been called "Polish cuffs."

Drab: Woolen cloth of dull, grey-brown color, or the color itself.

Dress uniform: Contraction of full dress uniform, the most formal wear for soldiers.

Embroidery: Expert needlework in silver, gold, or silk thread that was used for insignia.

Epaulet: Shoulder piece that indicated rank and branch of service.

Equipment: Accoutrements worn with the uniform.

Facings: Collars, cuffs, tails, and edges of the uniform in a contrasting color to the garment that indicated branch of service. This practice grew out of linings for coats that would be revealed when turned back.

Farrier: In keeping with the special function of its wearer, horseshoes were used as insignia in the British Army as early as the eighteenth century, and began to appear during the United States during the Civil War.

Fatigue: Work details performed by soldiers, such as wood cutting, construction, and the like.

Fatigue cap: Forage cap.

Fatigue uniform: Uniform worn for work details.

Ferrule: Lower end of a sword or saber scabbard.

Festoon: British term for the elaborate plaited cords worn on some headgear such as the Ringgold cap of the Mexican War or the 1872-pattern mounted artillery helmet.

Field dress: Campaign or combat uniform, akin to battle dress in the British Army.

Field grade officer: Majors, lieutenant colonels, and colonels.

Fifer: Musician who played the fife.

Flannel: Utility woolen fabric often with a cotton warp.

Flap: Evolved from the turnback at the cuff into a three-pointed decoration with buttons after the British fashion.

Flash: Patch of facing on collar.

Flounders: British term for interlaced and plaited knots at the end of a cap line or breast cord. The French referred to these as *raquettes*.

Foot artillery: Originally enlisted men assigned to an artillery unit who were not mounted, later referring to heavy or siege artillery troops as opposed to mounted artillery.

Footwear: Boots, bootees, shoes, and overshoes.

Forage cap: A light cloth cap with leather visor worn with the undress uniform.

Fore-and-aft: Bicorn hat, worn aligned along an axis front to back.

Frock; frock-coat: Long-skirted single or double-breasted coat.

Frog: Short leather sheath suspended or attached to a belt to hold a sword or bayonet scabbard. Also a coat fastening of braid or cord.

Frogging: Ornamental looping to fasten a jacket or coat.

Full dress: The uniform worn on formal occasions such as parades, ceremonies, and hops.

Geneva cross: In 1864, with the introduction of humanitarian laws of war, non-combatants began to be set off by a device that was the reverse of the Swiss flag.

Gilt: Thin metal coating of gold.

Greatcoat: Overcoat.

Grenade: Flaming bomb device used for artillerymen, grenadiers, and others in England, and for the Ordnance Corps in the United States, as well as on the tails of artillery officers' coatees prior to 1851.

Gum blanket; gumcloth: Water-proofed blanket or sheet.

Gutta purcha: Precursor of rubber used for waterproofing and other purposes.

Hat: Headgear with a brim all around the crown.

Hatchet: Devices worn by pioneers in the British and American armies.

Havelock: White cap cover with flap in back, or the flap only, added to protect the wearer from the sun. This accessory was not adopted by the Regular Army, although white forage cap covers were issued for a brief period to be worn with the stable uniform.

Hops: Military dance or ball.

Horse Artillery: Mounted artillery organization, also known as "Flying Artillery."

Horse shoe: Worn by the 1700s on headgear by farriers in the British Army and by 1864 on the arm, as was the case for some individuals in the U.S. beginning in the Civil War.

Jacket: Short, waist-length outer garment. Later a loose blouse or tunic.

Kepi: French from *kappe*, sometimes applied to the forage cap adopted in the United States in the late 1860s, although not necessarily a term of the period.

Kersey: A course woolen cloth, usually twilled.

Kersimere/keserymere: see Kersey.

Merino: A fine, soft wool from merino sheep, used for high quality cloth.

Knapsack: Foot soldier's pack; from the German.

Knot: Worn on the shoulder to indicate rank. Also suspended from the sword or saber.

Kossuth hat: Nineteenth century nickname sometimes applied to the 1855-pattern cavalry hat, and the 1858-pattern hat, also known as the "keg hat" and "Fra Diavalo hat" during the period, and more recently among some dealers and collectors as the "Hardee" or "Jeff Davis"

Lace: Flat braid used as trim, either of gold, or of worsted.

Leather stock: Stiff leather band worn around the neck.

Leggings: Leg covering adopted by some militia and volunteer units in the mid-1800s, but not issued to the Regular Army until the late 1880s.

Mohair: Stiff braid made from Angora goat wool.

Muslin: A general term for the lightest, most delicately woven cotton fabrics, but also can refer to similar, thin materials with an open weave in silk or wool.

Nankeen/Nankin: A twilled cotton cloth with a yellowish-brown tint, originally produced in Nankin, China.

Neck stock: Leather collar worn under the uniform coat or jacket. see leather stock

Needle: The point or aglet of an aiguillette.

Net: Meshed fabric of which the threads may be twisted, plaited, looped, or knotted.

Numbers or numerals: The numbers that designated regiments on coat collars and headgear.

Officer of the Day: Officer detailed daily to perform certain duties within the garrison.

Overalls: Loose trousers designed to be worn over other breeches or trousers.

Overcoat: Heavy outer garment for foul weather wear, sometimes called the greatcoat.

Patrol jacket: Jacket authorized for wear in 1867 for British officers being of blue cloth with black mohair trim.

Pioneer: Soldier who performed certain labor in the field such as felling trees to clear the line of march.

Piping: Narrow strip of material sewn into seams and along edges of garments, usually in a contrasting color. This strengthened the seams and often designated the wearer's arm of service.

Plait/Pleat: The term "plait" was used throughout the nineteenth century to refer to the technique of pleating or folding material. Also the woven cord on a cap or helmet.

Plastron: Panel at the center front of the chest usually made in contrasting color.

Plume: Originally a feather decoration for headdress, but also made of worsted tufts and horsehair.

Pompon/Pompon: Woolen tuft worn on a cap.

Poncho: Square cloth, usually rubberized or of material to repel moisture, with a slit in the center to allow the wearer to slip the item over his head.

Prussian collar: Standup collar on coat.

Rattinet: Another name for ratteen—a twilled thick woolen cloth, usually friezed or with a curled nap.

Roll collar: Collar cut to turn down or over as opposed to a stand collar.

Roundabout: Close-fitting sleeved jacket without tails that usually was cut just a few inches below the waist.

Sack coat: Loose fitting garment used for fatigue and campaign dress.

Saddler: Individual responsible for leather work in a mounted organization. In many European nations the insignia was a saddle, except in England where it was a horse's bit.

Sash: A scarf or cloth that originally displayed national colors early in the evolution of uniforms, but later became additional indicators of rank or function.

Satin: Silk with a diagonal weave to create a glossy surface on one side.

Sealed pattern: Official specimen approved as the model for other versions of the item as a means to maintain standardization.

Seamstress: Woman who sews by profession.

Self-covered: Covered in the same fabric as the garment.

Serge: Strong, twilled woolen or worsted cloth.

Service stripe: Half chevron to indicate long service, campaign service, or service in war.

Shako/Schako: Cylindrical military cap made of leather, felt, or a combination of the two materials. The term sometimes is applied to the 1851-pattern cap, that also was known as an "Albert Cap."

Shalloon: A closely wooven woolen material chiefly for linings; Also known earlier as chalon.

Shell jacket: Name sometimes applied to the jacket or roundabout worn by mounted troops, and sometimes called a drill jacket.

Shoulder knot: Epaulets without fringe, known in earlier times as "counter-epaulets."

Shoulder scales: Metal decorative items that affixed to the wearer's uniform coat or jacket at the shoulders.

Shoulder Straps: Insignia adopted in the early 1830s to denote the rank of officers on campaign and undress uniforms.

Slide: Moving loop used to keep saber knots, cords for headdress, and other items secured.

Slouch hat: Broad-brimmed hat favored in the American West and by certain troops in the Civil War.

Standing collar: Stiff, upright collar.

Stock: Neck stock.

Surtout: Orginally referred to a man's greatcoat or overcoat.

Talma: Wide-sleeved overcoat or cloak with hood to protect against inclement weather.

Tape: Cotton, linen, or other material used to make chevrons and trim for some uniforms prior to 1872.

Undress: Uniform worn for regular military functions or duties of a lesser degree than full dress.

Velvet: Silk fabric with short, dense, and smooth piled surface.

Ventilator: Cover for a small hole in headgear of various types of metal supposedly to promote circulation of air.

Vest: Waistcoat.

White metal: Alloy or mixture for enlisted insignia to match officer's silver.

Whiting: A preparation of finely powdered chalk used to whiten buff leather, etc. see Blanco

Wicker helmet: Sun helmets made of wicker covered with cloth starting in the 1850s India.

Woolen: Wool fabric made from carded fleece, which has not been further processed.

Worsted: Wool fabric in which the fibers have been aligned for a finer effect, as opposed to woolen.

LIST OF ABBREVIATIONS

AGO	Adjutant General's Office
A&NJ	Army and Navy Journal
AMWH	Autry Museum of Western Heritage, Los Angeles, CA
AHS	Arizona Historical Society, Tucson, AZ
ARSW	Annual Report of the Secretary of War
C&E Br.	Clothing and Equipment Branch, Quartermaster General Department
CCF	Consolidated Correspondence File, Records of the Quartermaster General
CSPM	Colorado Springs Pioneer Museum, Colorado Springs, CO
CSPRD	California State Parks and Recreation Department
ERG	Eugene R. Groves Collection
DCM	Douglas C. McChristian Collection
FAM	Frontier Army Museum, Ft. Leavenworth, KS
FLNHS	Ft. Laramie National Historic Site, Ft. Laramie, WY
FWSHM	Fort Worth Museum of Science and Industry, Ft. Worth, TX
GGNRA	Golden Gate National Recreation Area, National Park Service, Ft. Mason, CA
GO	General Orders
GM	Greg Martin Collection
HL	Huntington Library, San Marino, CA
HO	Hayes Otoupalik Collection
HP	Herb Peck, Jr. Collection
JCN	J. Craig Nannos Collection
JG	Jerome Greene Collection
JML	Joshua M. Landish Collection
KHC	Kurt Hamilton Cox Collection
KSHS	Kansas State Historical Society, Topeka, KS
LBNB	Little Bighorn National Battlefield, Crow Agency, MT
LC	Library of Congress
LR	Letters Received
LS	Letters Sent
MFB	Michael F. Bremer Collection
MTHS	Montana Historical Society, Helena, MT
MJM	Dr. Michael J. McAfee Collection
MNHS	Minnesota Historical Society, St. Paul, MN
MOHS	Missouri Historical Society, St. Louis, MO
NA	National Archives
NCMH	North Carolina Museum of History, Raleigh, NC
NF	Norm Flayderman Collection
NPS	National Park Service
NSHS	Nebraska State Historical Society, Lincoln, NE
OQMG	Office of the Quartermaster General
PAF	Paul Alan Feldman Collection
RB	Robert G. Borrell, Sr. Collection
RBM	Reno Battlefield Museum, Garryowen, MT
RG	Record Group
SEO	Stephen E. Osman Collection
SFTC	Santa Fe Trail Center, Larned, KS
SH	Scott Harmon Collection
SHSM	State Historical Society of Missouri, Columbia, MO
SHSND	State Historical Society of North Dakota, Bismarck, ND
SHSW	State Historical Society of Wisconsin, Madison, WI
SI	Smithsonian Institution, Museum of American History
TC	Tojhusmuseet (Royal Arsenal Museum) Copenhagen, Denmark
UHS	Utah Historical Society, Salt Lake City, UT
UPM	Union Pacific Museum, Omaha, NE
USA	U.S. Army (former Presidio Army Museum Collection)
USAMHI	U.S. Army Military History Institute, Carlisle Barracks, PA
USAQM	U.S. Army Quartermaster Museum, Ft. Lee, VA
USHS	Utah State Historical Society, Salt Lake City, UT
VJM	Mr. and Mrs. V.J. Moran
WC	Wes Clark Collection
WCC	Western Costume Company, North Hollywood, CA
WD	War Department
WJS	Dr. William J. Schultz Collection
WPM	West Point Museum, U.S. Military Academy, West Point, NY
WSHS	Wisconsin State Historical Society, Madison WI
WSM	Wyoming State Museum Historical Library, Cheyenne, WY

BIBLIOGRAPHY

Primary Sources

Unpublished

Autograph Letters. W.T. Sherman and P.H. Sheridan. Library of Congress.

Burt, Elizabeth. "Reminiscences of Elizabeth Burt." Typescript, Fort Laramie National Historic Site, 1912.

Circular No. 4. Surgeon General's Office. June 5, 1862.

Circular. Army of the Potomac. March 21, 1863.

Crosman, G.H. to Potter, R.W. April 15, and April 16, 1856. Joint Collection, University of Missouri, Western Historical Manuscript Collection. Columbia, State Historical Society of Missouri.

General Orders. Adjutant General's Office. 1848-1873.

General Orders No. 85. XVIII Army Corps. December 30, 1862.

General Orders. Head-quarters, Army of the Potomac. August 1862-August 1863.

General Orders No. 62. Department of the Cumberland. April 26, 1862.

General Orders No. 14. Army of the Tennessee. July 5, 1864.

Record Group 92. Reords of the Office of Quartermaster General. National Archives, Washington, DC.

Record Group 94. Records of the Office of the Adjutant General. National Archives, Washington, DC.

Record Group 107. Records of the Secretary of War. National Archives, Washington, DC.

Record Group 108. Records of Headquarters of the Army. National Archives. Washington, DC.

Record Group 112. Records of the Office of the Surgeon General. National Archives, Washington, DC.

Record Group 391. Records of U.S.Army Mobile Commands. National Archives. Washington, DC.

Record Group 393. Records of U.S. Army Continenal Commands. National Archives, Washington, DC.

Schofield, John M. Letters. Library of Congress.

Published

Alter, J. Cecil. Ed. *The Utah War Journal of Albert Tracy, 1858-1860*. Salt Lake: Utah Historical Society, 1945.

Annual Reports of the Secretary of War, 1861-1872. Volume I. Washington, DC: U.S. Government Printing Office, 1865-1874.

Armes, George A. *Ups and Downs of an Army Officer*. Washington, DC: n.p., 1900.

Bieber, Ralph P. Ed. *Frontier Life in the Army*. Glendale, CA: Arthur H. Clark, 1932.

Billings, John D. *Hardtack and Coffee*. Boston: George M. Smith & Co., 1888.

Brackett, Albert G. *History of the U.S. Cavalry*. New York: Harper & Brothers, 1865.

Callan, John F. *The Military Laws of the United States, Relating to the Army, Volunteers, Militia, and to Bounty Lands and Pensions from the Foundation of the Government to the Year 1863, To Which are Prefixed the Constitution of the United States. (With an Index Thereto,) and a Synopsis of the Military Legislation of Congress During the Revolutionary War* Philadelphia: George W. Childs, 1863.

"Clothing For Soldiers." *Philadelphia Inquirer*. January 7, 1888.

Bibliography

Custer, George A. *My Life on the Plains*. Norman: University of Oklahoma Press, 1962.

Dubois, John Van Deusen. *Campaigns in the West, 1856-1851*. Tucson: Arizona Pioneers Historical Society, 1949.

Hafen, Leroy R. Ed. *The Utah Expedition 1857-1858: A Documentary Account of the United States Military Movement Under Colonel Albert Sidney Johnston, and The Resistance by Brigham Young and the Mormon Nauvoo Legion*. Glendale, CA: The Arthur H. Clark Company, 1982.

Frazer, Robert W. Ed. *Mansfield on the Condition of Western Forts 1853-54*. Norman: University of Oklahoma Press, 1963.

_____. Ed. *New Mexico in 1850: A Military View*. Norman: University of Oklahoma Press, 1968.

General Orders. Adjutant Generals Department, 1846-1873.

General Orders. War Department, 1846-1873.

Hammond, Otis G. Ed. *The Utah Expedition, 1857-1858 Letters of Capt. Jesse A. Gove, 10th Inf., U.S.A., of Concord, N.H. to Mrs. Gove, and special correspondence of the New York Herald*. Concord: New Hampshire Historical Society, 1928.

Hill, Michale D., and Innis, Ben. Eds. "The Fort Buford Diary of Private Sanford, 1876-1877." LII *North Dakota History* No. 3 (Summer 1985): 2-40.

Hine, Robert V. and Lottinville, Savoie. Eds. *Soldier in the West: Letters of Theodore Talbot During His Services in California, Mexico, and Oregon, 1845-53*. Norman: University of Oklahoma Press, 1972.

Jacobsen, Jacques Noel, Jr. Ed. and Comp. *Regulations and Notes from the Uniform of the Army of the United States, 1857*. Staten Island: Manor Publishing, 1973.

Kimball, Maria Brace. *A Soldier-Doctor of Our Army James P. Kimball*. New York: Houghton Mifflin, 1917.

Kip, Lawrence. *Army Life on the Pacific: A Journal of the Expedition Against the North Indians...in the Summer of 1858*. New York: Redfield, 1859.

Langley, Harold. Ed. *To Utah With The Dragoons*. Salt Lake: University of Utah, 1974.

Long, Oscar F. *Changes in the Uniform of the Army 1775-1895*. Washington, DC: Army & Navy Register.

Lowe, Percival G. *Five Years A Dragoon And Other Adventures on the Great Plains*. Norman: University of Oklahoma Press, 1965.

McConnell, H.H. *Five Years a Cavalryman: Or, Sketches of Regular Army Life on the Texas Frontier, Twenty Years Ago*. Jacksboro, NC: J.N. Rogers Co., 1889.

A Medical Report upon the Uniform and Clothing of the Soldiers of the U.S. Army, 15 April 1868. Washington, DC: Surgeon General's Office, 1868.

"Movement of Troops." Sacramento *Daily Union*. May 29, 1860.

New Orleans *True Delta*. November 13, 1864.

Nelson, Henry Loomis. *The Army of the United States*. New York: B.M. Whitlock, 1890.

_____."Army Uniforms in the United States." *Harper's Weekly*. March 1, 1890.

_____. "Reform in Army Uniforms." *Harper's Weekly*. August 30, 1890.

"New Uniform for the U.S. Army." *Gleason's Pictorial Drawing-Room Companion*. March 22, 1852.

Parks, Joseph H. *General Edmund Kirby Smith*. Baton Rouge: Louisiana State University, 1954.

Regulations for the Army of the United States 1857. Staten Island: Manor Publishing, 1973.

Report of the Secretary of War, Communicating the Report of Captain George B. McClellan, (First Regiment United States Cavalry) One of Officers Sent to the Seat of War in Europe 1855 and 1856, Executive Document No. 1, Senate, Special Session. Washington, DC: A.O.P. Nicholson, Printer, 1857.

Special Orders. Adjutant General's Office, 1862-1865.

Taylor, William O. *With Custer on the Little Bighorn*. New York: Viking, 1996.

Tome, Robert. "The Fortunes of War." XXIX *Harper's New Monthly Magazine*. June 1864, 227-8.

Townsend, E.D. *Anecdotes of the Civil War in the United States*. New York: D. Appleton & Company, 1884.

United Service Gazette. April 13, 1850.

United States Army and Navy Journal. 1863-1873.

Viele, Teresa G. *Following the Drum: A Glimpse of Frontier Life*. Lincoln: University of Nebraska Press, 1984.

Zogbaum, Rufus Fairchild. "Army Uniforms." *Harper's Weekly*. May 4, 1897, 4.

Secondary Sources

Book and Monographs

Above and Beyond: A History of the Medal of Honor from the Civil War to Vietnam. Boston: Boston Publishing Company, 1985.

Allie, Stephen J. *All He Could Carry US Army Infantry Equipment, 1839-1910*. Ft. Leavenworth: Frontier Army Museum, 1991.

Ambrose, Stephen E. *Upton and the Army*. Baton Rouge: Louisiana State University, 1964.

Barnes, R. Money. *Military Uniforms of Britain the Empire, 1742 to Present.* London: Seeley Service & Co. Limited, 1960.

Bauer, Jack K. *The Mexican War 1846-1848.* Lincoln: University of Nebraska Press, 1992.

Bender, Averam B. *The March of Empire.* Lawrence: The University of Kansas Press, 1952.

Biegloe, David Nevis. *William Conant Church and the Army Navy Journal.* New York: Columbia University Press, 1952.

Brinckerhoff, Sidney B. *Boots and Shoes of the Frontier Soldier.* Tucson: Arizona Historical Society, 1976.

_____. *Military Headgear in the Southwest, 1846-1890.* Tucson: Arizona Pioneers' Historical Society, 1963.

Byrde, Penelope. *Nineteenth Century Fashion.* London: B.T. Batsford Limited, 1992.

Campbell, J. Duncan and Howell, Edgar M. *American Military Insignia 1800-1851.* Washington, DC: Smithsonian Institution, 1963.

Carmen, W.Y. *British Military Uniforms from Contemporary Pictures, Henry VII to the Present Day.* London: Leonard Hill, Ltd., 1957.

_____. *A Dictionary of Military Uniforms.* New York: Charles Scribner's Sons, 1977.

Chappell, Gordon. *Brass Spikes and Horsetail Plumes: A Study of the U.S. Army Dress Helmet, 1872-1904.* Gettysburg: Thomas Publications, 1997.

_____. *Search For The Well-Dressed Soldier, 1865-1890.* Tucson: Arizona Historical Society, 1972.

Coffman, Edward M. *The Old Army A Portrait of The American Army in Peacetime 1784-1898.* Oxford: Oxford University Press, 1986.

Cox, Kurt Hamilton and Langellier, John P. *Longknives: The U.S, Cavalry and Other Mounted Forces, 1845-1942.* London: Greenhill Books, 1996.

Cunliffe, Marcus. *Soldiers & Civilians: The Martial Spirit in America, 1775-1865.* New York: The Free Press, 1973.

Delano, Marfé Ferguson and Mallen, Barbara C. *Echoes of Glory Arms: and Equipment of the Union.* Alexandria, VA: Time-Life Books, 1991.

Davis, William C. Ed. *The Image of War 1861-1865.* Garden City, NY: Doubleday & Company, 1981-83. 5 Volumes.

Egner, Philip and Mayer, Frederick. Eds. *Songs of the United States Military Academy West Point, New York.* West Point: Egner and Mayer, 1925.

Elting, John R. Ed. *Military Uniforms in America The Era of the American Revolution, 1755-1795.* San Rafael, CA: Presidio Press, 1974.

_____. *Military Uniforms in America Years of Growth, 1796-1851.* San Rafael, CA: Presidio Press, 1977.

_____. *Military Uniforms in America Long Endure: The Civil War Period, 1852-1867.* Navato, CA: Presidio Press, 1982.

_____, Cragg, Dan, and Deal, Ernest. *A Dictionary of Soldier Talk.* New York: Charles Scribner Sons, 1984.

Emerson, William K. *Chevrons: Illustrated History and Catalog of U.S. Army Insignia.* Washington, DC: Smithsonian Institution Press, 1983.

_____. *Encyclopedia of United States Army Insignia and Uniforms.* Norman: University of Oklahoma Press, 1996.

Field, Ron. *Brassey's History of Uniforms: Mexican-American War 1846-1848.* London: Brassey's Ltd., 1997.

Flugel, J.C. *The Psychology of Clothes.* London: Hogarth Press, 1940.

Foner, Jack D. *The United States Soldier Between Two Wars: Army Life and Reforms, 1865-1898.* New York: Humanities Press, 1970.

Fuller, Claud E. *The Breech Loader in Service 1816-1917: A History of All Standard and Experimental U.S. Breechloading and Magazine Shoul der Arms.* New Milford, CT: N. Flayderman, 1965.

Ganoe, William Addleman. *The History of the United States Army.* Pishton: Eric Lundeberg, 1964.

Geertz, Clifford. *The Interpretation of Cultures.* New York: Basic Books, Inc., Publishers, 1977.

Goetzmann, William H. *Army Exploration in the American West.* New Haven: Yale University Press, 1965.

Carolyn T. Hornsberger. Ed. *Mark Twain at Your Fingertips.* New York: Beechhurst Press, Inc., 1948.

Howell, Edgar M. and Kloster, Donald E. *United States Military Headgear to 1854 Catalog of United States Army Uniforms in the Collections of the Smithsonian Institution,* Volume I. City of Washington: Smithsonian Institution Press, 1969.

Howell, Edgar M. *United States Army Headgear 1855-1902: Catalog of United States Army Uniforms in the Collections of the Smithsonian Institution.* Volume II. Washington, DC: Smithsonian Institution, 1975.

Jefferies, B.G. *Know Thyself or The Royal Path to Happiness.* New York: J.L. Nichols Co., 1903.

Johnson, David F. *Uniform Buttons, American Armed Forces, 1784-1848.* Watkins Glen, NY: Century House, 1948. 2 Volumes.

Katcher, Philip. *U.S. Infantry Equipments 1775-1910.* London: Osprey Publishing Ltd., 1989.

Kidwell, Claudia B. and Christman, Margaret C. *Suiting Everyone: The Democratization of Clothing in America.* (Washington, DC: The Smithsonian Institution Press, 1974.

Kieffer, Chester L. *Maligned General: A Biography of Thomas S. Jesup.* San Rafael, CA: Presidio Press, 1979.

Kouwenhoven, John A. *The Beer Can by the Highway: Essays on What's "American" about America.* Baltimore: Johns Hopkins University Press, 1988.

_____. *Made in America.* Garden City: NJ: Doubleday & Co., 1948.

Langellier, John P. *Bluecoats: The U.S. Army in the West, 1848-1897.* London: Greenhill Books, 1995.

_____. *Parade Ground Soldiers: Military Uniforms in the Collections of the Wisconsin State Historical Society.* Madison: State Historical Society of Wisconsin, 1978.

_____. *They Continually Wear The Blue: U.S. Army Enlisted Dress Uniforms, 1866-1902.* San Francisco: Barnes-McGee, 1976.

Laver, James. *British Military Uniforms.* London: Penguin Books, 1948.

Langner, Lawrence. *The Importance of Wearing Clothes.* New York: Hastings House, 1959.

Bibliography

Leonard, Thomas C. *Above the Battle: War-Making in America from Appomattox to Versailles*. New York: Oxford University Press, 1978.

Lord, Francis A. *Civil War Collector's Encyclopedia: Arms, Uniforms, and Equipment of the Union and Confederacy*. New York: Castle Books, 1965.

_____. and Wise, Arthur. *Uniforms of the Civil War*. Cranbury, NJ: Thomas Yoseloff, 1970.

Lurie, Alison. *The Language of Clothes*. New York: Random House, 1981.

McChristian, Douglas C. *The U.S. Army in the West, 1870-1880: Uniforms, Weapons and Equipment*. Norman: University of Oklahoma, 1995.

McAfee, Michael J. and Langellier, John P. *Billy Yank: The Uniform of the Union Army, 1861-1865*. London: Greenhill Books, 1996.

Marshall, Max L. Ed. *The Story of the U.S. Army Signal Corps*. New York: Franklin Watts, Inc., 1965.

Miller, Francis Trevelyan. Ed. *Photographic History of the Civil War*. New York: Review of Reviews, 1911. 5 Volumes.

Millett, Allen R. *Military Professionalism and Officerships in America*. Columbus: Ohio State University, 1977.

Millis, Walter. Ed. *American Military Thought*. Indianapolis: Bobbs-Merrill Company, Inc., 1966.

_____. *Arms and Men: A Study in American Military History*. New York: Putnam, 1956.

Mollo, John. *Military Fashion*. New York: G.P. Putnam's Sons, 1972.

Munden, K.W. and Beers, H.P. *Guide to Federal Archives Relating to the Civil War*. Washington, DC: National Archives, 1962.

Myerly, Scott Hughes. *British Military Spectacle: From The Napoleonic Wars Through The Crimea*. Cambridge, MA: Harvard University Press, 1996.

T*he Oxford Universal Dictionary of Historical Principles*. Oxford: The Claraden Press, 1955. 3rd Ed.

Peterson, Harold L. *The American Sword, 1775-1945*. Philadelphia: Ray Riling Books, 1965.

Porter, Horace. *Campaigning With Grant*. New York: Bonanza Books, 1961.

Phillips, Stanley S. *Civil War Corps Badges and Other Related Awards, Badges, Medals of the Period: Including A Section on Post Civil War and Spanish American War Corps Badges*. Lanham, MD: S.S. Phillips, 1982.

Polhemus, Ted and Proctor, Lynn. *Fashion and Anti-Fashion: An Anthropology of Clothing and Adornment*. London: Thames and Hudson, 1978.

Price, George F. *Across the Continent with the Fifth Cavalry*. New York: D. Van Nostrand, Publisher, 1883

Railsback, Thomas C. and Langellier, John P. *The Drums Would Roll: A Pictorial History of U.S. Army Bands on the American Frontier, 1866-1900*. Poole, England: Arms and Armour Press, 1987.

Rickey, Don. *Forty Miles A Day On Beans and Hay*. Norman: University of Oklahoma, 1966.

Risch, Erna. *Quartermaster Support of the Army: A History of the Corps 1775-1939*. Washington, DC: Office of the Quartermaster General, 1962.

Roach, Mary Ellen and Eicher, Joanne Bubolz. Eds. *Dress, Adornment, and the Social Order*. New York: John Wiley & Sons, Inc., 1965.

Rodenbaugh, Theo F. *From Everglade to Canyon with the Second Dragoons*. New York: D. Van Nostram, 1875.

Rudofsky, Bernard. *Are Clothes Modern?* Chicago: Paul Teobold, 1947.

Sadies, Stanley. Ed. *The New Grove's Dictionary of Opera*. Volume II. New York: Grove's Dictionary of Music Inc., 1992.

Sefton, James E. *The United States Army and Reconstruction*. Baton Rouge: Louisiana State University Press, 1967.

Shannon, Fred. *Organization and Administration of the Union Army, 1861-1865*. Glouster, MA: P. Smith, 1965. 2 Volumes.

Smith, Robin. *Brassey's History of Uniforms: American Civil War Union Army*. London: Brassey's, Ltd., 1996.

Spencer, Herbert. *The Principles of Sociology*. New York: D. Appleton, 1892. 2 Volumes

Steffen, Randy. *The Horse Soldier 1776-1943*. Norman: University of Oklahoma Press, 1978.

Stover, Earl F. *Up from Handymen: The United States Army Chaplaincy, 1865-1920*. Washington, DC: Office of the Chief of Chaplains, 1977.

Tily, James C. *Uniforms of the United States Navy*. New York: Thomas Yoseloff, 1964.

Todd, Frederick P. *American Military Equipage 1851-1872*, Volume I New York: Charles Scribner's Sons, 1980.

_____. *American Military Equipage, 1851-1872*. Volume II. N.P.: Chatham Square Press, 1983.

_____. *Cadet Gray*. New York: Sterling Publishing Co., Inc., 1955.

Urwin, Gregory J.W. *The United States Infantry: An Illustrated History, 1775-1918*. London: Blandford Press, 1988.

Utley, Robert M. *Frontier Regulars: The United States Army and the Indian, 1866-1891*. New York: Macmillian, 1978.

_____. *Frontiersmen in Blue: The United States Army and the Indian, 1848-1865*. New York: The Macmillan Company, 1967.

Veblen, Thorstein. *The Theory of the Leisure Class*. New York: Modern Library, 1934.

Wagner, Arthur L. and Kelly, J.S. Jerrold. *The United States Army and Navy*. Akron, OH: The Werner Company, 1899.

Weigley, Russell F. *The American Way of War: A History of United States Military Strategy and Policy*. New York: Macmillan and Company, 1973.

_____. *History of the United States Army*. New York: Macmillan and Company, 1967.

_____. *Quartermaster General of the Union Army: A Biography of M.C. Meigs*. New York: Columbia University Press, 1959.

_____. *Towards an American Army: Military Thought from Washington to Marshall*. New York: Columbia University Press, 1962.

White, Morton. *Social Thought in America: The Revolt Against Formalism*. Boston: Beacon Press, 1957.

Wilkinson-Latham, Christopher. *The Indian Mutiny*. London: Osprey Publishing Ltd., 1991.

Wilkinson-Latham, R.J. *Collecting Militaria*. New York: Arco Publishing, Inc., 1976.

Williams, T. Harry. *American at War: The Development of the American Military System*. Baton Rouge: Louisiana State University Press, 1960

Unpublished Works

Andrews, R.A. "Years of Frustation: William T. Sherman, The Army and Reform." M.A. thesis, Northwestern University, 1968.

Greiss, Thomas E. "Dennis Hart Mahan: West Point Professor and Advocate of Military Professionalism, 1830-1871." Ph.D. dissertation, Duke University, 1968.

Thomas, Donna M.E. "Army Reform in America: The Crucial Years, 1876-1881." Ph.D. dissertation, University of Florida, 1980.

Periodicals

Bailes, Howard. "The Patterns of Thought in the Late Victorian Army." IV *Journal of Strategic Studies* No. 1 (March 1981): 29-45.

Baird, L.C. "The Philadelphia Quartermaster Intermediate Depot," VI *Quartermaster Review* No. 6 (May-June 1927), 18-23.

Borrell, Robert, Sr. "U.S. Army Uniforms of the Civil War Part III: The Artillery." III *Military Images* No. 3 (November-December 1981): 9-15.

Chappell, Gordon. "Dress Hat of the First Regiment of Mounted Rifles, 1858-1861." XXII *Military Collector and Historian* No. 2 (Summer 1970): 58-9.

Curaton, Charles and Schultz, William. "Dating The Regulars." XVII *Military Images* No. 4 (January-February 1996): 8-11.

Emerson, William. "Leather Stocks in the U.S. Army." XXIX *Military Collector and Historian* No. 2 (Summer 1977): 62-3.

Flower, William Henry. "Fashion in Deformity." V *Humboldt Library of Popular Science Literature* 28 (1882): 2.

Haarmann, Albert W. "The Blue and the Gray." VI *Military Images* No. 6 (May-June 1985): 16-23.

Hamilton, C.S. "Jeffersonville Quartermaster Intermediate Depot History and Functions." VII *Quartermaster Review* No. 1 (July-August 1927), 3-9.

Hutchins, James S. "The Army Campaign Hat of 1872." XVI *Military Collector and Historian* No. 3 (Fall 1968): 65-73.

Katcher, Philip. "British Rifle Volunteers of the 1860's." I *Military Images* No. 1 (July-August 1979): 5-8.

_____. "'They were well thought of...' The Veteran Reserve Corps, 1863-1866." VI *Military Images* No. 1 (July-August 1984): 20-24.

Kloster, Donald E. "Uniforms of the Army Prior and Subsequent to 1872," Parts 1, 2. XIV *Military Collector and Historian* No. 4 (Winter 1962): 103-12; XV No. 1 (Spring 1963): 6-14.

Lang, Wendell W., Jr. "Corps Badges of the Civil War." VI *Military Images* No. 6 (May-June 1986): 16-25; VIII No. 1 (July-August 1986): 8-15; VIII No. 3 (November-December 1986): 16-26; IX No. 3 (November-December 1987): 6-15.

McAfee, Michael J. "Irregular Regulars." XVII *Military Images* No. 4 (January-February 1996): 34-36.

_____. "Militia of `61." VIII *Military Images* No. 1 (July-August 1986): 16-24.

_____. "U.S. Army Uniforms of the Civil War Part I: The Frock Coat." II *Military Images* No, 4 (January February 1981): 16-21.

_____. "U.S. Army Uniforms of the Civil War Part IV: The Jacket." III *Military Images* No. 6 (May-June 1982): 10-15.

_____. "U.S. Army Uniforms of the Civil War Part VI: Zouaves and Chasseurs." IV *Military Images* No.3 (November-December 1982): 10-15.

_____. "What Is A Zouave." I *Military Images* No. 2. (September-October 1979): 19-26.

Madaus, Howard Michael. "Massachusetts Mystery Medal." VIII *Military Images* No. 3 (November-December 1986): 14-15.

Osborne, Seward R. "They Wore An Orange Ribbon." XXXVIII *Military Collector and Historian* No. 1 (Spring 1986): 40-1.

Peladeau, Marius B. and Cohen, Roger S., Jr. "Corps Badges of the Civil War." XXIII *Military Collector and Historian* No. 4 (Winter 1971): 103-12.

Peterson, Mendel L. "American Army Epaulettes 1814-1872." III *Military Collector and Historian* No. 1 (March 1951): 1-14.

Townsend, F.C. and Todd, Frederick P. "Branch Insignia of the Regular Cavalry, 1833-1872." VIII *Military Collector and Historian* No. 1 (Spring 1956): 1-5.

Sperry T.J. "Winter Clothing on the Northern Plains." XLIV *Military Collector and Historian* No. 3 (Fall 1992): 116-120.

Styple, William. "The Kearny Medal." IX *Military Images* No. 3 (November-December 1987): 18-9.

Wike, James W. "Individual Decorations of the Civil War and Earlier," V *Military Collector and Historian* No. 3 (September 1953): 57-64.

Wike, John M. "The Wearing of Corps and Division Insignia of the Union Army, 1861-1865." IV *Military Collector and Historian* No. 2 (June 1952): 35-8

Williams, W.T. "History of Jeffersonville Quartermaster Intermediate Depot." V *Quartermaster Review* No. 4 (January-February 1927):10-20.

Winey, Michael J. "Clergy in Uniform." IV *Military Images* No. 6 (May-June 1983): 8-12.

INDEX

Also from the publisher

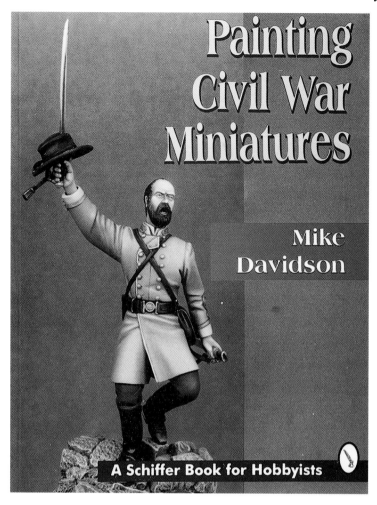

PAINTING CIVIL WAR FIGURES
Mike Davidson.

Miniature American Civil War figures have become extremely popular in the past few years. Using a clearly photographed step-by-step approach, Mike Davidson utilizes hobby paints and oils to bring these highly detailed miniatures to life. Mike also provides formulas for mixing a variety of Civil War uniform colors. While applied to a particular figure, the lessons and techniques learned from this book will enhance any American Civil War figure the reader may choose to paint.

Size: 8 1/2" x 11" 250 color photographs

64 pages, soft cover

ISBN: 0-88740-884-2 $14.95

CIVIL WAR RE-ENACTMENT
David and Joan Hagan.

Photographers David and Joan Hagan portray the Civil War drama through their poignant pictures taken during re-enacted battles.

Size: 8 1/2" x 11"

over 290 color photographs

112 pages, soft cover

ISBN: 0-88740-949-0 $19.95

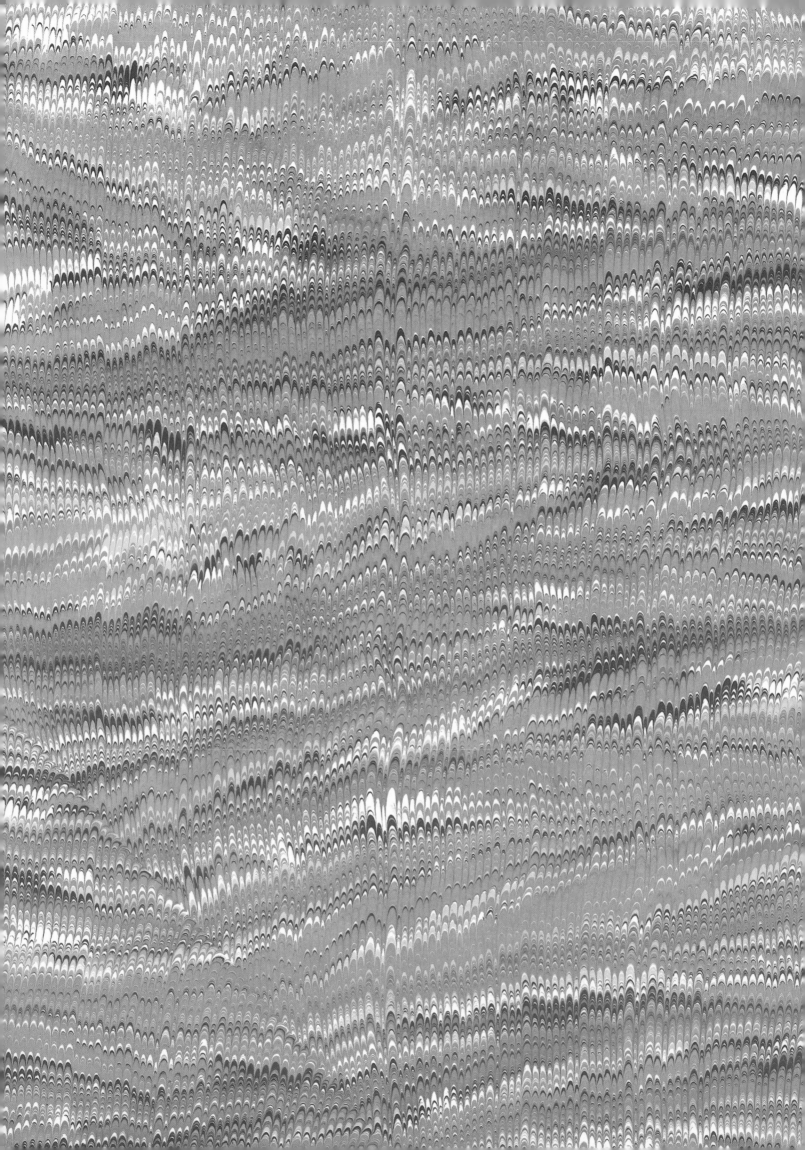